THE ROYAL DEMESNE IN ENGLISH HISTORY

by the same author

THE CROWN LANDS, 1461–1536
Historical Problems Series

THE ROYAL DEMESNE IN ENGLISH HISTORY

THE CROWN ESTATE IN THE GOVERNANCE OF THE REALM FROM THE CONQUEST TO 1509

B. P. WOLFFE

Senior Lecturer in History
University of Exeter

London

GEORGE ALLEN & UNWIN LTD

RUSKIN HOUSE MUSEUM STREET

First published in 1971

ISBN 0 04 942087 9

Printed in Great Britain
in 11 on 12 point Plantin type
by Alden & Mowbray Ltd
at the Alden Press, Oxford

To the Memory of
K. B. McFarlane

PREFACE

Every student of English history knows that medieval kings were expected to 'live of their own'. The history of the landed estate of the English Crown cannot be told without reference to that fundamental theory of the English constitution: the revenues of the English Crown are divided into ordinary and extraordinary, and were so divided time out of mind; extraordinary revenues are deemed to be derived from the proceeds of taxation, and our medieval kings were expected to live of their own from their ordinary revenues, the substance of which was derived from their royal demesne, crown estate, or crown lands. When I began my researches into the role of the crown lands in the government of late-medieval England it was generally accepted that this was indeed an ideal of the English middle ages which was already as ancient as it was impossible of achievement by the time of our later Plantagenet kings. But two awkward facts from the late-medieval period ultimately led me to question the whole of the accepted history of the English royal demesne, at least from the cataclysmic conquest of 1066. The division of the royal revenues into ordinary and extraordinary in the accepted sense was still unknown in England at the end of the fifteenth century. The notion of the king 'living of his own', when it did ultimately arise in the fourteenth century, was not in fact a protest against the king's misuse of his landed estate, as generations of historians have led us to believe, but the late-medieval Englishman's defence against the king's abuse of his rights of purveyance as a means of supplying the royal Household.

The long first chapter of this book is therefore perforce devoted to an exploratory re-examination of the role of the English royal demesne in the Norman and Angevin period, assisted by a brief look at the very different contemporary role of the Capetian royal *domaine* in the history of medieval France as portrayed by recent French historians. As Sir John Fortescue appreciated in the mid-fifteenth century, the differences between medieval French and English history can be more instructive than those apparent similarities which have generally been stressed by historians both from the French and English side. The fuller history of the English royal landed estate from Edward I to Henry VII on which this study concentrates can hardly be made credible without some such reconsideration of accepted theories about the earlier medieval period, even if this only succeeds in posing certain new questions to which specialists in the detailed history of this earlier period can provide more fully satisfactory answers.

The primary significance of the role of the English king as landowner from the mid-thirteenth century to 1399 lay in his position as the head of a numerous royal family: as its provider of English and Welsh estates consequent on the loss of the larger, continental Angevin empire. His secondary role as the dispenser of landed patronage outside the circle of the royal family was also a most important factor contributing either to political stability or political unrest according to how he disposed of these resources. But it was only between 1399 and 1461, after the vast private estate of the Lancastrian House had been brought to the support of the Crown, that the use and disposition of crown lands at last became a permanent, central issue of English politics. It was the subsequent period from 1461 to 1509 which first saw general acceptance of the idea that an endowed and inalienable royal landed estate ought to form the basis of monarchical stability and national financial solvency.

I am very conscious of the dangers inherent in attempting such a wide-ranging survey of one aspect of English history. Nevertheless it has proved a most fruitful approach for shedding new light on the politics and finances of late-medieval English governments. But the principal justification must be the emergence of certain generalizations about the whole of medieval English political life. Medieval England from 1066 was probably the most regularly and most heavily taxed country in Christendom and the English royal income was always essentially derived from taxation during the medieval period, in spite of the contrary, later theories of seventeenth-century politicians and modern constitutional historians. A continuous history of an English medieval royal demesne, in so far as it had any continuous existence, can only be presented, not in the context of royal finance, but of royal patronage. There appears to be no evidence to support the generally accepted view that restraint of the king's powers to alienate his lands was a general principle of medieval opposition to royal financial extravagance, while the undoubted significance of the crown estate in the national finances between 1461 and 1509 appears to have been unique and temporary. With Wolsey and Henry VIII the traditional medieval methods of dependence on taxation were quickly reasserted. Seventeenth- and eighteenth-century politicians and lawyers, followed by nineteenth-century constitutional historians, appear to have created a powerful and tenacious myth around the functions of the royal demesne in English medieval government which bears little relation to the more elusive truth which this book attempts to elucidate.

It is a pleasure to be able to acknowledge the many obligations incurred in writing this book. My wife has been a never-failing source of encouragement, a penetrating critic, and an indefatigable research assistant and typist. I owe debts of gratitude to many distinguished medievalists who have helped me since I first began the study of the royal demesne under the guidance of the late Bruce McFarlane, especially to Sir Goronwy Edwards who read and commented on the whole of an earlier draft of this work, to Dr James Conway Davies for invaluable insight into the use of exchequer records, to my teachers John Armstrong and John Roskell and to my colleague Frank Barlow. I am indebted to the editor and publishers of the *English Historical Review* for permission to use material from three papers which I published in the journal in 1956, 1958 and 1964. Finally I wish to express my thanks to the staffs of the Public Record Office, the Students' Room at the British Museum, and Exeter University Library for much assistance given beyond the call of duty.

B.P.W.

University of Exeter
November 1970

CONTENTS

PREFACE *page* 9
ABBREVIATIONS 15

I. THE ROYAL DEMESNE IN NORMAN AND ANGEVIN GOVERNMENT 17
1. Royal demesne and tallage 17
2. 'Ancient demesne' 24
3. Royal demesne and parliamentary taxation 26
4. Royal demesne and land revenue 30
5. Royal demesne and patronage 34
6. Contrasts in the role of the Capetian *domaine* 38
7. Restraint of alienation in England and the genesis of 'the king to live of his own' 40

II. A NEW ROYAL PATRIMONY. THE PLANTAGENET FAMILY ESTATE 1227–1399 52
1. Family endowments 52
2. Alienations outside the royal family 59
3. Finance and royal patronage 60
4. Exchequer and chamber administration 65
5. Parliamentary criticism 72

III. PATRONAGE, POLITICS AND FINANCE, 1399–1437 76
1. Parliament and the act of resumption of 1404 76
2. The financial survey of 1433 89

IV. THE BACKGROUND TO THE RESUMPTIONS OF 1450–6 97
1. The royal lands and the spoils system under Henry VI 97
2. Resumption as the panacea for financial reform 112
3. The collapse of royal government, 1437–50 117

V. THE RESUMPTIONS OF 1450–6 124
1. The Leicester act of resumption of May 1450 124
2. The act of resumption of March 1451 130
3. The 'Yorkist' act of resumption of 1455–6 138
4. The significance of the resumptions 140

VI. THE CROWN ESTATE OF THE YORKIST KINGS 143

1. Edward IV's acts of resumption 143
2. Receivers, surveyors and auditors of land revenues, 1461–83 158
3. Administrative changes in the central government under Edward IV 168
4. Richard III and the crown lands 180

VII. HENRY VII'S LAND REVENUES AND CHAMBER FINANCE 195

1. The collapse and re-establishment of the Yorkist land revenue organization 195
2. Lancastrian, Yorkist and Early Tudor land revenues compared 212

VIII. CONCLUSION 226

APPENDIX

A. LANDS OF THE ROYAL FAMILY, 1327–77 230

Queen Isabella, p. 230; Queen Philippa, p. 237; John of Eltham, earl of Cornwall, p. 239; Edward prince of Wales, duke of Cornwall and earl of Chester, p. 240; John of Gaunt, earl of Richmond and duke of Lancaster, p. 241; Edmund of Langley, earl of Cambridge and duke of York (1385), p. 242; Isabella countess of Bedford, p. 243.

B. THE PROPOSED CONFISCATION OF TEMPORALITIES OF THE CHURCH IN 1404 245

C. THE CROWN LANDS AS AFFECTED BY THE ACTS OF RESUMPTION, 1450–61 248

Beds. & Bucks., p. 248; Cambs. & Hunts., p. 249; Cumb. & Westm., p. 250; Devon & Cornwall, p. 253; Essex & Herts., p. 255; Gloucs., p. 257; Hants., p. 257; Hereford & the Marches of Wales, p. 259; Salop & the Marches of Wales, p. 260; Other lands in Marches of Wales, p. 261; South Wales, p. 261; Kent, p. 261; Lincs., p. 264; London, p. 267; Middlx., p. 270; Newcastle-on-Tyne, p. 271; Norf. & Suff., p. 271; Northants. & Rutland, p. 274; Northumbld., p. 275; Notts. & Derbys., p. 276; Oxon. & Berks., p. 278; Soms. & Dors., p. 280; Staffs., p. 282; Surrey & Sussex, p. 283; Warws. & Leics., p. 285; Wilts., p. 286; Worcs., p. 287; Yorks., p. 287; York, p. 288; Duchy of Lancaster, p. 289.

D. THE MANAGEMENT OF THE CROWN LANDS, 1461–85. LISTS OF OFFICERS WITH THE AREA OF THEIR CHARGE 290

Receivers, Surveyors, Supervisors and Approvers, p. 290; Auditors, p. 298.

INDEX 307

ABBREVIATIONS

B.I.H.R.	*Bulletin of the Institute of Historical Research*
B.M.	British Museum
C.L.	B. P. Wolffe, *The Crown Lands 1461 to 1536* (London, George Allen & Unwin, 1970)
E.H.R.	*English Historical Review*
Proc. and Ord.	*Proceedings and Ordinances of the Privy Council of England*, ed. N. H. Nicolas (London, 1834–7)
P.R.O.	Public Record Office
Rep. Dig. Peer	*Report from the Lords' Committees appointed to search the Journals of the House, Rolls of Parliament, and other records for all matters touching the Dignity of a Peer* (London, 1820–9)
Rot. Parl.	*Rotuli Parliamentorum*, ed. J. Strachey and others (London, 1767)
T.R.H.S.	*Transactions of the Royal Historical Society*

I
THE ROYAL DEMESNE IN NORMAN AND ANGEVIN GOVERNMENT

1. ROYAL DEMESNE AND TALLAGE

The landed resources of the medieval English monarchy are, by long-established custom among English historians, normally designated the 'royal demesne'. According to modern English constitutional law the revenues of the English Crown are divided into ordinary and extraordinary[1] and constitutional historians in general accept that this has always been so, at least since the Norman Conquest. Extraordinary revenue is deemed to consist of the proceeds of taxation, and it is a commonplace of English history that our medieval kings were expected to 'live of their own' from their ordinary revenue, the substance of which was derived from their royal demesne. In English history the essential landed prerequisite for a powerful and permanent medieval monarchy is generally considered to have been gained in one brilliant stroke of conquest by William the Conqueror and the record of it promptly enshrined in the *terra regis* of the Domesday Survey, the greatest land book of all times.

But the student of the medieval English royal demesne finds himself confronted at the very outset by a serious problem of semantics and definition. The earliest reference in Du Cange to an English royal demesne in a Latin form (*in dominicis regis*) is from Glanvill (*c.* 1187–9) and the *Revised Medieval Latin Word List* gives no example before 1241, a reference to ancient demesne (*dominicum antiquum regis*). *The Oxford English Dictionary* also gives a reference to ancient demesne as its earliest example in the Norman-French form (*auncienes demeynes*, 1292).[2] Professor Robert Hoyt, who has written the only modern monograph on the English royal demesne, begins his book with a conclusion that the typical medieval Latin term for this concept was the neuter plural *dominica regis*, denoting the *maneria regis*, and being the sum total of the rural royal estates organized as manors. Akin to these, but only 'demesne' in a less absolute, 'adjectival' sense were the highways, 'demesne forests' and 'demesne

1. E. C. S. Wade and Godfrey Philips, *Constitutional Law* (2nd ed., London, 1935), p. 220: 'The revenue of the Crown is divided into ordinary and extraordinary, the latter being derived mainly from taxation. The principal item of "ordinary" revenue, the total of which is nowadays negligible, is the income derived from Crown lands. . . .'

2. The Du Cange reference is in fact to a passage in the later Scottish *Regiam Majestatem* derived from Glanvill.

boroughs'. Professor Hoyt insists that the phrase 'royal demesne', describing as it did estates which had not been subinfeudated, expressed a feudal concept which is only intelligible for the period following the Conquest.[3]

The obvious first use for this seemingly handy definition is to test it out on Domesday Book, the sole surviving description of the king's landed possessions in English history before the sixteenth century and, indeed, since it was essentially the record of an alien conquest, the only record of its kind ever made. But the term *dominica regis* does not seem to have been used at all in Domesday Book. Was the common phrase *in dominio* its equivalent? One well-attested and clearly intelligible Domesday use of this phrase, adequately translated as manorial demesne, is clearly not directly relevant to this enquiry and can be set aside. There is an early definition in the *Dialogus de Scaccario* of this manorial demesne of the typical Domesday entry[4] 'Ibi nunc in dominio IIII carucae et XXX villani et III bordarii habent VIII carucas':

> 'You must know that "demesne" lands are those which are tilled at the cost, or by the labour, of the owner, and those held in his name by his villeins. For because villeins, by the law of the land, may not only be transferred by their lords from the lands which they actually till to other spots, but may even themselves be sold or otherwise disposed of: both they and the lands which they cultivate as service to their masters are rightly deemed to be demesne.'[5]

The other common Domesday use of *in dominio* occurs very often within the *terra regis* to designate land which King William himself held, as opposed to other land held by his tenants-in-chief *de rege*. In this sense this phrase may indeed appear to express what Professor Hoyt means by royal demesne. Yet it can hardly be taken *per se* to identify a royal demesne, because in some counties the king, like each of his tenants-in-chief, is merely stated to hold (*tenet*) his land. To consider *in dominio* as automatically implied within the whole of the *terra regis*, or to translate *terra regis* as 'royal demesne' would be to beg the question.[6] Until we can find specific examples of the concept 'royal demesne' used in the records of government we can hardly decide what contemporaries meant by it and we are bound to ask whether they would have understood it. In any case there would still

3. Robert S. Hoyt, *The Royal Demesne in English Constitutional History: 1066–1272* (Ithaca, N.Y., 1950), pp. 2–3, 6.

4. *Domesday Book seu Liber Censualis Willelmi Primi, Regis Angliae*, ed. Abraham Farley (London, 1783), i, 203(b).

5. *Dialogus de Scaccario*, ed. and trans. Charles Johnson (London, 1950), p. 56. It should perhaps be noted that this *Dialogus* definition of manorial demesne to include villeins' lands differs from the typical Domesday entry which places manorial demesne and villeins' lands in apposition.

6. It appears that Professor Hoyt does regard land described in Domesday Book as 'held *in dominio* by the king' and *terra regis* as identical terms for 'royal demesne' except when it refers to manorial demesne (*op. cit.*, p. 26).

be the problem of Professor Hoyt's designation of the king's cities or boroughs and the king's forests as associated royal demesne. Domesday Book clearly states, outside the *terra regis* in Herefordshire, that King William held the city of Hereford *in dominio*,[7] as he did many of his manors. There is surely no difference in kind, degree, immediacy or permanence of royal possession intended in its description outside the *terra regis* or in the use of 'habet' instead of 'tenet' here. Indeed, the record is actually concerned to make a special point of the completeness of the king's lordship in the case of the city of Hereford. There had been in Hereford twenty-seven burgesses of Earl Harold in the time of King Edward, but even then King Edward had had the three forfeitures for breaking his peace, housebreaking and assault *in suo dominio*, from every man in the entire city of Hereford, no matter whose man he might be. On the other hand the borough of Bath, three times referred to as a borough (*istud burgum huius burgi, de ipso burgo*) is described within the *terra regis* in Somerset.[8] Neither can we award a subordinate, associate, or 'adjectival' membership of a 'royal demesne' to the Domesday forests. One finds a single reference to the *dominicae forestae*, within the *terra regis* in Oxfordshire.[9] But there appears to be no difference in meaning between this reference on the one hand and all the other references to various forests as *foresta regis*, within or without the *terra regis*,[10] at least no more than one would discern in the English language between 'the king's own forest' and 'the king's forest'.

Thus, in spite of the prominence given to the *terra regis* in the final form of Domesday Book, there is in fact no collective noun used there which can be reasonably translated as 'royal demesne' within the terms of Professor Hoyt's definition. There is a reference to *dominica terra regis* in Domesday, but it is to the manorial demesne of the king's manor of Sutton Courtenay which the sheriff, Godric, had unlawfully ploughed with his own ploughs.[11]

7. *Domesday Book*, i, 179.
8. *ibid.*, 87.
9. *ibid.*, 154(b).
10. e.g. *ibid.*, 38(b), 184, 186, 221(b), 247(b).
11. *ibid.*, 57(b). There remain the *Dominicatus Regis* headings of the Exon 'satellite' Domesday. Professor Hoyt refers to one of these, 'Dominicatus Regis ad Regnum pertinens in Devenescira' as the heading of the *terra regis* section of the Exon Domesday survey of Devon (*op. cit.*, p. 10). But what is listed there under this heading is not the equivalent of the Devon *terra regis* of Domesday Book and will hardly fit his definition of royal demesne. The separate items are: manors held by King Edward at his death, his boroughs of Barnstaple and Lydford and the city of Exeter. The Devon *terra regis* of Domesday Book includes these manors and the two boroughs, but not the city, while two further categories of the Exon book have to be added to complete it: (1) a separate section of the Exon book headed *Dominicatus Regis in Devenesira* and further identified in both surveys as lands held either by Earl Harold or by Queen Edith at King Edward's death; (2) another separate section of the Exon book headed there *Terra Mahillis Regine in Devenesira* and further identified in both surveys as lands of Brictric at King Edward's death which had since been Queen Matilda's (died 1083). The relevant Devon headings and sections can be found in the printed version of the Exon book, *Domesday Book*, iv (Record Commission, 1816), beginning at pp. 75, 84 and 100. They are interrupted at p. 94 by the king's Somerset lands which had formerly been Harold's and Edith's and at p. 99 by the

Other important records are strangely unproductive of terms which one can translate with confidence as 'royal demesne'. The 'Leges Henrici Primi' uses the phrase *habet in dominio suo*, but uses it equally to describe both the land held by the king and by each of his barons.[12] Professor Southern has recently demonstrated the impossibility of relying on the expression *in dominio regis* or *in dominico regis* as an identification of royal demesne in charters of the Anglo-Norman period.[13] The *Dialogus de Scaccario*, while providing a definition of manorial demesne, has no reference at all to anything which can be translated as 'royal demesne', although it contains several references to what can only be translated as 'crown lands'.[14] Moreover, these 'crown lands' to the author of the *Dialogus* meant the lands held by the king's tenants-in-chief directly of him, the very opposite of Professor Hoyt's definition.

The twelfth-century pipe rolls are equally unproductive. There are occasional references made to reductions for scutage and other feudal aids, made because some land was then *in dominio regis*, but it is doubtful whether one can translate this otherwise than as 'in the king's lordship', meaning that the land was at that time in his hands.[15] Where these lands can be traced in Domesday they were then mainly lands of tenants-in-chief. The neuter singular *dominicum* is very occasionally used in the pipe rolls to designate a purpresture, an encroachment on the king's property, but in three cases which I have found, one refers to land in a borough and the other two refer to land in the king's forest of Cumberland.[16]

Somerset 'mansiones de comitatu'. The consolidated Devon *terra regis* of Domesday Book proper begins with the boroughs of Barnstaple and Lydford (*Domesday Book*, i, 100). Professor Hoyt is mistaken when he states (*op. cit.*, p. 17) that there is no parallel in the *terra regis* of the main Domesday to the 'clearly marked categories of "royal demesne", arranged according to *antecessores* (as in Exon Domesday)'. At least for Devon there are clear sub-headings for Harold's, Edith's and Brictric's (Matilda's) lands within the *terra regis* (*Domesday Book*, i, 100(b), col. 2; 101, col. 1; 101, col. 2).

12. William Stubbs's *Select Charters* (9th ed.), pp. 124, 125.

13. R. W. Southern, 'The Place of Henry I in English History' (Raleigh Lecture, 1962) in *Proceedings of the British Academy*, xlviii (1963), 161–2.

14. *Dialogus* (ed. Johnson): p. 29, 'in fundis suis que corone annominantur'; p. 93, 'habitantes prope fundos qui corone annominantur'; p. 96, 'Quidam enim de rege tenent in capite que ad coronam pertinent'. In each case the editor translates these references as 'crown lands', and so would I. In the third case there is a contrast made between the 'crown lands' held in chief (greater or lesser baronies) and those lands not held in chief and 'accidentally fallen into the king's hands' ('non quidem ratione corone regie, set potius ratione baronie cuiuslibet').

15. 'Et in dominio regis de Stoke quam rex tenet de feodo abbatiae [Westmonasterii] xxs' (*Pipe Roll 1 John*, N.S. 10, 1933), p. 86. A convenient list of these can be compiled by using the index of the *Red Book of the Exchequer* (ed. Hubert Hall, Rolls Series, 1896) 3 vols, under 'dominicum Regis', where they appear in the early thirteenth-century extracts from the pipe rolls of Henry II. It should be noted that when checked against the originals in the Pipe Roll Society's publications in each case the *in dominico Regis* of the *Red Book* is in fact *in dominio Regis* on the pipe roll.

16. *Pipe Roll 31 Henry II* (1913, no. 34), p. 153; *Pipe Roll 32 Henry II* (1914, no. 36), pp. 87, 99.

Neither will Professor Hoyt's identification of royal demesne fit the pipe rolls as regards tallage levied in the reign of Henry II. He affirms that a tallage of the royal demesnes (*tallagium dominicorum*) would not include boroughs as a matter of course.[17] But the officials of Henry II's Exchequer do not appear to have designated tallage as something levied *sui generis* or primarily on 'royal demesnes'. The *Dialogus* describes tallage as 'aids or gifts of cities or boroughs'.[18] The proceeds of this tax were entered on the pipe rolls, by counties, as derived from 'the king's lordships (*dominiorum*) and lands which were then in his hands', and they included under that heading his cities, boroughs and manors without any further or separate classification.[19] Now it seems to me to be a very significant fact that the historian of royal tallage, S. K. Mitchell, in describing tallage as 'a levy upon the royal demesne', defined his 'royal demesne' very differently from Professor Hoyt, and he did this in an attempt to fit his definition to the incidence of tallage. To Mitchell the 'royal demesne', urban and rural, consisted of land which the king had never enfeoffed by knight service: 'ancient demesne' (being the royal lands not enfeoffed at the time of the Conquest) plus lands which had since come into the king's hands 'by escheat, forfeiture, or during minority of a tenant, or by a vacancy through the action of feudal or other customary law'.[20] His 'royal demesne' was essentially a handy group designation to describe those areas of the kingdom which he found were paying tallage in the reign of Henry II.

Only when we turn to the rationalizing and speculative pages of Glanvill (*c.* 1187–9) do we find anything as early as the reign of Henry II at all akin to Professor Hoyt's definition. Glanvill certainly appears to say that a purpresture ('an unjustifiable encroachment on property of the lord king') could occur in three separate spheres: 'in dominicis regis', in public highways or watercourses by obstruction or diversion, or in a city of the lord king by building something.[21] Within a few years in the 'Form of Proceeding on the Judicial Visitation' of 1194 is included the instruction 'praeterea tailleantur omnes civitates, et burgi et dominica domini regis'.[22] Here at last is a reference to royal demesne which appears to fit in with Professor Hoyt's ideas,[23] at least as regards the cities, boroughs and manors of the royal demesne.

17. Hoyt, *op. cit.*, p. 3.

18. *Dialogus* (ed. Johnson), pp. 108–9. There are the 'auxilia' or 'dona', but there is no doubt that what is described here is tallage and the editor rightly indexes this reference under 'tallage'.

19. A good example is *Pipe Roll 34 Henry II* (1925, no. 38), pp. 42, 48, 60, 80, 89, 97, 99, 102, 110, 139, 144, 159, 167, 184, 212.

20. Sydney Knox Mitchell, *Taxation in Medieval England* (New Haven, 1951), p. 244.

21. *Glanvill*, ed. and trans. G. D. G. Hall (London, 1965), pp. 113–14.

22. Stubbs's *Select Charters* (9th ed.), p. 254.

23. This is the earliest instance cited by Professor Hoyt. His other examples are thirteenth-century (*op. cit.*, p. 108).

Was there in fact any concept of a royal demesne in English history earlier than the end of Henry II's reign? Did it have any earlier existence than that parallel developing concept of 'ancient demesne' which Professor Hoyt has so brilliantly demonstrated to have been the creation of the later twelfth and early thirteenth centuries and to which no specific references have been discovered earlier than the thirteenth century? Were developments in the sphere of royal taxation, aimed at all the king's subjects not holding by military tenure, basically responsible for the very creation of both these twin concepts of royal demesne and ancient demesne which came to have financial and legal substance only from the later twelfth century? To a student of government finance it appears that 'royal demesne' might in origin even be called a fiscal term; that it was the evolution of royal tallage which itself created the concept as a term in the workings of English government. The origins and nature of royal tallage in this context must therefore be discussed in some detail.

The recovery of lost 'royal demesne', its retention and its direct exploitation in rents and profits, played but a minor part in the vast increase in royal financial resources achieved between 1154 and 1215. This fact was grasped at the time by Gerald of Wales who explained why Henry II and his sons 'abounded in so much treasure':

> 'The reason is this, that as they had less rents they took care to make up the total by occasional incomings and relied more on accessory than on the principal sources of revenue.'[24]

If we add that what Gerald thought were accessory sources of revenue were really the principal ones all the time, and *vice versa*, we can explain what he shrewdly noticed thus: the potential resources available to the Angevins through their political power as kings were so great that, by comparison, their financial resources as landlords were insignificant. Most notable among their political sources of income was tallage, the tax which 'proved to be the most profitable of any for the strongest monarchy of Western Europe'.[25]

It used to be supposed that tallage was a levy successfully imposed by our Angevin and Plantagenet kings solely on a royal demesne whose inhabitants were subject to such arbitrary exactions like the villeins on the demesne of any feudal lord. Tallage according to Vinogradoff[26] was a private not a political right. While from the rest of the nation consent to taxation was found to be necessary or expedient in the form of the feudal aid at a very early stage, the lesser status and freedom suffered by the royal

24. R. L. Poole's translation in *The Exchequer in the Twelfth Century* (Oxford, 1912), p. 137, from the 'De Principis Instructione', ed. G. F. Warner in *Opera*, viii (Rolls Series, 1891), 316.

25. Carl Stephenson, *Borough and Town* (Cambridge, Mass., 1933), p. 164.

26. P. Vinogradoff, *Villainage in England*, p. 92, following Madox.

demesne rendered it peculiarly liable to arbitrary exploitation. The researches of Carl Stephenson into the origins of the English tallage and its continental equivalents have since demonstrated both its essential public and political basis. Domesday Book reveals tallage in England as a Norman importation which was not servile, levied at first not by the king, but only by the Norman barons on all those made subject to them, free and unfree, as an annual and heavy imposition. This was done by virtue of their seigneurial jurisdiction which was essentially delegated royal jurisdiction.[27] But the Norman king of England himself was in a unique position as regards taxation of which tallage was a part. He had the superior royal geld, the Anglo-Saxon legacy of regular royal taxation which applied to all lands in England by whomsoever they were held on whatever terms. He had no need of tallage it seemed, and those areas of England which he did not enfeoff, his royal manors and boroughs, far from being under-privileged were in fact specially privileged in the first place, in that they alone for a time escaped this additional burden which the baronage, by the tacit permission and approval of the king, exacted from their tenants.[28]

It was the growing prosperity of the kingdom and especially of English towns, a prosperity not reflected in the yield of existing taxation, which first drew the attention of the royal government to the revenue possibilities of a royal 'tallage'. At least from the reign of Henry I, the declining yield of Danegeld was supplemented by an *assisa communis* levied on a county basis.[29] To this had been added *auxilia* from various boroughs, an early sign of their growing prosperity. The obligations of military tenure owed by other sections of the community were already being commuted for a financial levy, scutage. The government of the dynamic Angevins took up and primarily developed these specialized levies each framed to exploit to the full a certain group interest in the community. By the side of scutage from the baronage was developed tallage, in the first place out of the *auxilia* of the thriving boroughs. To some degree in 1164–5 and generally for the first time in 1167–8 this was also extended to the king's vills and manors

27. C. Stephenson, 'The Seignorial Tallage in England' in *Mélanges d'histoire offerts à Henri Pirenne* (Brussels, 1926), ii, 465–74, although as Stephenson appreciates it later (by the thirteenth century) became a common doctrine of English law that payment of tallage meant servility.

28. C. Stephenson 'Taxation and Representation in the Middle Ages' in *Anniversary Essays in Medieval History by Students of Charles Homer Haskins* (Boston and New York, 1929) conveniently reprinted in *Medieval Institutions Selected Essays*, ed. Bryce D. Lyon (Ithaca, N.Y., 1954). When royal tallage was later levied it was occasional, not annual, and this later became a distinctive feature of ancient demesne tenure (see below, pp. 24–6). This distinctive feature of ancient demesne tenure was responsible for the fact that when a manor of ancient demesne was farmed out or granted away it could only be tallaged when the king tallaged his demesnes and then only with his permission.

29. See the document printed by C. H. Haskins in his note on 'The Abacus and the King's Curia' in *E.H.R.*, xxvii (1912), 101–6, and his comments and references given *ibid.*, p. 104.

and to those portions of lands in his hands by escheat through failure of heirs or forfeiture or during minority, which were not liable for the payment of scutage.

These were the developments which appear to have brought the concept of a royal demesne into the records of English government. The occasion for this royal tallage was the collection of the *auxilium ad filiam maritandam* and this levy became the pattern for all subsequent levies, though tallages did not always subsequently coincide with scutages.[30] Boroughs which were increasingly called upon to contribute to royal taxation sued for the privilege of farming the king's revenues within their boundaries. This was also the time when the special legal privileges of royal ancient demesne tenure began to be created, again in return for special obligations. Increasing economic prosperity and special privileges were thus made grounds for increased payments in taxes to the royal Exchequer. Increased fiscal obligations could be used as bargaining counters for special privileges. While the occasion for the damand for tallage was indeed arbitrary, this was only really so in the sense that the occasion for the demand for scutage was arbitrary: the exercise of the supreme power of political decision vested in the king. It was not the depressed position of a 'royal demesne', but the evident increasing prosperity of the towns which first provided the occasion for it. Historians now also stress the element of negotiation in determining the amount of this levy between the local royal commissioners and the communities of the boroughs, vills and manors concerned.[31] Again, the capacity to pay clearly affected the frequency of the demand. The old idea of an under-privileged royal demesne as the milch-cow of the Angevin monarchy must be discarded. On the other hand it does appear likely that the very concept of a royal demesne only acquired administrative significance as the result of the devising of tallage, a tax which drew certain categories of the king's subjects not liable for scutage into a special fiscal relationship to him, in the course of which they too developed certain privileges and vested interests.

2. 'ANCIENT DEMESNE'

The concept of 'ancient demesne' has now been re-examined by Professor Hoyt. He has demonstrated that the villein sokemen of ancient demesne were not relics of privileged conditions surviving from pre-Conquest days under the direct influence of a conservative king, as Vinogradoff and Maitland supposed.[32] 'Change and novelty' characterized the first appearance

30. Stephenson, *Borough and Town*, p. 163. For a somewhat different explanation of the origins of tallage see Hoyt, *op. cit.*, pp. 115–17.

31. S. K. Mitchell, *op. cit.*, the chapters on tallage *passim*.

32. Hoyt, *op. cit.*, pp. 192–207. P. Vinogradoff, *op. cit.*, p. 125. Pollock and Maitland, *History of English Law* (2nd ed.), i, 400.

of this special, privileged tenure of villeins of royal demesne during the twelfth and thirteenth centuries, not earlier. It was in fact a new form of tenure developed during the growing financial, judicial and administrative activity of the reigns of Henry II and his sons and did not stem from Anglo-Saxon conditions. Itinerant justices and other royal commissioners brought royal justice to the shires, including the king's boroughs, vills and manors, along with assessments to tallage, inquiries into the values of privileges and estates and by what warrant and on what terms they were held of the king. A definition of privileges in return for increasing obligations, mainly fiscal, had begun earlier in the royal towns, where a uniform status and burgage tenure had become general about the time of Henry I.[33] As regards the rural estates the monarchy increasingly farmed out its manors, either to the highest bidder, or to subjects and servants whom it desired to favour. A system of fixed farms with the possibility of increments added from time to time best suited its primarily political needs here. Direct royal economic exploitation of estates was, in any case, an extremely difficult proposition and no royal organization existed to render this possible. By a grant of a manor for a limited period the land was ohviously not lost to the Crown for ever. But neither was it lost for ever if alienated. It might be resumed. Especially was this so following the new emphasis on the duty of both king and subjects to work together for the recovery of lost royal rights and to preserve them inviolate, which was evident from Henry II's accession. Thus the king had a special, permanent interest in protecting the well-being of the peasantry on lands held in socage, directly under his control. He took his principal financial profit from these by tallage, that is, by taxation. A prosperous peasantry was therefore very much in his interest. It was of course open to him to grant out even the right of tallage along with the land to a royal grantee or farmer, if he wished to do so, or to reserve it to himself as he pleased. Hence in the twelfth and thirteenth centuries king, peasantry, farmers or grantees of royal demesne, all had an interest in the development and preservation of the special rights of a 'royal demesne tenure' which gradually became known as tenure in ancient demesne although, historically, it was not ancient at all.

Even if a manor were alienated a certain special, royal nature thus began to be inseparably attached to it. Its tenants continued to enjoy certain immunities from other forms of taxation, freedom from suit of shire and hundred court, which meant freedom from jury service and trial by combat outside the manor, and, later, freedom from contributing to the cost of the knights of the shire sent to parliament; freedom from the sheriff's jurisdiction and from the ordinary courts of common law in certain respects; also freedom from toll wherever they went. The villein sokemen of

33. Stephenson, *Borough and Town*, p. 136 ff. and pp. 160–1.

the royal manors actually developed a legal form of tenure superior to ordinary villeinage. By the mid-thirteenth century this had become 'ancient' demesne tenure, verified by the law courts by reference to what had been King William's on the day on which King Edward was alive and dead, according to Domesday Book. But the privileges of villein sokemen on this 'royal demesne' who Bracton considered held '*de domino rege a conquestu*', and, indeed, the very concept of 'ancient' demesne, had been unknown to Glanvill a century earlier.[34] There was naturally enough a close parallel between the privileges of royal burghal tenure and these somewhat later developing privileges of ancient demesne tenure.[35] The privilege whereby a villein could gain his freedom by sojourn unmolested for a year and a day on privileged soil applied only to privileged urban areas in the twelfth century. By the thirteenth century it had been extended to a rural royal demesne also.[36] Our Angevin kings thus participated in the development of a theory of ancient demesne right and created a new form of tenure unknown to earlier generations. This was an integral part of the exploitation of all their royal rights, but most notably their rights of taxation, and of their freedom to dispose of their lands as they wished, while yet preserving their royal prerogative unimpaired. Inevitably certain subjects derived benefits and vested interests from these developments, an unavoidable concomitant of the growing power of the monarchy.

The emergence of a concept of royal demesne in Angevin England thus seems to have been the product of fiscal changes, of developments in an expanding system of national taxation. The *terra regis* of Domesday had no subsequent history in England along the lines of the contemporary French *domaine*, the landed patrimony of the Capetian royal house, the essential fount and reserve of French military, financial and judicial royal power from which, over a period of five hundred years or more from 987, French kings and their domainal officials moved outwards to effect a piecemeal unification of France. From the Conquest of 1066 the English counterpart of the French *domaine*, if any comparisons are to be attempted, was the whole kingdom of England.

3. ROYAL DEMESNE AND PARLIAMENTARY TAXATION

Even the development and maintenance of a royal demesne as a separate taxation entity within which the royal boroughs were comprehended ceased to be in the king's financial interest from the middle of the thirteenth century. In the history of English taxation there was a rapid de-

34. Hoyt, *op. cit.*, p. 184.
35. James Tait, *The Medieval English Borough* (Manchester, 1936), pp. 343–4, though Tait found this a 'curious parallelism'.
36. Hoyt, *op. cit.*, p. 188.

velopment of new taxes on personal (movable) property between the Saladin tithe of 1188 and 1240. After this development had been resumed for the crusade of 1269 the initiative in the replacement of the old tallage within the royal demesne by this new national levy came from the king and his Council. In spite of claims for exemption from tallage, and complaints about its frequency, there are indications that the boroughs and the rural demesne would have preferred to continue their payments under the old tallage rather than be incorporated in the new tax.[37] But the government desired otherwise. Pipe roll entries show that in 1294, when the magnates and knights granted a tenth on the value of movable property in parliament, local commissioners negotiated an identical sixth, not only from the towns and vills of the royal demesnes but from other 'market towns' also. Likewise pipe roll entries show that the parliamentary seventh of 1295 on movables was paid by these same categories when the magnates and knights granted an eleventh.[38] This was the so-called 'model parliament' of magnates lay and ecclesiastical, lesser clergy, knights of the shire, citizens and burgesses, summoned with *plenitudo potestatis* to bind their constituents, and summoned, at least in the terms of the writs to the archbishops and bishops, 'because what touches all should be approved by all'.[39] In 1296, as a result of a similarly constituted assembly, cities and boroughs 'of whosesoever tenures or liberties they may be and of all our demesnes' paid an eighth when the magnates and knights granted a twelfth.[40] The manors or vills of the rural royal demesne had to pay up like the rest of the king's subjects, but where were their representatives?

It has been asserted that the political thought of the thirteenth century could amply cover such a contingency: that the *plena potestas* of the knights of the shire could be taken to bind the whole shire over and above the magnates and representatives of those cities and towns who consented for themselves; that in any case parliament as the community of the communities bound the whole nation.[41] Professor Stephenson has more wisely written in a slightly different context that to interpret the history of medieval taxation as following a set of rigid legal principles is entirely to miss the point.[42] We may indeed take it that 'the king's prerogative for the common utility of all'[43] was sufficient to cover this anomaly of a directly

37. S. K. Mitchell, *op. cit.*, p. 359.

38. R. S. Hoyt, 'Royal Demesne, Parliamentary Taxation, and the Realm' in *Speculum*, xxiii (1948), 61–2 and references given there.

39. D. Pasquet, *The Origins of the House of Commons*, trans. R. G. D. Laffan (London, 1964), p. 99.

40. Hoyt in *Speculum* (1948), pp. 62–3.

41. Gaines Post, 'Plena Potestas and Consent in Medieval Assemblies', *Traditio*, i (1943), 405–6.

42. Carl Stephenson in his essay 'Taxation and Representation in the Middle Ages' in *Anniversary Essays in Medieval History by Students of Charles Homer Haskins*, p. 307.

43. The phrase is Gaines Post's in *Traditio* (1943), p. 406.

unrepresented rural demesne which was indirectly bound by the knights of the shire to contribute (and at a higher rate) than the rest of the shires. But one aspect of this problem is particularly clear: there is no evidence to suggest that the men of the rural demesne themselves considered that lack of representation was a grievance. Tenants in ancient demesne were in fact very well satisfied that they managed to opt out of contributing towards the expenses of the knights of the shire,[44] and made no effort to secure their own representation.

There is one little difficulty in the way of accepting this explanation, but it is easily surmounted. While in the record of the parliament of 1306 the nominal roll consists of the names of the magnates lay and ecclesiastical present, followed by a statement that each county sent two knights and each city and borough two citizens or burgesses, the subsequent statement in that record of the taxation granted there couples with the citizens and burgesses granting the higher rate of tax 'others of the king's demesnes assembled and holding discussion thereon'.[45] But it is most unlikely that such representatives were really present on this occasion and their inclusion here was most probably only a legal fiction. In this respect it is perhaps as well to recall that back in 1225, 1232 and 1269 the royal demesne, cities and boroughs, had paid the taxes on movables granted by general assemblies in which no such categories were represented.[46] The device of exacting a power of attorney from city and borough representatives, a *plena potestas* to bind their constituents, had already been used for the first time in the assembly of 1268,[47] but only from 1283 did it become a regular requirement. The men of the royal demesne were not anxious to secure representative status comparable to that forced upon other sections of the community, but to retain the old ways. When Edward I found that he could levy this new, more profitable, general aid as frequently as the old scutages and almost as frequently as the old tallage he was ultimately led to depend on central representatives with *plenitudo potestatis* to grant it, because this avoided lengthy discussions and produced quicker and more substantial results than sectional bargaining. The men of the rural royal demesne were perforce included without special representation. The consolidation of the royal demesne with the rest of the nation for purposes of taxation simply did not present a constitutional problem as far as contemporaries were concerned, or at the very most only to a few civil servants as revealed by this slightly ambiguous, judicious wording of the official record by royal clerks in 1306.

44. Hoyt in *Speculum* (1948), pp. 68–9.

45. Printed by Pasquet from the L. T. R. Memoranda Roll, *op. cit.*, pp. 234–6.

46. S. K. Mitchell, *Studies in Taxation under John and Henry III* (New Haven, Yale U.P., 1914), pp. 389–90 for 1225 and 1232; p. 297 for 1269.

47. G. O. Sayles, 'Representation of Cities and Boroughs in 1268', *E.H.R.*, xl (1925), 580–5.

The knights of the shire were first clearly alleged to represent the rural royal demesne in 1316.[48] A distinction that only the economically and legally privileged 'ancient demesne' had the duty of paying at the higher rate of tax, together with the similarly privileged boroughs, and not those lands in the king's hands by escheat, by failure of heirs, forfeiture or during minority, is first discernible in the records of the grant of 1307.[49] Royal tallage lapsed by disuse in the meantime, though the king's formal right to it was never abandoned. The first two Edwards only levied it twice (1304 and 1312) while the proposed tallage of 1332 was cancelled, and that was the last heard of it,[50] except in those Welsh or palatine counties which did not send representatives to Westminster.

Thus from the early fourteenth century the royal demesne was hardly distinguishable from the rest of the country even in the sphere of taxation. It is true that areas paying at the higher rate of a tenth rather than a fifteenth, including the 'ancient demesne' manors, were noted on a separate section of the taxation roll,[51] but these areas never varied after 1336. In that year this tax on movables, parliamentary tenths and fifteenths, became a grant of a fixed sum and the allocation of proportional contributions from the separate communities became correspondingly fixed for all time. The assessment of 1332, as modified by bargaining in 1334, thus comprised the amounts paid ever after, from 1336 until the reign of James I.[52] Future developments, following a tradition already centuries old, lay mainly in the discovery and exploitation of new forms of taxation, not in the rejuvenation of a static or declining tax.

It follows that the question of whether or not land was ancient demesne or royal demesne became of very little interest to the Crown even from a taxation point of view after 1334. Whether the king as landlord lost or acquired a manor or town could henceforth make no difference at all to the taxes paid by the men of that manor or town. The very term 'ancient demesne' came to have little significance beyond the legal definition of a form of land tenure, of special interest only to those tenants who held land by it. The term is mentioned only seven times in the printed calendars of the patent rolls between 1370 and 1405, and all of them resulted from petitions by tenants for exchequer certificates which, by defining their tenure, confirmed them in the enjoyment of certain legal rights, whether the land was in royal or private hands.[53]

48. Hoyt in *Speculum* (1948), p. 66.

49. *ibid.*, p. 65.

50. See the final chapter 'The End of Royal Tallage' in Mitchell, *Taxation in Medieval England*.

51. J. F. Willard, *Parliamentary Taxes on Personal Property 1290 to 1334* (Cambridge, Mass., 1934), p. 71 and references to lay subsidy rolls in print given there.

52. *ibid.*, pp. 12–13 (subject to multiple grants and to deductions for hardship).

53. *Cal. Pat. Rolls, 1370–1374*, 322; *ibid., 1377–1381*, 213; *1381–1385*, 358; *1385–1389*, 276; *1399–1401*, 309–10; *1401–1405*, 61. Also cf. *Rot. Parl.* iii, 18, 617.

Thus the primary significance of the royal demesne in the workings of government under the Norman and Angevin kings lay not in its value as a fundamental source of land revenue or military strength, or as a nursery of royal administration and justice, but as a fiscal entity paying tallage, and declining in importance and passing into history when that tax disappeared as a unit from the nation-wide system. It left behind only a fossilized division on the tax roll and the concomitant relics of legal privilege as a form of land tenure in ancient demesne.

4. ROYAL DEMESNE AND LAND REVENUE

The idea of a medieval English royal demesne which first evolved as a unit of Angevin taxation finds no support in the generally accepted history of the evolution of English national finances. The belief that the greatest part of the expenses of the Crown were once defrayed by a land revenue which was squandered by the grants of successive rulers until it became negligible was enshrined in English statute as long ago as the reign of Queen Anne.[54] The historian of the revenues of the medieval kings of England observed in judgement on Henry II that the value of the lands he gave away, the *terrae datae*, greatly exceeded the total of the 'illegal' tallages he imposed: if he had refrained from giving so freely he might have saved his memory from the opprobrium of extortion.[55] Such strictures are based on a fundamental misunderstanding of the whole nature of English medieval government finance. It is a misdirected exercise to search the records of English government before the later fifteenth century for evidence of any sustained effort to make a royal demesne yield by estate management a cash income on a scale comparable to what royal taxation, direct and later indirect, provided, or to try to identify lost opportunities for such a policy. The constantly evolving and changing system of national taxation within which an Angevin concept of a royal demesne can alone be described, had expanded to produce an average of about £35,600 p.a. between 1307 and 1327.[56] Such elusive information as can be recaptured about the yield of land revenue from a royal demesne between the accession of Henry II and the fourteenth century suggests that this made only a comparatively minor contribution to the royal finances. Except in the sole instance of Domesday

54. Stat. 1 Anne cap. 1, sect. V (An act for the better Support of Her Majesties Household and of the Honour and Dignity of the Crown): 'And whereas the necessary Expenses of supporting the Crown or the greatest part of them were formerly defrayed by a Land Revenue which hath from time to time been impaired and diminished by the Grant of former Kings and Queens of this realm so that her Majesties Land Revenues at present can afford very little towards the Support of Her Government. . . .'

55. Sir James H. Ramsay, *A History of the Revenues of the Kings of England 1066–1399* (Oxford, 1925), i, 186.

56. *ibid.*, ii, 145–9. His average of £35,600 consists of lay subsidies £12,000, clerical subsidies £11,000, and customs £12,600.

Book no historian has in fact ever claimed to be able to provide a convincing estimate of this contribution in produce, sales of produce, farms and rents at any point within the whole of the medieval period. The nature of the records, even though they survive in profusion, appears to make this impossible and it seems very doubtful whether any medieval English government was ever interested in such information.

Traditionally the direct financial yield of the king's lands was accounted for on the pipe roll, almost entirely within the sheriffs' farms. The total theoretical value of these sheriffs' farms, before any deductions or allowances were made, was about £10,000 during the reign of Henry II and remained unchanged until the thirteenth century.[57] Before 1236 the form of account makes it impossible to itemize them, but a substantial amount had certainly to be deducted from this total for *terrae datae*, a write-off financially to the Exchequer,[58] at least from the accession of Henry II if not earlier. Parow calculated this at £4,574 1s 1d in 1169–70; according to Ramsay's figures, taken from the chancellor's roll for 3 John, the value of the *terrae datae* had risen to £6,816 11s 10d by 1200–1.[59] But, further, as the *Dialogus* states of the sheriffs' farms, 'tota non exurgit ex fundorum redditibus set ex magna parte de placitis'.[60] After 1236, according to Miss Mills, what was left of these sheriffs' farms consisted entirely of profits from hundred and shire courts, views of frankpledge, castle-ward, sheriffs' aid and like payments.[61] Although one cannot prove it, one cannot but suspect that for many years before 1236 these jurisdictional financial activities of the sheriff had already loomed large in the residue of his farm, after the *terrae datae* had been allowed for, by comparison with his operations as a royal land agent.

In the early thirteenth century certain additional profits (*proficua*) and an increment (*incrementum*) were extracted from each sheriff supplementary to his farm, but it has never been suggested that the sheriff's ability to pay these additional levies was due to an improvement in his position as a royal land agent. There is no evidence to suggest a reversal of royal policy which such an improvement would have entailed. In 1284 the form of account was at last changed to exclude the *terrae datae* from the total theoretical charge against him. After these changes the total charges against the sheriffs under these three headings (farm, profits and increment)

57. Poole, *op. cit.*, p. 134; W. Parow, *Compotus Vicecomitis Die Rachenschaftslegung des Sheriffs unter Heinrich II von England* (Berlin, 1906), p. 27; G. F. Turner, 'The Sheriff's Farm', *T.R.H.S.*, New series, xii (1908), 117–41. For the thirteenth century see Mabel H. Mills, 'Exchequer Agenda and Estimate of Revenue, Easter Term 1284', *E.H.R.*, xl (1925), 229–34.

58. Parow, *op. cit.*, p. 28; Poole, *op. cit.*, pp. 134–5, 158.

59. Parow, *op. cit.*, p. 49; Ramsay, *op. cit.*, i, 233.

60. *Dialogus* (ed. Johnson), pp. 64–5.

61. Mabel H. Mills, 'Experiments in Exchequer Procedure (1200–1232)', *T.R.H.S.*, 4th series, viii (1925), 151–170.

appear to have been a mere £4,000.[62] The reluctance of the Exchequer to write off these *terrae datae* in the account before this late date has been attributed to the possibility that they might return to the Crown and so to the control of the sheriff. But this did not happen. It is true that some degree of financial compensation was received by the Crown in the partial conversion to feefarms and the levying of stiff entry fines which were sometimes part of such arrangements, but the amount of land revenue which reached the Exchequer was not the over-riding consideration governing the disposition of the royal demesne.

S. K. Mitchell collected many instances of new arrangements made in the administration of the royal demesne under Richard and John, a period sometimes now considered to have been one of most energetic financial development of the demesne. We must remember, however, that his definition of the royal demesne included the boroughs and escheats, even if lands were only temporarily in the king's hands during vacancy or minority etc., and most of the examples he cited fall into these categories. His examples certainly show increments added to farms or substantial entry fines required for new agreements, indicating that a determined government could raise significant sums of cash in this way, and, of course, revealing the opportunities enjoyed by entrepreneurs in this field. Nevertheless, the increased financial yield to the Exchequer must be considered in the context of the much longer leases, perpetual leases, or feefarms, which were almost invariably the crux of such arrangements. A substantial fine might even secure a permanent, substantial reduction in the farm. Mitchell's conclusion that 'no uniform policy in administering the demesne' can be discerned, also suggests that political considerations continued to determine this in the ultimate event, although no chances of obtaining immediate cash payments were neglected, usually at the expense of the longer-term conservation of financial assets.[63]

There are now dozens of pipe rolls in print and they can be searched for accounts of royal land revenue, but it is a singular fact that such accounts as do appear on the pipe rolls or on their subsidiary documents, or are preserved as the result of special inquiries (accounts which are also listed in the Public Record Office *Lists and Indexes of Foreign Accounts*, *Ministers' Accounts*, and *Special Commissions and Returns in the Exchequer*) consist almost entirely of the issues of lands which were held only temporarily in the king's hands, whether they had accrued to him as a result of escheat, by failure of heirs, or by forfeiture, by vacancy in the case of ecclesiastical lands, or during the minority or idiocy of lay tenants-in-chief.[64]

No one has yet doubted that the sheriffs' farms at the date of Domesday

62. Mabel H. Mills in *E.H.R.*, xl (1925), 230–1.
63. S. K. Mitchell, *Taxation in Medieval England*, pp. 304–6.
64. *Public Record Office Lists and Indexes*, v, viii, xi, xxxvii.

had consisted for the major part of income from the royal lands under their control. It may be that the Exchequer kept an up-to-date detailed record of how sheriffs' farms were made up in the *rotulus exactorius* or *breve de firmis*, several times mentioned in the *Dialogus* but not described in detail. This is suggested by the unique survival of what appears to be a copy of the Herefordshire portion of it for the time of Henry I, detailing the royal manors concerned, with the stock they carried and their individual contributions to the farms paid by the sheriff.[65] The total income from land which William I had at his disposal has been calculated from Domesday Book to have been about £73,000, exclusive of the boroughs, and he is supposed to have retained out of this for himself, the royal family, his minor officials and personal servants, lands to the value of about £19,450, a like amount going to the endowment of the church and the rest to his tenants-in-chief, Norman and English.[66] No one doubts that he received his land revenues, whatever they amounted to, by means of the sheriffs' farms. But there is no way of telling what the total farm of the shires amounted to in Domesday. When information about the total shire farms does at last appear, in the isolated pipe roll for 1130 and then again in the continuous series from 1155, the low totals there revealed are in stark contrast to the apparently huge landed income which the Conqueror had enjoyed. This contrast has been most vividly brought out by Professor Southern, quoting (1) figures, by shires, for royal profits in Domesday; (2) subsequent shire farms for 1130 or earlier if known.[67] Also the figures given by Professor Southern for the apparently shrunken revenues of 1130 are before allowances and deductions such as *terrae datae* were made to sheriffs, which make the contrast even more remarkable.

Historians have previously offered only one explanation for this apparently rapidly wasting asset: massive alienation by William I's successors, differing only as to where they apportioned the main blame, either on Henry I on the one hand, or on Stephen and Henry II on the other. Professor Southern has now argued cogently for a new look at Domesday

65. *Hereford Domesday circa 1160–1170*, ed. V. H. Galbraith and James Tait (Pipe Roll Soc. 1950, N.S. 25), fol. 39 and p. xxxi of the introduction.

66. W. J. Corbett, *Cambridge Medieval History*, v, 508.

67. Southern, *op. cit.*, pp. 157–69 *passim*. Professor Southern's figures can be tabulated as follows:

	County						
	Essex	Heref.	Herts.	Leics.	Northants.	Oxon.	Wilts.
Domesday (min.) figure	£616	£335	£142	£156 10s	£573	£788	£1,460
Later farm (approx. in some cases)	£300	£165	£60	£100	£150	£350	£600

This did not apply to all counties. He has noted that in Kent and Worcs. there appears to have been some improvement.

Book itself, suggesting that in fact the king never did receive a huge land revenue on the scale of the Domesday valuation even in 1086, and that all William the Conqueror himself received was shire farms already approaching the lower scale of 1130 and subsequent reigns.[68] This may indeed, as Professor Southern concludes, present a picture of much less efficient government under the Conqueror than has hitherto been supposed. But to my mind, if accepted, it removes from the pages of English history the only remaining instance before the advent of the Yorkists and Tudors when a king of England can be alleged to have received a massive income from the direct exploitation of land revenues. It suggests in fact that the finances of English government within a few years of the Conquest were already orientated on the lines familiar to us at least from the Angevins to the Lancastrians: that they were based fairly and squarely on the proceeds of taxation in its various forms.

5. ROYAL DEMESNE AND PATRONAGE

In considering the true nature and significance of royal landholding in England from 1066 one must begin by stressing that the Norman Conquest conquered and unified the whole country in a sense and to a degree which never applied in medieval France or Germany. This is still true even if we accept that the real growth of royal power in England dated not from *the* Conquest but from what has recently been called the Angevin 'conquest' of 1154.[69] While it is undoubted fact that William I took over the *terra regis* of the Confessor and the lands of Harold, yet if we are to speak of a post-Conquest royal demesne in England as the equivalent of the Capetian royal *domaine* in France then it should logically be of the whole country, whether enfeoffed or not. The all-pervading nature of the Norman Conquest of England rendered superfluous a royal demesne set apart or preserved as an entity, with any kind of separate royal estate management or any special administrative system. In England there never was any reliance on demesnial resources as such, no gradual, persistent permeation of fiefs by officials of the royal demesne asserting the rights of suzerainty; no instances of a monarch, secure only on the basis of his royal patrimony, successfully playing off the particularisms of one region against another. From the time of the Conqueror and his sons, kingly power in England was squarely based on the all-pervading influence of the king's political rights; on a royal justice which was uniformly applicable to all parts of the kingdom; on a kingdom-wide obligation, according to status, to military

68. *ibid.*, pp. 164–9.

69. Frank Barlow, 'The Effects of the Norman Conquest', in Dorothy Whitelock, D. C. Douglas, C. H. Lemmon and Frank Barlow, *The Norman Conquest Its Setting and Impact* (London, 1966), pp. 160–1.

service and taxation, and on a royal, common law. Any special rights which the king had as the direct owner of estates which he did not enfeoff were certainly maintained like all his royal rights, but this was done entirely through the normal national apparatus of central control, working through the shires and hundreds, the sheriffs and itinerant justices. The king's own lands like the royal fiefs were subjected at the same time, and by the same methods and machinery, to one system of 'undifferentiated government'.[70]

Historians of an English 'royal demesne' from the Conquest must therefore beware of attributing to it an entity and coherence which it never possessed. It is surely due to no accident of survival that all the records referred to in print as recording its extent, its component parts, its economic and financial value, either merely cover bits of it or appear to supply information about it only incidentally to some other purpose. There are references in print to certain working compilations made from the pipe rolls between 1 Henry II and 3 Richard I giving lists of some royal manors tallaged, *terrae datae*, and manors in hand at certain dates.[71] There is a list of the total theoretical amounts of the sheriffs' farms for the separate shires payable at the Exchequer, with an attempt to list their constituent farms and feefarms and the dates, ranging from the first year of Henry II to 1230, when these items were first allowed for on the pipe roll as *terrae datae*.[72] The great inquiry of 1274 which produced the Hundred Rolls, and the subsequent enquiry of 1279, were the only ones approaching the Domesday Survey in scope and thoroughness, yet even they were essentially inquests into the usurpation of liberties and franchises and into the misconduct of officials, not into royal landholding or royal land revenues.[73] The record known as the *Nomina villarum* of 1316, which appears to enable us to pick out the names of the king's hundreds, cities, boroughs and towns (*ville*) at that date, makes no mention of the king's manors and was made to facilitate the provision of footsoldiers for the Scottish campaign.[74]

Nevertheless, elusive as a medieval English royal demesne may be to describe in terms of composition, extent, or yield in land revenues, convincing evidence of wanton alienation of crown lands or of disregard for the maintenance of royal rights over them never has been and never will be produced. At all periods all lands at the king's disposal had an inescapable political role to play and custom had already fixed the methods of their

70. Hoyt, *op. cit.*, p. 102.

71. *Red Book of the Exchequer*, ii, p. ccxiii.

72. *ibid.*, ii, pp. cclxiii–cclxv and pp. 779–97, but what Hubert Hall described as entries of farms due to the Crown under the regnal year when they were first put in charge on the Pipe Roll are in fact entries of *terrae datae* when they were first *allowed for* on the Pipe Roll.

73. Helen M. Cam, 'Quo Warranto Proceedings under Edward I', *History*, xi (1926), 143–8 and her book *The Hundred and the Hundred Rolls*, especially pp. 195–9.

74. *Rot. Parl.*, i, 351; printed by counties in *Feudal Aids* (6 vols, H.M.S.O., 1899–1921).

administration designed to fulfil this role certainly as early as the reign of Henry II.[75] A policy of relentless economic exploitation was generally unnecessary, impracticable and undesirable. A salaried keeper might be employed with all the profits and all the losses of estate management borne by the king. But to an increasing extent manors or urban areas were let out at farm for a fixed annual amount with a substantial initial fine exacted for the granting of the privilege. The practice of feefarming or perpetual leasing by which the king had the advantage of stability and low costs of collection became increasingly widespread. Clearly in making arrangements for the local management of the lands held of them by socage or burgage tenure the Norman and Angevin kings had to share the advantages with their subjects. Their financial profit came primarily from tallage, the possibilities of which increased as the prosperity of the unit taxed increased. Nearly all the farms of royal manors appearing in the pipe roll of 1130 remained unchanged for the rest of the century. Entry fines might on occasion be substantial, but it was the level of taxation, not the level of rents or farms, which mirrored the true rise in economic prosperity, and it was through taxation that the king shared in that prosperity.

The truth is that the reservoir of royal land which was filled by conquest in 1066 and was subsequently further replenished by forfeiture, purchase or escheat, was immediately drawn upon to meet those vital military and political needs which far transcended any advantages of direct royal landownership on a larger scale: the multiplication of tenants-in-chief and vassals and the sharing out of the responsibilities and expenses of government. The usefulness of ecclesiastics in this respect, demands of regal piety and provision for the welfare of the king's soul also required a substantial endowment of the Norman church in England.[76] Provision had to be made for the maintenance of members of the royal family, as already evident in Domesday Book. Next in importance came support and rewards for royal companions, councillors, ministers and servants, likewise evident in 1086. This could be and often necessarily was 'everlastynge in their heyres to their perpetuall memorie and honour'[77] when the king so chose, the prospect of which was the only ultimate way to command service. English history is littered with complaints of royal prodigality on this score, but no century earlier than our own would have thought of condemning this practice outright, on principle, as living on capital rather than interest. Such grants, as Professor Southern points out, certainly diminished the powers of the mighty Anglo-Norman sheriffs, but not necessarily of the

75. See S. K. Mitchell, *Taxation in Medieval England*, pp. 300–3 for the remainder of this paragraph and the references given there.

76. cf. R. B. Pugh, *The Crown Estate* (H.M.S.O., London, 1960), pp. 3–4.

77. Sir John Fortescue, *The Governance of England*, ed. Charles Plummer (Oxford, 1885), p. 136.

king.[78] Regular and appropriate salaries for government servants are a very modern institution indeed and many grants of crown manors from the beginning filled this need also on a rough and ready basis, not by permanent alienation but for terms of years or for life. These were, in effect, farms of land either fixed at an appropriate level to allow sufficient reward, or with the farm remitted altogether. If the manor or property was actually let to farm or put in charge of a keeper, then there might well be one or more pensions, payable directly from the farmer or keeper to the recipients. Finally, the financial residue would be paid into the central Exchequer of Receipt. The royal lands were consequently subject only to residual and intermittent exchequer financial interest and control. It was certainly the Exchequer's herculean task to keep track that in the ultimate event the king received all that was financially due to him, in whatever form, from this diversified system. But the efficiency of it must be estimated, if it can be estimated at all, by a combination of political, military, social and, only lastly, financial criteria. The medieval English Exchequer never was an office of land management and land revenue in the normally understood sense of those terms.

The infinite complexity which faces the researcher who would unravel from medieval English records financial data about royal land revenues satisfying to the modern mind, but not required by contemporaries, can be admirably illustrated from the indefatigable labours of Miss Mills who has, for example, printed and elucidated the Surrey membrane of the pipe roll for 1295, in so far as that task is humanly possible. One specific instance alone will spotlight the insuperable difficulties. Even Miss Mills has been unable to provide reasons for the fact that the farmer of Southwark and keeper of the manor of Banstead, both of them within easy reach of the Exchequer, and one of them actually a chancery official, were both still being charged with arrears of account for 1295 on the pipe roll for 1302–3, although according to the receipt rolls, they had already made due payment in 1295. In the case of the keeper of Banstead his debt was still being pursued in 1311–12 when it was removed to the special roll reserved for 'desperate debts'.[79] Such instances of, apparently, the most simple cases, where the Exchequer failed to keep track on royal farms, were of frequent occurrence.[80] They can only be understood if one accepts as one's starting point the premise that the medieval English Exchequer, whatever else it was, was not an office of land revenue, not a court or treasury of a royal

78. Southern, *op. cit.*, p. 166.

79. *The Pipe Roll for 1295, Surrey Membrane*, ed. and trans. Mabel H. Mills (Surrey Record Soc.), vol. vii, no. 21 (1924), pp. lxi–lxiii.

80. *Red Book of the Exchequer*, iii, 877; 'great arrears of many farms run at the Exchequer, for long time past, without remembrance being found of the cause' (section 29 of the Cowick Ordinances of 1323). If the following section 30 is read together with section 29 it is clear that the reference is to farms and rents of lands not to the sheriffs' farms.

demesne. Indeed our Norman and Angevin kings, secure in their enjoyment of the revenues of the whole kingdom, had no such office and no need of one.

6. CONTRASTS IN THE ROLE OF THE CAPETIAN *DOMAINE*

The contrasts in the role of the royal *domaine* in the history of medieval France are most striking and instructive and deserve brief consideration here because of the undoubted existence in late medieval France of a clear distinction between ordinary (domainal) revenues and extraordinary (national, fiscal) revenues, the product of fundamentally different factors in three centuries of French history. How far English historians have been influenced in their interpretation of English history by a knowledge of the clearer and simpler but very different history of the French *domaine* is difficult to determine.

During the first three centuries of Capetian rule from 987 the areas over which the kings of France exercised direct authority were not the kingdom of France but the royal *domaine*.[81] Income from their *domaine* constituted their total financial resources. It was almost impossible for the French king to establish direct relationships with his subjects outside the *domaine*, other than with his tenants-in-chief, until he had annexed a particular territory or fief to his *domaine*. Even the Capetian *domaine*, which was, in origin, the debris of their Merovingian and Carolingian heritage, may, on close examination, appear to have been as much a tangle of royal domainal rights and services as an immediate possession of directly held lands.[82] Yet it was always undeniably identifiable as a territorial concept, originally centred on Paris, Laon and Orléans,[83] for which there was no territorial counterpart in Norman and Angevin England. Outside it were the great 'sovereign' principalities and fiefs of Flanders, Champagne, Burgundy, Toulouse, Normandy and Aquitaine, whose rulers dispensed 'high justice'. In addition there were all the lesser but judicially and financially comparable autonomous units over which the royal successors of Charlemagne exercised only the intangible attributes of their kingship and their claims of suzerainty. Until the reign of Philip the Fair the royal income increased only in so far as the *domaine* extended more widely over the confines of the kingdom. Domainal revenues were indeed the French king's 'ordinary'

81. The history of the French royal *domaine* and of the extraordinary revenues to 1524 is thoroughly expounded by Ferdinand Lot and Robert Fawtier in *Histoire des Institutions françaises au Moyen Age*, ii, *Institutions royales* (Presses universitaires de France, Paris, 1958) with full bibliographies, to which should be added Maurice Rey's *Le domaine du roi et les finances extraordinaires sous Charles VI, 1388–1413* (S.E.V.P.E.N., Paris, 1965).

82. *Histoire des Institutions françaises*, ii, 100; W. M. Newman, *Le domaine royal sous les premiers Capétiens* (Paris, 1937), with maps.

83. Robert Fawtier, *The Capetian Kings of France*, trans. Lionel Butler and R. J. Adam (London, 1962), p. 77.

revenue, but this designation only came to have significance with the acquisition of an 'extraordinary' revenue for the first time, beginning in the last years of the thirteenth century, and derived from the whole kingdom of France in the shape of direct and indirect taxation, the *taille* and the *aides*. The very beginnings of these national, 'extraordinary' revenues, as opposed to domainal, 'ordinary' revenues were the achievement of Philip the Fair. Commutation of military service was first extended generally throughout the kingdom beyond the confines of the *domaine* by the same king.[84]

The same distinction between the rest of the French kingdom and the *domaine* also applied in the realm of justice. Before the reign of St Louis the *ordonnances* of the Capetian kings which were the product of royal power were still limited in application to the royal *domaine* alone. The Capetian kings had no monopoly of legislation and *ordonnances* promulgated by their great feudatories, though rare, do exist.[85] During the thirteenth century there were a few occasions, beyond instances of a religious or ecclesiastical nature, where the French king appears to have legislated in limited fields for the general body of his subjects beyond the confines of the *domaine*, but the most important factor in the development of the French royal legislative power was the prodigious expansion of the royal *domaine* from the reigns of Philip III and Philip IV, and of the effective suzerainty which went with it. St Louis' celebrated abolition of trial by battle had applied only to his *domaine*.[86] From his reign the royal domainal bailiffs and seneschals provided the means by which the royal power ultimately succeeded in penetrating the great fiefs until the judicial limits of the *domaine* extended to the boundaries of the kingdom, but this situation still had not been reached at the outbreak of the Hundred Years War. Among the latest Capetians and the earliest Valois a largely ineffective moral pressure, exerted through the court of the *Parlement*, was the only power which they had to limit the operation of private war among the 'sovereign' nobility of France.[87]

The medieval French royal *domaine* was thus territorially, financially and judicially an autonomous unit within the wider Capetian kingdom. During the fourteenth and fifteenth centuries, but not earlier, French domainal revenues came to be described as 'ordinary' revenues because of the new national 'extraordinary' revenues which were then added to them. The question of representation and consent by national and regional assemblies was undoubtedly closely associated with the origins of the 'extraordinary' revenues in France. The day when a king of France could summon an assembly of all his vassals in the kingdom of France had to wait until the *domaine* had, in effect, spread itself over the whole realm. Extraordinary or national revenues, as opposed to domainal resources, began to be employed

84. *ibid.*, p. 195–6.
85. *Histoire des Institutions françaises*, ii, 290–2.
86. *ibid.*, ii, 317–19.
87. *ibid.*, ii, 429–30.

in France from that point in the later middle ages when the Capetian royal *domaine* burst out from the limits of a great fief and placed at the disposal of the French kings territories vastly superior in extent and resources to anything previously envisaged by their administrators.[88] First imposed through new national assemblies, these extraordinary or national revenues were collected by a new system of administration built around the new *généraux* and *super-intendants des finances* and not by the old *trésoriers* of the royal *domaine*. Beside the domainal *chambre des comptes* was ultimately created the new *cour des aides* of the extraordinary revenues. The revenues of the *domaine* now became 'ordinary' and for two centuries the issues of the new, national, direct and indirect taxation composed the 'extra-ordinary' revenues. The latter, which were shared with the great lords of France, became permanent from 1439, and all vestiges of consent had long since disappeared when Francis I's administrative consolidation of the new with the old in 1523–4 removed all practical distinction between the ordinary and the extraordinary.[89]

It is thus easily understandable that a modern French historian should have construed certain advice given by St Thomas Aquinas to the duchess of Brabant, and illustrated by reference to the landed portion of the kings of Israel, as the expression of a generally accepted, universal, medieval theory that royal government ought to subsist on the issues of a royal *domaine*.[90] By contrast there appears to have been no such theory, or any basis of fact to support one, in medieval England where a concept that royal revenues were divided into ordinary (demesnial) and extraordinary (fiscal) still seems to have been unknown at the end of the fifteeenth century. Moreover, the English medieval notion that kings should 'live of their own' does not appear in origin to have had any association with the resources of a royal demesne.

7. RESTRAINT OF ALIENATION IN ENGLAND AND THE GENESIS OF 'THE KING TO LIVE OF HIS OWN'

The English constitutional theory that extraordinary revenue consists of the proceeds of taxation, and that medieval kings were normally expected to live on their ordinary landed revenue which constituted their own, was enshrined in statute during the aftermath of the Glorious Revolution, but the earliest succinct and full expression of it appears to be Sir William Blackstone's in his *Commentaries on the Laws of England*:

88. *ibid.*, ii, 549–50.

89. *ibid.*, ii, 274.

90. A. Colville, *Les Cabochiens et l'ordonnance de 1413* (Paris, 1888), p. 37, quoted and elaborated by M. Rey, *Le domaine du roi*, p. 41. Aquinas was quoting Ezechiel XLV, 8: 'principi erit possessio in Israel, et non depopulabuntur ultra principes populum meum', see *Opuscula Omnia necnon Opera Minora*, ed. R. P. Joannes Perrier, O.P., *Tomus Primus, Opuscula Philosophica* (Paris, 1949), p. 218.

'This may suffice for a short view of the king's *ordinary* revenue, or the proper patrimony of the crown; which was very large formerly, and capable of being increased to a magnitude truly formidable: for there are very few estates in the kingdom, that have not, at some period or other since the Norman conquest, been vested in the hands of the king by forfeiture, escheat, or otherwise. But, fortunately for the liberty of the subject, this hereditary landed revenue, by a series of improvident management, is sunk almost to nothing; and the casual profits, arising from the other branches of the *census regalis*, are likewise almost all of them alienated from the crown. In order to supply the deficiencies of which, we are now obliged to have recourse to new methods of raising money, unknown to our early ancestors; which methods constitute the king's *extraordinary* revenue [i.e. taxes]. For the public patrimony being got into the hands of private subjects, it is but reasonable that private contributions should supply the public service. Which, though it may perhaps fall harder upon some individuals, whose ancestors have had no share in the general plunder, than upon others, yet, taking the nation throughout, it amounts to nearly the same; provided the gain by the extraordinary, should appear to be no greater than the loss by the ordinary, revenue.'[91]

It was only with the publication of William Stubbs's *Constitutional History of England in its Origin and Development* between 1874 and 1878 that the earlier assertions of seventeenth and eighteenth-century politicians and lawyers were so vigorously reasserted and applied to the English middle ages with such a convincing air of academic detachment that they became articles of faith among modern constitutional historians.[92]

In fact no instance of the use of the expression 'the king to live of his own' has been quoted earlier than 1311 by any writer who has accepted the modern theories of the constitution woven round it. Stubbs, the 'perfect hedger', might possibly be taken as referring only to the fourteenth century when he described it as a principle 'constantly recurring',[93] but other influential writers even in his own day understood him to mean that this demand had been frequently met with 'throughout the whole of the medieval history of England'.[94] This indeed was a justifiable interpretation

91. William Blackstone, *Commentaries on the Laws of England* (7th ed., Oxford, 1775), i, 306–7. The first edition was published in 1765.

92. The conclusions of Blackstone summarized in the quotation above seem to me to be fundamental to the plan of Stubbs's *Constitutional History*, but they are most succinctly expounded by Stubbs in vol. ii (4th ed., 1896), from p. 541, in the chapter headed 'Royal Prerogative and Parliamentary Authority'.

93. Stubbs, *op. cit.*, ii, 543.

94. Charles Plummer, in his edition of Sir John Fortescue's *Governance of England*, p. 250. Unfortunately Plummer's page references to Stubbs's *Constitutional History* are to the scarce cabinet edition. The two references which he gives here (ii, 545 and 551) are ii, 574 and 581 in the 4th edition.

of Stubbs because he had himself also written that one principle of medieval constitutional growth 'as enunciated by the party opposed to royal assumption' was that the king should 'live of his own', 'supporting royal state and ordinary national administrative machinery out of ordinary revenue'.[95] There can be little doubt that Stubbs was in fact thinking along the same lines here as Blackstone and the statute makers of the eighteenth century. Thus a long and unbroken sequence of events could be presented, beginning with the supposedly enormous land revenues of the Domesday *terra regis*, passing through centuries of alienations by profligate or incompetent kings who were impervious to the repeated strictures of baronial opposition, down to incipient, like-minded parliamentary opposition in the later middle ages, and so on to the full flowering of the principles of constitutional limitation through control of the purse-strings in the post-Revolution era.

There are a number of stubborn historical facts which prevent the easy acceptance of this grand far-ranging concept, but even if these could be ignored one awkward paradox might have been seen to mar its logic: if any of our misguided medieval kings had successfully been made to follow the advice of his alleged critics and had thereby fortified himself with a huge inalienable landed estate and its concomitant revenues, then the path of constitutional progress would presumably have been blocked for all time. Stubbs indeed referred to this as the 'double application' of the alleged medieval principle,[96] whatever that meant, but the unavoidable implication that medieval men were fools to strive for something whose attainment would defeat their objectives does not appear to have worried him.

Probably the advocate of Stubbs's views who had most influence on professional historians was the classicist Charles Plummer, who in 1885 published the first and only modern scholarly text of the earliest treatise on the English constitution in the English language, Sir John Fortescue's mid-fifteenth-century *Governance of England*. In his encyclopaedic glosses on this medieval treatise Plummer unequivocally presented Fortescue as an exponent of medieval principles that revenues were divided into ordinary and extraordinary and that medieval kings ought to live of their own from ordinary revenues based on their royal demesne. Generalizations which claim to summarize and clarify centuries of history must not only stand up to detailed exposition of the facts for more limited periods, but must also emerge fortified by such examinations. Yet Fortescue's text, which certainly contains a lengthy discussion of the *expenditure* of our medieval kings under the heading ordinary and extraordinary, has no reference at all to their revenues being so classified. The fifteenth-century meaning of the word 'extraordinary' is shown by his definition of extraordinary charges: those which 'bith so casuelle that no man mey knowe hem in certaynte'.

95. Stubbs, *op. cit.*, ii, 541–2.

96. *ibid.*, ii, 543.

Moreover, the description 'Total of ordinary Revenue', in a contemporary statement, which appears to have been taken by his editor Charles Plummer from the parliament roll of 1433 by way of illustration and corroboration of Fortescue's views, proves to have been inserted into it by Plummer himself. The collective items which he so described consisted of all sources of revenue available to the Treasurer, except for the customs and subsidy of wool, tunnage and poundage, in a year when there was no direct taxation. They were the same items which Plummer himself had correctly described on the previous page, in the original words of an earlier statement of 1421, as 'casual revenues' (*Revenciones regni Angliae casuales*).[97] Indeed, to any fifteenth-century Treasurer indirect taxation appears to have constituted the most basic, permanent, reliable and regular revenues of the Crown, the yield of which could be carefully estimated over several years, as Lord Cromwell's budget statement of 1433 demonstrated. It was the so-called 'hereditary' revenues which were the uncertain, casual items of minor importance. Any view of ordinary and extraordinary revenues in England during the middle ages must take these factors into account.

The history of the royal demesne in England as sketched by Stubbs is basically an account of unsuccessful attempts to limit the king's power of alienation. The Conqueror's enormous resources, increased by William Rufus and Henry I, dissipated by Stephen, partly recovered by Henry II and again wasted by Richard and John, were, in Stubbs's view restored in some measure during the minority of Henry III, but wasted yet again when he came of age. The reign of Edward I was perhaps, by implication, a period of retrenchment. Edward II conformed to type and Edward III was an innovator only in so far as he 'made the nation sharers in his imprudence'. For Richard II the struggle against royal alienation ended in his destruction. Stubbs's whole discussion presupposes that the retention of a substantial royal demesne was a fundamental plank in the platform of baronial opposition as a prerequisite for royal solvency. The most obvious form of expression to which this policy gave rise was the outcry against royal favourites, usually foreign ones, raised at intervals of English history ever since the Conquest.[98]

Stubbs's picture of a long line of wrong-headed kings bent on the dissipation of their essential patrimony, of kings who did not care and of kings who could not help themselves, presents the institution of medieval kingship, which supplied the life-blood of the medieval body politic, in an unusually unfavourable and unconvincing light. The power freely to alienate land within the framework of such military and political con-

97. *The Governance of England*, pp. 212–13 and cf. p. 215. Note also Stubbs's calculation of the 'ancient ordinary revenue' of the Crown from the 1433 document (*op. cit.*, iii, 121).

98. W. Stubbs, *Constitutional History*, ii, 584 ff.

siderations as would secure and maintain a stable kingdom must have been a prerogative equally vital to William I and to all his successors. Domesday Book records, not the completion of a process of defining the king's own and his subjects' own, but simply one moment of time in a process of distribution and redistribution which proved to be never ending. One can question the personal abilities of successive kings and one can appreciate the development of concerted opposition to certain individuals as the chosen instruments of royal policies, but restraint of royal powers of alienation as a means to royal financial solvency running as a unifying thread through all the centuries of baronial opposition is a myth of Stubbs's own creating.

Recent scholarship has now dated the earliest statement of the inalienability of the estate of the king in England in its widest sense, meaning all manner of royal rights, to the accession of Henry II and has demonstrated that it was not in origin a limitation imposed on the king's own action, but a safeguard developed by royal policy to facilitate the disowning of irresponsible or incompetent royal agents. Among these might be numbered the king's predecessor on the throne. Already in early twelfth-century England the canon law was understood to forbid the alienation of the property of a see or an abbey by a bishop or abbot and to render such alienation, the wasting of the substance of what amounted to a 'corporation sole', void if it were made. Bishop Nigel of Ely, Henry's financial minister, may well have been responsible for transferring this concept to the Crown. The bishop's promise at his consecration was transferred to the consecration of the king.[99] The third recension of the *Leges Edwardi Confessoris* which contains the earliest statement of the king's duty to preserve intact all the lands, honours, dignities and liberties of the Crown and to recover those alienated, appears to date not from the reign of John, where it had been associated with the activities of the baronial opposition by Liebermann, Schramm and others, but from the early years of Henry II.[100] Henry II and his successors may well have taken an oath at their coronations, in the spirit of this declaration, which continued as an addition to the ancient three-fold oath until the form of the oath was further drastically revised for the coronation of Edward II in 1308.[101]

These are the views of Mr H. G. Richardson, and while his claim to have established the existence of a fourth clause in the coronation oath from 1154

99. H. G. Richardson, 'The Coronation in Medieval England', *Traditio*, xvi (1960), 151–74.

100. *ibid.*, pp. 166–9. Text in F. Liebermann, *Die Gesetze der Angelsachsen*, i, 635–6. See also P. E. Schramm, *A History of the English Coronation*, trans. L. G. Wickham Legg (Oxford, 1937), pp. 196–7; and G. Lapsley, 'The Interpretation of the Statute of York', *E.H.R.*, lvi (1941), 433–4 for the older view that this tract was a product of the baronial opposition to King John.

101. See Mr Richardson's paper already cited in footnote 99 and also his earlier paper 'The English Coronation Oath' in *Speculum*, xxiv (1949), 49–50, 62–3.

has not found universal acceptance, the most recent contributor on this subject, Mr Gaines Post, is just as concerned as Mr Richardson to stress the importance of the assertion of the inalienability of the *iura regis et regni* by Henry II and his advisors. He is inclined to attribute this more to the general twelfth-century revival of interest in the Roman civil law of Justinian, in line with parallel developments at the court of Frederick Barbarossa.[102] In any case it is now clear that this concept of the inalienability of royal rights grew out of the needs of royal policy and it would be absurd to suppose that the monarchy was either 'building a strait jacket for itself' or imposing on itself a constitutional limitation as regards the inalienability of the royal demesne.[103] The purpose was to establish the legality and justice of resumptions of rights and property in the aftermath of civil war and rival claimants to the throne. In such situations, as again during the minority of Henry III, the resumption of those royal lands which included castles was of prime importance. Alienations made reasonably with regard to the best interests of the Crown in more normal times were not unlawful. It is no surprise, therefore, to discover that later restrictions on royal alienation up to the fourteenth century were designed in the same spirit, not to limit the initiative of the monarch, but to protect the rights of the Crown against negligent or dishonest royal servants.[104] There appears to be no foundation for the view that such measures were forced upon any royal government by critics of royal policies.

Professor Hoyt has recently reinvestigated the question of alienation of the royal demesne from 1066 to 1272 and has written a story very different from Stubbs's account, at least for the period from Henry II's accession to the closing years of Henry III's reign. His thesis is that these kings and their advisers pursued a consistent, successful policy of consolidation and expansion of their demesne rights. Other recent writers agree with the view that later twelfth-century and thirteenth-century restraint against the

102. Gaines Post, 'Status Regis' in *Studies in Medieval and Renaissance History*, ed. W. Bowsky, i (University of Nebraska Press, 1964), especially the section 'The Roman Law and the "Inalienability" Clause in the English Coronation Oath', pp. 83–99.

103. Robert S. Hoyt, *The Royal Demesne*, pp. 147, 166.

104. In this category I place the oath, taken sometime before 1218 by Peter des Roches, Richard Marsh the Chancellor, and Hubert de Burgh the Justiciar, not to alienate any of Henry III's lands during his minority: *Foedera*, I, i, 163, quoted by H. G. Richardson in *Speculum* (1949), p. 56; also the oath to defend the royal demesne against alienation, taken by royal councillors and officers in 1257, conveniently printed by J. F. Baldwin, *The King's Council* (Oxford, 1913), p. 346; likewise Henry III's complaint against his baronial opponents' permitting the Lord Edward 'to squander what the lord king has given him as an endowment of the Crown of England': quoted by Hoyt, *op. cit.*, p. 164, from N. Denholm-Young, *Collected Papers on Medieval Subjects* (Oxford, 1946), p. 128. These strictures were directed against dishonest officials and disloyal or rebellious subjects alienating the rights and possessions of the Crown against the royal will. Only if they acquired them by reasonable warrant of the king could they expect to retain them. This doctrine is summed up in clause 6 of the Dictum of Kenilworth: see Hoyt, *op. cit.*, p. 164 and Stubbs's *Select Charters* (9th ed.), p. 408.

alienation of all manner of royal rights, and affirmations of the royal right and duty to recover such alienations where they had taken place, were assertions and developments of monarchical policy itself and not of its critics.

Professor Hoyt's own narrower theme, the creation of a special royal demesne right by these kings, which was primarily designed to enhance their cash revenues by the exploitation of their royal demesne, seems to me to be valid only as regards taxation within the general national framework of developing royal financial policies which were applied equally to all sections of their kingdom. But in any case, even if there was a sustained, purposeful effort especially directed towards permanently increasing the yield of the land revenues from the royal demesne within the limits of the period studied by Professor Hoyt, we have no figures to indicate that it was successful. Such figures as we do possess for the total revenues of the shires, which included the financial yield of the royal demesne other than taxation, suggest that they remained virtually unchanged from 1170 to the end of the thirteenth century and beyond.[105] The failure of such a policy, if indeed it existed, was due, not to the prodigality or incompetence of kings, but to the other unavoidable and more vital needs of the monarchy which their landed resources had to meet. The amount of land revenue reaching the Exchequer was never the overriding consideration governing the disposition of a royal demesne.

Inextricably associated with the belief that opposition to the prodigality of our medieval kings was responsible for the development of a concept of the inalienability of the royal demesne is the notion that medieval kings were expected to 'live of their own', or, at least, that they were all expected to try to do so and that, alas, as the centuries went by, hopes of attaining this goal inevitably grew dimmer and dimmer. Even historians who, unlike Stubbs, do not castigate our medieval kings for profligacy with their landed resources tend to assume that their subjects were at fault in expecting the impossible of them in this respect and should be roundly condemned for their impractical foolishness. These latter views are admirably voiced by

105. W. Parow, *op. cit.*, pp. 47–9, made the yield of what one might call the total shire revenues within which all the yield of the crown lands must have been comprehended about £13,500 in 1167–70 (issues of sheriffs' farms, cities and boroughs, honours in the king's hands, vacant temporalities, farms of manors, escheats, forests and profits of justice). Miss Mills, in *E.H.R.*, xl (1925), 230–1, similarly estimated the total royal revenue from the shires at betweeen £13,000 and £14,000 in 1284. Closely comparable estimates can be found for 1327–36 in *The English Government at Work 1327–1336*, ed. W. A. Morris and J. R. Strayer (Cambridge, Mass., 1947), ii; *Fiscal Administration*, 4–5; and for 1345–6 in Sir J. H. Ramsay's *A History of the Revenues of the Kings of England 1066–1399*, ii, 144–5, and table, p. 293, if receipts for the hanaper and profits of the mint and exchange are deducted in the two latter cases. Parow calculated the *terrae datae*, a financial write-off to the Exchequer, at £4,574 1s 1d in 1169–70 (*op. cit.*, p. 49). According to Sir J. H. Ramsay's figures, taken from the chancellor's roll for 3 John, they had risen to £6,816 11s 10d by 1200–1 (*op. cit.*, i, 233).

Dr Anthony Steel in round condemnation of would-be apologists for the foolish Commons of Richard II's reign:

> 'Thus while it has long been clear that the ancient slogan, "the king should live of his own", was even more at variance with the possible facts of the case in the fourteenth century than it had ever been before, yet when that stale clamour is loudly raised again by the Commons in the Ricardian parliaments, it is no more than mildly deplored by the classic historians: the child is naughty, they admit, but its adult splendours must excuse the *mal entendus* of its infancy.'[106]

The real question to ask is whether the 'foolish' subjects did expect any such thing.

Historians who have used the phrase appear to have taken little trouble to ascertain when this 'ancient slogan' first came into use, how frequently it was used, what it meant to contemporaries or, indeed, what they mean by it themselves. Its modern use, as applied to English history, comprehends certain assumptions: that the sources of royal revenue in England were divided, time out of mind, into 'ordinary' and 'extraordinary'; that the revenues of the royal demesne provided, or ought to have provided, the core of the former, and that aids or taxes, levied with some kind of consent, constituted the latter.

The earliest actual use of the specific phrase in English history recorded in print seems to be three instances in the Ordinances of 1311. Professor Hoyt, however, sees an earlier formulation of it by Henry III's baronage in what Stubbs described as a 'debate in the council of the nation' in 1242. The validity of the description depends on what it signifies to Professor Hoyt, but we must make it clear that the expression was not used on this occasion. The arguments in question were put forward in 1242 to justify the refusal of an aid to Henry III. According to Matthew Paris they were as follows: to the best of their knowledge the king still had the proceeds of the recent tax of one-thirtieth on movables unspent; in addition a great sum of money should recently have come from escheats, especially since the archbishopric of Canterbury and other rich sees had been vacant; itinerant justices had been imposing heavy crops of amercements recently, which the king had already admitted more than once were exactions which should not be taken as precedents; there was a truce at that time with the French king; only if King Louis broke that truce need Henry's financial requirements be reconsidered.[107] In short, they certainly made an emphatic plea for economy, solvency and good faith and declared that they found the king's need for further aid on that occasion to be unsubstantiated. But

106. Anthony Steel, 'Some Aspects of English Finance in the Fourteenth Century', *History*, xii (1928), 307.

107. Stubbs's *Select Charters* (9th ed.), pp. 360–2.

there was no suggestion there of any division or classification of revenues into normal or ordinary and, by implication, extraordinary, as Professor Hoyt suggests. Furthermore, I cannot share his surprise that there was no mention made at all of the 'revenues of the royal demesne' in Matthew Paris's 'long and detailed argument'.[108]

From 1311 the actual, contemporary use of the phrase and its equivalents can be studied in their specific contexts. The fourth and eighth Ordinances included in 'the king's own', by implication, the revenues of the customs 'together with all other issues and profits of the realm arising from any matters whatsoever'.[109] Now among the Ordinances of 1311 there is also a complaint that royal grants had impoverished the Crown (seventh Ordinance) but, significantly, the references to the king living of his own do not appear in that connection. In both the fourth and eighth Ordinances the desirability of the king living of his own is linked, not with dissipation of the royal demesne, nor with excessive taxation, but with the abuses of purveyance: iniquitous 'prises', requisitions and seizures of provisions, goods, transport, even labour, made by royal officers for nominal payments or for mere promises to pay, for the use of the royal Household or for the households of prominent members of the royal family. In the tenth Ordinance, again coupled with the plea that the king should live of his own, these illegal prises are even cited as a potential cause of rebellion and declared to be of recent origin. It is true that at the same time this tenth Ordinance refers back to the safeguards of Magna Carta in this respect (clauses 28–31), but this grievance does seem to have become particularly oppressive towards the end of Edward I's reign and during the reigns of his two successors. In 1332, when the king was granted a tenth and a fifteenth, it was stated to be given in order that he might be able to live of his own, and again without burdening his people with outrageous 'prises'.[110] Two contemporary Latin tracts, reliably dated about 1330, bitterly attacked these abuses of purveyance. The first expressed the opinion that these iniquitous practices began in 1289–90 and threatened the young Edward III with the fate of his father unless he put a stop to them.[111] This primary association of the plea that the king should live of his own with complaints against the evils of purveyance and the consequent intolerable burden the royal households imposed on the community was still being expressed in parlia-

108. Hoyt, *op. cit.*, pp. 161–2.

109. *Statutes of the Realm*, ed. A. Luders and others (London, 1810–28), i, 158–9: 'qe le roi puisse vivre de soen'.

110. *Rot. Parl.*, ii, 66.

111. *De Speculo Regis Edwardi III*, ed. J. Moisant (Picard, Paris, 1891), pp. 115, 122. For the correct dating of these tracts see J. Tait, in *E.H.R.*, xvi (1901), 110–15. At p. 115 of tract A the author dates the beginning of the iniquitous practice of royal buying at less than the fair price from 18 Edward I (1289–90). In Stubbs's day, owing to the incorrect dating of these tracts themselves, this reference was taken as 18 Edward II (1324–5).

ment a century after it had first been made.[112] During this first century of its expression, this plea seems to have meant literally what it said: the king's 'own' was anything and everything which was legally his, contrasted with what was not his, but the property of his subjects.

Other fourteenth-century instances bear out this interpretation. The *Anonimalle Chronicle* report of the Good Parliament of 1376 has a phrase which seems to be a near equivalent: the king should be able to live and govern the kingdom and maintain the war 'on his own resources', and not fleece his subjects for these purposes.[113] In 1380, embedded in a plea for governmental economy and for the appointment of wise councillors, was the hope that the expenses of the war might be supported 'en partie de soen propre',[114] which I take to mean from what the king already had, irrespective of its source. From the minority of Richard II we are dealing with the spending of ear-marked war grants with special war treasurers appointed to see that the money was not diverted to other uses. Here, for the first time, we have classification and appropriation, and this does mean that certain royal revenues were henceforth only the king's own in a limited sense, but it is not classification into ordinary and extraordinary revenues. Hence the Chancellor's remark to the second parliament of 1380 that the king had spent all that the last parliament had given him for that specific purpose on the cost of the army in France and much of his own besides.[115]

In 1381 a commission of reform under the duke of Lancaster was asked to take steps to reduce the numbers of men on horse and on foot in the king's Household, that the king might live honestly of his own in future.[116] In 1382 those about his person were exhorted to strive to enable him 'honestly and royally to live within the revenues of your realm, and that all manner of wardships, marriages, reliefs, escheats, forfeitures and all other commodities may be kept for your wars, and in defence of your realm and no part given to others; in support and aid of your poor Commons, and great honour and profit to you'.[117] Stubbs actually cited this instance as one example of the requests to the king 'to live of his own', and so it was,[118] but in asking the king's entourage to ensure that he lived within his revenues

112. *Rot. Parl.*, iii, 624 (1410). The complaint against prises of goods taken without payment for the Household, Chamber and Wardrobe was answered: 'Le roy vorroit volunters vivre de soens, et voet si tost come il poet.'

113. *The Anonimalle Chronicle 1333–1381*, ed. V. H. Galbraith, p. 81: 'od ses biens demesne et nyent raunsoner ses liges gentz de la terre'.

114. *Rot. Parl.*, iii, 73.

115. *ibid.*, 88; 'et oultre ce grantement del son propre'. For the development of the practice of the king's ministers declaring the special needs of the moment at the opening of parliaments during the reign of Edward III and for the appointment of war treasurers from 1377 see Stubbs's *Constitutional History* (4th ed.), ii, 595–9.

116. *Rot. Parl.*, iii, 101: 'qe nostre dit seigneur puisse vivre honestement de son propre desore enavant'.

117. *ibid.*, p. 139: 'viver deinz les Revenues de votre Roialme'.

118. Stubbs, *Constitutional History* (4th ed.), ii, 543.

in 1382 his subjects were certainly not asking them to renounce taxation. Nor were they suggesting that he could exist on the income which would be saved if he made no further royal grants of the kind specified. The fourteenth-century meaning of this phrase was that the king should live on what was lawfully his, within the limits of his current income from all sources, and not incur debts or seize other people's property: economy, solvency and fair dealing. A king who was seen to be honestly striving towards such ends would find his poor Commons not ungenerous.[119] Such a policy was most endangered by a peripatetic royal Household, inflated in size, abusing the rights of purveyance, and by royal councillors allowing revenues from whatever source to pass into private hands in preference to the pressing needs of war and defence and the legitimate claims of the king's creditors. Ear-marked grants should be entirely devoted to the special purposes for which they were asked and granted.

The believe that the demand that the king should 'live of his own' was an ancient slogan in English history by the fourteenth century, 'constantly recurring', thus seems to be without foundation. To castigate it as 'the stale clamour of the foolish Commons' is an unwarrantable aspersion on the Commons of Richard II's reign. It appears that the expression 'the king to live of his own' may even have been unknown before the early fourteenth century and that when it first appeared it constituted a plea for royal economy, solvency and honest dealing specifically directed against the abuses of purveyance, perpetrated by the royal Household, and directly associated neither with the resources of a royal demesne nor with protests against parliamentary taxation. Time out of mind kings of England had found that their powers of taxation, both direct and, later, indirect, could best be relied upon by expansion or diversification to meet their pressing financial needs. In the thirteenth century they had called parliament into existence primarily to facilitate the continuation of what was already at that stage a long-established trend in English government finance, stretching back to Henry II and possibly even to 1066. Medieval England was always a much taxed country. New taxes to tap new or increasing sources of wealth among their subjects had repeatedly and successfully replaced well-proved but declining older ones. The fourteenth century saw a golden age of this policy in its lucrative development of the possibilities of indirect taxation. There was, of course, much complaint and hard bargaining about taxation in fourteenth-century parliaments as every schoolboy knows, but there was also a mounting volume of bitter resentment against the constant

119. See for example *Rot. Parl.*, ii, 323 (1376), a plea for good councillors around the king and for economy; a belief that some of the king's entourage were feathering their own nests at the kingdom's expense; that they should be brought to justice; and a declaration that the king would find his Commons very ready to help him should it prove necessary after these reforms had been made.

evils of household purveyance which has received much less attention from historians. To fourteenth and fifteenth-century Englishmen the expense of government meant primarily the burden which an insolvent royal Household imposed upon them.

These were the circumstances in which informed public opinion at last began to demand greater overall royal financial efficiency; in other words, greater ability on the part of royal government to pay its way, to 'live of its own'. Fifteenth-century civil servants were to prove no less capable of inventing new taxes than earlier generations, but in the field of government finance the fifteenth century was to be remarkable for the growing climate of informed public opinion which demanded, in parliament, for the first time in English history, the development of a substantial crown landed estate to make a permanent, reliable contribution towards government solvency. During the most serious political crises of the Lancastrian period parliamentary acts of resumption to recover long lost or deeply pledged lands and revenues were to be persistently pressed upon Lancastrian governments and ultimately accepted. Although the fifteenth-century meaning of the phrase was still very different from that which politicians, lawyers and historians of later centuries have attributed to it, our Yorkist and early-Tudor kings consequently came to regard the concept of 'living of their own' as a serious, practical programme of political action in which a significant part was to be played by the financial development of their crown lands. The first undoubted appearance at the centre of English politics of the concept of a king living of his own primarily through the exploitation of his landed patrimony dates from the accession of the first king of England ever to possess an extensive, private, English landed estate in his own right: Henry IV, duke of Lancaster and Hereford, earl of Derby, Leicester, Lincoln and Northampton.

II

A NEW ROYAL PATRIMONY

THE PLANTAGENET FAMILY ESTATE, 1227–1399

I. FAMILY ENDOWMENTS

The primary significance of the role of English kings as landowners from the reign of Henry III to the usurpation of Henry IV lay in their development of a new English royal family estate. Historians have tended to look askance at this policy, or to doubt that it ever existed, because of the apparent folly of the consequent, inevitable creation of apanages for younger sons. This has been seen as the surest way of breeding over-mighty subjects and of alienating those royal resources which would best have helped the king to live of his own. It has even been asserted that its principal architect, Edward III, was aware of a traditional unpopularity attached to such a policy and therefore strove to spare the crown lands and to achieve the same results through politic marriages for his offspring.[1]

Contemporaries viewed the matter far differently. By 1399 conventions were firmly established that the principal function of the crown estate was to provide adequate endowment for all members of the royal family. When Henry IV was consolidating his usurpation he was able to rely on the support of petitions from the Commons in Parliament that his queen, his heir and all his sons should receive prompt landed endowment on the ample scales which had become customary by that date. During the later middle ages their duties as head of a royal family towards their queens, their heir, their younger sons and daughters, younger brothers and nephews generated and maintained a very powerful interest in English kings. A well-endowed royal family was an essential attribute of effective kingship. This royal family interest led to very substantial family acquisitions from time to time; certain conventions developed governing the circumstances in which alienations were permissible, and accidents of politics, or failure of family trees, often brought these lands back yet again into the hands of the kings themselves. In such instances, and especially when a dearth of royal children afflicted certain kings, public attention was undoubtedly focused on the employment of this newly augmented and consolidated royal demesne: on its disposal and on its permissible use or misuse outside the circle of the royal family.

Family acquisitions and consolidations of English and Welsh manors

1. T. F. Tout, *The Political History of England, 1216–1377*, pp. 427–31, where he is discussing 'Edward III's family settlement'.

were first made necessary by the shrinking of that much wider, continental 'family estate of the Plantagenets', the Angevin empire, still to some extent a fluctuating process for much of the thirteenth century, but finally hardening into the smaller concept of a kingdom of England with appurtenances during the reign of Edward I.[2] They began with the county of Cornwall (1227), later earldom and fourteenth-century duchy. There followed the county palatine and earldom of Chester (1246), augmented by Flintshire in the Statute of Wales (1284), and belonging inalienably to the king's eldest son from 1333 'with remainder to his heirs being kings of England'.[3] This was briefly made into a principality under Richard II. The de Montfort (1265) and Ferrers (1266) lands were added to the existing royal county and honour of Lancaster.[4] Further augmented by royal gifts to John of Gaunt and by the Bohun marriage of his son, the vast inheritance of the dukes of Lancaster returned to the Crown in 1399. The principality of Wales, which was united to England in 1284 and given to the king's eldest son by charter in 1301, must also be included here.

Conscious policy certainly lay behind the avidity with which Henry III pursued the opportunities presented by the dissolution of the patrimony of the Norman earldom of Chester when John le Scot died in 1237 leaving four female co-heirs. Likewise the partisan support of the royal courts was essential to Henry III's younger son Edmund in his pursuit of the Ferrers inheritance.[5] The terms of Henry III's final instrument for the endowment of his eldest son the Lord Edward, in 1254, are also significant of active royal concern in this respect: 'in such manner that the said lands . . . may never be separated from the Crown, and that no one, by reason of this grant made to the said Edward, may have any claim to the said lands . . . but that they shall remain to the kings of England in their entirety for ever'.[6] The same concern is evident in Henry III's complaint against the baronial council in 1261 that 'they permit Edward the king's son to squander what the lord king has given him as an endowment of the Crown of England, and which [lands] were conveyed to him so that they should not be separated from the Crown of England as appears by his charters'.[7] We now have a masterly exposition of how the operations of the laws of inheritance were assisted by royal sharp practice when Edward I defeated the

2. See John Le Patourel, 'The Plantagenet Dominions', *History*, l (1965), 289–308.

3. G. E. Cockayne, *The Complete Peerage* (new ed., London, 1910) iii, 435, where references are made to charters of 17 March and 16 May 1333.

4. The details can most conveniently be studied from the relevant articles in the *Complete Peerage*, and the references there given.

5. For Chester see R. Stewart Brown, 'The End of the Norman Earldom of Chester', *E.H.R.*, xxxv (1920), 26–54; for the Ferrers lands see R. Somerville, *History of the Duchy of Lancaster*, and for both, the article cited in footnote 8 below.

6. *Foedera*, i, 297, as quoted in translation by Le Patourel, *op. cit.*, 310–12.

7. Quoted in translation by Hoyt, *The Royal Demesne*, p. 164, from N. Denholm-Young, *Collected Papers* (Oxford, 1946), p. 128.

legitimate claims of collateral heirs to the landed inheritances of some of his wealthiest subjects. As a result the unfortunate comital families of Forz, Clare, Redvers, Lacy, Longsword, Bigod and Bohun were each subjected to a compulsory 'course of slimming' to the immense benefit of the royal family and himself.[8]

By the mid-fourteenth century custom already indicated that the principality of Wales should normally and in due course become the patrimony of the heir to the throne. In addition to the lands of the earldom of Chester (1333) the rich estates of the earldom of Cornwall were made part of his permanent endowment in 1337. Edward III's second son had recently died, so that on the eve of his great enterprise he had only one son left alive. His brother John of Eltham had also died in the previous year without heirs of his body, leaving his lands at the king's disposal. Thus Prince Edward was created duke of Cornwall with its possessions inseparably annexed 'to himself and his heirs first born sons of the kings of England'.[9] Here Edward was following the path marked out by Henry III and Edward I in confirming and strengthening the inalienability and coherence of the patrimony of the king's eldest son. Significantly one of the first undoubted references to the wide extent of the crown lands in a claim for reduced parliamentary taxation came at the accession of the Black Prince's infant son to the throne. His Commons in Parliament included the fact that he had inherited the lands of his father among the reasons for disbelieving in his professed poverty.[10]

The Plantagenet family estate of the fourteenth century consisted of lands, rents and feefarms which the king could use for the permanent endowment of the royal family or favoured royal servants. Other sources of landed income (wards' lands, vacant temporalities and alien priory lands) could not provide such permanent endowment either for life or in tail because of the temporary nature of the king's possession. Queens and the king's unmarried daughters were all endowed for life only. King's sons, brothers, and uncles were normally endowed with lands entailed upon them to the heirs male of their bodies, with reversion to the king and his heirs if their lines failed.

Amid the welter of temporary acquisitions of lands due to the accidents of wardship, to vacancy of sees, or to the intermittent wars which temporarily deprived foreign abbeys of their English lands, the Plantagenet family lands stand out in the records of government with a definite identity and surprising permanence. A unique starting point for the identification of this family estate is provided by the huge endowment appropriated by Edward II's queen, Isabella, at the nominal beginning of her son's reign,

8. K. B. McFarlane, 'Had Edward I a "Policy" towards the Earls?', *History*, l (1965), 145–59.

9. *The Complete Peerage*, iii, 435.

10. *Rot. Parl.*, iii, 35, no. 18.

to an annual value of 20,000 marks. How far these lands, rents and fee-farms were ever actually cleared of existing life grants or grants for terms of years during the three brief years when she held nominal possession of them all is not known. But this endowment, with the exception of some Welsh, Chester and Cornish estates, in effect constituted the whole of the permanent royal patrimony in lands, rents and feefarms. The purpose of this parliamentary appropriation was probably not so much to provide her with a cash income as to place the whole royal patronage at the disposal of a *de facto* queen regnant. Fifteenth-century kings were to achieve the same result in similar political crises by means of parliamentary acts of re-sumption.

Isabella's 'dower' is set out in detail in Appendix 'A' below, together with its subsequent history in the endowment of six other members of the royal family during the following fifty years. It cannot be claimed that the needs of the royal family invariably had precedence over all other claims upon these royal lands. The king's personal convenience or other important matters of royal policy might dictate exchanges and surrenders of various lands from time to time. For example, Isabella's lands included former Lacy lands to the value of about £1,700, which Alice Lacy, daughter of Henry earl of Lincoln and wife of Thomas earl of Lancaster, had quit-claimed to Edward II in the political vicissitudes of the previous reign. Some of these were later returned by Edward III to Henry of Grosmont, first duke of Lancaster. A reversionary grant of others ensured that they passed at Isabella's death to the heirs of William Montague, earl of Salisbury, the daring leader of the young Edward III's *coup d'état* of 1330. Again former owners or their descendants might subsequently recover possession in a new political climate. A king might require extensive lands to alienate in mortmain, for the performance of his will. But, generally speaking, the amount of patronage available to Edward III or Richard II depended on the greater or lesser degree to which the royal family made demands upon royal lands, rents and feefarms, while the small residual financial interest of the Exchequer in them was limited to the brief periods needed to replace one life grant by another.

It will be seen that Isabella's endowment included the whole of what were later to be the duchy of Cornwall estates in Cornwall and Devon, together with many of its later 'foreign' manors in other counties; Welsh lands and Chester lands. A degree of duplication in her successive grants does not appear to have been accidental, but was probably due to the fact that only the usufruct of the lands involved in the duplicated groups had originally been granted to her on behalf of her younger children. After the major grant of 1327 her acquisitive appetite was still not satisfied, for in May of that year 10,000 marks of a parliamentary grant was spent on purchasing the Montalt inheritance. Queen Isabella lived until 1358. Following her great 'surrender' of 1330 she was amply re-endowed by her dutiful son Edward III, but it is quite clear that he could never have assumed real power in his kingdom without the complete annulment of all her grants and the consequent resumption of patronage which took place in 1330. Only thus could he endow his own queen, his younger brother, his own children, the supporters of his *coup d'état* and later boon companions of his French adventure.

Except for a few royal residences and hunting lodges in the hands of salaried keepers, kings of England in the later middle ages did not retain immediate possession of any landed estate. The primary, recurrent charge on the crown estate was the endowment of successive queens. Queen Isabella had received the bulk of the possessions of Edward I's Queen Margaret at her death in 1318. In the redistribution of Isabella's lands from 1330 Queen Philippa was the chief beneficiary, receiving lands valued at about £3,850 a year immediately and a further £2,000 in 1359 after Isabella's death. Queen Philippa's lands were subsequently largely re-assembled to provide a dower valued at £4,500 a year for Richard II's Queen Anne. In the early years of Henry IV's reign the disposal of these lands in ways which prevented their being available for a new queen on this now accepted scale of 6,000 marks p.a. became a political issue. Henry IV's Commons in Parliament petitioned for a special act of resumption which the king accepted, in order to endow his Queen Joan with the lands which had belonged to Richard II's Queen Anne, subject only to the upholding of any grants he had made to his own sons.[11] The first beneficiary of the Lancastrian acts of resumption of 1450 and 1451 was to be Queen Margaret of Anjou.

Conventions also gathered about the composition and use of a landed patrimony for the heir to the throne. The lands which were later to form the duchy of Cornwall patrimony had first been brought into the very centre of political controversy in the destruction of Peter Gaveston by the Lords Ordainers. The Ordinances of 1311 were essentially an attack on the personal, political power which Gaveston exercised over royal policies in general, but a vital basis for the maintenance of this power was seen to be his endowment of royal lands. Edward II had striven to give him the endowment of a royal earl, to himself and his heirs in perpetuity, by making him the successor of his cousin Edmund of Almaine, earl of Cornwall, with entailed grants of the later duchy of Cornwall lands in Cornwall and Devon, the later duchy foreign manors in other counties and the later Lancastrian honour of Knaresborough. A second grant of these lands which limited the entail to the joint heirs of the bodies of Gaveston and his wife Margaret, grand-daughter of Edward I, did not make it less unpopular.[12] It was un-

11. *ibid.*, iii, 548, 555.
12. *Rep. Dig. Peer*, v, *Appendix* (London, 1829), pp. 12–14, 14–17.

acceptable to Edward II's baronage as an accroachment of royal power and dignity. The ultimate recipient of these lands during Edward II's reign was Queen Isabella, but Edward III, when he endowed his brother John of Eltham with lands to support the dignity of earl of Cornwall in 1330, granted him only the 'foreign' manors, with nothing in Cornwall or Devon beyond the nominal £20 p.a. from the issues of the county of Cornwall.[13] Perhaps the endowment of 1337 was already in mind. In any case the 'foreign' manors which John of Eltham held were reunited after his death with the 'home' manors in Cornwall and Devon in 1337 and the whole joined to the duchy of Cornwall 'so that they should never be therefrom severed, nor given to any other than the dukes of Cornwall, and upon the decease of such dukes if there should be no son to whom the duchy manifestly belongs, the same should revert to the king to be kept in his hands until a son and hereditary successor should appear in the realm, to whom the king willed that livery thereof should be given'.

These were the terms of the original grant of 1337 as quoted by Henry IV's writ to the escheator of Cornwall on 15 October 1399 whereby he dispossessed Richard II's uterine brother John Holand and his wife, Henry's own sister, of the major stake which they had acquired in the duchy lands in the south-west, an act which probably precipitated the rebellion of the Holand earls in January 1400.[14] The Holands were then in possession only of the duchy estates of Trematon, Calstock, and Saltash in tail, but had also acquired for life Tintagel, Helston in Trigg with Lanteglos and Helsbury, Tewington, Moresk, Helston in Kerrier, Bossiney and Trevailly, Restormel, Pelynt and Penkneth, Lostwithiel, Camelford and the waters of Fowey.[15] Richard II had certainly not heeded the requests of his first parliament that the issues of the patrimony of the heir to the throne should meantime be devoted to the national Exchequer, although he had only actually alienated Trematon, Calstock and Saltash from the duchy. But criticisms of alienations or misuse of the patrimony of the heir to the throne did not extend to the permanent endowment of the king's uterine brother from other crown lands. John and Elizabeth Holand had actually derived their permanent stake in the West Country primarily from arrangements which Edward III had made for the performance of his will. He had purchased the reversion of the considerable estate of James Audley of Heighley which included the manors of Blagdon, Lydford and Staunton (Somerset), Bovey Tracy, Northlew, Holdsworthy, Langacre in Broad Clyst, Barn-

13. For details of these grants and all other grants to members of the royal family between 1327 and 1377 see below in Appendix 'A'.

14. *Cal. Close Rolls, 1399–1402*, pp. 22–3; *Cal. Inq. Misc.*, vii, *1399–1422*, p. 58 (no. 100). The escheator of Cornwall took possession on the Monday before Christmas, 1399. The rebellion was timed for Twelfth Night, 1400, and misfired on the night of 4 January when the king heard of it.

15. *Cal. Pat. Rolls, 1391–1396*, pp. 102, 600; *ibid., 1396–1399*, pp. 22, 526.

staple, Combe Martin, Fremington and South Molton (Devon) and Tackbeare (Cornwall). But Audley did not die until 1386, when, with the approval of John of Gaunt, his father's principal executor, Richard II entailed these lands on John Holand and his wife Elizabeth, Gaunt's daughter, finding a measure of compensation elsewhere for Edward III's intended beneficiary, the priory of St. Mary's Graces by the Tower.[16]

Political exigencies prevented Henry IV from confirming Richard II's other tamperings with the patrimony of the heir to the throne, which seem to have been designed to compensate for the inroads which he had made on the resources of the duchy of Cornwall. The additions which he made to the lands of the earldom of Chester, when he elevated it to the dignity of a principality, consisted of valuable Arundel forfeitures (Holt, Bromfield and Yale, Chirk and Chirklands, Oswestry, Shrawardine, Dawley and Clun), which he 'inalienably' annexed to it. These were restored to Arundel's son and heir in 1399. From the possessions of the earldom Richard had previously alienated to John and Elizabeth Holand the lordships of Hope and Hopedale, Northwich and Overmarsh, but had subsequently arranged to recover these in exchange for a grant in fee to the Holands of other Arundel lands, the castle, honour and lordship of Reigate. The Commons in Henry's IV's parliament petitioned for the resumption of all grants for term of years, for life, or in fee, made from the lands of the principality of Wales and the earldom of Chester, for the benefit of Prince Henry.[17]

With the exception of alienations made from possessions now considered reserved for the king's eldest son and heir to the throne the endowment of Richard II's uterine brother John Holand, earl of Huntingdon, as a royal duke entitled to 2,000 marks of land[18] thus does not appear to have caused criticism. Similarly Henry VI's endowment of his uterine Tudor half-brothers after the resumptions of 1450 and 1451 was later to be accepted by contemporaries as only right and proper. Still less were criticisms raised against the alienations of crown lands for the permanent endowment of princes of the full blood, John of Gaunt and Edmund of Langley. Neither was criticism roused by Edward III's lavish life grants to his daughter Isabella, although only a small fraction of these were extended to her husband and the heirs male of their bodies. Edward's youngest son Thomas of Woodstock had to wait until the death of Richard II's Queen Anne for a substantial entailed grant (Burstwick in Holderness), but representations had already been made in the first parliament of Richard II that the king's uncles who were still 'poor in their estate' should be given fitting landed endowment.

16. *ibid., 1381–1385*, pp. 515–16; *ibid., 1385–1389*, pp. 494–5, *ibid., 1388–1392*, p. 364.
17. *Rot. Parl.*, iii, 353–4, 435, 441–2; *Cal. Pat. Rolls, 1396–1399*, p. 467.
18. *Rep. Dig. Peer*, v, *Appendix*, pp. 82–3.

2. ALIENATIONS OUTSIDE THE ROYAL FAMILY

An occasionally heavy but infrequent charge upon the king's landed patrimony occurred when he wished to establish or strengthen a stake in his realm for his most trusted political and military supporters as a reward for services rendered and to come. Following a political crisis or the launching of a great enterprise these calls upon the royal estate might even override the long-term interests of individual members of the royal family. Great ability and devotion in the royal service would probably first bring elevation to comital status with a grant of 1,000 marks p.a. at the Exchequer as an earnest of the king's intention to endow the new earl with suitable entailed lands of the same value. William Montague, Robert Ufford and William Clinton, essential agents of the young Edward's *coup d'état* of 1330, were respectively created earls of Salisbury, Suffolk and Huntingdon in 1337 on the eve of his great French adventure. Permanent rewards of land to sustain them in their numerous official and personal services to the king prior to 1337 had already been provided by the political misfortunes of other families, Lacy and Mortimer, or by such smaller expiring life grants of Edward III, or his father, which conveniently reverted to the Crown.[19] Montague's rewards for his dangerous services in 1330 had already exceeded the standard comital level. Thus in 1337 he was granted only reversions to himself and his heirs: Queen Isabella's Montalt purchases,[20] and valuable Warenne estates. The latter had been acquired in fee by Edward II for certain royal services rendered to the last Warenne earl of Surrey and then returned to their former owner for life only.[21] Besides certain reversionary grants Ufford was now given immediate possession in fee of lands worth over £400 p.a. in Norfolk and Suffolk, while Clinton received lands to the value of 500 marks p.a. in Lincolnshire, all of which had returned to Edward III on the death of his brother John of Eltham in the previous year.[22] Edward III's only other really substantial alienation outside the circle of the royal family was made in the same year to William de Bohun, a cadet of the family of the earls of Hereford. To support his new dignity as earl of Northampton he was to have reversionary grants of other lands acquired by Edward II of John de Warenne, earl of Surrey, lands which were held for life by the dowager countess of Pembroke and by Hugh Audley, earl of Gloucester, and his wife Margaret, grand-daughter of Edward I.[23] As it happened, failure of William de Bohun's line subse-

19. *Cal. Charter Rolls*, iv, *1327–1341*, pp. 210–22.
20. *ibid.*, p. 432–3.
21. References to agreements between Warenne and Edward II on the patent and close rolls are given by Tout in the *Dictionary of National Biography*, xx, 826.
22. *Rep. Dig. Peer*, v, *Appendix*, pp. 38–41; *Cal. Pat. Rolls*, *1334–1338*, p. 415; *ibid.*, *1338–1340*, p. 265.
23. *Cal. Charter Rolls*, iv, *1327–1341*, p. 401.

quently released the Warenne and Pembroke grants for the endowment of the king's son Edmund of Langley and thus ultimately brought them back into the possession of the Crown from 1461.

In the eyes of contemporaries such alienations, immediate or reversionary, constituted a legitimate charge upon the crown estate, the expression of a vital prerogative power which, if used wisely in the service of the Crown, could produce a much more valuable dividend in service and support than any lost potential contribution to the ordinary expenses of government, which could so much more easily be met by other means. It was very difficult even for Edward III to be prodigal in such grants because suitable lands were clearly in very limited supply and even the royal family had frequently to be supported from other more lucrative sources of income.[24] There was also a conventional limit set to the scale of reward. For example, William de Bohun's reversions to support the dignity of earl of Northampton were to be restricted if he should happen to inherit the Bohun earldoms of Essex and Hereford.

Such grants were not mere personal whims of a magnanimous king, cunning enough to make 'the nation sharers in his imprudence'. The stake of these earls in their localities, although not necessarily associated territorially with the title, was undoubtedly considered to be a normal and necessary part of the fabric of royal government, locally as well as centrally. Thus in the next reign Sir Simon Burley was given the task of reconstituting the Kentish patrimony of the Leybourne countess of Huntingdon there because Richard II's advisers considered that Edward III's dispersal of it in mortmain had gravely weakened the defence of the county.[25] Likewise when the new Ufford line of Suffolk earls unexpectedly failed, the inheritance was entailed intact in 1385 on Sir Michael de la Pole.[26] Such arrangements may be meaningfully decried or applauded by historians for their political results, which was also the viewpoint of contemporaries, but they cannot be effectively criticized as an irresponsible drain on the national finances.

3. FINANCE AND ROYAL PATRONAGE

How far can the residual value of royal lands, rents and feefarms to the Exchequer be estimated over any extended period of years during the

24. e.g. supplementation of dower from the customs, clerical subsidies and general exchequer assignment: *Cal. Pat. Rolls, 1334–1338*, p. 489; *ibid., 1338–1340*, pp. 112, 546; *ibid., 1340–1343*, p. 257 (all Queen Isabella); *ibid., 1330–1334*, p. 34; *ibid., 1345–1348*, p. 130 (Queen Philippa).

25. *Cal. Pat. Rolls, 1381–1385*, pp. 305, 367–8; *ibid., 1385–1389*, p. 37; *Cal. Inq. Misc.*, iv, *1377–1388*, no. 411; *ibid.*, v, *1387–1398*, no. 188.

26. *Rep. Dig. Peer*, v, *Appendix*, pp. 70–6, but in reversion after the death of Queen Anne. He forfeited his estates in 1388 and never had possession. They first came to his family after the restoration of his son, 15 November 1399 (*Rot. Parl.*, iii, 668).

fourteenth century? From the end of the twelfth century all manner of payments due to the king by way of fine or oblation for any agreement made with him were entered on the *oblata* or fine rolls, together with the details of the transactions concerned. Examination of any volume of the printed calendars of this splendid series of records during the thirteenth or fourteenth centuries leaves a firm impression that the only possible sources of significant amounts of royal land revenue, in number of transactions and size of payments, were wards' lands, vacant temporalities and alien priory lands. By contrast the history of those lands and land revenues which belonged absolutely to the king by way of inheritance, escheat, gift or purchase was recorded not as financial assets on the fine rolls but as preferential grants on the charter and patent rolls.

However, in the absence of the immediate authority of a preferential patent the interim formal, routine, exchequer method of administering those lands which belonged absolutely to the king was through leases made for a term of years, or for one or more lives, at the rate of the extent (the yearly value), ascertained either by inquisition or by search of exchequer records, payment being guaranteed by two or more mainpernours or sponsors. These arrangements were duly recorded on the fine rolls by authority of the Council or by bill of the Treasurer. A degree of patronage or preferential treatment might still be involved, as even these leases were often stated to be granted in view of faithful service rendered. Indeed there is evidence to suggest that a fourteenth-century exchequer extent had no relation to current economic value and normally undervalued the property.

The securing of an exchequer lease for a term at the rate of extent was the most reliable method of obtaining initial possession of a royal estate. But there were never sufficient estates available to meet even the accepted needs, according to status, of all the members of the royal family during Edward III's reign. This is evident from the considerable supplementary incomes paid to all of them from the issues of the customs and of lay and clerical taxation. Newly created earls were endowed at the rate of 1,000 marks p.a. in lands and rents; royal earls or dukes at 2,000 marks; but none of the fourteenth-century creations were ever lucky enough to get a full initial endowment. A favoured king's knight, banneret or baron might expect to receive a single substantial manor in fee fairly well on in his career and almost all other royal servants had to be content with life grants or with reversionary life grants subject to existing life interests. All could and did look for supplementation from the income of wards' lands, vacant temporalities and alien priory lands. Thus it was a privilege to secure any lease at the rate of the extent, although at certain times the death of a member of the royal family might temporarily release a host of royal lands, rents and feefarms into exchequer custody. For example, the largest single grant ever made during the fourteenth century, Queen Isabella's grant of 1 February 1327, to the value of £8,722 4s 4d, contained 119 separately extended units ranging in annual value from £7 to £800.[27]

The fourteenth-century fine rolls do, therefore, provide authentic information for illustrating both the extent of the residual operation of royal patronage after the needs of the royal family and other permanent endowments had been met, and the ultimate, residual financial income left at the disposal of the Exchequer. If we take the last thirty years of Edward III's reign from 1347, and exclude wards' lands, vacant temporalities and alien priory lands from the reckoning, then the total cumulative annual value of new leases made at the Exchequer (for manors, towns, hundreds, bailiwicks, forest lands, mills and fisheries) during these thirty years was rather less than £5,000. Visitations of the Black Death, which caused evident increases in the number of inquisitions *post mortem* recorded on the fine rolls, made no impact on the pattern of leases of crown lands. In the first fourteeen years of this period to 1360 new leases totalled only £762, of which £300 was due from the Channel Islands, a very doubtful source of income, and a further £130 of it was the estimated surplus value of Southampton castle with its appurtenant lands and the New Forest, taken from Queen Philippa and put into the hands of a competent soldier, Sir Richard de Pembridge. The queen had to be compensated by other grants. From 1361 there was a marked rise in the value of new leases, due entirely to three causes: the death of Queen Isabella in 1358; the acquisition of the Kentish lands of Juliana de Leybourne, countess of Huntingdon, which were leased direct to the existing tenants and not allowed to pass elsewhere because they were intended for the performance of the king's will; and the death of Queen Philippa in 1369. These three sources alone accounted for all except £580 out of a total of £4,200 in new leases made between 1361 and 1377.[28]

From the death of Edward III the Leybourne lands (value £636 10s p.a. in leases) were alienated in mortmain by his executors, together with a number of other manors then available, in order to perform the king's will. This concentrates attention on the other vital factor which determined the amount of the exchequer residual interest: how quickly did patronage remove the rest of these new leases from the exchequer records? The £5,000 worth of new leases made between 1347 and 1377 never did represent anything approaching that amount in annual exchequer revenue.

27. See Appendix 'A' below.

28. *Cal. Fine Rolls*, vi, vii, viii, *passim*. The Kentish Leybourne manors leased on the fine rolls were Dean Court in Thanet, Meres Court in Rainham, Packmanstone, Ham, Elham, Wateringbury and Leybourne, Harrietsham, Eastling, Barton Buckwell, Ashford, Wadling, Elmstone and Overland, Preston by Wingham, Gore in Upchurch, Coldbridge, and Bewper. For a fuller list of her lands, etc., obtained by Edward III see *Cal. Close Rolls 1360–1364*, pp. 393–4. For his will see *Cal. Pat. Rolls 1374–1377*, pp. 347–8 and *Collection of Wills of Kings and Queens of England etc.*, ed. J. Nichols (London, Society of Antiquaries, 1780), pp. 59–65.

With the exception of the Leybourne leases, which were significantly and uniquely made, not in the Exchequer, but on the lands concerned, by the Chancellor, William Wykeham, who travelled down to Queenborough for this purpose, the overwhelming majority of leases were made at Westminster to royal servants. The accession of a new king provides a handy point from which to survey the effects of patronage on exchequer leases. Sixteen new leases of crown lands appeared on the fine rolls during the first regnal year of Richard II.[29] A new reign meant that prudent lessees and grantees looked to the validity of their agreements and obtained confirmations of them under the authority of the new king. Sixteen new leases in one year may still appear to be a very small total, but a survey of the ultimate fate of these new leases of 1377–8 provides a more representative and more substantial selection for scrutiny than an attempt to survey in detail the tiny trickle of exchequer leases appearing on the fine rolls between 1347 and 1377, which were briefly swollen only on three occasions, by the deaths of two queens and by the acquisition of the Leybourne estates for alienation in mortmain.

The manor of Eastwood with the hundred of Rochford (Essex) had been valued at £100 when Queen Philippa held it. In 1374 a local man, supported by the king's tenants and bondmen there, obtained a nine-year stock and land lease of this manor at £61 6s 8d. The new reign now saw it newly leased to Thomas Oklee, clerk, at the same figure, for seven years, but on 1 August 1380 Aubrey de Veer, king's esquire, received it for life, rent free, at a valuation of £44 2s 1d, obtaining a separate, life, rent-free grant of the hundred in the following January. In 1377 the park of the manor of Bradninch, duchy of Cornwall land, with two water mills, fishings and some two hundred acres of arable, meadow and pasture, was let to William de Corby, king's esquire, for three years at £11 6s 8d. In February 1378 this was converted to a lease for the joint lives of himself and his wife. It appears that he had in fact been entitled to a pension of £10 p.a. from the receiver of the duchy of Cornwall since June 1376. In 1387 he surrendered this pension and received the Bradninch grant in survivorship, rent free.

In 1 Richard II the manor of Havering-atte-Bower (Essex) was confirmed on the unexpired portion of a four-year lease at £116 to Ralph Tyle, a king's yeoman. He also already held the keepership of the park there, and a life grant of £5 from the issues of the manor. He acquired the office of keeper of the manor at 2d a day wages in 1380. By this time the lease of the manor had passed to Alan de Buxhall, knight, Constable of the Tower of London, also at £116 for five years, but in May 1382 it was granted

29. See the index to *Cal. Fine Rolls*, ix, under Eastwood, Bradninch, Havering-atte-Bower, Isleworth, Somerton in Boothby, Walton-on-Trent, Woodrow, Brigstock, Leeds, Castle Rising, Mansfield, Bristol, Witley, Whitchurch, Moorend and Haselbury Plucknett, and in the relevant volumes of calendars of patent and fine rolls for the subsequent grants and leases.

for life to Queen Anne as part of her dower at a valuation of £100. The manor and hundred of Isleworth (Middlesex) was newly leased by Richard II's Exchequer to John de Ipre, knight, formerly controller of Edward III's Household, for six years at £123. But on 26 March 1378 he obtained an *inspeximus* of letters patent of 1372 confirming to him a grant of £100 out of the manor for life. On 18 July 1387 the manor passed to Queen Anne at a valuation of £100.

The king's manor of Somerton in Boothby and a moiety of the manor of Carlton le Moorland (Lincs.), was obtained on what appears to have been a stock and land lease at 50 marks for ten years in 1377 by John Auncell, knight. He was dead by 16 November 1380 and on 16 January 1381 Adam de Ramesey, a king's esquire, received a life grant of it for 50 marks a year. Four days later he received a grant of 40 marks p.a. for life out of the issues, at the same time surrendering an earlier grant of 40 marks on the stanneries of Cornwall. But on 15 February 1389 he surrendered the grant of 40 marks p.a. on Somerton and Carlton to Angetill Malore, king's knight, receiving back in exchange a grant of 40 marks p.a. on the issues of the duchy of Cornwall. A lease of 8 October 1377 gave Thomas Ardeyn, knight, the manor of Walton-on-Trent, part of the Montalt purchase, for ten years at £22. On 22 December 1377 he was superseded by a king's esquire, Richard de Hampton, with a life grant at the same farm. But £20 of this farm was to be allowed to him for life and on 10 May 1381 he was also pardoned payment of the surplus for life.

With the sole exception of the manor of Woodrow (Wilts.) which was confirmed in 1382 to John Roche, a king's knight, for ten years for 20 marks p.a. with an allowance of 13s 4d, when his original lease of 1377 expired, the story of these six units of royal land was repeated *mutatis mutandis* in the cases of all the other ten new leases of 1377–8. The manor of Brigstock (Northants.), leased for £46 for six years in 1377, passed to Queen Anne at the same valuation in 1382; so did the manor of Leeds, Kent, where the prior of Leeds had been paying £20 p.a. on a nine-year lease, already reduced by £5 by a life pension granted to John Quartayse since 1379. The demesne lands of the manor of Castle Rising (Norf.), which John Talman had obtained for seven years at 40 marks in 1377, were alienated to John duke of Brittany and his wife and the heirs of his body in 1378, when two king's esquires and two king's yeomen had consequently to be found annuities elsewhere. The lessee of the manors of Mansfield and Linby (Notts.), John de Burley, whose lease was made for two years at 100 marks p.a. in 1377, received a life annuity of 100 marks p.a. from them in 1378 because he was retained to stay with the king, and a month later at his request this was granted to his son. The farm of Bristol, granted to John Woderowe of Bristol for two years at £100 in 1377, passed to Queen Anne at the same valuation in 1382. John de Hermesthorp, clerk had a lease of the manor of Witley (Surrey) in 1377 for ten years at £33. The king's nurse, Mundina Danos of Aquitaine, first received a life grant of £30 p.a. from this farm and then the whole manor rent free for life in 1378, a grant which was extended in survivorship in 1381 to her husband Walter Rauf, the king's tailor. A lease of two-thirds of the manor of Whitchurch (Oxon.) for nine years at 20 marks, made in January 1378, was superseded four months later by an *inspeximus* and confirmation of an earlier grant to William de Drayton, an esquire of the king's father, for life, rent free, to the value of £20 p.a.

Some confusion existed about the legal position of Moorend (Northants.). The king's knight, Richard Waldegrave, staying with the king by agreement of the Council, received it for life rent free in 1377, but in February 1378 he found it necessary to take out an exchequer lease at the rate of the extent. An inquisition held in the following May because Alice Perrers had held some or all of it extended it at £30 and in fact it then stood enfeoffed for the performance of Edward III's will. However, in 1382 it passed to Queen Anne at a valuation of £20. Finally a lease of the manor of Haselbury Plucknett was obtained by William de Weston for ten years at £42 p.a. in May 1378. His mainpernours who were bound for £200 had their property seized in 1390 because the Exchequer had not received his farm. This manor, which Edward III had in fact granted in tail male to his daughter Isabella and her husband Ingram de Coucy, had subsequently been declared forfeit because of Ingram's defection to France. It is not clear whether the king's aunt ever recovered her interest in it, but from November 1385 the manor was in the hands of Michael de la Pole, rent free, at a yearly valuation of £43 6s 8d.

Thus the apparent original exchequer entitlement of over £700 annual rent from these sixteen units of crown property in 1 Richard II had been reduced within five years by the requirements of the royal family and the demands of patronage to a total of about £55 p.a.

4. EXCHEQUER AND CHAMBER ADMINISTRATION

The significance of the royal lands in the workings of English government during the thirteenth and fourteenth centuries thus lay primarily in supporting the king's family. Next in importance they provided a cement of patronage which, if prudently used, helped to bind together the political structure of the kingdom in loyal service to the head of state. Last of all, they made some intermittent, fluctuating and normally rather insignificant contributions to the current expenses of government. These expenses meant to contemporaries the living costs of the king's Household, Chamber and Wardrobe, and the salaries, as opposed to pensions and endowments, of his officers and servants. This order of priorities was naturally reflected in the pattern of their administration.

After an estate had been created to support a member of the royal family it acquired its own professional officers and when it reverted to the Crown it was not immediately broken up. The outstanding fourteenth-century example was the duchy of Cornwall, created for the king's eldest son Edward of Woodstock, the Black Prince, from 1337. This was exceptional in that its entity was preserved by charter and it was ever after administered as one separate unit, even when there was no heir to the throne to enjoy its revenues. Throughout the reign of Richard II it was under exchequer control. Less permanent examples occurred when a queen suffered confiscation of her estates or died. For example, Richard II's queen, Anne, died in 1394. She had held crown lands valued at £4,500 p.a.[30] In 1400 her receiver-general was still accounting for rather less than half of that total at the Exchequer, though new life grants, rent free, were rapidly disposing of his charge.[31]

Apart from the intermittent, residual nature of its financial interest in the units of the royal demesne, the great weakness of the Exchequer as an office of land revenue lay in its lack of permanent professional agents in the localities, the receivers, surveyors and auditors who served every large-scale private estate. It was dependent on a multitude of the king's subjects who were responsible as farmers for individual payments either locally by assignment or, to a minor extent, at the central Exchequer, and for separate, personal appearances there to clear the accounts, unless an attorney was employed at their own expense. The only debt collector of the central office was the non-professional sheriff who admittedly had an office staff, but himself came to hold office only for a year at a time and was appointed primarily to discharge essential governmental, legal and military duties in the shires, not to act as a royal land agent.

There were sporadic exchequer experiments to increase the financial yield of the royal demesne by special administrative arrangements, but these were always unsustained and stopped short of results because of the intervention of much more important political considerations. Special keepers were appointed for the 'ancient demesne' for the first time after 1236, but Professor Hoyt, who has re-examined the changes of these years, has found evidence only of these keepers piling up debts at the Exchequer and of a wider extension of the customary farming system for a fixed sum and term of years very soon after 1236.[32] In 1275 special stewards of the

30. *Cal. Pat. Rolls, 1381–1385*, pp. 125–7, 159, 192, 203, 511, 513, 528–9, 552, 567.

31. P.R.O., Exch., L.T.R., Misc. Rolls, E.358/17: 30 manors producing £1,250; 3 forest areas—£200; 9 feefarms—£600. At Easter 1401 he was exonerated from his duties and had no successor.

32. See Mabel H. Mills, 'The Reforms at the Exchequer (1232–1242)', *T.R.H.S.* 4th series, x (1927), 111–33. To the names of Warner Engayne and Walter de Burgh, Professor

king's demesnes, this time in three groups of counties covering the whole of England except Durham, Lancaster and Cornwall, were appointed, but the experiment seems to have been abandoned from about 1283,[33] most probably because the lands concerned were required for other uses. For purposes of better financial exploitation of the exchequer's residual interest in the royal demesne these experiments do seem nevertheless to have been along the right lines. Investigation of the venerable exchequer farming system, which merged so conveniently into the pattern of the other more important priorities which the royal lands had to meet, only serves to bear out this conclusion.

In farming arrangements, where no special terms were dictated by the king's grant, the basis of agreement was a valuation or 'extent' made by local men empanelled by the sheriff on instructions from the Exchequer. The method to be followed was ultimately laid down in an enactment of uncertain date called the statute *Extenta Maneria*.[34] It is doubtful whether in practice these detailed instructions were often carried out. During the fourteenth century the normal process of inquisition to ascertain the value of royal lands seems to have been no different from that which served for the everyday process of inquisitions *post mortem*. While the full identification of all the lands of the deceased in an inquisition *post mortem* was of vital interest to the heir if he wished to be sure of his title, their accurate valuation by the process of inquisition was of much less importance to him and tended to be a mere formality. The same traditional process of extent by inquisition applied to royal lands primarily for the purpose of valuation can hardly have been very effective. At the end of the thirteenth century it was certainly on occasion deemed unnecessary even to extend royal manors leased for life and in the king's hands by the death of the occupier, because their value was already known to the Exchequer.[35] Extents of royal lands became fixed and formal affairs held, not on the lands concerned, but in the county towns where the sheriffs had their offices, and the returns sent to the Exchequer were no more than a declaration of what the previous farmer had paid. Thus the process of extent by inquisition became less and less of a guide to the market value of a manor and one suspects that this process of fossilization was of very long standing.

Hoyt adds Robert de Crepping. Their terms of reference, quoted by Hoyt, are in *Cal. Pat. Rolls, 1232–1247*, pp. 146 f., 156; Hoyt, *op. cit.*, pp. 156–61.

33. E. R. Stevenson, 'The Escheator', in *The English Government at Work 1327–1336*, ii, *Fiscal Administration*, 116–18. Compare the enactment of uncertain date printed in *Statutes of the Realm*, i, 197(a).

34. *ibid.*, 242–3. The order in which inquiry and assessment was to be conducted was as follows: the buildings, demesne lands, foreign pasture, park and demesne woods, foreign woods, pannage and herbage, mills and fishings, freeholders, customary tenants, cottages and curtelages, perquisites of courts, patronage of churches, liberties and customs; cf. Britton, III, vii, para. 5: to be made by verbal testimony of the jurors and to be 'de claro'.

35. *Cal. Inq. Misc., 1219–1307*, p. 282, no. 936.

Detailed fourteenth-century evidence to support this view can be found, though it is scarce and, indeed, such evidence can hardly be plentiful at any period because one must find contemporary valuations of specific royal manors made by an alternative method to set against the extents. In 1318 the tenants of the manor of Brigstock unsuccessfully offered £50 a year to forestall another preferential grant when it returned to the king's hands, after being held by Queen Margaret at a yearly valuation of £41 10s.[36] In 1378 Adam Hartington and Richard Fillongley were appointed to survey all the king's lands south of Trent with special reference to alien priories, and to lease the premises to the king's advantage.[37] Hartington was a chamberlain of the Exchequer and Fillongley a surveyor and auditor of the Exchequer Court. They produced a number of detailed surveys[38] and valued the lordship, manor and park of Woodstock at £216 17s p.a. free of charges. The farmer, Sir Philip de la Vacche, was paying a farm of £127 16s 6d. This lower sum was indeed the normal farm, since Roger Elmrugge, king's yeoman, had held it before him at this figure, and annuities charged on the manor, or deductions to the farmer, would be allowed for out of it. Its normal value then for purposes of leasing, the accepted rate of extent for all transactions relating to it, was £127 16s 6d. This survey had therefore revealed a discrepancy between the market value and the farm, but this information was not allowed to affect the terms of Sir Philip's farm[39] and when Queen Joan was granted the same lands in 1403 their extent by inquisition appears to have fallen as low as £60 p.a. Nevertheless, it is highly significant, though at first sight it may appear incredible, that when Henry VII's Exchequer farmed out this lordship, manor and park in 1485 in the traditional manner it was at the fossilized rate of £127 16s 6d p.a., the identical sum being charged in 1378, plus an insignificant increment of 3s 6d.

There were similar commissions issued again in 1387, again primarily concerned with alien priorities but also again embracing some royal lands.[40] Among the surveys then made appeared the manor and town of Mansfield (Notts.), surveyed by two king's sergeants-at-arms and valued at 100 marks.[41] In this case the survey actually seems to have resulted in an increase of the farm to this figure for the next three years, but by 1433 the exchequer extent of Mansfield with Linby was only £35 2s,[42] while the account of Geoffrey Kneton (constable of Nottingham castle and clerk of the forest) of the towns and manors of ancient demesne in the 'Book of

36. *Cal. Fine Rolls*, ii, 365; *Cal. Pat. Rolls, 1301–1307*, p. 369.

37. *Cal. Pat. Rolls, 1377–1381*, p. 253.

38. P.R.O., Exch., K.R., 'Extents of Alien Priories', E.106/11/2. Also Chanc. Misc. Inq., C.145/219 mm. 2, 5.

39. *Cal. Pat. Rolls, 1377–1381*, p. 341; cf. *Cal. Fine Rolls*, vi, 343; *ibid.*, viii, 293–4.

40. *Cal. Pat. Rolls, 1385–1389*, p. 318.

41. P.R.O., E.106/11/11; see also E.106/11/3–8.

42. *Cal. Fine Rolls*, viii, 369; x, 182; xii, 8; xvi, 162.

Sherwood Forest', dated 1446–7, gives the extent of Mansfield as no more than £18 8s 2½d, and of Linby as a mere £6 15s 4d p.a.[43]

An instance from a different and unexpected source, the records of the parliament of 1386, indicates that normally there was a tendency for all new valuations by extent to go consistently to the advantage of the person placed in possession, and that this was quite well known at the time. Michael de la Pole, earl of Suffolk, had been given lands to a certain value by the king, who advised him to take them at the last previous valuations rather than to have new extents made because it might later be said that as Chancellor he was in a strong position to influence those who would make the extents. This he agreed to do. Nevertheless, he was subsequently accused in the parliament of 1386 of having defrauded the king by receiving lands which had a much higher actual than declared value. In answer to this accusation he told how he had accepted the king's advice and received them at their old valuations. But he swore that by so doing he had not defrauded the king, for if new extents had been made they would certainly have produced lower values than the old ones. Had he chosen to have been less honest and to have taken his grants at the rate of new valuations he could have claimed and received more royal land than he had in fact received.[44] Leases and grants made 'at the yearly rate at the Exchequer of as much as X used to render', 'at the rate of the extent', 'at the usual farm', or on some such similar terms thus in fact bore no relation to the true market values of the lands.

The organization and methods necessary for a financial exploitation of the land revenues of the royal demesne simply did not exist within the royal Exchequer. The medieval Exchequer, with its mere residual interest in royal manors, was not a land revenue office, or at most only to a very subsidiary and far from efficient degree. But we must ask whether any other royal office performed this function at any period before 1399. The possibilities inherent in chamber and wardrobe finance spring to mind, especially since it has recently been cogently argued that the Chamber, not the Exchequer, was the very 'centre and controlling organ of the financial system' in the eleventh and twelfth centuries.[45] Moreover, the meticulous and vast investigations of Tout into Wardrobe and Chamber do in fact demonstrate an identical, general state of control in the thirteenth and fourteenth centuries, if one can manage to discount his erroneous assumptions of political and administrative rivalries and of divisions between 'national' and 'private' financial organs and funds. This is not to suggest that

43. Nottingham University, Middleton MS., viii a, fols c. 15, 16; see also *Hist. MSS. Com. Middleton*, p. 245.

44. *Rot. Parl.*, iii, 216–17.

45. H. G. Richardson and G. O. Sayles, *The Governance of Mediaeval England from the Conquest to Magna Carta* (Edinburgh, 1963), p. 239. Their views on the origins of the Exchequer demand very serious consideration by all students of English medieval history.

the normal, well-used machinery for raising and spending the proceeds of direct and indirect taxation under exchequer supervision and control could be bettered by Chamber or Wardrobe. But it does seem that the making of loans and individual bargains with his subjects and the appropriation of cash for the king's immediate affairs belonged more conveniently and naturally to chamber and wardrobe finance at all periods of active kingship.[46]

Nevertheless, the prospect of discovering a royal land revenue office hidden in the Chamber or Wardrobe is inherently improbable for most of the medieval period, because throughout these centuries our kings continued to draw their income mainly from their rights of taxation; they concentrated their financial energies on the exploitation and development of these, not on the development of farms, rent and agricultural profits. The proceeds of taxation financed their chamber and wardrobe activities almost as completely as they did their Exchequer. Recent investigations which have highlighted the financial importance of Henry II's and John's chamber activities have only served to confirm this.[47] There is also sufficient evidence in the monumental pages of Tout to show that it held good for Henry III, Edward I, most of Edward III's reign and for the reign of Richard II.[48]

46. I do not doubt that the Exchequer had the ultimate task of scrutinizing accounts to see that the king was not defrauded. But this was essentially *ex post facto*: relentless, tenacious pursuit with all the possible rigours of the law for which the Exchequer was designed, but not a process of control and decision exercised on current spending. This seems to have been done at all times of active kingship in Chamber or Wardrobe as required. No attempted distinction between 'national' and 'private' offices will stand up to criticism because among the king's most intimate 'secret matters' at the heart of chamber and wardrobe finance were *sui generis* matters of the most urgent and vital national concern. As Tout himself says at one point (*Administrative History*, iv, 294) the most 'secret business' in the heart of Edward III was the prosecution of the war. Without a prolonged, detailed reinvestigation of his material it is very hard to prove Tout wrong in his frequent diagnoses of departmental rivalries. Similar situations in fifteenth and early sixteenth-century administration do not appear to have generated such rivalries.

47. J. E. A. Jolliffe, 'The Camera Regis under Henry II', *E.H.R.*, lxviii (1953), 1–21; 337–62; H. G. Richardson, 'The Chamber under Henry II', *E.H.R.*, lxix (1954), 596–611. J. E. A. Jolliffe, 'The Chamber and the Castle Treasures under King John', in *Studies in Medieval History presented to F. M. Powicke*, ed. R. W. Hunt and others (Oxford, 1948), pp. 117–42; R. A. Brown, '"The Treasury" of the Later Twelfth Century' in *Studies presented to Sir Hilary Jenkinson*, ed. J. Conway Davies (London, 1957), pp. 35–49. Jolliffe's articles are particularly important for the scale of chamber operations uncovered. Mr Richardson's article succeeds in dispelling the impression created by Jolliffe for the reign of Henry II that the Chamber was superseding a less efficient Exchequer and demonstrates that it was doing different kinds of work. The activities of the itinerant Chamber over fines, debts and profits in the localities detailed by Jolliffe for the reign of John were, of course, allowed for in exchequer procedure by writs of *computate* and *perdono* (see the *Dialogus* (1950 ed.), pp. 15–16, 32–3, 80). References (*Administrative History*, i, 107) which Tout thought might suggest one or two twelfth-century manors regularly accounting in the Chamber seem to me to suggest merely the allocation or granting of their issues to a chamber officer for his support.

48. See especially Tout, *op. cit.*, ii, 113–15; for the years 1282–4, a period of maximum 'extra-exchequer' receipt by the Wardrobe, where these receipts are shown to consist of the great customs, a parliamentary thirtieth and a thirteenth-century 'benevolence'.

Yet there is embedded in the mass of the *Administrative History* an excellent factual record of the first creation of a royal land revenue office in English history by the younger Despenser and Edward II,[49] paradoxically in the very reign which historians regard as the worst example of wanton squandering of royal landed endowments since the reign of Stephen. A revival of normal chamber activity very early in the reign of Edward II was financed by the loans of foreign bankers, the issues from Walter Langton's forfeited lands and from the Templar's lands. Later forfeitures were also channelled there. This process was much disrupted by the sudden, urgent needs of the Scottish campaign of 1322, and weakened by the normal restoration of entailed forfeited lands which custom and law required. Nevertheless, after allowing for all these factors, the unique feature of the period from 1322 was the permanent reservation of some fifty units, ranging down from the lordship of Burstwick with Holderness, worth 1,000 marks p.a., to single manors, tightly and exclusively administered by the Chamber as a central office of land revenue.[50] Besides the normal, local farmers and bailiffs there was built up a central staff of receivers, surveyors and auditors to visit, control, audit and develop the estates to the maximum profit of the king. In its brief four years of orderly development as 'the peculiar bulwark of the prerogative'[51] according to Tout, Edward II's Chamber achieved an annual 'permanent' land revenue of about £2,000, apart from all that it received *ad hoc* from other sources. The amount had little significance in itself, but the administrative innovations and the principles which lay behind them are of great interest. Understandably the local inhabitants of these lands who felt the impact of these new arrangements did not like them, and in 1327 they petitioned in parliament to be put back under exchequer control.[52]

This chamber estate was broken up by the revolution of 1326–7 and almost the whole of it appropriated by Queen Isabella. A partial revival followed from 1333 as the young Edward III began to assert himself, with the reservation of Burstwick once more and with other additions, most notably Carisbrooke castle and the Isle of Wight, in 1335. Forfeitures and escheats, wards' lands, alien priories, part of the Channel Islands and even certain Breton and Norman estates were added from time to time; chamber receivers, surveyors and auditors controlling the lands reappeared.[53] But though this revived process of land reservation to the Chamber continued

49. Tout, *op. cit.*, ii, 314–60.

50. These are listed under counties by Tout, *ibid.*, p. 352.

51. *ibid.*, iv, 265.

52. *Rot. Parl.*, ii, 432. This private petition, clearly the work of the interested parties, seems to be the grounds on which Tout based his statement that the chamber reservations were abolished in 1327 at the instance of the Commons (*ibid.*, iv, 296). This conclusion is quite unwarrantable.

53. *ibid.*, iv, 227–348 for all chamber activities in the reigns of Edward III and Richard II.

from 1333 to 1356 the impression remains that there were less lands permanently available than before 1326.[54] Notably from 1349 they began to disappear altogether, the chief beneficiary being Isabella, the king's eldest daughter. The royal family was increasing in numbers; Edward III was determined to be generous towards his nobility and others in pursuit of his great enterprise, which was in any case financed by direct and indirect taxation; the years of economic disorder following the Black Death were hardly propitious for the financial exploitation of royal landed estate. These were probably the reasons for the disappearance of Edward III's chamber estate rather than the other much less plausible explanations advanced by Tout in the tradition of Stubbs: departmental rivalries, superior administrative efficiency in the Exchequer, and an Exchequer too powerful for the king to be able to pit his more personal financial department against it with any degree of success.

5. PARLIAMENTARY CRITICISM

The royal lands of the English monarchy were thus employed in the service of the Crown during the thirteenth and fourteenth centuries according to a pattern of needs which placed first the needs of the royal family, second the rewarding of royal servants, and third, for which little remained, contribution to the national finances. Some of our most influential modern historians, most notably Stubbs and Tout, have asserted that contemporaries were consistently highly critical of this state of affairs, but there is only intermittent evidence in the chronicles and the records of government which can be made to bear this interpretation. Edward II was certainly condemned by his political enemies as well as by Stubbs for his alienations to Gaveston. On the other hand his experiment with a land revenue office in his Chamber passed unnoticed by contemporaries, except for those whose pockets were adversely affected, only to be bizarrely condemned by Tout, the historian who has most fully described it, as a potential danger to infant parliamentary liberties, designed to make the king independent of parliamentary taxation.[55] Stubbs drew a picture of the crafty Edward III, evading or breaking alleged rules against alienation of the royal patrimony and making parliament jointly responsible for his imprudence, but this view similarly amalgamates contemporary fourteenth-century facts with inappropriate constitutional proprieties drawn from a later age. In the case of charges of large-scale alienations made against Richard II, study of the printed *Calendars of Patent Rolls* suggests that his alienations outside the royal family were in fact on a very much reduced scale compared with the two previous reigns. The amount of land at the disposal of our Plantagenet kings during the thirteenth and fourteenth centuries does however,

54. There is a useful list of lands, *ibid.*, p. 245.

55. *ibid.*, ii, 355.

appear to have been on the increase as a result of conscious royal policy, but in normal times there was still precious little left over after the legitimate needs of the royal family had been met.

The beginnings of a persistent constitutional demand that royal lands should be made to provide a substantial contribution to the national finances, at the expense of patronage if not at the expense of the royal family, does not in fact appear to have much antedated the accession to the throne of the first really substantial royal landowner since William the Conqueror: Henry duke of Lancaster, in 1399, though it did have certain fourteenth-century antecedents. There certainly were references to the role of the king's lands in government in the fourteenth century. It is evident that 'gifts of land, rent, franchise (liberty), escheat, wardship, marriage or bailiwick'[56] were always the most desirable, normal and effective means available to the king for adequately rewarding his servants, great or small and for binding men to him. A draft on the central Exchequer for these purposes, which had to compete there with all the urgent demands of the king's great affairs, was a very uncertain and unattractive proposition indeed, acceptable to no one except as a stop-gap until something more permanent could be obtained. This was an inescapable fact of English government, and one would expect these gifts to be called in question at times of political crisis when personalities and financial difficulties were involved. Historians have quoted two outstanding fourteenth-century examples of this, in 1311 and 1377. The third Ordinance of 1311 required the Ordainers, who were taking over the government, to exercise great restraint over these gifts; the seventh gave them power to annul any which had been made since they received their commission. It seems that someone must actually have resurrected these Ordinances of 1311 for reuse at the accession of Richard II, because the two petitions of 1377 repeated the demands of 1311 almost *verbatim*. The Council on this later occasion were asked to examine the rolls of Chancery for evidence of gifts which had weakened and dismembered the Crown during Edward III's reign.[57] The purpose of such restraint, review and annulment in 1311 had been given as to acquit the king's debts and to relieve his estate. In 1377 the aims were stated rather more specifically: for the king's debts, to relieve the estate of the very honourable lords his uncles who were poor in their estate, for the confirmation of worthy grants and the punishment of unworthy grantees and, lastly, to obtain the means to reward those worthy servants of the late king who had so far gone unrewarded. Grants of royal lands and of the income and profits to be derived from them were potentially strong cement

56. The words of the third Ordinance of 1311.

57. *Rot. Parl.*, iii, 15–16 (nos. 47 and 48). For the striking correspondence and indeed verbal identity between extensive portions of common petitions in 1377 and the Ordinances of 1311 see J. G. Edwards, 'Some Common Petitions in Richard II's First Parliament', *B.I.H.R.*, xxvi (1952), 200–13.

to help to build a stable political structure. They could never be entirely abolished, although at times of weak or uncertain political direction and control they were inevitably called into question. They were undoubtedly part, but only part, of the king's own, but the criticism of their use or misuse recurring in times of unsuccessful government during the fourteenth century did not yet stem from any fundamental and generally accepted belief that the king ought to be able to meet the normal expenses of government from the revenues of his royal demesne, if only he could be prevented from giving it away.

There were requests, in 1343, 1381 and 1382, that the king should retain lands, rents, wardships, marriages, escheats, profits and forfeitures (there were slight variations in the list) for his wars, his debts, his great affairs and to lessen the burdens on his poor Commons. The replies stated that of course the king wished to save his own (1343), that he would exercise restraint through the advice of his Council (1381) and that he would do whatever his Council thought best for his honour and profit (1382).[58] Such general requests for economy were reasonable enough, but they could receive only such general and noncommittal answers because their implementation involved the most important priorities and prerogatives of government.

The earliest and indeed the only fourteenth-century instance that could possibly be interpreted as a definite claim that the issues of the royal demesne ought to provide sufficient for the king to live on comes from a copy of common petitions for 1340, found in the Winchester cartulary, but not on the rolls of parliament. Clearly, if we do so interpret it, then it was an absurd demand. It was a demand for an enquiry by sheriffs into all alienations and sales of royal lands, other than escheats or royal purchases, to be carried back to the time of Edward I. These were to be judged and tried in parliament and unreasonable ones re-seized into the king's hand: 'so that the king may live of his own without laying charges on his people'.[59] These Winchester petitions have an air of untutored authenticity about them and they may well have represented the views of the king's 'poor Commons'. If we interpret this as a limited demand that the king's landed resources should make some more substantial contribution to the national Exchequer than they were doing at that time, to help the king towards living of his own, then that demand seems to have been not unreasonable. Uninitiated as they may have been into the mysteries of statecraft, they were living and complaining at a unique period of maximum alienation of the royal patrimony outside the royal family when Edward III was endowing the chosen companions of his great adventure on a scale which sur-

58. *Rot. Parl.*, ii, 141 (no. 35); iii, 115 (no. 74); iii, 139 (no. 42).

59. *Chartulary of Winchester Cathedral*, ed. A.W. Goodman (Winchester, 1927), p. 132: 'issent qe le Roi puisse vivere de soen saunz charge de soen people'.

passed the alleged weak generosity of Edward II. Perhaps the climate of public opinion outside the circle of the king's companions and advisers was not then so very favourable to Edward III's royal giving as has generally been supposed, at least before the victories began.

There was certainly some shrewd sense in the next, undoubted reference to the financial potentialities of the royal estates when Richard II's Commons declined to believe in his poverty in 1378, because they knew that he had inherited all the lands of the prince his father.[60] But the same point made to his successor about the broad lands of which he stood possessed after his usurpation in 1399 had even more substance because his assumption of the throne had added to the royal resources the whole landed patrimony of the House of Lancaster. This point was indeed a very difficult one for Henry IV and his advisers to answer, because they had included in their condemnation of Richard the claim that he ought to have been able 'without oppressing his people, to live honourably from the issues of the kingdom and from the patrimony belonging to the Crown, when the kingdom was not burdened with the expense of wars'.[61]

One consequence of Edward III's 'family settlement', with its incorporation of the inheritances of the Lancastrian and March heiresses in the family estate of the Plantagenets, may well have been the royal factions of York and Lancaster. But equally the crown estate of the Yorkist and first Tudor kings was also essentially that earlier royal family estate of the fourteenth-century Plantagenets, as augmented by three marriages[62] and consolidated by the usurpations of 1399 and 1461. Indeed the units of administration in the books of Henry VII's Court of General Surveyors were still the original fourteenth-century seigneurial groupings of Edward III's family. The explanation of the differences in its employment by the Yorkists and first Tudors, and of changes in public attitudes towards it in the meantime must be sought in events of the intervening Lancastrian period.

60. *Rot. Parl.*, iii, 35 (no. 18).
61. *ibid.*, iii, 419.
62. John of Gaunt to Blanche of Lancaster, Henry of Bolingbroke to Mary de Bohun and Richard earl of Cambridge to Anne Mortimer.

III

PATRONAGE, POLITICS AND FINANCE 1399-1437*

I. PARLIAMENT AND THE ACT OF RESUMPTION OF 1404

When Henry Bolingbroke seized the Crown in 1399 he became the greatest royal landowner England had seen since the days of the Conqueror. As the heir of his father and mother he brought to the support of the Crown the vast estates of the duchy of Lancaster extending over most of the counties of England and Wales.[1] Through his wife he had a life interest by courtesy in half the huge possessions of his father-in-law, Humphrey de Bohun, earl of Essex, Hereford and Northampton, which were to vest in his son on his death.[2] As king he controlled six other great complexes of estates, each with their own treasuries: (1) the duchy of Cornwall with extensive lands in more than a dozen counties besides Cornwall and Devon; (2) the king's lands in North Wales; (3) his lands in South Wales; (4) the county and lordship of Pembroke with the lordships of Tenby, Cilgerran and Ystlwyf; (5) the counties and lordships of Chester and Flint; and (6) the lordship of Richmond in Yorkshire, which included many manors in Lincolnshire, Norfolk, Suffolk and Cambridgeshire besides the Yorkshire lands.[3] In

* I have incorporated in this chapter, with important modifications and additions, portions of an article which I published in *E.H.R.* (1958), entitled 'Acts of Resumption in the Lancastrian Parliaments'.

1. See *Cal. Close Rolls, 1360–1364*, pp. 201–11, for the lands of Lancaster which John of Gaunt inherited on the deaths of his father-in-law in 1361 and his sister-in-law in 1362. For the substantial gifts of crown lands which had augmented these estates see below, pp. 241–2.

2. There is a full list of Humphrey de Bohun's lands as drawn up in two lots by Anne countess of Stafford, for the final division between her and Henry V in 1421: *Rot. Parl.*, iv, 136–8. The earlier division had differed from this: *ibid.*, 138–40.

3. The chamberlains of North Wales (at Caernarvon), South Wales (at Carmarthen) and Chester each had their treasuries, the duchy of Cornwall had its treasury at Lostwithiel, there was a treasury at Richmond for the lands of the earldom and a treasury at Pembroke, *Cal. Pat. Rolls, 1401–1405*, p. 121, The royal lands in North Wales in 1399 were the counties and lordships of Caernarvon, Conway with the four commotes, and of Merioneth with the lordships of Criccieth and Harlech. Thomas Percy, earl of Worcester, was holding the lordship of Nevin and Pwllheli for life, and Henry Percy, earl of Northumberland, the county, and lordship of Anglesey for life: *Rep. Dig. Peer*, v, *Appendix*, 126–7. The royal lands in South Wales in 1399 were the county and lordship of Carmarthen with the lordships of Lampeter and Cantref, and the county and lordship of Cardigan with the lordships of Builth and Montgomery. Thomas Percy, earl of Worcester, held the lordships of Haverford and Newcastle in Emlyn for life. The Principality of Chester, created in 1397, was dissolved by act of parliament (Stat. 1 Hen. iv, c.3). These palatine counties of Chester and Flint included the castles of Chester, Beeston, Rhyddlan, Hope

addition there were the numerous other lands scattered throughout all the counties of England which were, in theory, farmed out from the Exchequer. The roll of the proffer for Michaelmas 1400, while professing to exclude certain lands which had been granted out for life or terms of years rent free, lists over a hundred separate lordships, manors and towns, the Channel Islands and the Isle of Wight, as charged to farmers or keepers.[4]

Contemporaries saw that Henry IV was a very great landowner indeed: much greater than his predecessor. At the same time they saw that he had few close relatives able to make legitimate demands upon the income from his lands. When he usurped the throne he had no queen and his sons were minors. Queen Joan, the widowed duchess of Brittany, only arrived in England in 1404. Even by 1404, when Henry met his parliament at Coventry, only his eldest son Henry (then aged seventeen), heir to the throne and king's lieutenant in Ireland, had received substantial endowments. Little provision had been made for the new queen or for the king's younger sons Thomas, John and Humphrey.[5] Yet the king maintained that he had exhausted his financial resources and the Commons were being repeatedly asked to dig deep into their own pockets to support him.

At the Coventry Parliament of 1404 a determined group of 'parliamentary knights' put forward a reasoned plan to resume into the king's hands all the landed resources which he and his predecessors had ever held in absolute possession since 1366. Their purpose was to strengthen the Crown financially, to place a significant part of the issues from royal lands at the disposal of the Exchequer in such a manner that they could be relied upon for a substantial and regular contribution to the royal income. The extent of the king's bounty was obvious to all. Let there be a full inquiry so that men with an honest sense of public duty might be satisfied. In this plan they roused strong opposition which came, according to the St Albans chronicler, Thomas Walsingham, from the temporal lords in parliament (i.e. the most powerful interests close to the king), and from the bishops.[6] The bishops' hostile attitude to these plans for reform, and

and Flint, and the manors of Shotwick and Frodsham. Henry IV ignored Richard II's grant of the Richmond lands to John duke of Brittany's sister and granted them for life to Ralph Neville, earl of Westmorland, 20 October 1399.

4. P.R.O., Exch., K.R., E.159/177, mm. 1–4. This figure does not include liberties, or cities and towns listed as paying feefarms. The practice of not listing these crown lands while granted for life or term of years, rent free, began in 1334 when the dowers of Queens Isabella and Philippa, the lands of John of Eltham and grants to Margaret countess of Kent, absorbed a major part of the whole.

5. Henry's sons were born in 1387, 1388, 1389, and 1391 respectively.

6. 'Annales Ricardi et Henrici IV' in *Johannis de Trokelowe et Henrici de Blaneforde Chronica et Annales* (Rolls Series), ed. H. T. Riley, pp. 392–4; *Historia Anglicana* (Rolls Series), ed. H. T. Riley, ii, 266–7; *Ypodigma Neustriae* (Rolls Series), ed. H. T. Riley, pp. 410–11. Professor V. H. Galbraith in his introduction to *The St Albans Chronicle 1406–1422* proves conclusively that Thomas Walsingham, the most important of contemporary chroniclers, was the author of all these three accounts.

indeed the chronicler's own, was determined when these same parliamentary knights also directed their attention to the lavish temporal endowments of the church. Would-be despoilers of church property were the enemies of bishops and of monastic chroniclers.[7] Moreover, according to Walsingham, some parliamentary knights were tainted with lollardy. We are indebted to him for his account of the activities of these parliamentary knights, but it is not surprising that no defence of their policy can be found in that quarter.

There is, however, an alliterative poem (dated 1403–6) composed by an anonymous author who expounded in popular form the policies which were being advocated with such vigour by the Commons in these parliaments. The author was no great believer in the powers of parliamentary knights, for he saw that the grievances which they took to parliament they most often brought back unredressed. Nevertheless, he regarded their views with respect: what they said was not to be classed with the ill-informed and irresponsible criticism of government he heard all around him, and they had a right and duty to make their views known.[8] His own statements of the need for strengthening the endowed revenues of the Crown merit quotation:

'For nedis moste oure leige lord like his estat
Haue for his houshold and for his haynous werres
To maynteyne his manhoode there may no man seye other,
But of his owen were the beste, who-so couthe hit bringge;'
(ll. 1664–7)

and again:

'Thenne of fyne fors hit foloweth as me thenketh,
That a certayne substance shuld be ordeynid
To susteyne this souurayn that shuld us gouerne.'
(ll. 1636–8)

He had no doubt about the causes of the king's political weakness and financial straits which at this time, and especially in the Coventry Parliament of 1404, provided an unusually favourable opportunity to air plans for reform:

7. See Appendix 'B' below.

8. *Mum and the Sothesegger*, ed. M. Day and R. Steele (Early English Text Society, 1936), pp. 27–78. After a round condemnation of irresponsible criticism he continues:

'I carpe not of knightz that cometh for the shires,
That the king clepith (i.e. calleth) to cunseil with other;
But hit longeth to no laborier the lawe is agayne thaym.'
(ll. 1460–2)

Professor Helen Cam accepts the date 1403–6 deduced by the editors for the composition of this poem, *Liberties and Communities in Medieval England*, p. 225.

'There is a librarie of lordes that losen ofte thaym-self
Thorough lickyng of the lordship that to the coroune longeth,
And weneth hit be wel y-do but wors dide thay neuer
Thenne sith thay gunne that game . . .'

(ll. 1626–9)

The king's advisers, knights of the Council, temporal lords and bishops had 'pulled the pears off the royal tree' and 'were licking even the leaves'. Half the king's livelihood and more was in their hands (ll. 1648–53).

Periods of determined personal rule by strong kings were the golden ages of medieval government. Just as in the later troubles of 1450 men would look back to the reign of Henry V, so now in these early years of the century the personal rule of Edward III in his prime had become a legend. Government was weak where once it had been strong. Therefore, contemporaries thought, the evident causes of current weaknesses could not have applied in that earlier period. Edward III must have been better endowed before the policies of the last forty years, 'these fourty wintre', began. So argued the author of the poem, and the sponsors of the petition for resumption did likewise. They proposed a resumption into the king's hands of all castles, manors, lordships, lands, tenements, fees and advowsons, feefarms, annuities, franchises, liberties and customs which had been 'membre et parcelle d'auncien Enheritance de la dite Corone' in the fortieth year of Edward III or since.[9] They believed that if there had been wanton misuse of the king's lands it had occurred since then. This period from 1366 to 1404 was sufficiently long to ensure that the vast majority of crown manors on lease or grant for term of years or life would have fallen in at least once within that time and so would be brought under the scrutiny of the act. The net was stretched to include all lands leased or granted for a term of years, for life, in fee simple, fee tail or conditional fee. Emphasis was thus not merely on grants in fee, i.e. alienations, but also on the leases and grants for life and term of years which were the normal means by which the king bestowed his favour and obtained some income from his lands. The information required to set an inquiry in motion could be found by a search of the records, a laborious but common enough practice in the Exchequer of the later middle ages whenever any kind of statistical information was needed.

The printed calendars of chancery rolls make the modern task of assessing the amount of alienation which had taken place between 1366 and 1404

9. *Rot. Parl.*, iii, 547–8; 'L'an due regne le Roy E, aiel nostre Seigneur le Roy q'or est XL et puis en cea', which is repeated as 'Douns ou Grantz que feurent parcelle del dite Corone le dit an XL ou depuis'. The king's answer, in English, took the Commons' request to mean 'al that longed unto the Coroune the fourty yere of Kyng Edward, and sithe hath be departed': *ibid.*, p. 549.

a comparatively simple one. From the evidence it appears unlikely that the value of all effective royal grants in fee made between these dates would have made a very appreciable contribution to the royal Exchequer. Of the entails received from crown lands by royal half-brothers, younger sons, uncles and their families during the reigns of Edward III and Richard II only in the case of Edmund Langley, duke of York, had they failed to come in again to the king by 1400. In any case the parliament was not opposed to grants made to members of the royal family, for they also petitioned that the queen, the king's younger sons, the Beauforts and Edward duke of York, should be better endowed. The period in question had opened with the grants to the notorious Alice Perrers, but they had been revoked by the first parliament of Richard II. The enforced sales of the 1388 forfeitures did not concern crown lands and were exempted from consideration by the Coventry Parliament. The forfeitures of the dukes of Gloucester and Norfolk, the earls of Warwick and Arundel and of Archbishop Arundel at the end of Richard's reign, and the grants made from them, had been very soon annulled, and though they represent numerous entries of grants on the patent rolls they had no effect on the crown lands. A list of the remaining royal grants of land in fee as they appear on the patent rolls shows that the grants to Michael de la Pole, first earl of Suffolk, far from being typical, were quite exceptional. It must also be remembered that, for the most part, he never had time to enjoy them and they only began to pass to his family after the restoration of his son in November 1399. Some of the other grants in fee were partly strategic in purpose, namely to Sir Simon Burley of the Leybourne lands in Kent, to Ralph Neville, earl of Westmorland, of lands in Cumberland and Westmorland, to Sir Francis de Courte of the castle and lordship of Pembroke and to Sir Hugh Browe of lands forfeited for treason with Owen Glendower. The rest were some twenty-five manors of which only Dunham (Notts.) and Headington (Oxon.) were not recent escheats. The Coventry Parliament itself considered the grants made to Ralph Neville and to George Dunbar, earl of the March of Scotland, as worthy to be exempted from the stop of annuities in 1405. Most of these grants were of single manors to king's knights and over a period of some forty years do not appear excessive and were probably only what such men had the right to expect for faithful service performed and the promise of more to come.

If these parliamentary critics were basing their case on a belief that large-scale, wanton alienation had taken place since the fortieth year of Edward III then they were therefore misinformed. However, they had good grounds for believing that the royal demesne had increased appreciably during that period, they could see that the royal family did not have it all by any means, and, if it had not been alienated, then they believed its profits were being salted away by others in the form of rent-free life grants or favourable leases for terms of years. In the circumstances of 1404 they cannot be dismissed simply as foolish or wrong-headed critics.

The basic purpose of the petition was to place the landed resources of the Crown at the disposal of the Exchequer so that they could be let out to farm again at their true value. The revenues so obtained were to have as first charges upon them the expenses of the Household, Chamber and Wardrobe and due provision for the queen's dower. Only after these charges had been met was the residue to be made available to compensate the dispossessed at the king's discretion. In other words the beneficial occupation of royal lands and the enjoyment of their profits were not in future to be given in lieu of fees and wages but were to be at the disposal of the Exchequer for the current expenses of government. Although it is not stated in so many words, this was the aim of the petition.[10]

This petition was no isolated incident in one unusual parliament, but the culmination of a campaign of criticism in successive parliaments which Henry and his ministers were finding increasingly hard to control.[11] By the autumn of 1404 the king's room for manoeuvre was most severely restricted. The expenses of consolidating his usurped authority had made a prompt and substantial parliamentary grant essential. Early in the year he had already met a parliament which had granted him little immediate supply and that under the most stringent conditions: a novel land tax of which only £12,000 was at the king's free disposal, the rest to be spent under control of four treasurers of war appointed in parliament and answerable to parliament.[12] This assembly had also launched a most outspoken attack on his lavish grants of lands and annuities and on the cost of his Household.[13] He had been driven by its obstinacy to proclaim a priority assignment of £12,000 for his household expenses spread over a wide range of existing revenues,[14] and by the summer of 1404 his financial embarrassment was so acute that he had to suspend payment of annuities.[15] The support of men of substance for the House of Lancaster was at best

10. Forfeiture of the lands, etc., concerned and three years imprisonment were to be the penalties for retaining anything covered by the operation of the act without authority of parliament. In future any royal officer who executed any gift or grant from these recovered royal possessions was to be liable to loss of office, complete forfeiture and also a sentence of three years' imprisonment.

11. For attempts in Henry IV's previous parliaments to resume or limit royal grants see *ibid.*, iii, 433 (1399), 458 (1401), 495 (1402). In 1400 his Council warned him to keep some lordships in hand lest the wasteful nature of grants made should prejudice his chances of generous parliamentary aid: *Proc. and Ord.*, ed. H. Nicolas, i, 108.

12. *Cal. Fine Rolls*, xii, 251–64. For evidence that the treasurers were effective see *Proc. and Ord.*, i, 220–2; warrants to them for payment dated 23 April 1404.

13. *Rot. Parl.*, iii, 523–4; *Eulogium Historiarum* (Rolls Series), ed. F. S. Haydon, iii, 399–400; 'Annales Ricardi et Henrici IV' (see above, footnote 6), p. 379.

14. *Rot. Parl.*, iii, 528 (1 March 1404); *Cal. Close Rolls, 1402–1405*, p. 343.

15. *ibid.*, pp. 377, 382 (cancelled under 5 July 1404 but finally issued under 28 August 1404).

lukewarm; he had no alternative but to come to some terms with his persistent parliamentary critics.

In negotiating a bargain under such financial stress Henry IV showed considerable cunning. In his reply he expressed his willingness, 'als sone as he wel may', to 'leve upon his owne' as the Commons desired. They had asked him 'to that entent that the Kyng myght better leve of his owne', to resume all that had belonged to the Crown in the fortieth year of King Edward and had since been granted away. But the essential information needed to carry out such a resumption was lacking. Therefore he intended to appoint a committee composed of certain lords spiritual and temporal, all the royal justices and sergeants-at-law and other persons he might wish to name, to put into execution all the articles of their petition 'als ferre as he may by the lawe of his land, or by his prerogatif or libertee'.[16]

Did this ambiguous undertaking amount to an acceptance of the resumption? Immediately following his answer on the roll are three entries in Norman-French (nos. 21–3) very closely related in content to this resumption petition and to the answer. At first sight they may appear to be more petitions of the Commons, especially as they in their turn are followed by further petitions received and answered in this parliament. But they are actually enrolled in the form of deliberations on the subject of the proposed resumption, most likely recorded in a council meeting. Alternatively, were they all that emerged from the deliberations of the promised committee? If so it must have been speedily convened and have speedily tendered its advice, because an order to give effect to one of these entries (no. 23) went out to the sheriffs on 17 November. The Commons granted supply on the 12 November and parliament was dissolved the next day.

These entries begin with a statement that it would be neither honest nor expedient for the king to revoke or resume outright any letters patent under the great seal, because of the clamour at home and abroad which would ensue. This presumably meant that a wholesale revocation of letters patent at the behest of parliament would further damage the prestige of his house in the country at large and in the eyes of foreign princes. The certain political damage of a resumption would outweigh the doubtful financial gain. But it was agreed (*accordez est*) that all who held annuities, fees or wages for life or for a term of years of the grant of Richard II or the present king should surrender one year's income from Easter 1404 to Easter 1405.[17] Next, holders of royal castles, manors, lands and tenements, rents and possessions granted for life or term of years by Richard or Henry IV should likewise surrender a year's income, subject to several important

16. *Rot. Parl.*, iii, 549.

17. *ibid.* Only the fees, wages and rewards of the Chancellor, Treasurer, Keeper of the Privy Seal, justices of both benches, Barons of the Exchequer, sergeants-at-law and the other royal law officers were exempted.

general and individual exceptions.[18] It should be noted that these two levies of a year's income were not to extend back as far as 1366, but to the accession of Richard II and were only to apply to grants for life or term of years. Finally (no. 23) proclamation was to be made throughout the kingdom requiring all holders of patents of grants for life or term of years made by any king since 40 Edward III to bring them in for scrutiny by the Council before Candlemas 1405 to the end that the deserving might be confirmed but the undeserving reduced or quashed.[19]

Were the Commons informed of these deliberations? Their inclusion on the roll of the parliament does not, of course, signify that they were. In the next parliament the Commons became very concerned about the authenticity of the roll as an accurate record of their petitions and answers. It is an obvious inference that this concern arose from their experiences in this, the previous parliament.[20] At all events the king's tactics at Coventry ultimately induced them to be generous. A further grant of the new land tax was voted, this time in the form of 20s tax on every £20 of income from land over 500 marks p.a., together with a lavish provision of two-tenths and two-fifteenths in the traditional form, plus an extension of the customs for two further years.[21] It would have been unusual by this date not to have extended the grant of the customs. Nevertheless, only Richard II, in 1398, had as yet ever received them for life. No doubt the king's reply to their resumption petition had much to do with this generosity.

It is difficult to say now exactly what the tortuous English of the royal answer meant. If delivered by itself it probably appeared to be a handsome acceptance. Why else should it be framed in English? But if read with the three following entries (21–3) in Norman-French appended to it then the picture is very different. At all events it was only the provisions of entries 21–3 which were actually put into effect. Instructions to levy one year's income from crown grantees were sent out to the shires on 21 January 1405.[22] But the king was in no position to offend any wavering supporters even by this limited measure. The returns made by sheriffs and escheators show that he exempted whom he pleased by writs *non obstante*.[23] Many

18. Exemptions from this second levy were made for all casualties (i.e. escheats, advowsons, wardships and marriages), for the queen and the king's sons, for confirmations or grants of annuities in parliament, and for castles assigned to meet the defence of the Scottish and Welsh marches and the coasts.

19. *Rot. Parl.*, iii, 549.

20. See *ibid.*, iii, 578 (no. 48) and also 585 (no. 65) where, on 22 December, the final day of the parliament, they obtained promise of an enrolment of record that a committee including twelve knights of the shire should be present at the enactment and engrossing of the roll.

21. *ibid.*, iii, 546–7; the previous parliament had insisted that all record of its land tax be destroyed to avoid creating a precedent. The Coventry parliament now allowed their grant of it to be enrolled.

22. *Cal. Fine Rolls*, xii, 288 (instructions to sheriffs and escheators throughout England).

23. See for example P.R.O., Exch., K.R., Sheriffs' Accts, E.199/8/49 (Devon); E.199/23/15 (Lincolnshire), E.199/42/41 (Surrey and Sussex).

other annuitants had already obtained their payments for the current year before the sheriffs and escheators received instruction to make the levy (21 January 1405) and the enrolled accounts show that the immediate yield, subject to these diminutions, could have been at the most a little over £600 and was probably less than this.[24] The sheriffs were also duly commanded to order the surrender for inspection of copies of all patents of life grants and grants for terms of years received from Edward III, Richard II or Henry IV.[25] This should have provided some material for the committee of enquiry to begin work if indeed it was intended to be a genuine committee of enquiry with a view to implementing a resumption. But there is no record that it ever met as such. Henry appears to have skilfully won the hearts of the Commons with his specious English reply—until his needs again compelled him to meet another parliament.

This assembly, which met in 1406, found the king's financial difficulties just as pressing as in 1404 and proved equally as determined as their predecessors. They seized the opportunity presented by the king's financial demands to substitute a full scheme of constitutional reform in place of the act of resumption apparently granted in 1404 but equally apparently never carried into effect. The Commons now realized that the king could not be trusted. It was also evident by now that he was a sick man. They therefore tried to put their trust in a Council which, they hoped, could be called to account in the next parliament. On this Council they proposed to base a most comprehensive scheme of reform. In the first session, before the adjournment, Henry made certain concessions which gave extra power to his Council as nominated by him in parliament. For the moment he surrendered his right to give orders direct to Chancery and Exchequer by promising to submit his warrants for endorsement by the Council. He reserved only the pardoning of criminals, appointments to offices and to benefices which should actually become vacant.[26]

Six days before the adjournment, which took place on 19 June, this strengthened Council was charged to discover by all means it could before the following Michaelmas the true value of all royal manors, lordships, lands and tenements let out for life, for terms of years or for the duration of war (i.e. also embracing alien priory lands), either at a fixed annual rent or at nothing at all. These lands were to be relet by the Council with the authority of parliament after Michaelmas 1406 at true value. The previous farmers were to have first chance of paying it. If they would not, the lands

24. P.R.O., Exch., L.T.R., Enrolled Accts, Misc., E.358/12.

25. *Cal. Close Rolls, 1402–1405*, p. 478; before Candlemas 1405 on pain of forfeiture.

26. *Rot. Parl.*, iii, 572(b), and see K. B. McFarlane's account of this document in the *Camb. Med. Hist.*, viii, 372. For a different but, I consider, unconvincing interpretation of it, which describes the king acting here as 'the inheritor of the Lancastrian tradition', see C. G. Crump, 'A Note on the Criticism of Records', *Bulletin of the John Rylands Library*, viii (1924), 146 f.

were to be taken from them after reasonable warning and compensation.[27]

There are no signs that this heavy task imposed on the Council was completed by them in the three-and-a-half months allotted. Parliament reassembled on 15 October and at the final meeting on 22 December thirty-one further articles for execution by the Council were ultimately accepted by the king.[28] These included additional measures to strengthen the power of the Council as the chief organ of government and to make it an effective instrument in the policy of retrenchment.

For the future the Treasurer of England, acting by advice of the Council, was to have full freedom to let to farm or to sell all lands, wardships, forfeitures, etc., in the manner appropriate to his office. From 17 December 1406 (presumably the date on which these thirty-one articles had received their final drafting and presentation) until parliament met again, no grant whatsoever, which gave away any source of profit to the Crown was to be made, under penalty of its loss and a fine of double the value, to be paid towards the expenses of the Calais garrison. There were to be two days each week, Wednesday and Friday, set aside by the king for receiving petitions, and all or at least some of the Council were to be present to receive and despatch them. This was, of course, to ensure conciliar control of grants. Severe penalties were to be imposed on any member of the Household or others who presented petitions to the king at any other time.

Even further drastic proposals were submitted which may suggest that the lords spiritual and temporal were at this time urging a similar course of action on the king,[29] but these were not entered on the roll and seem to have been merely discussed in the Council.[30] As the parliament drew to a close it became obvious that it was no easier to bind the Council than the king. Nevertheless, this time the Commons remained adamant in refusing supply. In the end the king's direct intervention secured the taking of oaths by the councillors, which were enrolled, but even this concession was not sufficient and the suspicious Commons now made an unprecedented and revolutionary demand; a personal guarantee from certain lords still present in the parliament that they would be individually responsible for refunding any money mis-spent. According to the St Albans chronicler, only the king's angry threats of violence, the refusal of the lords to co-operate and

27. *Rot. Parl.*, iii, 578–9. This measure also stated that annuities already charged on these lands, and grants of grace and favour already made rent free, would not be disturbed. Some care was thus taken in 1406 not to outrage existing interests but to concentrate on reform for the future.

28. *ibid.*, iii, 585–9.

29. See A. L. Brown, 'The Commons and the Council in the reign of Henry IV', *E.H.R.*, lxxix (1964), 24.

30. *Proc. and Ord.*, i, 283–7. These included the cessation of all grants for two years during which the secret and privy seals should not be valid instruments for making grants. Also an appropriation of £10,000 from the ancient revenues of the Crown to make ready money payments for prises taken for the Household, Chamber and Wardrobe; cf. the parliamentary appropriations of 1404 above, p. 81, and of 1439–40 and later described below.

the compelling desire of members to get home for Christmas at last produced a most reluctant grant after darkness on 22 December.[31]

This persistent, outspoken criticism of government by the parliamentary knights in the first six parliaments of Henry IV, directed towards securing effective and economical rule, had indeed been most remarkable. The usurpation of 1399 had dealt a heavy blow to royal authority. The new king's health was visibly failing under the strain of consolidating his usurped power, his government was harassed by serious rebellions and it was proving prodigiously expensive. In a sense the parliamentary enactment of deposition in 1399 had been as much a charade as the deposition of Edward II in parliament in 1327. Henry IV was king by conquest in 1399 and there was certainly no conferment of a parliamentary title to the throne. Yet the scope and influence of parliamentary criticism had vastly increased since 1327. The legacy of the Commons in parliament, inherited from the reigns of Edward III and Richard II, could not be ignored in any prolonged and acute political crisis: their share in the processes of legislation through petition; their constant presence in the parliamentary arena where decisions on the highest matters of state were declared and expounded, if not decided; their essential and regularly exercised role in the granting of all forms of taxation. A very significant difference between the depositions of 1327 and 1399 was thus the prolonged period of searching criticism in the Commons which followed after 1399. These criticisms were directed not towards reversing the fact of the usurpation, which would have been far beyond their aspirations or their competence, but towards making the usurper's government efficient and solvent. The accession to the throne of the most powerful private landowner in the kingdom directed attention towards the more efficient use of the king's landed patrimony as a partial solution of his financial difficulties. In the words of the poet 'a certain substance should be ordained to sustain this sovereign that should us govern'. Those same critics also directed attention towards a disendowment of the church, ostensibly, though insincerely, if we are to believe Walsingham, as a further means of relieving the king's professed poverty. Parliamentary legislation and the authority and supervision of the king's Council were to supply the means by which the king would thus 'live of his own'.

It is very difficult to say what effects all this had on royal policies, but it does seem to have assisted the restoration of the king's traditional authority. Royal grants which diminished the revenue do seem to have shown an appreciable drop from October 1406.[32] There was a noticeable change in the personnel of the Council: for the next twelve months attendance was

31. The *St Albans Chronicle 1406–1420*, ed. V. H. Galbraith, pp. 2–3.

32. For the evidence, and for the rest of this paragraph, see A. L. Brown, *op. cit.*, pp. 23–9.

restricted to those who had taken the oath, with the notable addition of Prince Henry. But at the end of that time the Commons were 'firmly put in their place' in the parliament of 1407 and the councillors were released from their oaths. The prince and his friends may have forced the ailing king into a period of semi-retirement in which his household expenses were moderated. But whether the king or the prince was in control it does seem that some greater measure of 'good and abundant governance' as the Commons desired it, was henceforth provided. The new king surmounted his crisis of confidence, although the effort entailed ruined his health and hastened his death. Aided or superseded by his able son Henry IV succeeded in crushing his rebels and winning over the English aristocracy and gentry to the support of his house. An almost undisputed succession was secured for Henry V. More effective political control in itself brought a measure of economy. A further resumption of £10,000 yearly out of annuities granted by letters patent under the great seal was enacted at the instance of the Commons in Henry V's first parliament as a contribution towards the annual expenses of the Household, Chamber and Wardrobe, although this measure was subject to a proviso of exemption in favour of those who held heritable annuities.[33] There was very little alienation of crown lands outside the royal family between 1404 and 1437. The Lancastrian royal family was growing up and its numbers were increased by the addition of two queens, Joan of Navarre and Catherine of Valois. Younger sons (later uncles) and queens had to be provided for.[34] Perhaps Henry V showed some solicitude for his manors. At least he was the first king to purchase land since Edward III[35] and was not disposed to part with English manors when he could so easily give away French lands. But, above all, a popular sovereign was able to arouse a favourable public opinion for a new adventure in the heady field of French conquest and plunder. Had his health allowed it, no doubt Henry IV would have done the same himself as early as 1407.[36] Thus the royal demesne did not reappear at the storm centre of politics for some years.

33. *Rot. Parl.*, iv, 5.

34. Both Queen Joan and Queen Catherine had dowries to the value of 10,000 marks p.a. (*ibid.*, iii, 532–3; iv, 202–6). Queen Joan's imprisonment on a charge of sorcery and witchcraft in 1419 seems to have been connected with alleged attempts by her Breton servants to discover the secrets of the realm and reveal them to their compatriots. She was not brought to trial and was kept in honourable confinement for three years. Her dower lands were confiscated and the government saved a considerable sum of money thereby. At Henry V's death, in accordance with his wishes, she was restored, so that from 1422–37 there were two queens each costing 10,000 marks *p.a.* (see A. R. Myers: 'The Captivity of a Royal Witch: the Household Accounts of Queen Joan of Navarre, 1419–21', in the *Bulletin of the John Rylands Library*, xxiv (1940), 263–84).

35. For example Chirk and Chirklands, bought from his grandmother, Joan de Bohun (as daughter and heir of Richard earl of Arundel), in 1418 for 4,000 marks: *Cal. Pat. Rolls, 1416–1422*, p. 172.

36. E. Perroy, *The Hundred Years War* (London, 1951), p. 218.

Even the accession of an infant king in 1422 and the prospect of a long minority did not shatter this new-found political stability. After its splendid victories abroad there was no rivalry to the succession of the Lancastrian House and the royal dukes were loyal to the infant prince. The Council, therefore, had to face up to the prospect of governing the country and conducting a major war under the leadership of the royal uncles for a very long time to come. This prospect produced a number of improvements in conciliar organization and the development of a certain *esprit de corps* which the much publicized rivalries of Humphrey duke of Gloucester and Cardinal Beaufort have tended to obscure. Indeed, when one considers the events of earlier and future minorities in English history one cannot but think that the achievements of the Lancastrian royal family and their supporters during these critical years have received an unmerited bad press from historians. Power may corrupt, but it can also induce responsibility.

An inevitable condition on which the Council accepted its new charge in 1422 was that only they should be informed by the Treasurer and Chamberlains what the king had in his Treasury, and that all appointments to office or benefice, all grants of farms of crown lands, wardships and marriages, should be made by them.[37] But there were also inevitable limitations on their power to dispense the royal patronage. Lands could not now be alienated, or even granted for life, until there was a *de facto* as well as a *de iure* king again, i.e. until 1437, when Henry VI reached his majority. The Council declared in 1434 that 'they dared not give away the king's inheritance', in reply to a request by Bedford.[38] Plummer was mistaken in thinking that in 1422 they changed the terms of grants of offices, made 'quam diu se bene gesserit' by Henry V, into life grants. The council minute in effect merely stated that both grants during pleasure, and life grants made by Henry V were confirmed.[39] The spate of surrenders of grants during pleasure for their replacement by grants for life from 1437 is ample proof of the Council's limitations in this respect.[40] The king's patrimony was traditionally at the disposal of those who provided the government, but the Lancastrian Council of the minority did not have the legal power to waste Henry VI's inheritance. If Henry V's grandiose French schemes had

37. *Rot. Parl.*, iv, 176; *Proc. & Ord.*, iii, 17.

38. *ibid.*, iv, 226–7. There is, however, one case of grants in fee being made to the royal dukes Bedford and Gloucester on 8 July 1433. Bedford's dukedom and his earldom of Kendal, held for life, were surrendered to the young king, who granted them anew to him and the heirs of his body. Likewise Gloucester's dukedom and his earldom of Pembroke. No doubt these only were considered uncontroversial.

39. C. Plummer, *Fortescue on the Governance of England*, p. 326 (notes to Chapter XVII), where he quotes from *Proc. and Ord.*, iii, 23. The Latin sentence, taken as a whole, does not bear this translation. Nicolas, *Proc. and Ord.*, i, p. vi, in his chronological table did not take it so.

40. See the *Calendar of Patent Rolls, passim*, around this date.

proved capable of fulfilment and if his son had inherited the political acumen of his house, then the much maligned government of the minority would not have appeared to later generations as the inevitable prelude to the ensuing chaos and disaster. At all events the use and abuse of the king's landed patrimony did not again become the centre of political controversy until the collapse of Henry VI's personal government from 1449. Then and only then did parliamentary criticism once more begin closely to follow the pattern of the years 1399 to 1406, but this time with more easily discernible and more permanent results.

2. THE FINANCIAL SURVEY OF 1433

The belief that Lancastrian royal finance reverted to the traditional pre-1399 pattern once the prolonged crisis of authority of 1399 to 1407 had been surmounted can fortunately be tested by material of a new kind for the minority of Henry VI. Four years before he officially came of age the fullest declaration of the state of the royal revenues known for medieval England was enrolled on the parliament roll at the petition of the Treasurer, Ralph lord Cromwell.[41] The novelty of this statement really lies only in its enrolment on the parliament roll which has ensured its complete survival, because a similar statement in summary form survives for as early as 1362–3[42] and we know that the Lords in parliament, if not the Commons, were supplied with figures from this or from another one in 1365 to help persuade them to make a grant of the wool subsidy at a higher rate.[43] During the Lancastrian period a 'state of the realm', an assessment of the year's revenue and expenditure, may well have been produced annually, at least from 1401. In addition to the 1362–3 statement two of these earlier Lancastrian statements survive in sufficient detail for useful comparisons to be made with the figures supplied by Cromwell's exchequer staff in 1433.[44] All these estimates supplied to the king's ministers by their experts

41. *Rot. Parl.*, iv, 433–8, preceded and followed by petitions in which Cromwell explained the purpose of the declarations.

42. *E.H.R.*, xxxix (1924), 412–13, printed by T. F. Tout and Dorothy M. Broome as part of a note entitled 'A National Balance Sheet for 1362–3 with documents subsidiary thereto'.

43. *Rot. Parl.*, ii, 285(b).

44. *Proc. and Ord.*, ii, 172–80 (1415–16) and ii, 312–5 (1421). Other incomplete survivals or references to such statements will also be found *ibid.*, i, 154, 342; ii, 7–13, 96–7; iii, 322. In addition there is a statement among the causes for summoning a Council in 1437 that the king's progenitors were accustomed at the beginning of the year to 'purvey by the assent of his great council for all necessaries and charges . . likely to fall and ensue all the year after' (*ibid.*, v, 65). It seems that the parallel 'état par estimation' in France did not begin until the middle of the fifteenth century: see G. Dupont-Ferrier, *Études sur les institutions financières de la France à la fin du moyen âge*, ii, 192–7. It has been pointed out that such a declaration was prescribed by the Walton Ordinances of 1338 (see J. L. Kirby, 'The Issues of the Lancastrian Exchequer and Lord Cromwell's Estimates of 1433', *B.I.H.R.*, xxiv (1951), 121, note 3. For some later statements see below, p. 114.

at the time deserve to be treated with respect, but the completeness of the 1433 statement gives it a unique value in the history of English medieval government finance. Figures from four of these estimates are compared in the first two of the three following tables, with some rearrangement of items and some combining of totals in order to obtain the necessary correspondence. The relevant detailed evidence from the 1433 statement is tabulated in Table 3.

The Treasurer's purpose in presenting this budget for enrolment on the parliament roll in 1433 was to secure a firm authorization from the Council, backed by parliament, to prefer payment and to retain funds in hand for the current expenses of the king's Household, Chamber, Wardrobe and necessary works. These necessary works were for the upkeep of the royal palaces, etc., where the king and his Household were resident or likely to be resident, not for war or defence against the French. The dangers to the position of royal ministers from the activities of an insolvent royal Household, living off the land by an abuse of prerogative power, were never far from the thoughts of Lancastrian Treasurers. This preferment would inevitably be at the immediate expense of any annuities, fees and rewards to individuals, among them some of the greatest in the land, for which no assignments had yet been made. According to Treasurer Cromwell, who explained the position in two petitions accompanying the declaration, the burden of having constantly to decide between their importuning and the current needs of government was too heavy for him to bear alone without clear, unequivocal, conciliar direction. Their total demands alone, over and above the allotted charges shown in the first table, exceeded the total current needs of the king's establishment. Furthermore, there were the heavy current needs of military garrisons in the Scottish marches, Calais, Aquitaine, etc., whose importuning was doubtless rendered somewhat less pressing by distance. Finally there was an accumulation of debts which constituted a truly forbidding total, but these had been put off at least once already and so could be put off once more for the present.

Medieval governments were hardly, if ever, subject to pressures exerted by international finance and they could not be bankrupted by creditors who were their own subjects. The immediate financial crisis of 1433, if it was a crisis at all, was principally one of priority of assignment. Stubbs admitted as much when within a few sentences of describing the situation as 'alarming if not appalling' he wrote that 'a single annual grant of a fifteenth would be sufficient to balance revenue and expenditure and would leave something to pay the debt'.[45] Tout equally found the similar situation as revealed by the 1362–3 statement 'very alarming' but we should perhaps remember in his case that he was writing in 1924 with the post-war budget deficits very much in mind and this no doubt made it especially difficult for

45. Stubbs, *Constitutional History* iii, 121.

Table 1

Revenues (England and Wales)		1362–3 *Marks*	1362–3	1415–16	1421	1433
Customs	gross	57,310	£38,206 13s 4d	£47,333 13s 4d	£40,676 19s 9¼d	£30,799 2s 7¾d*
	charges	10,400	£6,933 6s 8d		£5,195 7s 7d	£3,756 2s 9¼d
	net	46,910	£31,273 6s 8d		£35,481 12s 2¼d	£27,042 19s 10½d
Other revenues (apart from direct taxation)	gross	13,087 5s 5d	£8,724 18s 9d	£9,633	£15,066 11s 1d	£23,047 11s 4d
	charges	6,552 8s 4d	£4,368 8s 4d		£10,754 10s 1½d	£14,183 0s 4½d
	net	6,384 10s 5d (sic)	£4,356 10s 5d		£4,312 0s 11½d	£8,864 10s 11½d
Total	gross	70,397 5s 5d	£46,931 12s 1d	£56,966 13s 4d	£55,743 10s 10¼d	£53,846 13s 11¾d
	net	53,294 10s 5d (sic)	£35,629 17s 1d		£39,793 13s 1¾d	£35,907 10s 10d

* I have included in this total an item of £76 17s for the customs of wines at the ports from alien merchants which Cromwell listed separately.

Table 2

	1415–6 (gross)	1421 (gross)	1430–1 (gross)	1431–2 (gross)	1432–3 (gross)
Great and small custom	£6,133 6s 8d	£6,414 10s 3¼d	£7,780 3s 1½d	£6,996 16s 0¾d	£6,048 0s 8d
Tunnage and poundage	£10,000	£8,226 10s 9½d	£6,920 14s 5d	£6,998 17s 10d	£6,203 1s 6d
Subsidy on wool	£31,200	£26,035 18s 8½d	£20,151 13s 3¼d	£16,808 7s 9½d	£14,259 2s 3¼d

Table 3

1433 Other Revenues (England & Wales)	Gross	Charges	Net
Sheriffs' farms / Farms worth less than 40s	4,476 10 8¼	3,773 2 5¼ (Sheriffs' farms, Farms worth less than 40s, Law court fines)	1,903 8 3
Law court fines (green-wax)	1,200 – –		
Escheats (excluding wards and marriages)	500 – –		500 – –
Feefarms (towns and manors)	3,612 11 3	2,978 1 –	634 10 3
Farms of wards' lands	1,604 19 11	6 13 4	1,598 6 7
Farm of duke of Norfolk's lands	1,333 6 8		1,333 6 8
Farms worth 40s or more	983 7 5¾	79 10 –	903 17 5¾
Subsidy and ulnage of cloth	720 10 1	542 6 –	178 4 1
Hanaper of Chancery	1,668 3 4	1,530 10 8½	137 12 7½
Tower Mint	465 19 9¼	378 11 5	87 8 4¼
London Exchange	66 13 4		66 13 4
Exchange for Roman Curia	13 6 8		13 6 8
Coroner and Marshal of Household	26 5 –	8 – –	18 5 –
Alien priories	277 5 –	72 – –	205 5 –
Duchy of Cornwall	2,788 13 3¾	2,637 12 6½	151 – 9¼
South Wales	1,139 13 11	669 8 6½	470 5 4½
North Wales	1,097 17 3	506 18 11½	590 18 3½
Chester	764 10 2¾	719 19 6¾	44 10 8
Exchequer fines	100 – –		100 – –
Windsor Castle	207 17 5¼	280 5 10½	– 72 8 5¼*
Totals	23,047 11 4	14,183 0 4½	8,864 10 11½

* I have included this deficit figure here for the sake of the balance, but it was an over-assignment, and, as such, was not included in Cromwell's total. Cf. below p. 115. (next chapter).

him to avoid reading a modern financial crisis into a medieval deficit. There was one interesting element common to the 1362–3 and the 1433 statements, and absent from the two statements for Henry V's reign. Both in 1362–3 and in 1433 the Exchequer was having to make do with a reduced rate of wool subsidy.

Comparison of these four statements shows at once that from the period when Edward III was still in his prime, a period which the parliamentary knights of 1404 had regarded as a golden age of royal solvency, indirect taxation based on the wool subsidy provided the bulk of English government revenues. This permanent dimension, fully developed by the exigencies of Edward III's war finance, alone supplied more money annually, even in a 'crisis' year, than the yearly average which Edward II's government had been able to command from all sources of direct and indirect taxation combined.[46] The second table shows to what extent this indirect taxation came from the wool subsidy. It is generally accepted that the amount of raw wool exported, on which this tax was based, had been in constant decline since roughly the date of the first budget quoted here, though the rapidity of the decline had varied, and had become particularly dramatic about 1430.[47] Nevertheless, the most important factor in explaining variations in revenue from indirect taxation seems to be the political fact of the rate of tax granted. In spite of the decline in the kind of export trade which was the greatest producer of revenue, Henry V's total of indirect taxation in 1415–16 was much higher than Edward III's had been in 1362–3. Edward III, after more than a decade of grants at the rate of 40s, was reduced to 20s on each sack or 300 woolfells from Michaelmas 1362;[48] from 1413 Henry V enjoyed 43s 4d on each sack or 240 woolfells from denizens and 50s from aliens. The life grant which he obtained from his grateful subjects after Agincourt confirmed this 43s 4d rate for denizens and raised the rate for aliens to 60s.[49] But from 1422 the government of the infant Henry VI was only granted 33s 4d from denizens and 43s 4d from aliens.[50] By 1432–3 Henry VI's gross revenue from the wool subsidy was nearly £12,000 p.a. less than Henry V had been receiving at the end of his reign.

On the other hand, Cromwell's totals show that this decline in indirect taxation had to some degree been offset by an increase in the gross total of other revenues listed in his budget (i.e. excluding direct taxation), although charges upon these had shown a similar, proportionate growth. This increase appears to have taken place after the early years of Henry V's

46. See above, p. 30, n. 56.
47. A handy table is provided by Dr A. R. Bridbury in his *Economic Growth, England in the Later Middle Ages* (London, 1962), p. 32, giving figures by decades from 1281–1540.
48. *Rot. Parl.*, ii, 229, 252, 265, 271, 273.
49. *ibid.*, iv, 6, 64.
50. *ibid.*, iv, 303, 342.

reign and examination of the separate items of these other revenues in Cromwell's budget, as set out in the third table, suggests an explanation. The patrimony of the king's eldest son (Cornwall, Wales, Chester) gradually reverted to exchequer control when Prince Henry succeeded to the throne and was heavily assigned by 1433 (represented by about £5,800 gross and about £1,200 net, in Cromwell's statement). In the circumstances of 1433 even this remaining £1,200 would make further very attractive assignments, and a note of Cromwell's shows that a further £590 of it was in fact already assigned to the seneschal of Aquitaine, Sir John Radclyff, for the next twelve years. As it happened no royal heir was to be born for another twenty years. The major part of the rest of the increase in the total of other revenues since 1415 can only have been due to the completely casual escheats and unpredictable windfalls of lands temporarily in hand (about £3,500 gross from escheators' issues and wards' lands in 1433, almost completely unassigned). Cromwell specifically excluded vacant ecclesiastical temporalities from his budget without explanation, but we cannot tell whether any were included in 1415–16 or in 1421. It is significant, though it should be an obvious point, that the least predictable and most casual items among these other revenues were also the ones which bore the lowest long-term assignments.

In this respect, as in others, Cromwell's figures are revealing as regards the crown lands proper, or royal demesne. They are represented by farms worth 40s or more and totalling less than £1,000 gross, almost entirely unassigned. Exchequer custody of these was clearly brief, inconsiderable in amount and very 'casual'. Strictly speaking we ought to add to these the farms worth less than 40s (included by Cromwell in the composite total for sheriffs' farms and fines of green-wax because they were accounted for through the sheriff). Since 1236 the sheriffs' farms themselves had included no royal land revenues. These 'minute farms', as they were called, resulted from many petty forfeitures and escheats to the crown scattered all over the realm of the kind which can be identified in any volume of the printed *Calendars of Miscellaneous Inquisitions*. They may have amounted to a maximum of about £500 gross in Cromwell's budget, though his grouping of charges here makes it impossible to give a net amount for them.[51] Finally we must add the feefarms or perpetual leases of towns and manors, the only permanent section of royal demesne as far as the Exchequer was concerned, totalling about £3,600 gross, of which some £3,000 was assigned in annuities. Much of this was assigned in the most permanent sense of all, since Cromwell noted that about £1,200 of these

51. For the composition and total of sheriffs' farms in the later medieval period see Miss Mills in *T.R.H.S.*, 4th series, viii (1925); and in *E.H.R.*, xl (1925). See also above, pp. 31, 32. The figure she gives for sheriffs' farms in *E.H.R.* (1925) is £3,983 16s 11d. Cromwell's total of £5,676 10s 8¼d also included £1,200 profits of green wax.

assignments were in heritable annuities. Thus the contribution of the royal demesne to the 'national' revenues was patently of comparative insignificance in 1433, in spite of the increasing amount of land at the king's disposal.

There remains one interesting item which Cromwell partly detailed in his budget but carefully excluded from his totals, presumably because he had no authority or control over it: the revenues of the duchy of Lancaster (£4,952 13s 3¼d gross, £2,544 4s 8⅛d net). This is the only one of the six great complexes of estates listed at the beginning of this chapter as belonging to Henry IV at his accession in 1399 and otherwise remaining unaccounted for in 1433, since the Richmond lands had meantime passed in fee to the duke of Bedford and the Pembroke lands likewise to the duke of Gloucester. Had Henry V died without issue his wish had been that the duchy of Lancaster should also be divided between his two brothers. Mention of this intention recalls that the primary function of crown lands was to provide for the royal family. Apart from the two royal uncles in 1433 these were the widowed duchess of Clarence, and two queens dowager. Both Queen Joan and Queen Katherine were entitled to dowers of 10,000 marks p.a.[52] Katherine was enjoying some duchy of Lancaster revenues (£4,360 9s 7d net in 1432) as well as income from North Wales and from the duchy of Cornwall. Henry IV had wished his Queen Joan, whose landed income came mainly from alien priories, to be provided for from the duchy after his death, but this had not happened. Indeed Henry V had confiscated her dower and it had only been restored to her in accordance with his dying wish, by the government of the minority. The greatest single 'family' charge on land revenues in 1433 however was about £6,000 p.a. obtained from very extensive duchy of Lancaster lands placed in the hands of feoffees by Henry V for the performance of his will. These feoffees received £114,000 from this source between his death and Michaelmas 1441. Under pressure they were making very substantial loans towards the conduct of the war from time to time, but all these loans had to be and were repaid.[53]

Cromwell's budget of 1433 thus reveals that Lancastrian governmental finance on the eve of Henry VI's majority had entirely re-established the pattern which had existed under Edward III. After Henry IV had been constrained to pay lip service to a reorganization of royal finance, designed to enable him to 'live of his own', which would give a new prominence to the economical deployment of his land revenues, the victorious Henry V had nevertheless found the solution for his financial difficulties in the

52. See above, p. 87, n. 34.

53. Robert Somerville's *History of the Duchy of Lancaster*, i (London, 1953), gives a succinct account of all the vicissitudes of the duchy in what he calls this 'period of dismemberment' under Henry V and Henry VI. The figures quoted will be found on pp. 206 and 208 and details of the feoffees' lands and Queen Katherine's lands on pp. 339–40.

traditional resources of heavier taxation. By contrast, Henry VI's ministers, who henceforth were to find themselves conducting only unsuccessful war, would be brought under increasing pressure to release the whole income of the great duchies of Lancaster and Cornwall to the Exchequer. Ultimately when this proved quite insufficient they would be constrained to attempt to free all existing, deeply pledged resources of the Crown from all encumbrances and to recover those which this king alienated. Contemporaries thought royal solvency could only be achieved, if at all, by controversial parliamentary acts of resumption which began to be attempted in earnest only from 1450.

IV
THE BACKGROUND TO THE RESUMPTIONS OF 1450–6

I. THE ROYAL LANDS AND THE SPOILS SYSTEM UNDER HENRY VI

When James I was searching for means to increase his revenues he employed Sir Robert Cotton and others to examine and report on any records of his predecessors which might suggest ways and means. The history of the crown lands received much attention. There is, for example, a report on fifteenth-century acts of resumption, as they appeared to this early seventeenth-century antiquary and politician, summarized thus: 'the state held it more just to help the king out of his own than to burden the commonwealth, and therefore gave way by parliament to the king to improve up his lands, though in lease, provided that the lessee should have the refusal of the bargain if he would'.[1] Another report was intended to persuade the king to preserve and extend the practice of farming out his manors to the local gentry at feefarm, and to dispense with the services of all professional officers other than sheriffs and escheators, the ancient servants of the Exchequer, in the administration of his lands. This treatise, by 'an eschequier man' stressed the unwelcome high cost of officials contrasted with the advantages to be gained for his majesty from bargains with 'ready and hearty undertakers amongst the gentry and nobility who have any place of residence near any of his majesty's manors and the king's security the better since their abilities will settle the fee farm rent upon more land than purchase'.[2]

The pretentions of the exchequer man's title[3] belie the fact that his primary reason for writing was to defend the privileges of his office. But an administrative act of 1438 on which he concentrated his attention makes a good starting-point for an examination of the disposition of crown lands during the personal rule of Henry VI. He had come upon a privy seal writ, undoubtedly after a great deal of searching, which he cited in support of his contention that the employment of professional officers to manage royal estates was 'unprofitable and discommodious to the Crown and contrary to

1. B.M., MS. Cotton, Cleopatra, F.VI, fols 54–5, and *passim*, for Sir Robert Cotton's views on crown lands.

2. B.M., MS. Cotton, Titus, B.IV, fol. 246.

3. 'The true cause and remedy of a dangerous consumption in his majesties revenue discovered by an eschequier man.'

the customs of ancient times'. It was dated 5 May 16 Henry VI, and relieved Robert Whittingham of his appointment as receiver-general of the duke of Bedford's lands, which had reverted to the Crown on Bedford's death in 1435. Rather fuller quotation of the original than would have served the ends of the exchequer man and an examination of the historical context of this writ reveal reasons for Whittingham's dismissal quite different from the financially preferable alternative of more economical and efficient management which our seventeenth-century author professed to see in it.[4]

Throughout the later medieval period great numbers of manors were brought together from time to time under a receiver-general and auditors to provide an income or endowment for some member of the royal family, a queen, a younger son, a brother or an uncle. Likewise when a member of the royal family who held such large amounts of crown lands died without heirs qualified to inherit under the terms of their grants, that receiver-general was reappointed by royal letters patent or replaced by a royal nominee. His new task, however, was not to exploit their revenues for the Crown but to preside over the dispersal of the lands to royal grantees. For example, Roger Westwood, who was appointed supervisor or receiver-general of Queen Anne's lands by Henry IV on 18 December 1399,[5] was exonerated from his duties at Easter 1401 and had no successor. The numerous lands Westwood administered did not come back into exchequer control; they passed to some of those whom Henry IV desired to reward or felt constrained to honour. A similar period was now taken to dispose of the lands of John duke of Bedford. Robert Whittingham had been appointed royal receiver-general on 6 February 1436 and was exonerated from his office by this writ of privy seal to the Barons of the Exchequer on 5 May 1438. It is perhaps significant that when Bedford's brother Humphrey duke of Gloucester died without legitimate issue in 1447 no receiver-general was required at all, even for one or two years. His wife's condemnation for witchcraft and for treason as aiming at the king's life meant that the whole of Humphrey's lands were completely at the king's disposal and they were dispersed among Henry's intimates mainly within a few days of his uncle's death.[6] Nevertheless this general process, if not the

4. P.R.O., Exch., K.R., Mem. Rolls, E.159/214, 'brevia directa baronibus', 16 Hen. VI, Easter m.1d; 'et que nous avons grantez la greindre partie des dites terres et seignuries ad divers persones par quele encheson il bien semble que le dit office nest pas depuis plus proufitable pur nostre proufit et que les gages quelx il prent de nous par celle cause purront bien estre abbruggez et que noz Eschetours purront bien lever annuelment les Revenues de ce que depuis remanent en nous mains dicelles terres et seignuries par loure offices par maniere come il ad este avant ces heures'. Privy Seal. Westminster 5 May 16 Hen. VI.

5. *Cal. Pat. Rolls, 1401–1405*, 121; P.R.O., Exch., L.T.R., Misc. Rolls, E.358/17; cf. above, p. 66.

6. Humphrey duke of Gloucester, died on 23 February 1447. His widow was barred from receiving any dower or jointure on 3 March (*Rot. Parl.*, v, 135). Some idea of the speed

speed with which it was carried out, or the amount of alienations involved, was quite normal.

Only in the event of a reserved rent being placed upon such lands would the Exchequer retain any interest in them although it would be the Treasurer's standing duty to let to farm at the rate of the extent any manors still remaining ungranted by the king when a receiver-general's services were dispensed with. Further preferential grants made by the king would automatically supersede such exchequer farming arrangements. Thus in Treasurer Cromwell's statement of 1433 the total value of farmed lands only amounted to about £1,000 p.a. gross and the Treasurer normally had no authority to 'improve up the king's lands in lease' as Sir Robert Cotton put it. The disposition of crown manors was decided by the success or otherwise of petitions presented to the king and organized for submission and endorsement in the first instance by the clerks of his signet office, if not actually written out by them. An attempt to compute a financial value for the king's preferential grants was no part of exchequer responsibilities. They were not mentioned in any of the Lancastrian declarations of the state of the realm, except that in the fragment of the earliest known Lancastrian declaration (dated by Sir Harris Nicolas as being not later than July 1401) the exchequer clerk who computed the charge of annuities on the revenues at £24,000 p.a. by estimation entered this figure as being 'over and above the castles, manors, lordships, lands and tenements granted by our lord the king'.[7]

The amount of exchequer revenues derived from crown lands was thus a subsidiary consideration depending on the terms of bargains which were more often political than financial. In the case of a weak king like Henry VI there might be no element of bargain in them at all. Sufficient evidence exists to demonstrate that exchequer valuations of royal lands, based on inquisition and extent supplemented by record evidence, allowed financial returns to farmers far beyond what we would regard as a reasonable percentage on the farms they paid. It therefore seems unlikely that even a farmer who was paying the full exchequer rate of the extent would have to resort to any extortion from his tenants in order to obtain a handsome return. Perhaps this is why complaints of exploitation at the hands of a farmer or grantee from the tenants on crown manors are so rare. One example of complaints can be cited from the lordships of Pembroke and

with which his lands were dispersed can be obtained from the entries of grants on the patent rolls (*Cal. Pat. Rolls, 1446–1452*, 43–5). He had made very ample provision for Eleanor Cobham. Had she lived and been allowed to receive her dower and jointure she might have been a power in the land comparable to Jacquette dowager duchess of Bedford. Queen Margaret and Suffolk were the chief beneficiaries: *Foedera* (1727 ed.), xi, 155; *Rep. Dig. Peer*, v, 240, 254–5, but Buckingham, Say and Sele, and Sudeley did well also. York successfully claimed some lands which Humphrey had continued to hold since his (York's) minority.

7. *Proc. and Ord.*, i, 154.

Cilgerran when they were in hand by resumption in 1450, but it should be remembered that the last holder of them had recently been murdered and was the target for every man's abuse. On this occasion the gentlemen and commons of these lordships petitioned the king that debts to the last grantee, William duke of Suffolk, should not be exacted and 'considering the great oppressions, extortions, misgovernances, misprisions and other great inconveniences that have been had by (i.e. suffered at the hands of) farmers and their servants by colour of their farm and service, of the which they were never bold nor never durst ask remedy', that the king would keep the lands in his own hands, or if he did grant them out, that he would grant them to the queen, who already held Haverfordwest.[8] Even if taken at face value this instance seems to have been the isolated exception rather than the general rule.

There is quite a lot of information for the reign of Henry VI about the profits which recipients of crown lands might expect. For example, Ralph lord Cromwell held on various terms many crown manors, some of which were duchy of Cornwall and Richmond lands. There exists a useful valor of his manors, for an unspecified year.[9] The head of the roll and most of the Nottinghamshire account is badly damaged, but the rest is in good condition and his issues, less necessary expenditure, can be compared with the payments he made to the king and with valuations or extents, made for the Exchequer under the resumption acts of 1450–1.

The duchy of Cornwall's manor of Castle Rising (Norfolk) was a stock-and-land lease. Cromwell held it for ten years, paying £20 p.a., and was to have allowance for all necessary repairs.[10] By an earlier grant he already held the offices of constable of the castle, of keeper of the forest, chace and warren, and of steward of the lordship there for life, which carried joint

8. P.R.O., Augmentations Office, E.314/1, Petitions, Hen. VIII–Ed. VI, where it is wrongly dated to Hen. VIII. From its language and spelling (e.g. 'Moounteyngnes' for mountains), it is clearly much earlier. The reference to Suffolk as the last farmer, and to the act of resumption, date it exactly. It has a wider interest than crown lands, concerning as it does Suffolk and the administration of the Welsh Marches, and conflicts of English law with the 'law of the mountains'. This document is not the original but a copy of Ancient Petition S.C.8/338/E.1197, made at a very early date, when the original was much more legible than it is now.

9. P.R.O., Special Collections, Rentals and Surveys, S.C.11/822. This valor is in fact an account of a year's income, less expenditure. It includes the fees of the offices he held for life and of the chamberlainship of the Exchequer, which he had to himself, his heirs and assigns. In this year (date unspecified) he enjoyed an income of £2,263 5s 10½d net cash from land and office, according to this document. The date must be between 1446, when he received the last of his manors from the king (Castle Rising), and his death in January 1456. There is mention of a payment for a fifteenth, but parliament granted fifteenths and tenths in 1445–6, 1449 and 1453. I do not find any record of the royal grant of Somerton, which must have been of one-third only, or of Chorley. It is possible that the rents paid to the king for these two manors were feefarms. This valor is the type prepared by auditors, combining 'the static view of the ordinary extent with the currency of an open annual account' (R. Somerville, *op. cit.*, i, 107–8 describing them seventy-five years earlier).

10. *Cal. Fine Rolls*, xviii, 11.

fees of £19 10s 10d p.a. taken out of the issues of the manor. The valor shows that for the twelve months on which it was based, after all other wages, fees and repairs had been met, it produced £70 6s 9d '*clare, ultra reprisas*'. This sum included his fees, so that if we assume that he actually paid the £20 p.a. farm (the accounts of the receiver-general of the duchy show Castle Rising as worth nothing in these years) he received two-and-a-half times as much as he paid to the king. It is most likely that the only payment the king received for the manor in the year of the valor was a two shillings levy for a fifteenth. With effect from Cromwell's death Castle Rising was leased out by the Exchequer for twenty years at £20 1s 8d p.a. indicating that these highly favourable terms were not peculiar to him.

In Lincolnshire Cromwell had a freehold grant of two-thirds of the manor or lordship of Burwell from 1442, with the reversion of the third part after the death of Bedford's widow. These two-thirds were valued by the Exchequer in the resumption accounts of 1451 at £42 p.a. From Michaelmas 1456 after their resumption they were leased out by the Exchequer for ten years at £41 13s 4d. Now the valor of Cromwell's lands show that in the year in which it was made these two parts had been worth £105 12s 5¼d, their value '*hoc anno clare*'. In yet another example of a royal grant revealed by this valor Cromwell was paying £9 farm to the king for the manor of Somerton in Lincolnshire. His profit here was put in the valor at £20 19s 10d after the king's rent and other charges had been met.

In 1451 the Exchequer valued two-thirds of the manor of Leadenham, also in Lincolnshire, with its knights' fees and advowsons at £8 p.a., obtaining this information from the reversion roll. In 1442 these two parts had been alienated to Lord Cromwell freehold. The valor shows that in his possession they were worth a clear £11 18s 9¾d not including the advowson of Fulbeck church. Two-thirds of the royal manor of Washingborough (Lincs.) also appear in the valor worth a clear £50 8s 0½d to him. He had never paid any money to the king for Washingborough. At first he had a grant of £40 p.a. from it; then he received the two-thirds of the manor for life, paying no rent and rendering no account; later, in 1442, he had a freehold grant of these two parts, with the reversion of the third part on the death of Bedford's widow. After the 1456 resumption had annulled these grants, and with effect from Michaelmas 1457, John viscount Beaumont secured both the two-thirds of Leadenham and the two thirds of Washingborough together in a sixteen years lease at £20 p.a.

Humphrey duke of Buckingham had a number of crown manors, but unfortunately an excellent rent-roll for his lands in fifteen counties and London does not include the manors he had obtained from the Crown.[11] However, at the bottom appears an annuity charged on the sheriffs of several counties, the whole of which was three years in arrears. This

11. P.R.O., Special Collections, Ministers' and Receivers' Accts, S.C.6/1305/4.

instance serves to show how very much more valuable was a grant of land where the grantee actually had control of the sources of income, than any cash annuity to be paid by a royal officer, whose total commitments in this respect might far exceed the resources at his command. Buckingham had other receivers and no doubt the crown manors were in their hands. The residuary account of the duke of Bedford's lands shows that the manor of Atherstone (Warws.), which was extended at £26 13s 4d under the resumption acts of 1450–1 and which Buckingham held for life, rent-free and without rendering account, had been worth £41 12s 1d to the duke of Bedford as accounted for by Bedford's rent-collector, Clement Draper. To this sum must also be added the issues of a meadow called Hallesyche, 8s, and of a court estimated at 35s, for which Draper was not responsible.[12] From 25 March 1451, when the resumption acts had introduced a temporary element of financial competition into grants of royal manors, the Exchequer leased this manor for ten years at £33 6s 8d p.a. jointly to John Heton, Buckingham's receiver-general, and to the same Clement Draper the rent-collector there.

The history of a valuable complex of manors in Somerset and Dorset between 1443 and 1457, known as Matthew Gurney's lands,[13] will serve further to demonstrate the degree of profit to be had by those who were in a position to obtain the farm of crown lands. Henry V had granted these lands for life to John lord Tiptoft, but had enacted that they were to be inseparably joined to the duchy of Cornwall along with other lands by reversion at Tiptoft's death.[14] This was lavish compensation to the duchy for his own alienation of its manor of Isleworth to the nuns of Syon. Tiptoft died in 1443 and the Gurney lands were extended at £123 13s 10d in his inquisition *post mortem*. But Edmund Beaufort, then marquis and later duke of Somerset, managed to obtain a grant of the Gurney manors on 4 October 1444 from Henry VI for himself and the heirs male of his body, together with Bedford's former Richmond lands of Bassingbourn and Babraham (Cambs.) for which Somerset was prepared to surrender an earlier grant of £417 14s p.a. made to him at the Exchequer of Receipt. This surrendered sum was now declared inseparably annexed to the duchy instead, which must have been an absurdly poor bargain indeed for the duchy and for any future duke of Cornwall.[15]

Resumed by the acts of resumption of 1450–1 these Gurney manors were valued by extent at £198 3s 3d on 21 June 1451.[16] Somerset was not

12. *ibid.*, S.C.6/1038/1 (15–16 Hen. VI).

13. Midsomer Norton, Withycombe and Laverton, Farrington Gurney, Welton, English Combe, Stratton on the Fosse, Stoke under Hampden, Curry Mallet, Milton Falconbridge, a moiety of West Harptree and of Shepton Mallet (Soms.) and Ryme (Dors.).

14. *Rot. Parl.*, ii, 141 (1421).

15. *ibid.*, v, 446(b) and *Cal. Pat. Rolls, 1441–1446*, p. 419.

16. P.R.O., Exch., L.T.R., Sheriffs' Seizures, E.379/175.

dispossessed at once, but was made liable for this sum at the Exchequer from the date of the resumption. The acts had, however, introduced an entirely new element of competitive bidding at least temporarily, into the process of disposing of crown lands. Three times (20 June 1450, 16 December 1450 and 20 September 1451) a syndicate headed by the young duke of Exeter took out a ten year lease of them, beginning on the terms 'at a yearly farm of the extent, or as much as may be agreed upon between them and the Treasurer by Christmas next . . . with proviso for increase of the farm' (i.e. if any would pay more), and ending with a lease for 370 marks p.a. (£246 13s 4d) for the Gurney lands and 100 marks for the Cambridgeshire lands.[17] On 6 September 1452 Somerset was able to secure a new rent-free, entailed grant.[18]

Here the matter rested until they were again resumed by the resumption act of 1455–6. Somerset had recently been slain at St Albans and his widow now petitioned the Council on behalf of the heir, Henry, for the upholding of the original entailed grant. The Council replied that the family might revert to the original cash grant at the Exchequer but that their claim to the lands failed.[19] The widow, however, began the process of securing a seven-year lease of the Gurney lands at the Exchequer, beginning on 18 March 1456 with exactly the same general terms as in the earlier lease to the duke of Exeter and his associates,[20] but ending up at the quite different rate of extent of £123 13s 10d which proved to have been taken from the inquisition *post mortem* made on the death of John Tiptoft in 1443.[21]

This was, no doubt, a smart move, but her success was not complete. She had been forestalled in two of the Gurney manors: by Lord Chief Justice Fortescue at Farrington Gurney, where he had secured a twenty-year lease at £13 16s 8d p.a. on 17 March 1456,[22] and by William Browning, a servant of Richard duke of York, at Curry Mallet. He had bound himself to a seven-year lease there for £14 14s 10d p.a. on 14 March 1456.[23] Thus the 'rate of the extent' which in 1450–1 entitled the Exchequer to £246 13s 4d now only five years later entitled it to £152 5s 4d, for the same lands. From 3 September 1457 the dowager duchess surrendered her lease. This was, in fact, because the infant Prince of Wales had been given possession, although the cancellation merely stated that she surrendered her letters patent at the king's request.[24] Ministers' accounts show that these lands had a receiver, Richard Flint, by Michaelmas 1456, who secured a

17. *Cal. Fine Rolls*, xviii, 175, 182–3, 238.
18. *Cal. Pat. Rolls*, *1452–1461*, pp. 18–19.
19. P.R.O., Chancery, Parliament and Council, C.49/61, m.34.
20. *Cal. Fine Rolls*, xix, 154.
21. P.R.O., Exch., L.T.R., Sheriffs' Seizures, E.379/174; P.R.O., Exch., K.R., Miscellanea, E.163/8/6, which is part of the record of an account rendered at the Exchequer by the dowager duchess.
22. *Cal. Fine Rolls*, xix, 157.
23. *ibid.*, xix, 158.
24. *Cal. Pat. Rolls*, *1452–1461*, pp. 293, 390.

major part of the issues for 1456–7 in spite of all these legal changes and uncertainties.[25] He paid £200 to the receiver-general of the duchy of Cornwall for the prince's use. The dowager duchess of Somerset received £45 14s 1d from divers ministers; her son Henry duke of Somerset received another £16 13s 4d; the Lord Chief Justice retained his farm of £13 6s 8d in his own hands, apart from any profits he made; Flint took wages of £6 13s 4d, and paid a parker at Curry Mallet, who had failed to get his wages on the manor, £3 0s 10d. The prince and the farmers thus had at least £275 14s 1d in cash between Michaelmas 1456 and Michaelmas 1457. In addition, the officers had their wages and £7 15s 5¾d was carried over, balance in hand, to Flint's account for the following year.

One other instance may perhaps be quoted. In 1451 the Lord Treasurer's Remembrancer, Thomas Thorp, was paid an extra £10 for scrutinies and labours connected with the resumption. As a result of his work, he furnished a report to the Treasurer showing that the latest extents of manors held by William de la Pole, late duke of Suffolk, were £136 p.a. less than the last previous extents.[26] These figures do not indicate that the period of Suffolk's prominence in the Council had been one of declining land values and agricultural profits. Royal leases and grants made during the personal rule of Henry VI 'at the yearly rate at the Exchequer of as much as X used to render', 'at the rate of the extent', 'at the usual farm', or on some such similar terms, afford no indication of the true market value of the lands concerned.

It may be asked why, if these crown manors were worth so very much more to the farmers than they had to pay, did not other local men outbid them as Sir Robert Cotton had implied would happen in James's reign? It is quite clear that this did not happen under Henry VI, except in the unique situation of the acts of resumption of 1450–6. To some small degree this was perhaps a penalty of centralization of control, because leases could only be taken out through the Exchequer at Westminster. But the fundamental reason was that the king's lands hardly ever came on to the market. Farmers were not chosen for financial reasons. Reversionary grants made during the lifetime of previous occupants, or opportune petitions, submitted by those with the necessary knowledge and access to the king the moment a vacancy occurred, ensured that very few competitive bids could be made or be accepted by the Exchequer. One specific grant, of the keeping of the lordship and castle of Berkhamsted in 1447, vacant on 5 August by the death of the duke of Exeter, shows how pickings went to those with the earliest information and most ready access to Henry VI. Edmund

25. P.R.O., Special Collections, Ministers' and Receivers' Accts, S.C.6/1095/7 (35–36 Hen. VI).

26. P.R.O., Exch. of Receipt, Issue Rolls, E.413/781 (Mich., 29 Hen. VI under date 8 April, 1451).

Hungerford and Gilbert Parr received Berkhamsted in survivorship and had their patent sealed and engrossed on 7 August.[27] But this was no long-standing reversionary grant. It was secured by petition as the duke lay on his deathbed, and then implemented by a direct warrant under the signet which was dated at Osney on 5 August, by-passing the privy seal. In the words of this signet warrant to the Chancellor the king 'understanding now late that our cousin John duke of Exeter was either dead, or in point to die, and not fully ascertained how it was with him, showed our grace unto our trusty and well beloved knight Sir Edmund Hungerford, one of our carvers, and to Gilbert Parr, one of the squires for our body . . .'.[28]

The issues of the crown lands were consumed by the personnel of Henry VI's court and government and their dependents in grants of favour in fee, for life, for term of years or during pleasure, over and above their annuities in fee or for life, pensions, offices, fees and wages. However, the consequent unreliability of valuations by extent was not a development peculiar to the reign of Henry VI. An instance from the career of an earlier de la Pole, Richard II's minister, recorded on the parliament roll of 1386, has already been quoted, indicating that contemporaries were then aware that new valuations of royal lands by extent normally went to the advantage of the person placed in possession.[29] It is also possible to produce fourteenth-century examples of exchequer extents which can be shown to bear no relation to the true values of the lands concerned, although evidence is harder to come by than it is for the reign of Henry VI.[30] This is not necessarily because the practice of concealed preferential leasing was then less common, but because fewer private estate documents survive for earlier periods, and one must find alternative contemporary valuations made by a different method to set against the exchequer valuations by extent.

The important point to grasp is that financial atrophy in the management of the crown lands, which was the inevitable by-product of their constant political use, was not normally a matter of serious controversy. In the hands of a strong, effective king the practice was part of the cement of political cohesion. What such a ruler did with his estates, within certain accepted conventions, was a vital part of his prerogative power. He had no need to exploit and develop their issues for the current expenses of the king's government. Evidence of the true nature of the exchequer farming

27. *Cal. Pat. Rolls, 1446–1452*, p. 84.

28. P.R.O., Chanc., Warrants for the Great Seal, C.81/1370/50; *C.L.*, doc. no. 1.

29. *Rot. Parl.*, iii, 216–7; cf. above, p. 69.

30. cf. above p. 68. Alternative valuations to exchequer extents given in the printed calendars of patent and fine rolls for the fourteenth century have been found in the following documents: P.R.O., Exch., K.R., 'Extents of Alien Priories', E.106/11/2, 3–8, 11; Chanc., Misc. Inq., C.145/219/2, 5. Certain extents, printed in the *Calendar of Inquisitions Miscellaneous*, vol. vi, can be contrasted with valuations given in a near-contemporary valor now among the duchy of Lancaster records at the Public Record Office (D.L., 41/4/18).

system for the period of Henry VI's personal rule is more plentiful than at any earlier time, partly because of the great flood of estates at his disposal within a comparatively short period, but mainly because a unique failure in general political direction produced parliamentary acts of resumption which constituted a new source of information on this subject. Grants, sales and exchanges of royal lands became the subject of heated controversy in parliament from 1449, not merely because of his failure to control the normal political spoils system, but because of his total inability to provide purposeful government. The royal responsibility was unjustly laid at the doors of those who benefited most from his lavish, indiscriminate generosity.

Land hunger among the Council and the personnel of the royal Household does seem to have been kept within reasonable bounds under Henry V, and during the minority also, if only by the checks and balances operated by the mutual jealousies of the great. But from 1437 the king's lands could once more be alienated. Suitors already had direct access to the young king by 1438. Lord Cromwell was the first of their own number to be given a grant in fee (the manor of Sutton by Chiswick, Middlx.) in October 1437.[31] Two years later Henry sold Chirk and other lands to Cardinal Beaufort. Henry certainly had the right to sell his land if he wished, or if he could be persuaded to do so. Other churchmen besides the Cardinal now began to consider the needs of their favourite foundations. Some lay members of the Council, like James Fiennes, lord Say and Sele, and Humphrey Stafford, duke of Buckingham, covered their acquisitions by making the king a small gift of land for one of his own foundations, by way of exchange. Others in a favourable position to sue for grants, like John Holand, duke of Exeter, pleaded grants to their ancestors by earlier kings in support of their requests.[32]

An unusually comprehensive picture can be given of Henry VI's grants of crown lands because they were three times annulled by act of parliament between 1450 and 1456. The returns made by sheriffs and escheators to writs of inquiry sent out by the Exchequer in pursuance of these acts of resumption show what these grants were, who held them and on what

31. *Cal. Pat. Rolls, 1436–1441*, p. 117.

32. Alien priory lands which had provided much of Queen Joan's income were naturally a favourite purchase during these years. Archbishop Chichele paid £1,000 to Henry VI for the manor of Weedon Lois (Northants.), for All Souls (P.R.O., Anc. Petitions, S.C./132/6595). John Frank, 'clerk of the rolls in the Chamber', paid £1,000 for the manor of Wadley and Littleworth (Berks.), for Oriel College, Oxford (*ibid.*, S.C.8/132/6596). Archbishop Kemp paid 300 marks for the manor of Newington (Kent), for the college of St Gregory and St Martin at Wye (*Rot. Parl.*, v, 305). Humphrey duke of Buckingham gave the king the patronage of Fordingbridge church in return for the manor of Penshurst and other manors in Kent (*Rot. Parl.*, v, 309). Lord Say gave a reversion of Monkecourt (Kent), to Henry and acquired the manor of Witley (Surrey), by agreement instead (*Cal. Pat. Rolls, 1441–1446*, pp. 140, 161, 187). The duke of Exeter secured the alienation of the manors of Tremanton and Calstock and the burgh of Saltash from the duchy of Cornwall, on the plea of an earlier grant dated 25 January 1393.

terms. Apart from the information disclosed by these local inquisitions, the Exchequer filled in gaps by search of records (i.e. the originalia rolls, the reversion rolls, ministers' accounts, and the pipe rolls).[33]

It has thus been possible to examine the terms on which 169 persons held 192 grants of these lands and properties in 1450. The holders were those whom the Exchequer considered directly responsible to the king and his officers under the terms of the acts. In some cases the information required only came to light after further returns had been made pursuant to the act of resumption of 1456. The lands concerned ranged in size from whole lordships like Pembroke, and groups of many manors like the Gurney estates in Somerset and Dorset, to parcels of 50 acres or less, single messuages with portions of land in the open fields, properties in London such as dwelling houses or wharfs, and salmon fisheries, which were obviously also very valuable. The majority were single manor units.

The whole of the crown lands was not represented. The returns covered most of England, but none have been found for North Wales, Chester, or the duchy of Lancaster. The acts only applied to lands etc., leased or granted since the beginning of the reign, that is 1 September 1422. Lands in hand, of which there were a number under the direct management of the officers of the duchies of Cornwall and Lancaster, of the lordships of Chester, Flint, and Richmond, and probably under the chamberlains of North and South Wales, were not affected, though annuities or offices held there were covered by the acts. Some holders of crown lands, but surprisingly few individual holders, were exempted from the operation of all three acts of resumption which were passed in 1450, 1451, and 1456, and so their holdings were not mentioned in the returns. The outstanding example was Queen Margaret.[34]

Study of these returns reveals how many of the most valuable royal lands had been alienated outside the royal family between 1440 and 1450. These would have been permanently lost to the Crown and royal family but for the acts of resumption. Among these alienations were a number of duchy of Cornwall manors, the whole of the lordship of Pembroke and its members, and most of the great lordship of Richmond. Undoubtedly the duchy of Lancaster had only escaped large-scale alienations because of the demands of two large enfeoffments (to fulfil the terms of Henry V's will, and also of

33. I have compiled a consolidated list of grants as affected by these three acts of resumption, together with their subsequent history to 1461, in Appendix 'C' below. The main manuscript sources are P.R.O., Exch., L.T.R., Sheriffs' Seizures, E.379/175 (enrolled accounts for the act of 28 Hen. VI); *ibid.*, Escheators' Accts, E.357/41 (enrolled accounts for the act of 29 Hen. VI); *ibid.*, Sheriffs' Seizures, E.379/174 (enrolled accounts for the act of 33 Hen. VI). Details of the regrants are found mainly on the fine rolls.

34. In 1450 she held the lordships and manors of Feckenham (Gloucs.) Berkhamsted (Herts.), Milton and Marden (Kent), Marlborough with Savernake forest, Devizes with the forests of Melksham, Pewsham and Chippenham (Wilts.), and Haverfordwest (South Wales), none of which were mentioned.

Henry VI's will, the fulfilment of some of the terms of which was begun long before his death); also because of the provision for the dowers of two queens (Catherine of Valois and Margaret of Anjou), made upon it with only a short interval between.

The remaining lands in the list of 1450 were almost all granted out on life leases, for joint lives, or for long terms of years. The total farms paid to the Crown for all these lands fell far short of £1,000. Moreover, a large part even of this sum was remitted in annuities to the holders or paid out to others. A few examples will make this clear. Robert Dawson, a yeoman of the Crown, and William Haydock, a customer, paid £40 p.a. for the manor of Eltham, Kent. Out of this sum John Trevelyan, a king's sergeant, had wages as a parker there of 6d *per diem*, Robert Berd of Kent, the steward, had £2 p.a., Robert Dawson received back 3d *per diem* as a parker, Richard Dalby, king's sergeant, had an annuity of £6 13s 4d, and John Haukeston, clerk of the household chapel, had another 10 marks p.a. It is quite possible that the £11 remaining of the rent was also given away to other members of the Household.[35]

Other similar cases were common. John Penycock, the king's esquire, who had a grant of the manor of Walton on Thames at £15 p.a. for life (the manor was extended at £23), had an annuity of £15 p.a. on the farmer of the same manor (i.e. himself). In Westmorland Thomas Colt and John Tunstall paid £33 2s 6d p.a. for a number of manors of the lordship of Kendal. But Richard earl of Salisbury had an annuity of 50 marks paid by them, and he had surrendered a lease of these lands in order that they might have them. Similarly in Nottinghamshire, John Cockfield, William Heton, Robert Cowsell, and William Stanlowe, paid £40 12s p.a. for the manors of Mansfield, Clipstone, and Linby. The receipt rolls show that Ralph lord Cromwell regularly took this farm as part of his fee for attendance at the Council. Cromwell was the previous lessee, and had made these arrangements to ensure that his fee would always be forthcoming.

An analysis of the status of the 169 beneficiaries of this distribution of crown lands shows them to have been 16 members of the nobility, 21 knights, and 132 esquires, gentlemen, yeomen, or below, mainly esquires and gentlemen. Only 13 of these grantees are completely unidentifiable, and the lands they held were almost negligible in size and value.

An attempt to discover the interests in common of these holders of crown lands shows that there were nine great lords concerned: the dukes of York, Somerset, Buckingham and Exeter, the marquis of Suffolk and the earls of Salisbury, Devon, Warwick and Oxford. If we exclude these, seventy-four of the remaining total, headed by Viscount Beaumont, and

35. These farmers were often exempt from any obligation to carry out maintenance work on buildings or on the land, which meant that the king's lands did not even pay for their own upkeep.

Lords Cromwell, Beauchamp, Sudeley, Say, Stourton, and Dudley, were members of the king's Household in 1450. Another fifteen may be classed as 'country members' of the Household, described as king's knight, esquire, or servant, holding one or more offices on the principal royal manors and clearly closely connected with the central Household, though not continually resident members of it.[36] Another ten were officers of the Exchequer or Chancery, and six were customers. Five may be described as officers of the duchy of Lancaster, one as an officer of the honour of Richmond. Another fifteen were members of one or more parliaments between 1439 and 1459, who had no known household connection, whatever their sympathies and uses may have been in their localities. Thirteen were minor persons unidentified, there was a chaplain and two clerks having no known connection with the Household, a citizen of London, a pensioner, a minor local official and a falconer. There remained fourteen who were mainly men of some substance, but whose recorded activities lay only in their own localities. This analysis classifies each person once only. They could be put into different groupings. For example, twenty-two held offices of the duchy of Lancaster in 1450, and another ten at some date during the reign.

In 1450 the king's landed patrimony was thus distributed entirely through the Household. For all its vaunted *esprit de corps* it is a mistake to regard the fifteenth-century Exchequer as an office with any independent power or policy of its own. It appears merely to have recorded and acted upon the decisions and arrangements made by the king in his Household. At all events the higher exchequer officers made their way through the Household. With the exception of the bishop of Carlisle (appointed Treasurer in 1446), all the Treasurers between 1433 and 1452 (Cromwell, Butler, Fiennes, Beauchamp) had previously been household chamberlains, and Butler, Fiennes, and Beauchamp were each of them king's household chamberlain when they took over the Treasurership. Cromwell, before his appointment as Treasurer in 1433, had been chamberlain with the young king abroad. On his resignation from the Treasureship he preserved some influence at the Exchequer. In 1443 he was given one chamberlainship of the Exchequer to himself, his heirs and assigns.[37] This

36. In this connection a passage in some lesser known household ordinances of 1445 should be noted: 'All manner of the king's squires and surplus of officers exceeding the number of appointment must resort to the king's court at the five feasts of the year, at Parliament, great councils, or for coming of strangers and at other times necessary as the case requires by the discretion of the steward or of some of the sovereigns of the king's house' (P.R.O., Chanc., Miscellanea, C.47/3/36). These ordinances bear the sign manual of Henry VI. They have now been printed from a fuller copy in the British Museum (Lansdowne MS. I, fols. 86a–93b) by Dr A. R. Myers in *The Household of Edward IV*, pp. 63–75. This passage is para. 19 on p. 66 in Dr Myers's version. Note also para. 20 on the same page to the effect that among those surplus to establishment the ones best provided for in the localities should be sent home in preference to those who had less of the king's gift.

37. *Cal. Pat. Rolls, 1441–1446*, p. 158

office he held until his death in 1456 and his appointee William Appletrefeld continued to hold it for some time afterwards.[38] In addition, Cromwell was king's chamberlain in the Household at least from 18 May 1451.[39] Other members of the exchequer staff like the under treasurer, Thomas Brown, king's esquire, farmer of Havering, steward of Middleton and Marden, had strong household connections. In these circumstances there could normally be no conflict between Exchequer and Household.

The young king had been alienating his crown lands to the principal members of his Household from about 1440 at an unprecedented rate. These were available for disposal in great numbers after the deaths of his uncles. The endowment received by the marquis of Suffolk was the outstanding example. After Suffolk, Viscount Beaumont and Lords Beauchamp, Cromwell, Sudeley, Say, Stourton, and Dudley received the most. In each case they naturally acquired crown lands lying mainly in their respective local spheres of interest: Beauchamp and Sudeley in Gloucestershire, the West Country and the Southern Marches, Beaumont in Lincolnshire, Cromwell in Lincolnshire and Nottinghamshire, Stourton in Wiltshire, Dudley in Staffordshire and Shropshire, Say in Kent, Surrey, and Sussex. Each of these noble king's servants were men of substance in their own right, but they were little if any greater than knights of the Household like Sir Edmund Hungerford, who received crown lands in Wiltshire and Berkshire, or Sir Thomas Stanley of Knowsley in Lancashire, who was granted the lordships of Mold and Hawarden and made more powerful in Cheshire and the northern Marches of Wales. Less powerful perhaps was Sir Robert Roos, who was given extensive crown lands in Northamptonshire, and probably equal to him in influence were some king's esquires; for instance, John Hampton in Staffordshire, John Norreys in Oxfordshire and Berkshire, John Say in Essex, and John St Loo in Somerset and Dorset. Household service provided a ladder for rapid advancement, and even a yeoman of the king's cellar like William Ludlow received the castle, town, and manor of Ludgershall (Wilts.) to himself and his heirs male. He had every chance of becoming a powerful king's knight. The crown lands alienated to all these household officers so far mentioned were all granted in tail male, with the exception of Cromwell who had no sons and always received his land in fee simple.

These men also had a share of the more numerous rent-free grants for life which the lesser members of the Household enjoyed. However, not only crown lands, but also crown offices, were at their disposal. These were

38. P.R.O., Exch. of Receipt, Receipt Rolls, E.401/849, 857 (King's Chamberlain's Rolls for Easter 1456 and Easter 1457).

39. *Cal. Pat. Rolls, 1446–1452*, p. 452: 'William Worcester' in the *Annales* (*Letters and Papers illustrative of the Wars of the English in France*, ed. J. Stevenson, Rolls Series, vol. ii, pt. ii), referred to him as such in April 1452 and the Household Ordinance of 13 November 1454 included him, with his establishment, as king's household chamberlain.

available to them with the fees and profits charged on crown lands throughout the country, including the numerous duchy of Lancaster appointments. They also received annuities, paid locally from feefarm rents, and through the sheriffs, bailiffs or farmers of crown lands and properties. Privileges and immunities enhanced the value of their own lands and of the crown lands given to them. Opportune petitions secured them valuable wardships and forfeitures great and small. All this was accompanied by an equally lavish distribution of honours. The extraordinary numbers of creations to the peerage made at this time stand out. Of seventeen creations to baronies by letters patent or charter before the Reformation ten were made between 1441 and 1449. In addition between the same years there were five earls created, two marquises and five dukes.[40]

A distribution of crown lands and revenues outside the circle of the great princes of the blood on the scale made by Henry VI probably had no precedent, with the possible exception of Edward III's less widely distributed munificence in the preliminary stages of the French war. Even then the patrimony of his eldest son and heir had been enhanced, not diminished, while success in war had soon brought mounting governmental prestige. Such a volume of lands had in fact never been available to any king before within such a comparatively brief period. At this time of growing national humiliation Henry VI was bereft of both royal family and authority. The disappearance from the scene of Queen Joan of Navarre and Queen Katherine of Valois in the same year that he came of age, and also of the three royal dukes,[41] who had no legitimate issue, had left the feeble king with no near relatives around the throne, except his own young and alien queen (Margaret of Anjou) and his two half-brothers (Jasper and Edmund Tudor) who were minors.

This favoured group interest within the nobility and gentry, receiving grants stretching throughout the land, and identifiable as the personnel of the royal Household, were inevitably identified also with the policy of national humiliation which resulted from Henry VI's personal assumption of government. They were the channels of the royal authority at the centre and in the localities. They were frequently at the king's side, whereas the opportunities and influence of the greatest councillors like York and Buckingham, who admittedly shared the royal bounty to some degree, were intermittent. Powerful in the king's Council and administration and the recipients of royal favour in their own localities, the household men yet appear to have had little control and influence over public opinion, especially as it was expressed in the House of Commons. When the mount-

40. There is a list of the baronies in Appendix 'A' of the *Complete Peerage*, vii, 703. The rest are taken from *Rep. Dig. Peer*, *Appendix*, v and the *Calendar of Charter Rolls*, vi, *passim.*

41. Clarence died in 1421, Bedford in 1435 and Gloucester in 1447.

ing costs of unsuccessful war rendered an impoverished and ineffectual king utterly dependent on parliamentary grants their endowments from the royal patrimony made them especially vulnerable to personal attack.

Of the 153 commoners who were holding crown lands in 1450, fifty-four sat at least once in the parliaments which met between 1439 and 1459, but not more than twenty-seven in any one parliament.[42] Their numbers were highest in the Bury Parliament (the occasion of the disposal of the duke of Gloucester's lands); in the first parliament of 1449 when, in spite of persistent demand for an act of resumption no act was passed; and in the Reading Parliament of 1453, the most amenable of Henry's parliaments. Their numbers were lowest in the parliament of 1450–1 which passed the most drastic of the acts of resumption. In this parliament there were only seven recorded holders of crown lands and only three of these (Thomas Barton, John Norreys and Sir Thomas Stanley) were members of the king's Household. But the average total membership of the Commons in these years was about 270. Had this group of king's men been bound together by close political aims, and by a purposeful policy one might have expected them to have exerted an influence out of proportion to their numbers. There is no evidence that they were so bound, and the determination of the Commons to put through acts for the resumption of crown lands is not surprising when one sees how few House of Commons men were personally affected.

2. RESUMPTION AS THE PANACEA FOR FINANCIAL REFORM

In the disastrous final stages of the Hundred Years War angry men stigmatized Henry VI's disposition of the royal lands and revenues as a wanton misuse of royal resources. We may seriously doubt whether a very substantial, permanent contribution to the national finances could be secured by any resumption such as they proposed, however drastic it might be. On any historical view which extended back beyond 1437 the weight of evidence was against them. Nevertheless, the ensuing acts of parliament can-

42. The following is an analysis by parliaments of those holders of crown lands in 1450 who were also M.P.s 1439–59:

Parliaments	1439	1442	1445	1447	1449 (1)	1449–50	1450–1	1453	1455	1459
Probable total membership	264	268	268	272	276	278	280	286	286	250
No. of names missing	156	0	146	0	2	6	12	8	82	83
No. of holders of crown lands present	10	15	8	21	27	12	7	18	15	11
No. of these who were also members of the Household	7	10	5	16	16	8	3	13	9	10

not be explained away as mere partisan weapons of political pique and spite. They were seriously intended as financial reforms, put forward in the wider circumstances of general national crisis by men of goodwill, however limited their vision. A calmly reasoned financial case for them is found in chapter eleven of *The Governance of England*.[43] Here that staunch Lancastrian servant Lord Chief Justice Fortescue expressed the essence of the financial reasoning behind the plea for a resumption when it began to be pressed upon Henry VI's government in parliament from 1449: the king had held, sometime or another since his accession, lordships, lands, tenements and rents near in value to one-fifth part of the total value of such resources in England, excluding the possessions of the church. Of course he could not have retained them all; heirs had rights at law; some men had served him so notably that they were entitled to a permanent reward such as the king's own honour required he should give them; members of the royal family had to be suitably provided for.[44] Nevertheless, for lack of ready money the king had sometimes rewarded men with land where a cash payment would have sufficed; by the importunity of suitors some had been rewarded above their merits. Ill-considered and undeserved grants ought to be resumed. It was currently thought that if this were done and if such rewards were confined in future to money, to offices, or at most, to grants of land for life, then the king would have sufficient livelihood to maintain his estate. However, should this prove not to be so in the event, then Fortescue gave his own view (and he was most emphatic about it), that public opinion would then be ready to make up the deficiency in the royal livelihood by negotiating the grant of a sales tax on the current Burgundian and French models, provided that guarantees were given that no such alienation of royal lands and revenues, including the proceeds of the new tax, should ever be allowed to happen again.[45]

The serious financial intention of the resumption demand cannot be doubted. Indeed, the title given to one version of the 1451 resumption petition which appears in Richard Arnold's commonplace book is 'A provision by Act of Parliament to bring King Henry out of a debt of £372,000'.[46] Alleged facts and figures about the king's revenues were com-

43. *The Governance of England* (ed. Plummer) pp. 135–7. The chapter heading is 'Here is shewid, what off the kynges livelod given awey, mey beste be taken a geyn'.

44. The reference is actually to the endowing of the king's 'moste worshipfull brotherryn'. On my reading of this chapter this reference must be a later modification for Yorkist times, because Henry VI had not yet endowed his Tudor half-brothers. Indeed, it was only the resumption acts of 1450–1 which made their endowment possible.

45. 'A subsidie uppon suche comodities off his reaume as bith be forre specified' (p. 137). This is a reference back to the previous chapter at the top of p. 133 where he had switched from discussing the possibility of a sales tax ('such manner off subsidie') to the discussion of the potentialities of land revenues which led him to advocate a resumption.

46. Richard Arnold, *The Customs of London*, ed. F. Douce (London, 1811), pp. 179–86. Ramsay mistook this for a copy of the 1450 resumption petition.

mon talk from 1449, most probably derived in the first instance from those who heard declarations of the state of the realm which were made in parliament at Winchester and at Westminster in 1449, and at Leicester in 1450, but not entered on the parliament roll.[47] Two brief sets of figures survive from 1450, but they have only one item in common, and their meaning is a matter of some conjecture. The 1450 resumption petition stated that the king was 'endetted' in £372,000 and that his 'lyvehode in yerly value was but £5,000', while household charges were £24,000. One version of the articles against Suffolk, which put the king's debts at a mere £26,000 and his expenses at £32,000 p.a., also contains the much more easily intelligible statement that Henry 'may dispend but £34,000 of the which the Kyng hath no more in hond but £5,000'.[48] The figure of £5,000, common to both sets of figures, thus seems to represent not the current yield of the whole of the revenues of England, nor the total yield of 'a *basic* royal revenue, from farms and lands', as it has recently been interpreted,[49] but either the cash in hand at the Exchequer at some date in 1449 or 1450, or the estimated value at that date of all items of revenue remaining unassigned.

Cromwell's estimate for what the king might 'dispend' in 1433 had been £35,366 2s 0½d, his total charge to be met had totalled £225,314 16s 8d, and Cromwell's allowance for current household expenses had been £13,678 12s 11d. Tabulated thus the alleged position in 1450 appears credible in face of the cost of a losing war which had now at last entered its final, disastrous stage:

	Current charges and outstanding debts	Current net income
1433	£225,314 16s 8d	£35,366 2s 0½d[50]
1450	£372,000	£34,000

47. The preamble to the 1450 resumption petition (*Rot. Parl.*, v, 183) states that the figures there quoted came from a declaration of the state of the realm made to the Commons at the previous session at Westminster. Entries on the issue rolls show that such declarations involved the attendance of exchequer officials at parliaments to convey the record to the Treasurer there, and to expound it, no doubt to the Council. See, for example, part payment of £150 on 21 July 1449 to Thomas Brown Esq. (under-treasurer) for his labours at the Winchester session of the previous parliament (P.R.O., Exch. of Receipt, Issue Rolls, E.403/775, Easter, 27 Hen. VI); £10 on 9 March 1450 special reward to Hugh Fenne, clerk of John Somer one of the auditors of the Exchequer for labours in preparing a state of the realm 'in presenti parliamento dicto domino Regi et concilio suo demonstranda' (*ibid.*, E.403/777, Mich., 28 Hen. VI) and 60s expenses paid on May 19 1450 for the same Hugh Fenne's attendance at the Leicester parliament on the Treasurer's orders in connection with a declaration made to the Lords and Commons there (*ibid.*, E.403/779, Easter, 28 Hen. VI).

48. Printed by C. L. Kingsford, *English Historical Literature in the Fifteenth Century*, p. 360.

49. By E. F. Jacob, *The Fifteenth Century, 1399–1485*, p. 445. Plummer, *op. cit.*, p. 220, described it as 'the amount of the whole ordinary revenue'.

50. This figure represents what Cromwell considered to be the total of the unassigned financial resources of the crown at the time of his calculations. It is a combination of his estimate of the unassigned portion of the customs (£26,966 2s 10½d), plus his total for the

Increase in household expenses between 1433 and 1450 was to be expected since we are here comparing a minority with what was, in theory, adult kingship. Henry V spent most of his time abroad on campaign so that there is no comparable figure for the Household in the financial estimates of his reign, but in the somewhat restricted circumstances of 1410–11 the estimate for Henry IV's Household had been £16,000 p.a.[51] However, in view of the unreliable terminology in which the 1450 figures survive one cannot be sure that the £24,000 p.a. for the Household in fact represented only current expenses. It may have included debts. Cromwell's £13,678 12s 11d for current household expenses had been accompanied by another £11,101 0s 7d for its debts. Only the discovery of the original declarations for 1449 and 1450 would enable a true comparison to be made with the position in 1433.

Certainly when Fortescue and others talked of the paramount need for the king to have 'livelihood sufficient for the maintenance of his estate' they meant primarily for the maintenance of his household establishment in the widest sense of Household, Chamber, Wardrobe and works. These were the ordinary, principal, 'national' expenses of government, followed by the wages of the great officers and councillors and then by the cost of maintaining garrisons in the Scottish marches, in Calais, in Ireland and elsewhere. The ideal of medieval government was a splendid, solvent, well-ordered royal Household. The negation of medieval kingship was the king who 'helde no Householde ne meyntened no warres'.[52]

There was much emphasis on the need to make the Household solvent in the parliaments which met between 1433 and 1450. The same parliament of 1433 in which Cromwell presented his comprehensive financial review was told before their adjournment (13 August) that there was no more money available for current household expenses until they reassembled on 13 October. They instructed the Treasurer to place a ceiling of £2,000 on

unassigned portions of the other revenues (£8,399 19s 2d), both figures appearing in *Rot. Parl.*, iv, 435. It does not coincide with my figure for current net income for England and Wales given above p. 91, Table 1, because: (1) Cromwell's statement included Ireland, Aquitaine and Calais; (2) he included in his calculation of the figure £8,399 19s 2d only the unassigned portions of each separate unit of account. He did not include as a deficit to be set against other unassigned resources any over-assignment on a particular unit. This was because an assignment which had failed to get paid through lack of funds at the source assigned for payment could be ignored until it had been reassigned through the Exchequer and honoured. As it happens such a case occurred only once in the items given in my Table 3, p. 92 above. I have marked this as a deficit there (£72 8s 5½d under Windsor Castle) to make the totals of that table balance for modern eyes. But the explanation of this discrepancy serves as a salutary caution for anyone attempting to use as an income and expenditure account a medieval statement consisting of assigned revenues which had secured payment, unassigned revenues, recurrent unmet charges, outstanding debts and dishonoured assignments.

51. *Proc. and Ord.*, i, 342.

52. *An English Chronicle of the Reigns of Richard II, Henry IV, Henry V and Henry VI*, ed. J. S. Davies (Camden Soc., 1856), p. 79 under the year 1459–60.

the total of all payments of assignments allocated up to 20 July 1433. Only payments due to those who had lent the king money were to be exempt in order to give priority to current household expenses.[53] In the parliament of 1439–40 much more significant restraints on the free disposal of revenues were conceded: an appropriation of the issues of the duchies of Cornwall and of that part of the duchy of Lancaster not in the hands of Henry V's feoffees to current household expenses for five years;[54] one-quarter of a tenth and fifteenth specifically appropriated for ready money payment of household expenses;[55] and those portions of the duchy of Lancaster revenues still in the hands of the feoffees also appropriated, under certain conditions, to pay the king's debts and to lessen the grievance of household purveyance.[56] In 1442 attempts were made in the Commons to extend this appropriation of the revenues of the two great duchies to current household expenses for a further three years and to add a further annual appropriation of 5,000 marks on the customs for this purpose. The petition, which was accompanied by a plea for new controls on the abuses of household purveyance, was answered evasively.[57] Such matters were now too high for the Council once the king had assumed direction of affairs.

In the parliament which first met on 12 February 1449 assignments for wages of household personnel which had not been honoured on the customs were transferred to the issues of wardships, marriages and vacant temporalities.[58] Again there was complaint about the flagrant abuse of the right of household purveyance, this time against a certain purveyor of horses who was turning a life grant of an office to unscrupulous personal profit.[59] But this assembly was most notable for its persistent agitation for a large-scale act of resumption. It was this demand which led to its dissolution at Winchester on 16 July 1449.[60] Less than four months passed before another parliament had to be called, and in temper this assembly was even more determined than its predecessor. A new type of household appropriation was now drawn up at the instance of the Commons which it was hoped would be much more difficult to set aside in favour of other charges. This

53. *Rot. Parl.*, iv, 420–1.

54. *ibid.*, v, 7. As a result of these measures the controller of the Household acknowledged receipt of £7,192 18s 10d in 1441–2 and £8,481 12s 8¾d in 1443–4 from the receivers-general of the two duchies: P.R.O., Exch., K.R., Various Accts, E. 101/409/9, 11.

55. *Rot. Parl.*, v, 32.

56. *ibid.*, v, 8–9. Cf. the parliamentary appropriations of 1404 and the proposals of 1406 above, pp. 81–5.

57. *Rot. Parl.*, v, 62–3.   58. *ibid.*, v, 157–9.   59. *ibid.*, v, 154.

60. There is no mention of this petition on the roll of the parliament but the account of this first parliament of 1449, found in Robert Bale's Chronicle (*Six Town Chronicles*, ed. R. Flenley (Oxford, 1911), p. 125), stresses the insistence of this parliament on a resumption, and states categorically that this insistence caused its dissolution. This chronicle, according to Flenley and C. L. Kingsford, is a noteworthy contemporary account for the years 1449–51 and most precise in its chronology. Robert Bale was probably a citizen of London, a lawyer, and a judge. (See C. L. Kingsford, *op. cit.*, pp. 95–9).

measure detailed individual items to be derived from specific farms and feefarms throughout England and Wales, from the ulnage, from the customs and subsidies at the ports and from various other sources totalling £11,002 6s 1d p.a., all to go entirely to the current expenses of the king's Household, the arrangement to endure for seven years. It was specifically stated to be designed to relieve the king's subjects of the grievous burdens they had long suffered through the requisitioning of their goods and chattels for the Household without due payment. It included the direction that the receiver-general of the duchy of Lancaster should pay his surplus revenues, over and above the queen's endowment, fees, wages, reparations, costs and necessary expenses, to the treasurer of the Household for seven years from 7 May 1450.[61] Most significant of change in this respect, it also gave the oversight of the receiver-general's account of the duchy revenues to a board of three, consisting of the steward, treasurer and controller of the Household, thus foreshadowing in this single instance the later chamber finance of Edward IV. A long petition for a resumption followed, as the only means of ensuring that heavily pledged revenues were indeed freed for household use.[62] The demand for an act of resumption had by now aroused great interest and widespread support in the country at large. It was seen as promising some relief from the constant drain of direct taxation[63] which the country could probably afford, but which brought no returns in the way of national prestige, solvent or effective government at home, or favourable conditions for trade or military enterprise abroad. Its achievement came to epitomize all hopes of government solvency and of relief from the constant abuses of household purveyance and from all the other evils of weak and corrupt government which were the subject of growing complaints in successive parliaments.

3. THE COLLAPSE OF ROYAL GOVERNMENT, 1437–50

The political bankruptcy of Henry VI's regime made a resumption

61. P.R.O., Exch., K.R., Mem. Rolls, E.159/227 (29 Hen. VI), 'communia', Mich. m. 17. I owe this reference to Professor E. F. Jacob. The version printed in *Rot. Parl.*, v, 174–6, is accurate as far as it goes but is incomplete, details of more than £5,000 of the assignment being omitted. R. Somerville, *History of the Duchy of Lancaster*, i, 215, wrongly gives the commencing date for the duchy assignment as 7 May 1451.

62. *Rot. Parl.*, v, 183–5.

63. The average had been a complete tenth and fifteenth every two years since 1429. This aspect of the resumption was seized upon in John Hardyng's rhyming chronicle (ed. H. Ellis, p. 401). As a result of it he says: 'taxe ceased and dymes eke also, In all Englande then raysed were no mo'. He himself lost an annuity of £10 by the resumption. This 1450 parliament refused to make any grant in the traditional form ('we can, may, nor dare not, in any wite charge your said people with such usual charges as afore this time to you have been granted in your parliaments'). Instead it granted a graduated property tax on the 1404 model, appropriated to defence, to be paid to four specially appointed treasurers and not to be treated as a precedent (*Rot. Parl.*, v, 172–4).

practical politics in 1450. Behind the government's lack of funds lay the deeper lack of 'governance', or, as it was sometimes expressed, lack of 'politique rule and governance'. The emptiness of the public purse and the alleged universal degeneration in law and order at this time were only the most obvious signs of this deeper *malaise* which was inseparably tied up with the conduct of the French war.

That 'not unworthy manifestation of national consciousness',[64] Cade's rebellion, in all its humiliation, frustration, and bewilderment, admirably illustrates this fundamental consideration. Led by an ex-soldier from France, supported by a former squire of the body of Henry V who had fought at Agincourt and with many other men of substance among its supporters, this patriotic rising originated in one of the most densely populated, most politically conscious and normally most prosperous areas of England. Astride the great highway from London to Dover, its coasts open to French pirate raids and its trade and industry immediately subject to the severe depression which accompanied the final collapse of English continental power, the rebellion was sparked off by a wild fear of reprisals for the murder of Suffolk. The fallen minister's headless body had been cast ashore by Kentish seamen and put under guard by the sheriff, William Crowmer. He allegedly threatened to make all Kent into a deerpark, with the co-operation of his father-in-law the Treasurer of England, Lord Say, from his Kentish seat at Knole. No better example of the unity of domestic and foreign affairs in fifteenth-century England could be provided. The simultaneous disturbances in other parts of the country also concentrated on rabbling those leading ecclesiastics whom Henry's subjects closely identified with Suffolk, the losing war, or the French queen. The financial waste of Lancastrian government between 1437 and 1450, conspicuous though it was, would never have been followed by the acts of resumption passed in parliament from 1450, if it had not been for Henry VI's feckless misconduct of all the nation's affairs which culminated in the fall of Rouen in October 1449 and the Kentish rebellion of 1450.

The degree to which Henry VI was personally responsible not only for his grants, but also for all the disastrous policies which led to the crisis of 1450, has not been sufficiently allowed for in modern accounts of this period and must therefore be briefly considered here before we turn to describing the passing and effects of the Lancastrian acts of resumption. An understanding of the position of the Council in fifteenth-century government is fundamental in this respect. In November 1437 the Council felt bound to make provision for the young king to assume supreme direc-

64. Helen M. Lyle, *The Rebellion of Jack Cade* (Historical Association Pamphlet, General Series no. 16, 1950), p. 22. The rest of this paragraph is based on the useful summary of the causes and composition of this rebellion provided by Miss Lyle in this pamphlet.

tion of affairs of state. They began modelling the necessary changes in their own hitherto supreme powers on the commission which Henry IV had given to his Council in 1406.[65] On that occasion, it must be remembered, an adult king had personally made a voluntary surrender of some of his prerogatives to the Council.[66] The Council minute of 13 November 1437 began as an English translation of the French of this earlier document. But it then went on to add certain vital clauses which put the young Henry VI in full possession of all the normal prerogative powers of English kingship, leaving the Council as advisers and executants, with discretion only in routine matters, and only then provided that no serious disagreement arose among themselves.[67] The Council's own reference to 1406 is therefore misleading. From 1437, as a result of these changes, the effectiveness or otherwise of the role of the Council depended on the personal character, enterprise and industry of the king. What some historians have seen as conciliar or curialist cliques under Henry VI would have been hardworking conciliar committees under Edward IV or Henry VII. The original day-to-day minutes of the Council, in rough draft or fair copy, only survive up to 1444, and attempts which have so far been made to ascertain the rise and fall of political influence among councillors both before and after this date, according to the place of meeting, the various attendances, and the nature of the business transacted, do not stand up well to close scrutiny.[68] An ineffective king inevitably meant a weak and ineffective Council. The fifteenth-century Council drew its lifeblood from the king. Indications are that Henry VI allowed his Council little power and, but for a few sporadic and capricious efforts, did little governing himself. Hence the chronic lack of purposeful direction from 1437 which became acute from about 1445.

In the crisis of 1450 contemporaries in general, outside governmental circles, thought that an innocent king had been robbed of his resources and deceived by unscrupulous advisers. But the writings of those contemporaries who were best informed, such as his household chaplain and his Lord Chief Justice, suggest that the trouble arose from the king's own personality and behaviour. There is a revealing picture of the daily court life of this unworldly, ascetic youth who had been king from his cradle,

65. *Proc. and Ord.*, v, 71–2.

66. *Rot. Parl.*, iii, 572–3, and see above pp. 84–5.

67. The differences are made clear by a careful collation of the two documents of 1406 and 1437. If they are read side by side it will be seen that additional clauses appear in the 1437 document in the last four lines on p. 313 and the first nine lines on p. 314 of *Proc. and Ord.*, vol. vi. These clauses, in effect, removed the restrictions placed on the royal power by the document of 1406.

68. J. F. Baldwin, *The King's Council*, p. 189, was the first to state the view that 'A very material change in the affairs of the council is connected with the rise of the earl of Suffolk' which he dated from about 1444. Subsequent writers have merely followed him in this. I personally find the evidence he put forward for this view unconvincing, especially in his use of the council minutes. His interpretation of the peace negotiations from 1444 has been proved inaccurate by Kingsford.

drawn not by his detractors, but by his loyal household chaplain John Blacman.[69] In it we see Henry in his twenties already living a life dedicated to poverty and Christian charity, purposefully aiming at perfection in devotional exercises to the exclusion of state affairs; a king for whom the exercise of kingship lay in supervising the morals of his courtiers and testing the godliness of ecclesiastics aspiring to preferment. Many years later his Lord Chief Justice at this time, Sir John Fortescue, looked back with foreboding at his experiences of this earlier period, when Henry VI was briefly restored once more to the throne in 1470. From his exile in France he was quick to seize the opportunity to advise the earl of Warwick which the departure for England of his pupil, the Lancastrian prince of Wales, then presented. He warned Warwick not to allow the hapless king to make any grants at all until there was a responsible Council established to consider petitions. Outside the Council it was essential to ensure that 'the king not be counseled by men of his Chambre, of his Householde, nor other which can not counsele hym'. It is not too much to say that the whole of this later memorandum to Warwick was composed on the basis of his earlier, personal experience of the danger to the Lancastrian cause inherent in Henry's ready accessibility and uncontrolled largess.[70] Indeed, one of the principal themes of Fortescue's major work the *Governance of England* is the desirability of constant conciliar supervision over royal grants, and the need to undo the harm already done by indiscriminate royal bounty. After allowance has been made for the restrained language necessary in a work intended for presentation to a fifteenth-century king and for alterations consequent on its ultimate presentation to Edward IV *faut de mieux*, the *Governance* seems to belong mainly to these years before 1450 when acts of resumption were as yet untried.

Until 1445 almost the only marks of Henry's personal control of affairs of state were his grants. On several occasions these seem to have shocked the collective good sense of the Council, whatever its individual members may have got from him privately. As early as February 1438 the council minutes contain reminders to speak to the king about his grants of a pardon and two offices which had cost him 3,000 marks.[71] But the more important the grant the less likely would the Council feel able to advise him. His own good sense or lack of it became more important according to the magnitude of the transaction. The offices concerned in 1438 were in the lordship of Chirk. On 25 May he sold the lot: castle, manor and lordship, together with other valuable lands, to Cardinal Beaufort for £8,900.[72] This was particularly unwise, if only because of the contrast with his father, Henry V,

69. *Henry the Sixth, A Reprint of John Blacman's Memoir with Translation and Notes*, by M. R. James (Cambridge, 1919).

70. Printed by Plummer as Appendix 'B' to *The Governance of England*, pp. 348–53.

71. *Proc. and Ord.*, v, 88–9.

72. *Cal. Pat. Rolls, 1436–1441*, pp. 276, 311.

who had bought Chirk for cash in 1418.[73] Fortescue cited this as the most glaring example of wanton alienation he could think of: 'Wherof never man see a precedent and God defend that any man see more such hereafter.'[74] Blacman quoted Henry's later adamant refusal of a substantial gift from the Cardinal's executors for his own use or to relieve the burdens and necessities of the realm, because Beaufort had been good to him in his lifetime. He also recorded the amazement of the executors at this answer.[75]

In 1450 Beaufort's heir was to claim that the sale of Chirk had been done in the Council[76] and so it may have been, but the probable conciliar reactions if it was so done are suggested by another comparable but well-documented instance. On 30 March 1443 John Beaufort, duke of Somerset, asked Henry in the Council at Eltham for 1,000 marks of land, the better to maintain his estate and to serve him. There was a good attendance, including Gloucester: 'in the whiche matier my saide lords being present absteigned hem in alle wise to speke nor durst not avise the kyng to depart from suche livelode ne to open their mouthes in suche matiers'. The king told him he could have land to the value of 600 marks, to himself and the heirs male of his body.[77] Later, on 28 May the wary Treasurer Cromwell refused to show Somerset, on his own authority, the 'books of such lyvelode as that he may gyve' that he might make his choice, without first getting the recorded agreement of the other five councillors present.[78]

Nevertheless, in spite of the difficulties, personal dangers and rivalries inherent in meddling with matters which were too high for them the Council were driven to make some attempt to supervise Henry's grants. A lengthy memorandum, apparently composed sometime in 1444, was designed to give them an oversight of his signet letters through the agency of the Keeper of the Privy Seal. They proposed to bind themselves by a special oath for this purpose.[79] This memorandum was actually authenticated by the royal sign manual, but even if it was at first accepted as a degree of conciliar supervision Henry soon made quite clear his determination to exercise complete personal freedom in all such matters by means of whatever warrants he might choose.[80]

It does not appear that Henry VI, apart from his distribution of largess, had much inclination at all for public business before 1445. But John Blacman's intimate description of court life is no picture of a timid, sainted

73. See above, p. 87.
74. *The Governance of England*, p. 134.
75. *Henry the Sixth* (ed. James), pp. 10, 32.
76. *Rot. Parl.*, v, 187.
77. *Proc. and Ord.*, v, 253.
78. *ibid.*, v, 281.
79. *ibid.*, v, 316–20.
80. *ibid.*, p. vi, and p. cxci, where the privy seal writ declaring the unquestionable validity of all his instruments, dated at Windsor on 7 November 1444, was first printed by Nicolas from the patent roll for 23 Henry VI. It was the custom of the privy seal office, when transmitting a signet office warrant, to adopt in its own instrument the place and date of the original signet warrant. Where a privy seal writ was dated at a royal palace or elsewhere away from Westminster this suggests that the original came from the signet office.

recluse. Henry, if simple-minded, was nevertheless ominously extrovert and censorious in those pious pursuits which interested him. From 1445 he conceived a novel interest in the conduct of the French war and began to pursue a policy of peace at any price, perhaps from genuine conviction, but most likely moved by the desires of his new queen.

By 1444 a hopeful, realistic peace policy had at last gained wide acceptance among his chief councillors, even though the reluctance in some influential quarters was obvious enough. C. L. Kingsford's scholarly account of these years,[81] now unjustifiably neglected, demonstrates how in Council and in parliament up to June 1445 this general consensus of opinion, embracing Gloucester, York and Suffolk, was founded on a belief that peace negotiations could be, and were being, conducted from a position of strength. This had been the English mood at the truce of Tours (May 1444) and lay behind the approving demonstrations at the arrival of the new queen in London in February 1445. On 4 June Suffolk received a singular demonstration of thanks from the Commons and Lords in parliament for his 'conservation of the peace in the king's laws within this realm, in repressing and expelling all manner, [of] riots and extortions within the same', for his knightly courage in the wars, for his honourable efforts to secure peace, and for the truce, so beneficial to trade. His efforts to use the truce to strengthen garrisons etc., in case further negotiations failed, was put on record. Gloucester, with other lords, rose in his seat to support the testimonial.[82] Once again the unity of the sphere of domestic and foreign affairs within which government prestige was gained or lost is apparent from this incident, though the contrast with the 'lack of governance', irresponsibility, and treachery alleged in 1450 could not be more striking.

Historians stress the basic unreality of Henry V's grandiose treaty of Troyes once the Burgundian and Armagnac feud had been healed and the full potential of France could be realized, but the immediate causes of the English crisis of 1449–50 went back no further than 1445. In July 1445 the French ambassadors reported the greater warmth which they received from the king than from his ministers and were made aware of the king's personal displeasure with his uncle Gloucester.[83] The fated surrender of Maine was first personally promised by Henry in October 1445, although he could only secure its half-hearted implementation even in March 1448. In the meantime the public degradation of his heir presumptive, his uncle Gloucester which brought on his death, seems, like the surrender of Maine, to have been his personal policy. There resulted four years of vacillation, procrastination, countermanding of orders and general conciliar confusion which

81. 'The Policy and Fall of Suffolk' in *Prejudice and Promise in Fifteenth Century England* (Oxford, 1925), pp. 146–76.

82. *Rot. Parl.*, v, 73–4.

83. Kingsford, *op. cit.*, pp. 159–60, quoting Stevenson, *Wars of the English in France* (Rolls Series), i, 110–11.

embraced Suffolk and the general in the field, Edmund Beaufort, as well as those councillors usually branded as hostile to peace. Henry's own wilful efforts gave to the single-minded French those military advantages which led to the catastrophic fall of Rouen in October 1449 and the utter collapse of English power in Normandy.

Unfortunately Kingsford treated Henry VI almost with as much deference and respect as was generally accorded him by his ignorant subjects. In the eyes of the Kentish rebels, although they complained that he considered himself 'above his laws to his pleasure',[84] his servants were to blame for teaching him so. His 'false Council' and especially the 'false progeny and affinity of the duke of Suffolk'[85] were responsible for everything that was amiss with Lancastrian government. Miss Hastings has warned us that men of substance in fifteenth-century England expected of the law not perfect justice, but the furtherance of their own objectives.[86] Yet the special pleading of the petitions and depositions of Suffolk's local enemies tend to be accepted at face value by modern writers, even if made by those whose 'insatiable covertise' in the royal service matched Suffolk's own.

That personal animosities among the Council were generated by these desperate five years of futility cannot be doubted. But the recipients of the king's bounty proved ineffectual in Council, in parliament and in their localities, not because of their own inabilities, rivalries, irresponsible greed and lack of patriotism, but because they were the agents of a royal master whose conduct was the very negation of kingship. Outrageous grants and financial stringency would never have made a parliamentary resumption practical politics without the political inanity and bankruptcy of Henry VI's personal rule.

84. *Three Fifteenth-Century Chronicles*, ed. James Gairdner (Camden Soc., 1880), p. 94.

85. *ibid.*, pp. 96–7.

86. Margaret Hastings, *The Court of Common Pleas in Fifteenth Century England* (Ithaca, N.Y., 1947), p. 237.

V

THE RESUMPTIONS OF 1450–6*

I. THE LEICESTER ACT OF RESUMPTION OF MAY 1450

The parliamentary act of resumption which received the king's assent at Leicester early in May 1450 was the result of persistent importunity by the Commons since the previous November.[1] Second only to their humiliation of the duke of Suffolk, the scapegoat for Henry VI's inanity, a resumption had become the Commons' panacea for all the nation's grievances: heavy taxation, the abuses of purveyance as exercised by the king's Household, and, through the great losses which many royal servants would undoubtedly incur by it, the effective punishment of all those stained with responsibility for lack of governance at home and the disasters abroad.

The subject inevitably aroused almost nation-wide interest. Oriel College, Oxford, petitioned for exemption when they heard 'as the common fame runneth' that there was to be a resumption.[2] A copy of a resumption petition was considered suitable material for inclusion in the commonplace book of a London citizen.[3] The gentlemen and commoners of Pembrokeshire received news of the passing of the first act with joy, but made haste to petition the king to safeguard their own interests.[4] So did the people of the Isle of Wight, who feared that an unpopular steward, recently dismissed, might seize the occasion of a resumption to get himself reinstated.[5] Tenants might refuse to pay their rents because of the resumption.[6] The Kentish rebels, who rose in arms while parliament was still sitting at Leicester, put a resumption high in their demands, claimed that those nearest the king were preventing the acceptance of the parliamentary

* This chapter is a revised and amplified version of part of my article, 'Acts of Resumption in the Lancastrian Parliaments,' published in *E.H.R.*, October, 1958.

1. 'And the commons of the parliament [i.e. which first met on 6 November 1449] laboured evermore that the king should admit and receive to have his resumption': *Six Town Chronicles*, p. 126. The chronicler thus regarded this agitation particularly as a continuation of the struggle waged in the previous parliament, when he had described the duke of Suffolk as the chief opponent of a resumption (*ibid.*, p. 125).

2. P.R.O., Special Collections, Anc. Petitions, S.C.8/6372A.

3. The imperfect copy of the 1451 petition referred to above, p. 113, appearing in Richard Arnold's commonplace book between a papal bull and a recipe.

4. 'thanks be al myghty God it [Pembrokeshire] is in our soverign lordes handes' (P.R.O., Augmentations Office, E.314/1), see above, p. 100.

5. '. . . it is noised here that by the Resumption this Isle shall stand in the king's hand, etc' (*Rot. Parl.*, v, 204–5).

6. The tenants of the prior of Christchurch, Canterbury, in Ludgate, London (*Cal. Pat. Rolls, 1452–1461*, p. 106) did so on the grounds of the 1451 act.

resumption petition, and professed to be acting in support of parliament's efforts.[7] Resentment against holders of crown lands and revenues who would suffer most from a resumption figured prominently in political lampoons:

'Ye that have the kyng to demene,
And ffrauncheses gif theyme ageyne,
Or else I rede ye fle;
Ffor ye have made the kyng so pore
That now he beggeth fro dore to dore,
Alas, hit shuld so be.'[8]

When Suffolk was removed from the political scene by the efforts of the Commons, Cromwell, Say, Beauchamp, Sudeley and the rest decided to try a limited policy of concession to their critics. Consequently they advised Henry to accept the resumption petition to quieten the persistent importunity in parliament, confident that they could best defend the interest of those most threatened by allowing and supervising a resumption 'in summe, but nat in alle'. These were the words of John Crane sending the news of its acceptance from the parliament at Leicester on 6 May 1450. He also mentioned the spate of private bills being submitted, many of them, no doubt, for exemption from the act, and told his master to hurry if he had any of his own to put forward.[9]

The petition for a resumption of all grants made since the first day of the reign (1 September 1422), together with fifteen modifying and largely uncontroversial clauses, was finally turned into an act of parliament simply by appending a brief royal assent to it.[10] The first grievance listed by the

7. Kingsford, *English Historical Literature*, p. 360; *Three Fifteenth-Century Chronicles*. ed. Gairdner (Camden Soc., New series, xxviii, 1880), p. 95; *Six Town Chronicles*, ed. Flenley, p. 130.

8. Political Songs (Rolls Series), ed. T. Wright, II, 229, the first verse of 'A Warning to King Henry', cf. verse 5:

'So pore a kyng was never seene,
Nor richere lordes alle bydene;
The communes may no more.'

These verses end with two latin lines:

'O rex, si rex es, rege te, vel eris sine re rex;
Nomen habes sine re, nisi te recte regas.'

9. *Paston Letters* (1904, library ed.), ii, 148 (no. 121).

10. Petition and royal assent: *Rot. Parl.*, v, 183–6 with modifying clauses printed as follows: (i) The queen. (ii) Eton and King's Colleges. (iii) The provisions of the king's will. (iv) Alien priory lands granted to churches, monasteries, colleges, hospitals, chantries. (v) Grants given specifically to maintain a dignity (e.g. viscount) on an accepted scale. (vi) Purchases made by Cardinal Beaufort for St Cross, Winchester. Interest in any possessions owned by any person before 1 September 1422 though that person only obtained possession of it after that date. Letters patent for restitution of lawful inheritance. Discharge of towns, etc., for over-payment of farm. (vii) Grants made by Henry VI to replace grants made by his predecessors and lost through no fault of the grantee. (viii) Ex-

petitioners in their preamble was once more the abuse of purveyance ('takyng of vitaile to youre Houshold, and other thinges in your said Reaume, and noght paied fore'), followed by heavy taxation and lack of execution of justice. They specifically stated the purpose of the proposed resumption to be 'the contentyng and paiement of the expenses and charges of your Houshold, and all your other ordinarie charges', with resumptions of revenues made in Calais to be assigned for wages of soldiers and garrison maintenance there. They asked that every source of revenue resumed should be made inalienable in the future. The king qualified his assent by excluding Calais and Ireland from the operation of the act and by reserving the right to add any provisos of exemptions he considered necessary, on the understanding that they were put in writing during the remaining life of the parliament.

We know that the act had only recently been passed on 6 May 1450 and parliament was dissolved about 8 June.[11] Added to the roll were 186 provisos of exemption.[12] From dates upon the original petitions for exemption it appears that the time limit set for admitting exemptions was no mere formality. Almost all those enrolled were reviewed by the Lords spiritual and temporal during the remaining life of the parliament at Leicester. The petitioners knew that even if the king accepted late petitions after the dissolution of parliament their legal validity might be doubtful. Hence perhaps the somewhat elaborate subscriptions put on two petitions for household men not presented in time, designed to prevent their validity being questioned.[13] No other petitions bear subscriptions of this kind and the latest date found on others is 6 June. The resumption was to take effect from 6 November 1449, the day on which the parliament had been assembled, and to cover all the royal grants of Henry VI's reign from the first day of the reign to the date of dissolution of the parliament (about 8 June 1450) unless exemption was obtained under the terms of the act.

When one considers that the act would render doubtful the legal validity

changes of land made with the king if a fair exchange. (ix) All lands which yielded their full value to the king as at the time of the grant. (x) Lands for which the king was a trustee. (xi) Wages at the scale operating under Henry V for the Chancellor, Treasurer, Keeper of Privy Seal, Barons of Exchequer and other officers. (xii) Letters patent to children born overseas to English fathers of foreign mothers granting rights of inheritance. (xiii) All grants to All Souls College, Oxford. (xiv) Grants to towns of freedom from the jurisdiction of the admiral of England or the wardens of the Scottish Marches. (xv) Grants of murage to towns.

11. *History of Parliament, 1439–1509, Register*, p. 115.

12. *Rot. Parl.*, v, 186–99.

13. Thomas Parker's, dated 8 August, was subscribed: 'per dominum cardinalem de mandato Regis infra parliamentum signeto facto' and bears the sign manual. The petition from Thomas Pope, whose proviso follows Parker's on the roll (*Rot. Parl.*, v, 198(b)), and so was probably of the same date or later, was marked 'per signetum factum in parliamento per testimonium J. Stanley et B. Hawley et aliorum': P.R.O., Chancery, Parliament and Council, C.49/62/51, 52.

of most of the royal grants entered on the patent, charter, and fine rolls between 1422 and 1450 a total number of 186 exemptions is not surprisingly large in itself.[14] Many of the exemptions had little if any connection with the alienation of crown lands and revenues. There were matters like the restitution of bishop's temporalities, letters patent of naturalization, and debts and obligations of state.[15] A number of provisos are accounted for by the royal approval given by patent under the great seal to family arrangements from which the king could only have profited by outraging accepted conventions.[16] Confirmations of benefactions touching the king's interest, made to the church by the king's family or others of his subjects, accounted for a number of exemptions. In many cases these exemptions concerned reversions of alien priory manors which contemporary opinion felt should not remain permanently in lay hands. Some exemptions were for charters granted to towns which involved civic authority and dignity or arose out of mere economic necessity due to flood, inundations of the sea, tempests etc.[17] A number of legitimate rewards for valuable public services were exempted, as these services had been costly to the doers.

Read consecutively on the parliament roll all these exemptions may give an impression of excessive largess and benevolence on the part of a medieval king to those who were set in authority under him, but in fact they represented no more than his normal duty. The crucial exemptions were personal ones for members of the government and their supporters, that is, for the household men. These exemptions actually appear at first sight to have been less likely to make the act ineffective than the other exemptions, because some of them specifically state that the grantees were to surrender certain of their grants. Nevertheless, what they gave up was only a fraction of what they retained. Further consideration of their exemptions reveals how they hoped to placate the interests clamouring for resumption while actually consolidating their own position about the king.

The original Commons' petition for a resumption had probably been under discussion for about six months before it was accepted. At some time before individual petitions for exemption began to be submitted a confer-

14. Students of the Lancastrian period, in the absence of contrary evidence, have assumed that the high number of 186 exemption clauses was sufficient to make the act ineffective. This should be contrasted with the claim of Professor J. D. Mackie that Henry VII in 1485 'found means to enrich the Crown by an enormous act of resumption', *The Earlier Tudors* (Oxford, 1952), p. 63. The act of 1485 contains 461 clauses of exemption. See below p. 198.

15. e.g. debts to Leonard lord Welles as Lieutenant of Ireland, to John earl of Shrewsbury as Steward of Ireland and to Humphrey duke of Buckingham as Captain of Calais.

16. e.g. to John viscount Beaumont, in possession of the lands of his wife's family the Bardolfs; to John Holt of Aston, Warws., as the heir of his cousin Margery; the settlement of the lands of the Beauchamp earls of Warwick; the dower and jointure of Jacquette, widow of the duke of Bedford and the interests of her husband Lord Rivers; to William FitzAlan, earl of Arundel, in the recovery of his family lands.

17. There were twelve grants to towns among the exemptions.

ence or committee of household men appears to have determined what each of their members should give up and what he should retain. This is shown by a contemporary document containing a list of 101 members of the Household headed by Beaumont, Say, Sudeley, Cromwell, Beauchamp, St Amand, Stourton, Hungerford, and Stanley, stating the amounts which the king had granted them to keep and also those which he had been moved to resume.[18] The form of the original petitions for exemptions submitted by some of the household men who appear in this list show that before they submitted these petitions they had been told what they would be allowed to keep and what they must be resigned to losing.[19]

The household men thus gave up only what they had agreed among themselves and with the king to surrender. Some of their surrenders can be seen enrolled in their provisos on the parliament roll and appear to amount to about £700 p.a. in total value. But Cromwell, Say, Sudeley and other chief ministers were given exemption in the widest possible terms on the roll and it is only from the paper list of 101 members of the Household that we know that they had agreed to give up anything. A combination of amounts from these two sources shows that these household men who held most of the crown lands and endowed revenues firmly in their grasp were prepared to make surrenders worth about £1,800 p.a. The amounts to be retained, as listed in the paper list, total rather less than £3,750, including a few reversions. These figures take no account of profits made from lands held at the rate of the extent, or wardships, *ad hoc* gifts of forfeitures, or innumerable special allowances and privileges which came the way of these men. Nevertheless, as a valuation of lands held rent free and of fees from offices at the ancient rate, it may well be a reasonably accurate figure.

Apart from the surrenders, totalling about £1,800 for the whole Household, this act of resumption could have had little immediate or ultimate effect on the state of the king's finances. Administrative action was dilatory and ineffective, though no doubt this was partly due to the disturbed state of the capital and countryside. No copy of the act was sent to the Exchequer until 15 October 1450, though exemptions were reaching them by 13 August 1450.[20] The Exchequer did not begin to send out its writs to the sheriffs ordering local enquiries about holders of crown lands and revenues until the spring of 1451.[21]

18. P.R.O., Exch., K.R., Miscellanea, E. 163, bundle 8, no. 14: 'Paper roll of resumptions by the Crown.'

19. These are in the main to be found in P.R.O., Chancery, Parliament and Council (C. 49), but some are in Ancient Petitions (S.C.8).

20. P.R.O., Exch., K.R., Mem. Rolls, E.159/227 (29 Hen. VI), 'communia', Mich., m.23; *ibid.*, 'brevia directa baronibus', Mich., m.2.

21. The dates of the Exchequer writs sent to the sheriffs under this act can be partly ascertained from their enrolled accounts called 'Sheriffs' Seizures' (P.R.O., Exch., L.T.R., E.379/175) and their *particule compoti*, some of which are in P.R.O., Exch., K.R., Various Accounts, E.101/330. Of 20 writs whose dates are given there 13 went out between 16 and

Nevertheless, in spite of its shortcomings, the acceptance of this first act of resumption at Leicester in May 1450 had actually brought about a state of great uncertainty among holders of royal lands and offices. There were even members of the Household ready to profit from the expected misfortunes of their colleagues. Many of the land-hungry gentry and nobility were prepared to take a chance on the market. 'As for the Duche on this side Trent', wrote Thomas Denys to John Paston, on 13 May 1450, 'Sir Thomas Tudenham had a joynte patent with the Duke of Suffolk, which, if it be resumed, Sir Thomas Stanley hath a bille redy endossed therof.'[22] At an earlier date (16 April 1450) John Hampton, an esquire of the body, had already prudently surrendered a life grant of Kempton manor in Middlesex and paid an increment to have it converted to a twenty-five-year lease. His colleague Thomas Daniel lost a rent-free life grant of Geddington (Northants.) and Lord Rivers took out a ten years lease of it at £28 p.a. as early as 2 June. Stephen Cote, a valet of the Chamber, who held the manor of Westley (Suffolk) for life at a rent of 13s 4d, found himself superseded on 3 June by two ushers of the Chamber who were willing to pay £5 p.a. for a twelve-year lease. By 20 February 1451 he had recovered it by offering £5 13s 4d for a twelve year lease himself.

Suffolk's family were not allowed to retain any of the royal lands which he had been given, whether granted for term of years, for life, or in fee. An esquire of the body, Philip Wentworth, was appointed receiver of the lordship of Cilgerran (18 May 1450), and Lord Beauchamp took out a twelve-year lease of the county and lordship of Pembroke (31 May 1450). There was some competition for Suffolk's manor of Swaffham in Norfolk. His Oxfordshire lands[23] were taken over by Lord Sudeley from Michaelmas 1450.

The dukes of York and Somerset who were abroad were both affected by this act of resumption. York had an exemption for his lieutenancy of Ireland only, and Somerset only for the lands he held as heir of his uncle, Cardinal Beaufort.[24] It appears that the king's ministers acted without partiality for

27 March 1451, 1 on 20 June 1451 (Kent), 1 on 7 November 1451 (Norwich), 2 on 3 December 1451 (Devon, Dover and Cinque Ports), 1 on 4 December 1451 (Worcs.), 1 on 7 December 1451 (Westmorland) and 1 on 13 February 1452 (Cumberland).

22. *Paston Letters*, ii, 150 (no. 123). Denys was referring to the stewardship of the duchy south of Trent.

23. Woodstock, Handborough, Wootton and Stonesfield.

24. The manors of Bassingbourn and Babraham which Somerset held in tail male were leased to Thomas Cotton, a citizen and draper of London, for twenty years (7 June 1450). Three months later the duke of Exeter and three others took out a lease on them for ten years. On 20 June 1450 the manors known as Gurney lands in Somerset and Dorset, which Somerset also held in tail male, were leased to Exeter and four others for ten years. John Everdon took a lease of York's manor of Hadleigh on 18 May, but on 7 September surrendered it and this too passed to Exeter. Lands and rents in Great Wratting, another of York's manors, were leased to Hugh Fenne, clerk of the Exchequer (25 May 1450). The king ordered Lord Beauchamp to see to the rule of the Isle of Wight which York held, and

either in their own scramble for self-preservation and, no doubt, for the preservation of what they considered to be the king's vital prerogative right.

A new parliament was summoned to meet on 6 November 1450. Taking stock of the position at this date we find that the sheriffs had as yet received no writs from Chancery or Exchequer to order inquisitions pursuant to the act of resumption. The Exchequer itself had only received a copy of the act some three weeks before. Nevertheless, there had been considerable activity in the transaction of new leases. A number of the king's subjects who had not been on the spot when the act was passed had good reason to feel aggrieved because the lands they held from the king had been given to others. Even York and Somerset appear to have been treated in this cavalier fashion. The men about the king had not only handled the rebellions of the summer with firmness and skill, but had also managed to preserve their hold over the king's patrimony in spite of almost nation-wide support for the efforts of the Commons in parliament to secure a drastic resumption. Although the king's chief minister, Suffolk, had been destroyed and the Treasurer, Lord Say, murdered by the mob, the rest had closed their ranks and, at the price of comparatively small concessions, were actually turning the resumption to their own advantage.

2. THE ACT OF RESUMPTION OF MARCH 1451

Such a half-hearted resumption was sure to come under fire as soon as a new parliament met and political circumstances favoured the government's parliamentary critics when this new assembly was summoned to Westminster for 6 November 1450. Late in August Richard duke of York, the king's most powerful subject, had returned unbidden from Ireland, had forced his way into the king's presence with an armed escort, had openly censured the policies of the last few years and had demanded changes. When the first session of the new parliament was only a fortnight old he and his kinsmen Norfolk and Warwick brought strong forces to the capital. York was reported to desire 'meche thynge qywch is meche after the Comouns desyre':[25] his chamberlain Sir William Oldhall was chosen Speaker. Edmund Beaufort, duke of Somerset, the next male heir of John of Gaunt and Suffolk's close associate, had in the meantime become the king's foremost counsellor. But on 1 December York's influence prevailed at court and the duke of Somerset was placed in 'protective custody'. York

Beauchamp was made steward there for life on 7 June 1450. The foreign accounts show that a receiver, Thomas Chamberlain, a valet of the Chamber, was appointed with effect from 6 November 1449 on 27 June 1450, but that he only acknowledged responsibility for the issues from the Nativity of St John the Baptist (24 June) 1450. Until that date York's officers continued to collect the rents. Full details of resumptions, together with new leases, taken mainly from the fine rolls, are given in Appendix 'C' below.

25. *Paston Letters*, ii, 174 (no. 142), dated October 1450.

had taken little part in politics at home or abroad before 1450. Now his successful intervention emboldened the advocates of resumption to put forward another petition because, as they justly claimed, the act of the previous parliament had 'not been effectually had'.[26]

Though the attitude of York no doubt increased its chances of success, this new petition was essentially a continuation of the policy consistently advocated in the two previous parliaments. It was in fact the petition which had already been accepted at Leicester in the spring of 1450, now submitted all over again but subjected to a very careful revision in the meantime. While much of the wording was repeated exactly, there were significant alterations. Whereas, for example, the original petition had made a generous exception for the king's new scholastic foundations at Eton and Cambridge this revised petition, while making some exemption for them, described their endowments as 'over chargefull and noyus'. A new request was made that all exchanges of land to which the king had been a party should be reversed. Most important of all, there was a clause in the new petition requesting the appointment of a committee to supervise all the king's future grants, consisting of the Chancellor, the Treasurer, the Keeper of the Privy Seal and six lords of the Council, who were to write their names on all letters patent authorized by them. Any person accepting letters patent not so subscribed would render himself liable to loss of title to all his freehold lands.[27] All grants etc., made by Henry from the first day of his reign (1 September 1422) to the last day of the new parliament were to be again annulled with effect from 6 November 1449, the operative date specified in the earlier act of 1450.

Judging from the bold temper of this petition, it was presented during the first session of the parliament, when the king was temporarily overawed by York's presence and prestige and in fact appears to have submitted to some form of conciliar control.[28] The Commons' petition was framed in the spirit of that moment when the king's prestige was low.

The answer to this resumption petition most probably came some time later and was framed in different circumstances. Shortly after Christmas Henry felt strong enough to have Somerset released from the Tower. His intention was to establish a balance between his two most powerful subjects. Both York and Somerset were employed on commissions of oyer

26. *Rot. Parl.*, v, 219(b).

27. cf. Fortescue's advocacy of conciliar supervision of grants in *The Governance*, pp. 143–4, 150, 153–4, 156; also *ibid.*, p. 349 and especially p. 351 (his advice to Warwick in 1470).

28. Thereby fulfilling a promise to York to appoint a 'sad and substantial Council, giving them more ample authority and power than ever we did before this': the king's answer to York's bill of complaint, *Paston Letters*, i, 84. Evidence that for a time the king did submit to a measure of conciliar control is supplied by a royal writ to the Exchequer dated 25 January 1451 cancelling an earlier restriction upon the validity of warrants not passed by advice of the Council, *Proc. and Ord.*, vi, 104.

and terminer in the troubled area of the south-east. Somerset was made Captain of Calais. Parliament, prorogued on 18 December, was summoned to reassemble on 20 January 1451. But the king left London on 28 January and made a royal progress in the south-east, a most unusual act for Henry VI. On 23 February he returned to London and 'rode right royally through the city'.[29] The petition for resumption now received a favourable but firm and considered answer. It was not accepted wholesale, like its predecessor, with a brief royal assent. This act of resumption consists of a detailed reply to the petition: those portions of the petition not specifically accepted were declared to be rejected, among them most notably the proposed supervising committee of the Council to licence the king's grants. Exchanges of land made by the king were to stand. His scholastic foundations at Eton and Cambridge were to have full immunity. The new act covering grants from the first day of the reign to the end of the parliament was to take effect, not from 6 November 1449, but from Lady Day 1451. The exemptions which the Commons had themselves made to their petition were accepted and the king reserved the right to add what further exemptions he pleased during the remaining life of the parliament. Parliament was again prorogued on 29 March, reassembled on 5 May, and was dissolved some time between 24 and 31 May, by which date the king had added forty-three provisos of exemption in all.[30]

Sir James Ramsay was quite mistaken in assuming that all the 186 provisos of exemption made to the previous act of resumption at Leicester in the spring of 1450 also automatically applied to this new act.[31] In fact none of those 186 exemptions, least of all the personal ones which had largely rendered the earlier act ineffective, applied to the second act unless specifically re-enacted as exemptions to it. The forty-three provisos of exemption to the new act, with very few exceptions, were framed on general not personal lines. The chancery and receipt rolls show beyond any possible doubt that the resumption, which had been begun half-heartedly at Leicester in the previous summer, was now made effective.

On 2 August 1451 writs were sent out by the Chancery under the great seal in patent form to sheriffs and escheators throughout England, containing a copy of this act and the exemptions, and ordering inquisitions to be held under their joint supervision pursuant to this new act. Identical instructions also went out to the chancellor of the county palatine of

29. *Chronicles of London*, ed. C. L. Kingsford, p. 162.

30. Petition, answer and provisos of exemption are printed in *Rot. Parl.*, v, 217–25. The petition had provided for exemption for the queen, limited exemption for Eton and King's Colleges and Pembroke Hall, Cambridge, grants of alien priory lands in 'spiritual men's hands', leases made by treasurer's bill at truly competitive rates, salaries of officers of state, law officers, and civil servants, money due to the duke of Buckingham as Captain of Calais, and grants to corporate bodies of various kinds.

31. *Lancaster and York*, ii, 139–40.

Lancaster, the constable of Dover and Warden of the Cinque Ports, the constable of Calais and the mayor and escheator there, and to the chancellor of Ireland for transmission to all sheriffs and escheators in Ireland. All lands, tenements, annuities, privileges, franchises, and offices, granted by the king since the first day of his reign (1 September 1422), were to be taken into their hands with effect from 25 March 1451 and extents made. Details of these extents were to be sent to the Exchequer on the morrow of All Souls Day under penalty of £1,000. This time the escheators, not the sheriffs, were to be held accountable for the issues of the resumed grants.[32] When these writs of great seal were sent out some of the sheriffs had still not received the writs under the exchequer seal ordering similar inquisitions to be held pursuant to the previous act. The two acts were now operated concurrently. The second act supplemented the first; it did not render it void. The sheriffs held inquisitions and made returns for issues falling within the scope of the first act between 6 November 1449 and 25 March 1451 and they and their successors were held accountable for these.[33] The escheators and their successors rendered accounts from 25 March 1451 based on separate inquisitions held jointly by sheriffs and escheators under the terms of the new act.[34]

Action at Westminster did not wait upon sheriff's and escheators' returns. The act of parliament destroyed the validity of grants and leases the moment it was passed. Exemption from it could only be obtained while parliament was sitting. By 1 June 1451 the parliament had dispersed, and only forty-three exemptions had been made. Consequently there was a spate of new leases of crown lands taken out in June and July 1451. In the last three months of the year, when the sheriffs' and escheators' returns were being received at the Exchequer, the number of these new leases suddenly rose again. At least eighty-five new leases were made in 1451. Then the rate fell sharply until stimulated again by a further resumption in 1455 which to some extent further supplemented the two earlier acts.

As a result of the acts of 1450 and 1451 there were at least seventeen cases of alienated estates and properties recovered and let out to farm for terms of years at the rate of the extent, several cases of alienated estates kept in hand after recovery, and at least forty cases where life grants were changed to leases for terms of years only. In addition, a number of life grants resumed were not granted or farmed out again, and in at least thirty-five cases leases for terms of years were shortened and/or the farms raised. All new leases were made subject to a condition imposed by the act of resumption of 1451, namely that the rate of the extent should be the basis,

32. *Cal. Fine Rolls*, xviii, 229–30.
33. The enrolled accounts are P.R.O., Exch., L.T.R., Sheriffs' Seizures, E.379/175.
34. The enrolled accounts are P.R.O., Exch., L.T.R., Escheators' Accts, E.357/41.

but that any man who would offer to pay more without fraud should have the lease in preference, unless the holder would himself match or surpass the competitive offer.[35] Some resumed lands were for the time being retained in the hands of local officers, as in the case of the duchy of Cornwall lands, where this could easily be done. In other instances where farmers or grantees were displaced and the lands kept in hand, special officers and auditors had to be appointed.[36]

There appears to have been no political discrimination against would-be lessees of the resumed lands. In many cases the existing holders, including the household men, took them back on the new terms. A marked increase in the number of jointly-held leases and even syndicate leases, many to men who made no appearance on the political scene, suggests that financial considerations were now briefly allowed to be of primary importance.

The act of 1451 also annulled various liberties and privileges and also many annuities, not merely on land, but on other sources of revenue including the customs at the ports. The very greatest suffered in this way, including both York and Somerset, as well as most of the household men. The patent rolls show that many of these annuities were quickly regranted and back-dated to 25 March 1451. But the escheators' particulars of accounts and enrolled accounts under this act list over seventy annuities which were now resumed and were not regranted or replaced by others, as far as search of the chancery calendars can show.[37]

Without the resumption the parliamentary appropriation made in 1450 for current expenses of the Household from the revenues of royal lands, sheriffs' issues, feefarms, customs, ulnage etc., to the total of £11,002 6s 1d p.a. would most probably have been quite ineffective. It is very difficult to find evidence from the chancery calendars or exchequer records that any of the amounts charged on the king's lands in this appropriation were available when it was made. For example, in the case of seventeen items examined there seems to have been only about £150 available in May 1450 to meet a charge of almost £2,700. However, the same records show that from Easter 1451 there was certainly £1,700 available in the case of these seventeen items, due to the resumption of rent-free grants, grants at

35. New leases counted between the years 1450 and 1458 total: 1450, 16; 1451 and 1452, 102; 1453 and 1454, 24; 1455 and 1456, 40; 1457 and 1458, 22. They range from whole lordships like Pembroke and substantial groups of a dozen manors or more like the Gurney lands to single tenements in London. For full details see Appendix 'C' below.

36. e.g. the king's lands in the counties of Cardigan and Carmarthen and the honour of Richmond lands in Lincolnshire, Norfolk, Suffolk, and Cambridgeshire.

37. *Particule compoti* are in P.R.O., Exch., K.R., Various Accts, E.101/330, nos. 2, 3, 5, 6, 8, 10, 11, 12, 13, 15, 16, 17, and *ibid.*, Escheators' Accts, E. 136/238/3. The enrolled accounts are *ibid.*, L.T.R., Escheators' Accts, E. 357/41. These sources together do not provide a complete set of returns under the act. For a list of the resumed annuities see my Oxford D.Phil. thesis 'The Crown Lands and the Parliamentary Acts of Resumption, 1399 to 1495', pp. 326–8.

nominal rents and annuities and to the making of new leases.[38] Sheriff's issues, feefarms, customs and ulnage appropriated to the Household in 1450 were similarly freed by the resumption of annuities.

The immediate effect of the resumption on the national finances can best be gauged from the receipt rolls. Prior to the resumption not only were cash payments by farmers or keepers of crown manors at the Exchequer negligible but assignments made on them were almost equally so. As a result of the resumption, farms and rents from the resumed lands reappear on the rolls as sound assignments for current household expenses, for the defence of the borders and the payment of debts.[39] The prayer of the Commons that the resumption might 'take good and effectuell conclusion' had thus at last been answered. There could now be little cause for complaint. While declining to accept those portions of the petition which infringed his prerogative the king had been moved to further a genuine resumption. The uniquely lavish grants and alienations of 1437–50 were almost entirely undone. York, Somerset, and other great nobles, lords, knights, and esquires of the Household had surrendered grants in fee and grants for life in a manner quite unprecedented in English history. The rates of farm for crown manors had been significantly increased by competitive leasing. In addition there was a marked reduction in the value of annuities and pensions on the king's lands, on feefarms and on the issues of the counties, on the ulnage and on the customs and subsidies at the ports. Henry's parliamentary critics thought that the crown lands, effectively administered, could provide a worth-while contribution to the current expenses of the king's Household. Throughout their efforts to achieve a resumption, solvency in the royal Household had been central to their aims, the heart of the more general idea that the king should 'live of his own'. If the king's resources were still gravely inadequate for the

38. i.e. details of grants, leases and annuities for Bradwell, Hadleigh, Havering (Essex and Herts), Kingsthorp, Fawsley, Geddington, Brigstock (Northants.), Swaffham (Norfolk), Bassingbourn, and Babraham (Cambs.), the Gurney manors (Soms. and Dors.), Woodstock, Cookham and Bray (Oxon. and Berks.), Marston Maisey (Wilts.), Rockingham Forest (Northants), the counties of Cardigan and Carmarthen (S. Wales), Pembroke and Cilgerran lordships, Isle of Wight manors. See below, Appendix 'C'.

39. This statement is based on an examination of the receipt rolls from Michaelmas 1446 to Easter 1452 (P.R.O., Exch. of Receipt, E.401/796, 800, 804, 807, 808, 811, 814, 816, 820, 821, 824, 827). Note especially assignments made on the king's lands in the two periods May–August 1451 and June and July 1452 for John Stourton, treasurer of the Household, John Merston, treasurer of the king's Chamber, William Cliffe, clerk of the works, Henry Percy, warden of the East Marches, William Cotton, clerk of the Great Wardrobe, for money owed to Richard duke of York, and for fees and wages of the officers of the Exchequer etc. Very few were cancelled. Dr Steel in his book *The Receipt of the Exchequer, 1377–1485*, makes no reference to this significant change on the receipt rolls except for a brief note on p. 237 under Easter 1451 that 'all the larger drafts were unexpectedly on the hereditary revenues'. Following Ramsay he summarily dismisses the resumption, describing the act of 1451 as 'even more useless' than its predecessor of 1450: *op. cit.*, p. 236.

legitimate expenses of government he now had a very strong claim on the generosity of parliament.[40]

The next parliament, which first met at Reading on 6 March 1453, was indeed the most co-operative assembly Henry VI ever summoned. His stock had undoubtedly risen throughout the country. King's men were more acceptable in the constituencies;[41] the knights of the shire were more co-operative than ever they had been before. One is reminded of Fortescue's affirmation that the king who made a thorough resumption by act of parliament would be amply rewarded: 'And yff it [the king's livelihood after a resumption] wolde not than be so gret, I holde it for undoubted that the people off his lande woll be well wyllunge to graunte hym a subsidie, uppon suche comodites off his reaume as bith be ffore specified, as shall accomplishe that wich shall lakke hym off such livelod.'[42] Henry had made the gesture. No new kind of taxation such as Fortescue anticipated might be required was actually forthcoming,[43] but this assembly did respond with an act of generosity for which there were only two precedents in English history:[44] a life grant of the subsidy on wool, the tax on aliens and of tunnage and poundage. In addition they raised the rate of subsidy from denizens by 10s a sack to 43s 4d, the level enjoyed by Henry V, and demonstrated their patriotism by raising the level for aliens to the unprecedented figure of 100s. By the end of its second session the king had been granted one-and-a-half tenths and fifteenths and a force of 13,000 archers, apparently for service at home. On 2 July 1453 he thanked the Commons in

40. This 1450–1 parliament made no grant of supply. In addition to the resumption it enacted that a strict priority payment of £20,000 for two years from Christmas 1450 should be enforced for the defence of the realm on the customs of London and Southampton with exemptions only for the wages of the Calais garrison and for those who had lent the king money, with special mention of the Merchants of the Staple: *Rot. Parl.*, v, 214. This measure prevented payment of £1,000 p.a. of Queen Margaret's dower in 1451 and 1452 (*ibid.*, v, 258–60).

41. There certainly was a higher number of members of the Household elected to this parliament. Professor J. S. Roskell gives the following figures: 47 members of the Household (20 knights and 27 burgesses) being 17 per cent of the total House of Commons elected in 1453 compared with 17 members of the Household (3 knights and 14 burgesses) being 6 per cent of the total House of Commons elected in the 1450–1 parliament: *The Commons in the Parliament of 1422*, p. 136.

42. *The Governance of England*, pp. 136–7 and cf. p. 143.

43. A sales tax on the Burgundian and French models, *ibid.*, p. 133.

44. To Henry V immediately after Agincourt and to Richard II at Shrewsbury during the so-called tyranny (1398). This new sense of interest and purpose between king and Commons also resulted in a display of hostility towards the over ardent supporters of York and of loyal enthusiasm towards the king hitherto unknown during his reign. An 'act of resumption' was passed known only from its recital on the roll of the 1455–6 parliament which repealed it as casting doubts on the allegiance of some of the king's subjects: *Rot. Parl.*, v, 329–30. It was directed only against those who had taken the field at Dartford with York, and those who had contrived to be specially exempted 'by name of baptism' for fee simple grants from the resumption of 1451. This latter provision can have affected very few men: Ralph lord Cromwell and possibly one or two others. It is not a true act of resumption but rather a fore-runner of the acts of forfeiture and attainder.

person, a new departure for Henry VI, like his recent royal progresses. Special efforts were now being made to present him to his subjects as a public-spirited, effective monarch. The parliamentary roll specifically records the words of the brief sentence which he addressed to the Commons 'ore suo proprio'. The Chancellor then followed him to declare what great personal labours Henry had made in the cause of law and order on behalf of his Commons during the parliament and on his progresses, in order that they might carry back favourable reports of him to their homes.[45]

The limited but real success in their financial aims had to be balanced against the real danger to the king's prerogative inherent in acts of parliament calculated to restrict his power freely to dispose of his landed patrimony. One of Fortescue's most specious arguments in *The Governance* is that restraint on the king's powers of alienation would, in fact, be no restraint of the prerogative.[46] No action had been taken on the request of the first resumption petition that the resumed revenues should be made inalienable. In this Reading parliament the royal family were now endowed with the best of the resumed lands and there is no evidence that the advocates of resumption saw any contradiction here.[47] In March 1453, following a petition of the Commons, the king's two half-brothers Edmund of Hadham and Jasper of Hatfield were solemnly declared legitimate, created earls, and endowed with the lands of Richmond and Kendal and of Pembroke respectively.[48] They also received a number of other resumed manors in 1453 and 1454. When provision had had to be made for Queen Margaret's dower in 1446 there had been no land available with which she could be endowed and she had received only a general reversionary claim on the king's lands. Since the resumption the assertion of her reversionary claim had temporarily secured her the lordship of Pembroke lands, but in 1453 she surrendered her claim to these and by authority of parliament received a permanent endowment of other resumed lands in part satisfaction of her dower.[49] As a result of these arrangements for the royal family the parliamentary appropriations on the hereditary revenues for the

45. *Rot. Parl.*, v, 236.

46. *The Governance*, p. 121.

47. Compare the situation in the early years of Henry IV's reign when the same parliament which petitioned for a resumption also petitioned for a better endowment of the queen, the king's younger sons, the Beauforts and Edward duke of York: *Rot. Parl.*, iii, 547, 612; and when Queen Joan received an increase in income from crown lands it was specifically stated to be pursuant to the request of the Coventry parliament: *Cal. Pat. Rolls, 1405–1408*, p. 438. For the similar request in 1377, also coupled with a demand for a resumption, see J. G. Edwards, 'Some Common Petitions in Richard II's first Parliament', *B.I.H.R.*, xxvi (1953), 203, 207.

48. *Rot. Parl.*, v, 250–4.

49. *ibid.*, v, 260–3. For Queen Margaret's lands see also *Foedera* (1727 ed.), xi, 155; *Cal. Pat. Rolls, 1446–1452*, p. 559; *ibid.*, *1452–1461*, p. 340. The accounts of the keeper of the Wardrobe of the Household show that Queen Margaret's receiver, under her obligation to pay £7 a day to the expenses of the king's Household, contributed nearly £12,000 in the eight years from Michaelmas 1446 to Easter 1454 (E.101/409/20).

expenses of the Household would clearly be affected. The appropriation of 1450 was in fact annulled from 17 April 1454 and a new detailed appropriation for the Household substituted with a reduced ceiling of 10,000 marks p.a.[50]

3. THE 'YORKIST' ACT OF RESUMPTION OF 1455–6

To end the story of the Lancastrian resumption at this point on a note of success and co-operation between king and parliament would, of course, be unrealistic. While it is certainly true that in some ways the summer of 1453 must have appeared the most auspicious point in Henry VI's period of personal rule, in others it was the most disastrous. Even the final loss of Gascony may have been a blessing in disguise, but the king's first attack of helpless insanity, which followed within a brief time of his speech of thanks to parliament,[51] was an overwhelming catastrophe. This was probably due to enforced constant attention to affairs of state since 1450 which proved entirely beyond his powers to sustain. It brought to nothing all attempts to create a strong and solvent kingship and shattered any illusion that this could ever be attained under such a king. Politics degenerated into an open struggle for power between York and the queen.

In these radically changed circumstances less than two years passed before a petition for a further resumption was submitted.[52] This petition was presented in the first session of the 1455–6 parliament which ended on 31 July 1455.[53] Less than two months previously the Yorkist lords had taken the field against the king's Household at St Albans. As a result they were in forcible control of the government, were apprehensive lest parliament would not approve their actions and had made strenuous efforts to influence the elections.[54] Undoubtedly their endeavours were sufficiently successful

50. *Rot. Parl.*, v, 246–7. The details of the assignment given appear to be incomplete. They do not amount to 10,000 marks. The exchequer copy (K.R., Mem. Rolls, E.159/231 (33 Hen. VI), 'communia', Mich., m.39), is identical, but a copy in Ancient Petitions (S.C.8/24/1187 B) has an additional item at the end of the list which is crossed out.

51. Possibly in July and certainly by early August 1453.

52. The accounts of the keeper of the Wardrobe of the Household show a spectacular and unique drop in receipts from the Exchequer from Easter term 1453. £6,105 7s 1½d for Michaelmas Term 1452 was well above average. For Easter Term 1453 receipts were only £552 0s 4d (E.101/409/20). They substantially recovered by 1455: Easter 1455 £5,390 12s 8½d; Michaelmas 1455 £5,205 1s 10¼d (E.101/410/15). The accounts for most of 1454 do not survive.

53. *Rot. Parl.*, v, 300–20 (petition, answer and 143 provisos of exemption). The petition undoubtedly belonged to the first session (9–31 July 1455). *The History of Parliament 1439–1509, Register*, p. 217, erroneously places it in the third session. The act took effect from Michaelmas 1455 and the petition requested this operative date in the form '. . . from the Fest of Seint Michell th'Archangell next comyng . . .'. It could not have been presented in the second session which did not begin until 12 November 1455.

54. See Stubbs, *op. cit.*, iii, 178 and references to *Paston Letters, Proc. and Ord.* and *Rot. Parl.*, there cited.

to enable them to give an anti-Lancastrian bias to this petition.[55] Yet it is important to realize that all sections calculated to infringe the king's prerogative were carefully removed before this petition was accepted. The act itself in its final form cannot therefore be considered partisan.[56] However, in the autumn of 1455 the king again became totally incapacitated[57] and York held the office of Protector from 17 November 1455 until 25 February 1456 when the king appeared in person in parliament and relieved him of it. Consequently for much of the period during which petitions for exemption were being submitted to the Lords spiritual and temporal the Yorkist lords were in complete control.[58] How they used this act of resumption to carry out a thorough reduction of annuities and pensions still held by members of the king's Household is shown by the survival of the original petitions for exemption as submitted by grantees, with the comments of the 'Lords spiritual and temporal' upon them, scaling down their grants before any exemption was allowed.[59]

When it was known that the king was recovering it was thought in some quarters that this resumption would not go forward, a view which adds support to the belief that it was being applied in a partisan manner.[60] However, it was carried out,[61] its effects on annuitants and pensioners being

55. For example, the resumption of all duchy of Lancaster lands placed in the hands of feoffees either by the king or his father to perform their wills was specifically requested; the petition also requested that Queen Margaret's dower should not exceed 10,000 marks; no exemptions were requested for the king's two half-brothers Jasper and Edmund Tudor; the petitioners sought to have any exemptions the king might wish to make sent to them first for their approval.

56. It was accepted, saving the king's prerogative in all things; a request in the petition that the penalty of the Statute of Provisors and a forfeiture of 1,000 marks should apply to all who contravened the act was specifically rejected; the king reserved the right to make such exemptions as he pleased by advice of the Lords spiritual and temporal, to be put in writing during the lifetime of the parliament; and there was to be no question of submitting these provisos of exemption for the Commons' approval. Complete exemption was made by proviso for the queen and for the king's two half-brothers.

57. There appears to be no evidence that he was actually insane: see J. R. Lander, 'Henry VI and the Duke of York's Second Protectorate, 1455 to 1456', *Bulletin of the John Rylands Library*, xliii (1960–1), 46–69.

58. Parliament was dissolved on 12 March 1456.

59. P.R.O., Special Collections, Ancient Petitions (S.C.8) and Chancery, Parliament and Council Proceedings (C.49) *passim*. Examples of these are given in my D.Phil. thesis Appendix 'C', pp. 345–8. None of the original personal petitions for exemption from this act bear the king's sign manual. Almost all those for exemption from the 1450 act do so.

60. *Paston Letters*, iii, 75 (no. 322); 9 February 1456, John Bocking to Sir John Fastolf, 'The resumpsion, men truste, shall forthe, and my Lordes of Yorkes first power of protectorship stande, and elles not, etc.'

61. Inquisitions held by sheriffs and escheators under writs of great seal dated 10 July 1456. The enrolled accounts rendered by the sheriffs are P.R.O., Exch., L.T.R., Sheriffs' Seizures, E.379/174, continued in *ibid.*, E.379/177. An example of *particule compoti* is P.R.O., Exch., K.R., Sheriffs' Accts, E. 199/30/27 (Norfolk and Suffolk). It shows that the sheriff and escheator also received copies of exemptions and that they held inquisitions at Ipswich on 24 September 1456 and in the shire house at Norwich on 26 September 1456.

mitigated to some extent by means of letters patent under the great seal, regranting what had been resumed and back-dating the regrants to Michaelmas 1455. A certain number of new leases, operative from Michaelmas 1455, began to be taken out in November 1455.

The preamble to the act again deplored the insolvency of the royal Household in the strongest language so far used, the burden of its purveyance upon the king's subjects, the encouragement given to the king's enemies by its dishonourable reputation and by his subjects' open resentment at its conduct, and contrasted this situation with the worshipful, noble, and honourable estate of the Household kept in the days of that victorious prince of most noble memory, his father, Henry V. Once more this new act of resumption was closely associated with new detailed appropriations for the expenses of the Household, which follow it immediately on the roll, again stressing the primary purpose of these resumption proposals.[62] The king again exercised his undoubted prerogative right by setting aside the best of the estates resumed under this last Lancastrian act of resumption for the endowment of the infant prince of Wales.[63] The impact of this act on the crown lands was not very great, not primarily because of partisan action and its subsequent annulment, but because of the effective resumption of 1451: as a result of it the residue of crown lands which were not now held by the royal family had already been almost entirely leased out for terms of years at the rate of the extent plus the best increment obtainable under the exchequer farming system. Further financial improvement in this quarter could only be made at the expense of the royal family, or result from new acquisitions of crown lands, or from more effective methods of administration and financial exploitation.

4. THE SIGNIFICANCE OF THE RESUMPTIONS

These Lancastrian parliaments were thus characterized by their growing reluctance to make money grants without some evidence of retrenchment; by their persistent endeavour to obtain a more stable and purposeful direction of public affairs; by their close contact with public opinion; and by their eager response to any gesture of co-operation from the throne. In this setting their acts of resumption, especially in 1450 and 1451, must

62. *Rot. Parl.*, v, 320–1; *Cal. Pat. Rolls, 1452–1461*, pp. 295–8. These combined appropriations totalled £6,520 9s 5d for the year 1455–6, i.e. almost 10,000 marks as in the previous parliament.

63. Notably the Gurney lands in Somerset and Dorset. This resumption also freed the duchy of Cornwall and Welsh lands from certain grants. When the infant prince of Wales was endowed with the duchy and principality and with the earldom of Chester in this parliament (*Rot. Parl.*, v, 293–5) assignments made on these lands for the king's Household were specifically reserved and all surplus revenues above a sum for the prince's own household were also to be employed for the expenses of the king's Household and for no other purpose.

be treated as the seriously intended measures which they undoubtedly were. In 1451 a stage was temporarily reached in the history of the Commons in parliament when they were able to insist that the conspicuous waste and abysmal failures arising from Henry VI's misconduct of national affairs would be no longer tolerated. The final disasters of the great foreign adventure had produced a political and financial crisis even more acute than in the years 1404–6, and this provided the opportunity to achieve drastic retrenchment and reform. Had the Commons been demanding that all normal expenses of government should be met out of the revenues of crown lands and feudal dues and that national expenditure should be commensurate with those revenues then they might legitimately be considered foolish and impractical critics. But they were not demanding this. They believed that the 'king's own', efficiently administered through an Exchequer backed by parliament, could be made to finance a just, stable and solvent 'governance' of the realm. Living on the king's own meant, simply, living on all manner of resources which were legally his. As the Cade rebels complained, the opposite of this was the king who treated the bodies and goods of his subjects as if they were his own; this could not be good law they maintained because 'the contrary is trew, for then nedyd hym nevar perlement to syt to aske good of his comonys'.[64] The essence of this demand had come to be the financing of the royal Household by means of specific appropriations backed by acts of resumption, embracing every possible source of royal income which they thought could be recovered.

A more detailed examination of the Lancastrian acts of resumption than was possible to Stubbs and Ramsay suggests that although they were forced upon an unwilling government in the first instance, they were in the end made effective to a significant degree. The amount of alienation of crown lands and revenues between 1437 and 1450 had been unique and had undoubtedly mirrored the weakness and ineptitude of Henry VI's government. Nevertheless, the resumption of these lands and revenues in the interest of retrenchment and solvency, in spite of the enthusiasm of parliament and Sir John Fortescue for this course, might have done more harm than good, by depriving the king of the means of exercising his legitimate and vital political influence, not only at the centre, but also locally in the shires. The detailed history of the acts passed, however, shows that even under such an ineffectual ruler as Henry VI his professional advisers were able to ensure that these crucial interests were in fact safeguarded at every stage against undue restriction and against partisan exploitation in the legislation which resulted, until the manifest recurrent insanity or total incapacity of the king introduced new problems which were beyond the constitutional resources of the age. While the king's vital power of alienation was thus preserved, the resumptions of 1450 to 1456 do seem to have

64. *Three Fifteenth-Century Chronicles* (ed. Gairdner), p. 95.

marked a turning point in rewards for high office received by fifteenth-century royal servants. The myth of an early Tudor preference for middle-class servants has been exploded, but the fact remains that the barons, viscounts, earls, marquises and dukes of Henry VI's personal government obtained through royal service elevation in social rank and commensurate landed endowments on a scale never again equalled by the royal knights and esquires of the Yorkist kings and Henry VII. In this sense the Lancastrian resumption legislation was a successful expression of public opinion against one aspect of conspicuous waste in government which had reached a peak in 1450.

As regards the crisis of royal authority due to the personal character and ability of Henry VI, which was made acute by recurrent attacks of madness or total mental and physical incapacity, this impasse was only surmounted by the accession of a strong young king in 1461 who was in full possession of his faculties and victorious in battle, a king who surrounded himself by men influential in the House of Commons, many of them commoners, able and not afraid to take the initiative in government under his leadership. The policies of parliamentary opposition in the Lancastrian parliaments then became governmental policies under the Yorkists. Here lies the answer to the obvious query as to what became of the Commons' dogged determination after 1461. Yorkist kings and Commons, unlike their Lancastrian predecessors, found themselves able to unite in a policy of resumptions and forfeitures accompanied by a reorganization of royal lands and revenues designed to strengthen the monarchy along the lines so persistently advocated in Lancastrian parliaments.

VI
THE CROWN ESTATE OF THE YORKIST KINGS

I. EDWARD IV'S ACTS OF RESUMPTION

A large-scale reassessment of English government during the Yorkist period is badly needed.[1] Bishop Stubbs first published his account in the *Constitutional History* in 1878. Until very recently more modern writers on matters of government did not evince the same deep belief in the relevance of individual character and, even more so, of personal morality to the issues under discussion, beliefs which made Stubbs somewhat too prone to rely on the vivid anecdotes of Tudor chroniclers. Much of the original colour and force of his narrative therefore disappeared from later accounts. Nevertheless, his general theme remained intact: the period was still described as the twilight of constitutional government in the medieval sense, and as the early dawn of a 'New Monarchy'. Whereas Stubbs saw in the person of Edward IV 'a spirit defying and ignoring constitutional restraints', Jolliffe made the nation itself a partner in a desire to forsake the 'normal constitutional government of the day', whose form was described as 'a council of notables, a right course of common law, the king to live of his own'.[2] Parliament of that time was still described as a discredited institution. Stubbs wrote of the manipulation of parliamentary institutions and quoted Hallam in support of a belief that the reign of Edward IV was the first in our history which saw no single enactment to further the liberty and security of the subject. Jolliffe wrote of a decline of parliament accompanied by a lack of public interest and a widespread failure of confidence in institutions. He quoted Professor H. L. Gray whose analysis of so-called Commons' petitions attempted to show a marked decrease in the amount and importance of such legislation.[3]

The most recent general accounts do suggest that a more realistic picture of the nature of Yorkist government is at last emerging. Professor Wilkinson

1. For a brief attempt to summarize the results of recent research see my *Yorkist and Early Tudor Government, 1461–1509* (Historical Assoc. 'Aids for Teachers', no. 12, 1966, reprinted 1969).

2. J. E. A. Jolliffe, *The Constitutional History of Medieval England* (1937), p. 490.

3. H. L. Gray, *The Influence of the Commons on Early Legislation*. The mistranslation of 'communes petitiones' as Commons' petitions, and the assumption that petitions under that heading were the work of the House of Commons is a most serious mistake in a book which draws its conclusions from a classification of measures on the rolls of parliament. A common petition was not necessarily either sponsored or adopted by the Commons before being submitted to the king.

now stresses the Yorkist kings' constant awareness of their need for the approval of public opinion, and their conscious promotion of the good of the realm.[4] Professor Chrimes now emphasizes the revived importance of the king from 1461 as the actual, rather than merely the nominal, source of administrative action.[5] Even while Jolliffe was writing, important suggestions for a new line of approach were being made by Pollard, but they seem to have passed unnoticed. In 1936 Pollard suggested that the apparent eclipse of parliament under Edward IV was due rather to the impotence of the Crown under Henry VI than to the suppression of parliament under Edward IV; that Edward IV recovered an initiative in public legislation last exercised by Edward I; that perhaps for the first time here was a king more at ease with the Lower than the Upper House of parliament; an excellent speaker himself, adept at establishing a new relationship of confidence between the king and the Common House; that from 1461 parliament ceased to regard the government as the enemy which it had become under Henry VI, and a new concept of the Crown in Parliament was born.[6]

A study of the crown lands and of parliamentary interest in them under the Plantagenet, Lancastrian and Yorkist kings certainly does not support the older interpretations of the events of 1461–85, any more than it does the concept of a medieval 'constitution'. A 'council of notables' in the late-fourteenth and the fifteenth centuries was indeed the only possible substitute for kingship during the minority, sickness, or imbecility of the king, but at all other times the king chose and directed his Council unhampered by any conventions. The importance of a 'right course of common law' throughout English medieval history certainly cannot be doubted, especially as regards the ownership of land. But it is still hard to discount the distorting influence of seventeenth-century political and legal antiquarians whose determined searches for precedents in the medieval period influenced the course of modern historical writing through Hallam and Stubbs. The antiquity of a medieval concept that the king should 'live of his own' has been greatly overstressed and its true meaning distorted ever since Sir Robert Cotton carried out elaborate researches into, and deductions from, medieval records during the reign of James I. This expression probably arose in the first place in the fourteenth century from the hated abuse of household purveyance by which the king fraudulently converted to his own use the goods and chattels of his subjects. Its close association with household purveyance was maintained to the end of the Lancastrian period, when parliamentary acts of resumption appeared to offer the best means of achieving household solvency, and when the recovery of lost resources of

4. B. Wilkinson, *Constitutional History of England in the Fifteenth Century, 1399–1485* (1964), pp. 138–68 *passim.*

5. S. B. Chrimes, *Lancastrians, Yorkists and Henry VII* (1964), pp. 96–148 *passim.*

6. A. F. Pollard, *Parliament in the Wars of the Roses* (Glasgow University Publications, xlii, 1936), pp. 12, 15, 18–19, 28.

the crown lands became the principal objective of these acts of resumption. Stated in general terms this concept meant that the king should attempt to live within the limits of his income from all sources and be seen to be striving towards that end. No government before 1461, either of king or Council, had ever paid even lip service to a notion that the king's ordinary expenses should be met out of the revenues from his crown lands and feudal dues and be commensurate with those revenues. Such a notion is pure seventeenth-century politics. There was no form of medieval constitutional government, tacit or expressed, which included the axiom that the king should 'live of his own' in this sense.

The Lancastrian assemblies were endeavouring to invigorate a weakened monarchy by increasing its endowed revenues. Unfortunately such a plan itself required a strong king. When Henry IV had failed them in the early years of his reign they could do no more than put their trust in conciliar government, though not even the weakest of kings had ever consented to rule under any form of conciliar tutelage. The Council certainly had great power in England between 1406 and 1437 due to the partial incapacity of Henry IV in his later years, to the absences abroad of Henry V in pursuit of the foreign conquest which he felt to be necessary for the establishment of his house, and to his early death, which left an infant to succeed him. But this was a period when traditional policies were naturally followed at home and therefore no concerted policy of husbanding or augmenting the king's land revenues was ever apparent. Nevertheless, the Council had no power to alienate royal lands, and mutual suspicions and jealousies kept some check on their wanton misuse. During the personal rule of Henry VI a combination of weak and purposeless authority at the centre, of a royal family few in numbers and low in prestige, of expensive and unsuccessful foreign war, and of frequent parliaments called to grant heavy taxes, fostered the spirit of informed criticism in the Commons. At this time a lavish distribution of the king's favours and an alienation of his lands and revenues without precedent in English history, gave grounds for a mounting outcry against an insolvent royal Household living off the land, and against the burden of direct taxation. It led to parliamentary appropriations on all manner of revenues from the customs, crown lands, tenths and fifteenths etc., for current household expenses and, ultimately, to the passing of parliamentary acts of resumption, which were supported, from whatever motives, by Richard duke of York.

There is, indeed, much to be said for Pollard's view that with the accession of Edward IV the king recovered the initiative in public legislation which was expected of the monarch, and which had last been exercised by the strong Plantagenet kings. The policies of parliamentary opposition under the Lancastrians do indeed appear to have become governmental policies under the Yorkists. Thus parliament was able to work with the king rather than in opposition. There can be no doubt about the partnership developing between the Crown and Yorkist parliaments, whether we see in it merely a restoration of a much older tradition, or whether we regard it as something new, arising from the higher status and reliability of parliaments which had been attained during the time of testing and development which Lancastrian 'lack of governance' had provided.

The events of 1449–56 had partly arisen out of a resistance to further parliamentary taxes until policies were radically changed and government made effective. Stubbs thought that the frequent Lancastrian parliaments were a mark of constitutional advance and the less frequent parliaments which sat longer under the Yorkists he considered to be evidence of parliamentary manipulation by the king. Yet in spite of Stubbs's belief that subservient parliaments never refused or begrudged any tax to Edward IV, the fact remains that the incidence of direct parliamentary taxation asked for and received under the Yorkist kings was less than half the yearly average enjoyed by Henry V and Henry VI.[7] Although both Henry VI and Edward enjoyed grants of indirect taxation throughout their reigns, Henry VI had to wait for a life grant of it (the wool subsidy, and tunnage and poundage) until the thirty-first year of his reign and the seventeenth year of his majority. That Edward IV received this favour in the fourth year of his reign should be taken as a measure of the Commons' greater confidence in Edward, rather than as evidence of their increasing subservience.[8] The frequency of Lancastrian parliaments had been generally conditioned by the dependence on parliamentary grant. In co-operation with his parliaments, and with all other interests willing to help him, Edward IV and his advisers set about devising other forms of revenue not so dependent.

In 1467 Edward IV addressed the Commons in person. He began as follows, his words being recorded on the parliament roll:

> 'John Say, and ye Sirs, comyn to this my Court of Parlement for the Comon of this my Lond. The cause why I have called and summoned

7. During the 48 years of the reigns of Henry V and Henry VI parliament granted 26⅔ tenths and fifteenths and a number of special land taxes. During the 24 years of Yorkist rule the whole of the direct parliamentary taxation granted (including the experiments of 1463 and 1472) was equivalent to only 6¾ tenths and fifteenths, reckoning one tenth and fifteenth as equivalent to rather less than £32,000. To say that the yearly average in the Yorkist period was half the average in the Lancastrian period is therefore making a generous estimate of the total amount of Yorkist taxation, because some of the Lancastrian taxes were granted without the hardship deduction which became normal from 1433 onwards (i.e. they were unqualified grants, yielding in theory rather less than £38,000 instead of rather less than £32,000). In 1433 parliament began to deduct £4,000 from each whole tenth or fifteenth for allowance to certain areas on the grounds of hardship experienced by them in meeting taxation. In 1445–6 this deduction was permanently raised to £6,000 for each whole tenth and fifteenth granted and all the Yorkist grants were at this higher rate of deduction.

8. See above, p. 136, and below, p. 197.

this my present Parlement is, that I purpose to lyve uppon my nowne, and not to charge my Subgettes but in grete and urgent causes, concernyng more the wele of theym self, and also the defence of theym and of this my Reame, rather than my nowne pleasir. . . .'[9]

The articles which the Yorkist lords had sent to the archbishop of Canterbury in 1460 and published at large had included the complaint that Henry VI had no 'livelihood of the Crown of England whereof he may keep his honourable Household, which causeth the spoiling of his said liegemen by the takers of his said Household, which livelihood is in their hands that hath been destroyers of his said estate and of the said common weal'. These articles went on to request that 'it will please his said good grace to live upon his own livelihood',[10] and not 'find his said Household upon his poor commons without payment'. When one recalls the earlier support given by York for the Commons' identical demands in the resumption struggle of 1450 and later, one might almost describe the royal affirmation of policy to parliament in 1467 as made in a Yorkist tradition of constitutional principles, which Edward IV was pledged to follow. There can be no doubt that the king's words on this occasion made an impact on his listeners and that they did express a policy with which he came to be personally identified, because George Neville, Clarence, and Warwick thought it worth while to quote them against him as an unfulfilled promise in the manifesto which they issued from Calais on 12 July 1469.[11] This speech should not be dismissed as mere lip service to a time-worn constitutional ideal which Edward thought would please the subservient Commons. It appears rather to have been a proffer of alliance in an attempt to give effect to policies repeatedly advocated in the Lancastrian Commons and now favoured by a strong young king who was in full possession of his faculties, victorious in battle, in royal descent not inferior to his Lancastrian predecessors, and surrounded by commoners who proved able and not afraid to take a lead in government under his direction. Prominent among such men were Sir John Fogge, Sir John Scott, John Elrington, Thomas Colt, Sir Thomas Vaughan, Sir John Say, Sir Richard Fowler, Sir Richard Croft, Peter Beaupie, Nicholas Sharpe, Nicholas Leventhorpe, Avery Cornburgh, Geoffrey and Maurice Kidwelly. In the offices of treasurer of the Chamber, treasurer of the Household, under-treasurer of England, king's solicitor, chancellor of the Exchequer, keeper of the Mint, and in the highest offices of the duchies of Lancaster and Cornwall and of the earldom of March they shared control of the government of England. Some were soldiers, some lawyers; all were capable administrators and might even be called permanent

9. *Rot. Parl.*, v, 572.
10. *An English Chronicle*, ed. J. S. Davies (Camden Soc., 1856), pp. 86–7.
11. Printed by J. O. Halliwell in the notes to his edition of *Warkworth's Chronicle* (Camden Soc., 1839), p. 51.

officials. It is significant that in an age of revolution all of those mentioned, with the exception of Sir Thomas Vaughan, died in their beds. They were the lay successors of the competent clerical administrators employed by the king in an earlier age. Under their guidance, and with royal support, government became less factious and controversial. Such men survived to serve Richard III and Henry VII, and trained others to take their places. They can be found among those exempted from each of the king's parliamentary acts of resumption which played an important part in policy. Most of them were also House of Commons men, symbolizing in their two functions a basic identity of interest between the king and the Commons. Such men played a vital part in conscious efforts to provide a measure of that 'good governance' which the wider body of their fellows were demanding in parliaments as the price of loyalty and service to the king.

The malaise of English government between 1437 and 1460 was largely cured simply by the usurpation of the strongest and ablest male member of the larger royal family, once he had succeeded in establishing his authority. In the words of K. B. McFarlane 'the [civil] war was fought because the nobility was unable to rescue the kingdom from the consequences of Henry VI's inanity by any other means'.[12] In the favourable new climate of purposeful kingship which followed the Yorkist victory, Edward IV's professional advisers made significant changes in the organization of government which do appear to have been designed to enable the king better to live of his own in the sense in which public opinion at that time understood and demanded such a course of action. An office in the king's Chamber was developed to take the place of the Exchequer as the controlling organ of government finance. From 1461 its coffers were fed by certain land revenues collected for it by special receivers, and other sources of revenue besides the issues of crown lands later made even more significant contributions to chamber resources. In the latter part of the reign two extensive units of regional government were established, one for Wales and the West, based on the young prince's council at Ludlow, and the other for the Scottish border and the North of England, based on Richard duke of Gloucester and his council there. Both of these were largely financed from their endowments of land revenue. As regards Edward IV's central royal Household it appears to have set new standards of economy and solvency for most of his reign. The constant moans of parliaments during the Lancastrian era against the abuses of household purveyance ceased to be recorded on the parliament roll between 1461 and 1483. The Yorkist endeavours to avoid the notorious 'shabby indigence' and 'expensive inefficiency' of Henry VI's Household, and to achieve economy and efficiency by means of effective regulations and ordinances, has recently

12. 'The Wars of the Roses', in *Proceedings of the British Academy*, L, 97 (Raleigh Lecture on History, 1964).

been thoroughly explored by Dr Myers.[13] According to Dr Myers's figures the cost of the royal Household in the closing years of Edward IV's reign was lower than it had ever been in the reign of Henry VI or was to be under Henry VII. From 1462 all exchequer farms and feefarms worth 40s or more were put in charge of special receivers for payment direct to the treasurer of the Household. From 1466 all the issues and profits of the king's coinage and mines in the duchy of Cornwall and the customs and subsidies on tin and lead were appropriated to current household expenses.[14] Edward also began the practice of supplying the treasurer of the Household with working cash direct from his Chamber. The queen's household was made to function on a much reduced financial scale compared with the households of the Lancastrian queens.

Unfortunately Yorkist chamber finance was secret finance, and any attempt to produce figures for the contribution which land revenues made to the cost of government is even more difficult in these changed circumstances than under the Lancastrians or earlier. It is possible to cite many instances where payments were made to the treasurer of the Household or into the king's own coffers, some of them substantial, but no annual estimate or total can be given. There is some evidence that the Yorkist Exchequer continued to produce declarations of the state of the realm,[15] but these do not appear to have survived, and, in any case, the Exchequer under the Yorkist Treasurers of England was no longer in possession of all the relevant information required to compile a comprehensive statement such as Lord Cromwell, and probably his Lancastrian successors, had presented to the Council and parliament. There is, in fact, nothing to suggest that the amounts of land revenue received by Edward IV's government were ever sufficient to demote direct and indirect taxation as the main sources of public finance. Indeed, the reappearance on the parliament roll in 1483, less than three months before his death, of a detailed exchequer appropriation of £11,000 to the current expenses of the Household, which is once again there stated in the old Lancastrian phrases to be made by the king in response to the Commons' complaints of the grievous burden of household purveyance, suggests that Edward's disposition of his lands and their revenues at the end of his reign did not leave sufficient from this source even to meet his household expenses. Out of this assignment of £11,000 only £4,500 was to be contributed by land revenues, the rest coming mainly from the customs. Richard III, by contrast, apparently in comparative affluence as a landowner, was able to set aside nearly £12,000 p.a. from his lands for the current expenses of his Household, but with the

13. A. R. Myers, *The Household of Edward IV* (Manchester University Press, 1959). The figures are on pp. 45–6.

14. *Cal. Pat. Rolls, 1461–1467*, p. 519.

15. Cited by J. R. Lander in *B.I.H.R.*, xxxii (1959), 150.

accession of Henry VII this contribution from land revenues was reduced to under £10,000 and further reduced to £6,000 in 1495.[16] Such figures must be taken to demonstrate the limited financial importance of the crown lands in all three reigns, even under the purposeful management of these kings.

Nevertheless, an inability to produce figures for the total land revenues of Edward IV does not lessen the importance of administrative changes taking place during this reign in which royal lands were very much concerned. These administrative changes are discussed at length in the two following sections. But Edward's policies were to quite a considerable extent debated in parliament and by its authority declared and publicized. Before discussing their impact on the machinery of government it is desirable to consider them in so far as they were revealed in parliamentary legislation.

Following his speech to the Commons, made early in June 1467, the king submitted to them a schedule or proposal for a resumption drawn up in the form of an act of parliament. On 1 July through their Speaker the Commons recalled his declared disposition and intention to live of his own when they returned this bill to him with their assent to it. Through his Chancellor, Edward thanked them for their labours upon it.[17] Each of his two previous parliaments (of 1461–2, 1463–5) had also passed acts of resumption, fortified by acts of attainder and forfeiture where necessary. The first of these, in 1461, took the form of a petition to which the royal assent was given. It is described in the marginal heading on the roll as a 'declaration of the royal title and restitution to the same'. According to the official formula it was presented to the king *per prefatos Communes* and agreed by him *ad requisitionem Communitatis predicte*: 'at the request of the Commyns beyng in the same parliament'. It was, therefore, from the evidence of the roll of the parliament, a petition by or on behalf of the Common House,[18] although its content and wording suggest that Edward's professional advisers played a considerable part in drafting it. The act itself bears no designation as an act of resumption. It is only in some of the exemption clauses appended to it that it is so described. It was designed to declare the king's legal title to the throne, his assumption of it from 4 March 1461 and the taking into his hands of all the possessions[19] of his predecessors, starting with those held by Richard II on 21 September 1399 and embracing everything held or granted away by the Lancastrian kings. All this was done with effect from 4 March 1461, with no back claim made to any issues

16. See below, p. 196. 17. *Rot. Parl.*, v, 572–6, 618. 18. *ibid.*, v, 463–75.

19. No single comprehensive term was considered appropriate to describe these. They are listed as castles, manors, lordships, honours, lands, tenements, rents, services, fees, feefarms, knights' fees, advowsons, gifts of offices, fairs, markets, issues, fines, amercements, liberties, franchises, prerogatives, escheats, customs, reversions, remainders and all other hereditaments with their appurtenances.

from them enjoyed by anyone before that date. However, the 'moderations, provisions and exceptions' made by Edward IV to this act consisted not only of various grants made by the Lancastrian kings which, on consideration, he did not propose to disturb, but also confirmations of his own grants to offices, lands and revenues made since his accession. This shows that the act was taken legally to invalidate his own grants made between 4 March 1461 and its acceptance by parliament on or before the prorogation on 21 December 1461.

Its main purpose was, however, to give Edward undisputed legal title to all the possessions and rights of the Crown, while freeing him from any automatic obligation to observe arrangements and dispositions made by the 'usurping' kings of Lancaster. Obviously this act could not quite achieve all that was required, particularly since no 'resumption', 'declaration' or 'assuming' could make Edward undoubted heir to the lands of Lancaster. Therefore it was closely followed by an act of attainder against specific individuals, headed by Henry VI, by which the lands and possessions of Lancaster became Edward's like any other forfeited estates, and were declared a body corporate, continuing to be known as the duchy of Lancaster.[20] Subsequent to the passing of this act of attainder against Henry VI and his supporters, a further twenty-two articles in the form of petitions were deemed necessary to confirm various acts of his Lancastrian predecessors or of himself after due consideration and modification where necessary. Another one was respited for further consideration and one was refused outright.[21]

The form of this act of attainder differs significantly from the act of resumption. It is prefaced on the parliament roll by a statement (in Latin) that: 'A certain schedule containing the form of an act was exhibited to the aforesaid Lord King in the present parliament. . . .' The act is followed by the statements that this schedule was transported to the Commons, their assent was declared and then, the measure having been read, heard, and fully understood in parliament, the king, by the advice of the Lords spiritual and temporal gave his assent. This schedule was therefore a draft of an official bill, first placed before the king by his advisers, sent to the Commons and then to the Lords for approval, and then receiving the final royal assent together with any provisos of exemption or qualification which the king subsequently approved. The form of this act of attainder is important because all three of Edward's later acts of resumption followed it exactly.[22] In short, after the first petition of the Commons for a resumption the king took the initiative in this kind of legislation for the rest of his reign.

20. *ibid.*, v, 476–83.

21. *ibid.*, 489–93.

22. For purposes of comparison of the introducing words see *ibid.*, v, 476, 514, 572, and vi, 71. For the final enacting formula see *ibid.*, v, 482–3, 517, 576 and vi, 73–4.

The most important lands recovered to the Crown by these acts of 'declaration', 'assuming', 'resumption' and attainder in 1461, apart from the duchy of Lancaster, were the lands of Queen Margaret, the Tudor lands (i.e. the crown lands which had been bestowed by Henry VI on his half-brothers Jasper and Edmund Tudor), and the Beaufort lands like Chirk and Chirklands (which had passed from the crown in fee simple to the Cardinal, and so to his heirs the Beaufort dukes of Somerset).

The resumption acts of 1465[23] and 1467[24] continued the policy of augmenting the king's own. They resumed into the king's hands all lands etc., which he had held at any time since the first day of his reign, by virtue of the Crown, as part of the duchy of Lancaster, the duchy of Cornwall, the principality of Wales, the earldom of Chester, and as the heir of his father, Richard duke of York. The 1465 act excluded from its operation the dispositions which Edward had made of lands forfeited by those attainted in 1461, with the exception of the lands of Henry VI and Queen Margaret, but the subsequent acts of 1467 and 1473[25] included a review of all his grants of attainted lands made throughout his reign.

All these Yorkist acts of resumption were partly intended to improve the king's finances. The 1467 act was introduced into the Commons by the king as an earnest of his intention to 'live of his own'. The 1473 act had sandwiched within it a provision for reviewing all outstanding royal debts alleged to have been incurred between 4 March 1461 and 1 December 1470 and charged on the revenues of York and March, Lancaster or Wales. These were now to be paid off, provided they proved genuine, in equal instalments spread over twenty years. The most reliable of the Yorkist chroniclers, who was no slavish admirer of Edward, described this 1473 act as part of the king's personal endeavours to amass a treasure worthy of his royal estate 'de propria substantia propriaque industria sua' and stated that the king applied the whole of the revenue of the lands which he resumed to supporting the expenses of the Crown. But the same chronicler, when describing the autocratic tendencies of his rule in his latter years, noted that much of the royal self-confidence came from his careful placing of his castles, manors, forests and parks throughout the kingdom in the keeping of his most trustworthy servants. According to the chronicler his control in this respect was so effective that the shrewdest malcontent, wherever he might be, found himself charged with any disloyalty to his

23. *ibid.*, v, 514–48. To take effect from 2 February 1464 and to annul all grants of the king from his accession to that date, unless exempted.

24. *ibid.*, v, 572–613. All grants of Edward IV from his accession to be void from Easter 1467 unless exempted.

25. *ibid.*, vi, 71–98. Resumption from 21 December 1473 ('From St Thomas the Apostle that shall be in the year 1473') of everything held by Edward IV on 4 March 1461 or later, unless exempted. Enrolled accounts for all Edward IV's acts of resumption are in P.R.O., Exch., L.T.R., Sheriffs' Seizures, E.379/176, 177.

face before he could cause trouble.[26] One cannot doubt that the financial yield of his lands was important to Edward, but his acts of resumption were primarily important to him as instruments of political control through the exercise of patronage.

The two acts of 1465 and 1467 were intended in the first place to complete the endowment of the royal family in the persons of the king's two younger brothers, George and Richard (already partly accomplished after the 'resumption' of 1461), and of his queen, Elizabeth Wydeville. The act of 1465 specifically excluded a large body of crown manors and feefarms intended for the queen from being made the subject of exemption from the act. During the year ending at Michaelmas 1467 the queen's receiver-general, John Foster, handled receipts of over £4,500 p.a. from royal land revenues.[27] After the resumptions of 1461 and 1465 George duke of Clarence, the elder of the king's two brothers, had an income of 5,500 marks p.a. guaranteed out of lands at the disposal of the Crown, and the prospect of reversions worth another 1,000 marks. He was given lands in Kent, Wiltshire, Somerset, Dorset, and Gloucestershire, and succeeded to the lands which had been given to Edmund Tudor, earl of Richmond, in the previous reign. Clarence's position was consolidated from newly forfeited lands stretching across the whole of the southern counties and in the North.[28] The endowment of Richard, the younger of the king's brothers, did not proceed so smoothly. The king's first thoughts were to endow him in the West of England, the Welsh Marches and in the North. His obligations to the Herberts forced him to withdraw his grant of the lordship of Pembroke and its dependencies. At first he gave Richard the whole of the Richmond inheritance, then withdrew it in favour of Clarence. Richard was finally left with Gloucester and Corfe (but Clarence had St Briavels and the Forest of Dean), and with the Beaufort lands. To these were added appropriate forfeitures.[29] Before many years had passed the treachery of Clarence

26. The Croyland chronicle, as printed in *Rerum Anglicarum Scriptores*, ed. W. Fulman (Oxford, 1684), i, p. 559, 562. This is the part usually described as the second Croyland continuation, whose author is credited by Kingsford with an 'inner knowledge of political events' during the last ten years of Edward IV's reign (*English Historical Literature*, p. 184).

27. P.R.O., Exch., Treas. of Receipt, Misc. Bks, E.36/207. The principal grants to Queen Elizabeth are in *Cal. Pat. Rolls, 1461–1467*, pp. 430, 433, 445, 463, 464, 525; *ibid., 1467–1477*, pp. 419, 539, 540, 543, 561, 562, 566; *ibid., 1477–1485*, p. 169. She was deprived of her lands by Richard III: *Rot. Parl.*, vi, 263; *Statutes*, ii, 498 ('An Act for Annulling Letters Patent made to Elizabeth, late Wife of Sir John Grey').

28. The principal grants to George duke of Clarence, are in *Cal. Pat. Rolls, 1461–1467*, pp. 198–9, 212–13, 226, 328, 331, 362, 366, 388, 452–5, 484; *ibid., 1467–1477*, pp. 88, 330, 457–8, 594. The patent of 18 March 1472 included a clause that neither by authority of parliament, nor in any other way, should any lands hitherto granted to him be taken away. No patent under the great seal could save him, however, against the act of resumption of 1473 or the attainder of 1477. His attainder is in *Rot. Parl.*, vi, 193–5, signed with two sign manuals of the king.

29. The principal grants to Richard duke of Gloucester, are in *Cal. Pat. Rolls, 1461–*

gave Edward cause to reflect that his first thoughts on the endowment of his brothers might well have been in the best interests of his throne.

The purpose of the last Edwardian act of resumption in 1473, within a general review of grants, was two-fold: to undo the considerable rearrangements of crown lands and revenues which the advisers of Henry VI managed to effect in the short six months of his Readeption, and, with parliamentary authority, peacefully to curb the power of George duke of Clarence, who, a traitor to his royal brother, had been intimately concerned in those rearrangements. In this latter task the king and his advisers were at first only partially successful. Five years later (in 1478) a parliament was called specially to endorse the fulfilment of this policy, which had had to be pursued, in the attainder of Clarence, to a conclusion almost certainly not contemplated when it was first begun.

Bishop Stubbs deplored the end of Clarence as the 'summing up and crowning act of an unparalleled list of judicial and extra-judicial cruelties . . .'; '. . . no voice was raised for Clarence; no tax refused or begrudged'.[30] Stubbs's eloquent lament for the passing of Lancastrian 'constitutional' government should not be allowed to obscure the really important issues involved in this truly unparalleled destruction by the King in Parliament of a brother who had been, until a few years before, the heir presumptive to the throne. Edward had always kept a careful eye on the nature and extent of the possessions of his subjects. Even apart from the wider measures of resumption and forfeiture he was able on a number of other occasions to take back what he had once given and to effect exchanges of lands among the recipients of his gifts.[31] He was also able to find money to buy land when it came onto the market.[32] Effective powers of persuasion, purchase and intimidation were vital to any medieval king who aspired to control the activities of the over-mighty subject. Edward's own brother Clarence, in whom he had placed the maximum power and trust, had revived this

1467, pp. 197, 212–13, 228; *ibid., 1467–1477*, pp. 94, 139, 179, 260, 266, 297, 466, 483, 549, 560; *ibid., 1477–1485*, p. 90. Later as Edward tried to curb the power of Clarence so he increased the power of Richard who had received the entailed Neville (i.e. Salisbury) lands in the North. The division of the inheritance of the unfortunate dowager countess of Warwick (i.e. Beauchamp or Warwick and Spencer lands) between Clarence and Gloucester is in *Rot. Parl.*, vi, 100.

30. *Constitutional History* (4th ed.), iii, 226, 281.

31. The following are a few examples: Lord Sudeley surrendered Sudeley castle to Edward. Geoffrey Gate surrendered the royal manors in the Isle of Wight to Anthony Wydeville lord Scales, in exchange for some lands in Essex belonging to Richard Wydeville earl Rivers, and Jacquette his wife (1465). John Neville surrendered the earldom of Northumberland in 1470 by word of mouth. In 1475 Sir William Stanley received Chirk and Chirklands held by Richard duke of Gloucester, who received Skipton in Craven, Yorks., held by Stanley. In 1479 Edward took back the county and lordship of Pembroke and members from William Herbert for the prince of Wales and compensated him with the Gurney lands in Soms. and Dors. recovered from Clarence.

32. e.g. 2,600 marks for part of the lordship of Holt in 1478 (P.R.O., Exch. of Receipt, Warrants for Issue, E.404/76/4, m.23) mainly from a clerical tenth.

danger in its acutest form: the over-mighty subject spawned from the innermost circle of the royal family. Clarence showed a complete disregard for the king's wishes in his marriage to the eldest daughter of Warwick. During the Lancastrian Readeption he acted with the basest treachery when he entered into a compact of support for the Lancastrian cause. This guaranteed him possession of a major part of the crown lands of England including all the earldom of Richmond lands, together with most of what his brother had already given him, and most of the lands held at that time by his brother's queen, Elizabeth Wydeville.[33] After Edward's restoration, Clarence seemed to be almost beyond his control.

Edward had power to use a parliamentary act of resumption against the greatest lord when he wished to do so. Some years prior to the Neville family's desertion he had given them a demonstration of that power.[34] It may be that Clarence defied him in 1472–4 when he tried to take back from him by resumption some of the lands he had previously given. Royal officers charged with the duty of making effective the parliamentary act of resumption of 1473 may have met with obstruction and rough treatment at the hands of Clarence's officers.[35] With effect from 1474 the king's agents were successfully recovering crown lands held by Clarence in Nottinghamshire and Derbyshire, backed no doubt by the power of the royal castle of Nottingham,[36] but elsewhere in the shires they had little success. On 18 July 1474 Clarence even secured a confirmatory grant by patent of many, though not all, of the crown lands he held.[37] While stubbornly hanging on to all the king had given him he was at the same time avidly pursuing every scrap of the vast Warwick inheritance, in spite of the king's great anger.[38]

Edward feared that Clarence had the power and intention to disturb the peace of the kingdom and possibly usurp the throne. The open contest

33. *Cal. Pat. Rolls, 1467–1477*, pp. 241–3 (3 March 1471).

34. In 1467 Edward spent Christmas at Coventry where he 'restituit archiepiscopo [i.e. George Neville] terras de Penely et Widestone ab eo prius ablatas per resumptionem': 'William Worcester', *Annales* (Rolls Series), in *Wars of the English in France*, ed. J. Stevenson, ii, 789.

35. The king's surveyor and receiver for Soms., Dors., Devon and Cornwall (where Clarence held many crown lands including the Gurney manors), Geoffrey Kidwelly, feared to be maimed or murdered and asked the king to discharge him from his office: P.R.O., Exch., K.R., Mem. Rolls, E.159/252, 'brevia directa baronibus', Mich., 15 Ed. IV, m.17d.

36. See below, p. 166.

37. *Cal. Pat. Rolls, 1467–1477*, pp. 457–8. Notable absences from the confirmations included his lands in Notts. and Derbys. and the Gurney lands in Soms. and Dors. The Croyland chronicler states that many attributed the new dissension between Edward and his brother to Clarence's resentment at his loss of Tutbury and many other lands under the general resumption (*Rerum Anglicarum Scriptores*, i, 561, under date 1476).

38. In 1473 Sir John Paston wrote: 'The Duke of Clarence maketh him big in that he can, showing as he would but deal with the Duke of Gloucester: but the King intendeth, in eschewing all inconvenients, to be as big as they both and to be a styffeler atween them. And some think that under this there should be some other thing intended, and some treason conspired. So what shall fall can I not say': *Paston Letters* (Library ed.), iii, 38.

between Clarence and his brother Richard for the Warwick lands and this more dangerous and uneasy contest between Clarence and his brother the king continued unresolved for several years, but on 16 January 1478 a parliament was at last summoned to pass an act of attainder against Clarence. His execution did not follow immediately[39] and it was the Speaker of the House of Commons who urged upon the king the need to have it speedily carried out. As Stubbs wrote, no voice was raised in parliament in support of Clarence. The Commons had no cause to defend him. Where the policy of strengthening the Crown through general acts of resumption met resistance a parliamentary act of attainder proved effective even against this most powerful and privileged of the king's over-mighty subjects.

Before turning to the administrative side of Yorkist policy towards the royal lands, it is necessary to say something about the numerous clauses of exemption appended to each of Edward's acts of resumption. In 1461 there were 86, in 1465 288, in 1467 282 and in 1473 221. Here a word of warning will not be out of place. Writers on the Lancastrian and Yorkist periods, following Sir James Ramsay, have uncritically assumed that the numerous exemptions made from all acts of resumption before 1485 rendered the acts ineffective. If these acts were rendered ineffective by a maximum of 288 exemptions, what about Henry VII's act of resumption in 1485 which had 461 exemptions? Yet this act of 1485 has been called 'the great act of resumption' by Professor Dietz, and other historians of the Tudor period have been even more lavish in praise of its effectiveness.[40]

Each of these exemptions was the result of separate petition. When an act of resumption was pending common prudence prompted many people to assure their position by a petition for personal exemption. Any person who, in the past, had made a bargain with the king, had secured royal approval under the great seal to alienate lands or to change an interest in a grant, or had been the recipient of some royal favour or grant by patent, might desire the security of a special proviso without waiting to study the legislation proposed. This explains why some of the personal exemption provisos appended to these acts of resumption were also covered by general exemptions made in the body of the acts, and so appear superfluous.

An exemption was no formal thing. There can be no doubt that to petition for, and perhaps obtain, a special proviso could be a lengthy and costly

39. Edward signed the warrant for the execution of sentence on 7 February 1478 in parliament: *Rot. Parl.*, vi, 195.

40. F. C. Dietz, *English Government Finance, 1485–1558* (University of Illinois, Studies in the Social Sciences, ix, no. 3, 1920), p. 21; K. Pickthorn, *Early Tudor Government, Henry VII* (Cambridge, 1949), p. 17; Professor J. D. Mackie, *The Earlier Tudors 1485–1558* (1952), p. 63, states: 'the fact is that he (Henry VII) found means to enrich the Crown by an enormous act of resumption'.

business. Abbot Wheathampstead's archdeacon spent five weeks at Westminster making sure of the abbey's exemption to the 1461 act.[41] Nevertheless, time and money were considered well spent in view of the vexation which might otherwise follow at the Court of the Exchequer, even if no worse were to befall. Litigation against third parties, who were only too ready to intervene if any prospect of disputing an existing title presented itself, was a further probability to be avoided. Whether or not the king himself exacted a special fee for giving his approval to an exemption is not known. But Edward IV's interest in them was close and personal. From the evidence of hundreds of original provisos which passed to the clerk of parliament and his staff for enrolment, and which survive,[42] there does not seem to have been a single one during the whole reign which was not signed by Edward himself.

An act of resumption affected much besides crown lands, grants of offices, wardships etc., and many of these exemption provisos were only concerned indirectly with the king's lands and revenues. A comparison of total numbers of provisos appended to successive acts is perhaps some slight guide to the relative effectiveness of the acts, but even then detailed study is necessary before reaching conclusions. The comparatively low number of 86 in 1461 was because the act was framed to annul Lancastrian grants and was directed against Lancastrian grantees. The considerable rise to 288 four years later is readily explained by Edward having in the meantime made long-term arrangements for the disposition of his patrimony. These arrangements included sales of forfeited lands, necessary or unavoidable rewards to those who had supported Edward's bid for the throne, or had not actively opposed it, grants of protection afforded to cities and towns, churches, monasteries, colleges, and hospitals, widows and dependents against the vicissitudes of political fortune, grants of income to officers of state and civil servants, obligations to city merchants, and special protection for certain interests like those of the royal family, which the acts of resumption were specifically designed to foster.

Edward IV began a new policy of retaining many forfeited lands for financial development in the hands of professional officers, but these exemption provisos show that he also sold some forfeited lands outright for cash. There is an interesting proviso in 1467 for no less a person than Thomas Vaughan, treasurer of the Chamber, above which is written: 'these be the considerations that have moved us to grant unto our trusty and well beloved squire . . . etc.'. The king's reasons follow: Vaughan had served his father, Richard duke of York, loyally, and had suffered banish-

41. *Registrum Abbatiae Johannis Whethamstede* (Rolls Series), i, 415–18.

42. Most of the originals are bound up in files: P.R.O., Chancery, Parliament and Council, C. 49/54–65. Some, however, are among the Ancient Petitions class and can partly be identified by the Public Record Office list of Ancient Petitions in English.

ment and attainder for his sake under Henry VI; his only payment both for this and subsequent service to the king had been the grant of Sir Thomas Browne's forfeited lands, the possession of which was causing him expensive lawsuits against other claimants who had already recovered some of them from him. But this trusted chamber servant had also 'paid to us for the same lands and tenements £1,000 in money, to his utter undoing if the said land and tenements should now be resumed from him'.[43] The enrolment of this proviso on the roll of the parliament omitted these explanations.[44] There may possibly have been many more similar sales which appear on record only as munificent grants to those whom Edward delighted to honour.

Most of the clauses of exemption from the act of 1465 were repeated as exemptions from the subsequent act of 1467, when the total number fell slightly. In 1473 numbers of exemptions fell more substantially by sixty-one. Edward had been driven into exile and had had to recover his throne in the meantime. His obligations towards the Nevilles and their associates and to all those who had proved wanting on that occasion had therefore been removed. They received no provisos of exemption in his last act of resumption and this accounts for the substantial fall in the number of provisos. Most important among those who had secured exemptions in previous acts, but not in the last Yorkist act of resumption, was George duke of Clarence.

Under the Lancastrian kings parliamentary proposals for a resumption had been strenuously resisted by the king's government. With the accession of Edward IV they thus became governmental measures, part of a new policy intended to strengthen the monarchy both politically and financially in the interest of more stable, effective rule. How this policy worked in practice can best be illustrated by an account of the local and central administration of the king's lands during the Yorkist period.

2. RECEIVERS, SURVEYORS AND AUDITORS OF LAND REVENUES, 1461–83*

Edward IV's relations with his parliaments and the legislation of his reign indicate that he studied ways and means of providing a more effective kingship by avoiding the mistakes of his predecessor. This was also true in other directions, in that the battlefield once more became an effective and congenial instrument of royal policy. The serious nature of rebellions

43. P.R.O., Chancery, Parliament and Council, C.49/54/67.
44. *Rot. Parl.*, v, 587.
* The description of Yorkist chamber finance given in the remainder of this chapter is a revised and amplified version of my earlier account printed in *E.H.R.*, 1956, as 'The Management of English Royal Estates under the Yorkist Kings'. It supersedes that earlier account.

raised by some of his most powerful and ambitious subjects inevitably diverted his attention from the everyday needs of royal administration. But informed opinion continued to advocate the achievement of greater royal control over appointments and rewards and to look to the greater freedom of royal action which royal solvency would make possible. The importance which his contemporaries attached to the crown lands in both these respects cannot be doubted and it seems unreasonable not to accept that Edward shared their views.

Three acts of resumption, in 1465, 1467 and 1473, were important instruments for securing and maintaining his political grip on his kingdom as the best of the contemporary chroniclers realized. It must be doubted, however, whether any of these acts made any appreciable difference to the state of the royal finances. Certain other administrative acts concerning the crown lands might also be dismissed as indicating no more than sporadic, *ad hoc* efforts to raise money. For example, in 1464 Edward made a levy of one-quarter of a year's income from all persons holding lands, annuities, offices and pensions for life or during pleasure, under penalty of forfeiture for non-payment.[45] There was an isolated example of a special enquiry into decayed farms and rents on the king's lands throughout England in 1473.[46] But there is other evidence which indicates administrative changes and which cannot be dismissed as having no long-term significance. For example, in 1462 the Treasurer and Barons of the Exchequer were ordered to omit from the summons of the pipe all demands for farms and feefarms worth 40s p.a. or above, and eight regional officers called receivers and approvers, alias surveyors, were appointed to eight groups of contiguous counties with orders to collect all such exchequer farms and feefarms which were to be devoted solely to the expenses of the treasurer of the king's Household. These men had authority to make new leases where appropriate.[47] No precedent for such a general supervision of exchequer farms and feefarms by special salaried officers existed in English history later than the thirteenth century. The careers of the men appointed suggest that they had considerable administrative and financial experience and ability. It is true that their accounts, as enrolled in the Exchequer, show that they did not succeed in providing the treasurer of the Household with

45. *Cal. Close Rolls, 1461–1468*, pp. 230, 259. This levy applied only to lands etc., of a yearly value of 10 marks or more.

46. Commission to various persons throughout England to inquire into decayed farms and rents on the king's lands (*Cal. Pat. Rolls, 1467–1477*, pp. 405–8, 429–30, 18 August 1473).

47. Their appointments, as enrolled on the patent and fine rolls dated 24 and 26 February 1462 (*Cal. Pat. Rolls, 1461–1467*, pp. 110–11; *Cal. Fine Rolls, 1461–1471*, pp. 63–4) were to 'all the king's lands' in specified counties but the accounts they rendered show that they only concerned themselves with the farmed lands. The order to the Barons, dated 19 February 1462, is on the King's Remembrancer's memoranda roll for Hilary, 1 Ed. IV, 'brevia directa baronibus', m.23d.

more than £2,000 p.a. in any one year.[48] Nevertheless this evidence of change within that citadel of tradition the Exchequer is especially interesting when viewed in conjunction with other parallel developments in other branches of the royal administration. In 1472 these receivers were replaced by a further team with the same charge.[49] Some of these were later given authority to declare their accounts on oath before the Barons of the Exchequer, or exonerated from accounting there.[50]

New arrangements were also made for the duchy of Cornwall estates in 1461. The duchy revenues had been greatly depleted under Henry VI by the terms of leases made in the Exchequer at Westminster and by grants of favour from duchy lands secured by members of the king's Household and others. In 1461 Edward IV set up a kind of duchy council, sitting locally, with responsibility to demise at farm all the duchy lands on leases of twenty years or less. Apart from the two titular heads (Lord Hastings, the receiver-general, and Humphrey Stafford of Southwick, the high steward) this body consisted of professional men: Geoffrey Kidwelly the deputy receiver-general, Thomas Clemens the steward, John Broke and Thomas Aleyn the auditors, and William Menwennek a local lawyer. The powers of this body were renewed in 1469 and a new one was appointed by Richard III in 1483.[51]

But it is when we turn to consider lands which, for various reasons, came newly into the possession of the king of England in and after 1461 and which were not under the control of the Treasurer and Barons of the Exchequer, that more far-reaching innovations become apparent. These provide strong grounds for believing that Edward IV and his advisers were in fact creating a new system of royal estate management and organization intended to make a substantial and reliable contribution to the king's income quite independent of what he received through the Exchequer. These royal plans appear to have been modelled on the normal methods of con-

48. Foreign Accounts, 2 Ed. IV, D, E, F; 3 Ed. IV, B; 4 Ed. IV, A, D. After this date no further enrolments of their accounts were made on the foreign account rolls of the Exchequer.

49. Two sets of appointments were made, first on 26 March 1472 and then on 4 August 1472 with some adjustment of areas: *Cal. Pat. Rolls, 1467–1477*, pp. 329, 347–8.

50. e.g. Richard Spert (P.R.O., Exch., K.R., Memoranda Rolls, 'brevia', Easter, 15 Ed. IV, m.10); William Brent (*ibid.*, Trinity, 15 Ed. IV, m.8); Geoffrey Kidwelly (*ibid.*, Mich. 15 Ed. IV, m.17d); Robert Plomer (*ibid.*, Trinity, 16 Ed. IV, m.5); Thomas Hunt and John York (*ibid.*, Mich., 17 Ed. IV, m.3d). Some time between 1472 and 1476 Maurice Kidwelly, described as the king's receiver in Soms., Dors., and Wilts, certainly collected issues from the Gurney manors (P.R.O., Special Collections, S.C.6/1123/2). Geoffrey Kidwelly, who had asked to be relieved of his office for fear of violence against him, had originally been appointed to Soms. and Dors. where the Gurney manors were (see above, p. 155). These manors, granted for life to Clarence in 1464, were not included in the regrants he received after the act of resumption of 12 Edward IV.

51. *Cal. Pat. Rolls, 1461–1467*, p. 201; *ibid., 1467–1477*, p. 197; *ibid., 1477–1485*, p. 461.

temporary, large-scale, private estate management which had provided his income when he was earl of March.

The owner of a considerable estate in fifteenth-century England usually employed several professionally trained officers to control his revenues from the centre: a surveyor, a receiver, and one or more auditors. The training and qualifications for all three posts were largely identical because the office of surveyor was quite frequently combined with the office of receiver, while there were instances of a receiver of one complex of estates holding the post of auditor to another and unconnected group of manors in a different part of the country. There were undoubtedly certain families which specialized in estate management, for example, the Heton family, mainly employed by the Stafford dukes of Buckingham, the Leventhorpes in the duchy of Lancaster service, the Kidwelly and Sapcote families, prominent in the royal service from 1461. In this sphere the key man was the receiver, or receiver-general, directly responsible to the lord for supplying him with money. In his hands lay the collection of revenues from farmers, bailiffs, reeves, rent collectors or other officers in charge of separate manors, the payment of such officers and (where no surveyor was appointed, and perhaps with the concurrence of the lord's council) the replenishment of stock, the making of new leases, the ejection of insolvent or bad tenants, the authorization of repairs etc. He supplied money for the lord's household, paid his creditors, his jeweller's bills etc., and journeyed with large sums of money wherever the lord required it. He normally retained substantial sums in his own possession from year to year as a working balance.

The accounts of these men in private service can be studied in the Public Record Office in cases where their documents, together with the lands they administered, later came into the possession of the king. There is a good example for 1480–1 in the account of Harry Griffith, receiver to William Catesby in Warwickshire, Northamptonshire and Leicestershire. Other examples are the accounts of Gregory Westby, receiver-general to Margaret lady Hungerford in the early years of Edward IV's reign; of John Heton, receiver-general of Anne duchess of Buckingham (1463–4) and of John Harcourt her receiver in Staffordshire, Shropshire and Chester (1470–1).[52] There are also some similar accounts of the officers of the

52. P.R.O., Special Collections, Ministers Accts, and Rentals and Surveys, S.C.6/1117/16; S.C.6/1119/14, 15; S.C.6/1117/11; S.C.11/604. Other useful references to private accounts of the mid-fifteenth century will be found in *B.I.H.R.*, xxvi (1953), 'The English Baronage and the Income Tax of 1436' by T. B. Pugh and C. D. Ross. For fifteenth-century methods of estate management and the information to be derived from the accounts of receivers-general and from valors (auditors' reports) the following should be consulted: R. Somerville, *History of the Duchy of Lancaster, 1265–1603*, vol. i (1953); C. D. Ross and T. B. Pugh, 'Materials for the Study of Baronial Incomes in Fifteenth Century England', *Econ. Hist. Rev.*, 2nd Series (1953); R. H. Hilton, *Ministers' Accounts of the Warwickshire Estates of the Duke of Clarence 1479–1480* (Dugdale Soc., 1952); Joel T.

king's mother, Cecily duchess of York and of other members of the royal family at the Public Record Office.

Auditors were men well qualified to make a survey of the lord's lands, to draw up a valor and to advise on problems of estate management. Some of the royal auditors who were especially prominent during the reign of Edward IV served private lords as well as the king. John Luthington, royal auditor in North Wales, Chester, Lincolnshire, and the duchy of Lancaster was at the same time in the service of Richard duke of Gloucester; John Eltonhead, auditor of some of the Richmond estates from 1461 had previously been auditor for Lincoln's Inn, for the duchy of Cornwall and for a number of private lords; John Touke who joined the royal service in 1478 had been auditor to the duke of Clarence and to Margaret lady Hungerford.

It is well known that in England the most extensive and successful instance of this system of estate management during the later middle ages was the duchy of Lancaster, with lands extending over most of the counties of England and Wales, all controlled by an integrated staff of trained administrators. The dukes of Lancaster as kings of England from 1399–1461 had allowed little if any interference from the royal Exchequer in the affairs of the duchy. On the other hand, there is no evidence that they had made attempts to extend the benefits of the duchy system to cover the royal lands under exchequer control. They were careful to keep their Hereford estates separate from the Exchequer and in 1414 incorporated them in the duchy.[53] In marked contrast Edward IV, who, as earl of March had himself received his income by such a system, appears to have seen every reason for introducing as much as possible of these tried practices of private estate management into the working of the royal land administration. Richard III continued and extended his brother's policies. Many of the new appointments of receivers, surveyors, and auditors between 1461 and 1485 which these changes involved were ultimately enrolled on the patent rolls, but the activities of these royal officers can only be described from a variety of other record sources. The most important of these are accounts which were drawn up by 'foreign' auditors, that is, by auditors who were employed outside the jurisdiction of the Exchequer and thus 'foreign' to it,[54] and a series of privy seal writs which originated in the signet office and are enrolled among the 'brevia directa baronibus' on the king's remembrancer's memoranda rolls.

An early example of new royal organization was a complex of estates

Rosenthal, 'The Estates and Finances of Richard, Duke of York, 1411–1460', *Studies in Medieval and Renaissance History*, ed. W. M. Bowsky (Lincoln, U.S.A., 1965), ii, 115–204.

53. R. Somerville, *Duchy of Lancaster*, i, 177 and references given there.

54. Not to be confused with the 'foreign' auditors of the Exchequer itself who were so described because they audited accounts which were not part of the main Exchequer account, the sheriffs' accounts on the pipe roll. See below, p. 176.

newly created in 1461 mainly out of the earldom of March lands, with, in addition, some lands of the duchy of Lancaster, some of the Crown, and some lands which were in the king's hands by reason of the minority of the heir of Humphrey duke of Buckingham. These lay in ten counties of Wales and the Marches. John Milewater was appointed to be receiver-general and his accounts were audited at Hereford by John Luthington who received 5s *per diem* as king's auditor for North Wales and Chester. Milewater's accounts began at Michaelmas 1461 with the entry that there were no arrears to account for because this was the first appointment of a receiver-general for all these lands together. These accounts can be summarized as follows:

Michaelmas 1461–Michaelmas 1463

Total receipts	£1,520 12s 10d
Paid by warrants of the king	£560 7s 1d
Paid to the king's own coffers in three instalments, acquittances being given at Fotheringhay, Westminster, and Coventry	£820
His own fees and expenses at £60 p.a. and £20 to Thomas Colt, chancellor of the earldom of March	£140
Balance in hand	5s 9d

Michaelmas 1463–Michaelmas 1464

Total receipts (incl. arrears of 5s 9d)	£988 13s
Paid by warrants of the king (including maintenance for Henry duke of Buckingham and Humphrey his brother and a payment to Edmund Shaw, goldsmith, of London)	£361 4s 2d
Paid to the king's own coffers in instalments, acquittances being given at Pontefract, Northampton, Westminster, and Stamford	£548
Repairs to Ludlow castle	£5 10s
Surplusage	£6 1s 2d
(Subsequent receipt of £25 and payments and allowances of £34 9s 4d raised the surplusage to £15 10s 6d)	

Michaelmas 1464–Michaelmas 1465

Total receipts	£848 17s 9d
Paid to the king's coffers by signet warrant	£66 13s 4d
Paid out by warrants under the signet, one privy seal warrant, one warrant under the seal of March, by indenture to various officers of the king, and al-	

lowed for Milewater's own fees, expenses and surplusage of previous account etc.	£837 9s 9d
Surplusage, for which the king was in his debt	£55 5s 4d

In September 1465 Edward gave some of these lands to his queen, but they all remained under control of the same competent receiver-general and the major portion of the issues continued to be disposed of at the king's command. In 1467–8 the queen received £435 13s 4d from Milewater, but £667 3s 3½d was paid out as the king directed by warrants and as cash paid into his own hands.[55]

Many forfeited estates were also placed under the control of receivers and special auditors at the beginning of Edward's reign. Among the most important of these were the Richmond and Beaufort lands, the Roos lands, the lands formerly of the earl of Northumberland and of James earl of Wiltshire. Other lands for which similar appointments were made included those of the duchy of York and those of the earldom of March in East Anglia, the Home Counties, Cambridgeshire, and Huntingdonshire.[56] In 1462 the sequestered temporalities of the bishopric of Durham were placed under control of the treasurer of the Household, the controller of the Household and Thomas Colt; these commissioners were ordered to render their accounts, not at the Exchequer, but before special auditors acting in the exchequer of the bishopric of Durham.[57]

That the same organization applied to wards' lands can be seen in the case of the estates of the Talbot earls of Shrewsbury. Owing to the accident of two minorities they were at the king's disposal for most of his reign. Richard Fowler, king's solicitor, and later chancellor of the Exchequer and chancellor of the duchy of Lancaster, was first appointed receiver-general of them, but was later replaced by John Milewater and other receivers: Richard Croft, John Swift, and Thomas Stidolff. They accounted at Hereford, Sheffield and elsewhere before Richard Grenewey and probably other special auditors.[58]

Edward IV intended similar arrangements for the control of Clarence's forfeited lands in 1470. Walter Blount lord Mountjoy, Master Richard Martin, Henry Ferrers and John Hewik were designated 'our auditors to

55. P.R.O., Special Collections, Ministers Accts., S.C.6/1305/15, S.C.6/1236/9, 10, 11, in chronological order. Brecknock, Hay, Huntingdon (Herefs.) and part of Newport (Mon.) were the lands given to Queen Elizabeth: *Cal. Pat. Rolls, 1461–1467*, p. 464. After the figure of £667 3s 3½d for total outgoings by royal warrants in 1467–8 appears a higher total of £826 7s 3½d, partly oversewn at the join of two membranes and partly erased. This appears to represent a false start to a new membrane and is not part of this account; *C.L.*, doc. no. 7.

56. *Cal. Pat. Rolls, 1461–1467*, pp. 18, 26, 129.

57. The arrangements made for the bishopric of Durham are in *ibid.*, p. 215, dated 28 December 1462. Edward restored the temporalities to the bishop, Lawrence Booth, on 17 April 1464; *ibid.*, p. 347.

58. *ibid.*, pp. 40, 91; *ibid.*, *1467–1477*, pp. 397, 411, 442. *C.L.*, doc. nos. 12(e), 12(i).

direct, guide, oversee, examine and approve for our most avail and profit all such livelihood as late was George the duke of Clarence and now belongeth to us in the counties of Stafford, Derby, Leicester and Northumberland and to make levy to our use as well of all the arearage that late belonged to the said George duke of Clarence as of all the revenues and profits of the same livelihood and also to guide, rule and establish all manner [of] officers, ministers, farmers and tenants etc.'.[59]

Not all forfeited, resumed and escheated lands were placed under such skilled professional control. Undoubtedly Edward IV let some of these lands out to farm to private persons for lump sums. But these arrangements were seldom made through the Exchequer and the proceeds were usually paid direct into the king's own coffers. Receivers and auditors were appointed for all the large estates coming into his hands with the express purpose of preventing them from passing into the exchequer farming pool. This applied even in cases where, like the Beaufort and Richmond lands, many of the forfeited manors and lordships had been crown lands for most of their history.

Special arrangements were made for the administration of various other large estates, notably those which began to pass under royal control from 1472 onwards. In that year Edward IV took back from George Neville, archbishop of York, the royal lordships of Woodstock, Handborough, Wootton and Stonesfield, with the hundred of Wootton, in Oxfordshire. The king's trusted servant Richard Croft was made receiver and surveyor there and exempted from rendering any account of his office at the Exchequer. At the same time Thomas Aleyn was appointed to audit Croft's accounts at Woodstock together with the accounts of subordinate ministers.[60] The 'tightening up' effect of Croft's arrival to 'attend the guiding'[61] of the king's lands there is illustrated by a petition submitted to the king by the master and scholars of Balliol College on 17 May 1474. They complained that the receiver of the lordship of Woodstock and its members had begun to demand a rent of 4s for twelve acres of meadow at Steeple Aston, where a rent of 1s 3d had been paid since 1339. What is more, he had levied a distress upon their hay lying in the meadow, in order to obtain the higher rent. However, in this case the king granted their petition to continue pay-

59. P.R.O., T.R., Council and Privy Seal, E.28/91/65. I owe the reference to this Treasurer's bill to Dr Robin Jeffs, who also drew my attention to the fact that it is incorrectly designated 'post 17 Edward IV' in the Public Record Office file, and identified it as belonging to 1470, between the appointment of John Tiptoft, earl of Worcester as Treasurer 10 July, whose autograph signature it bears, and Henry VI's restoration (3 October). Commissioners were appointed to seize the lands of Clarence and other rebels on 25 April 1470; *Cal. Pat. Rolls, 1467–1477*, pp. 218–19 (*cf.* above, p. 155); *C.L.*, doc. no. 10.

60. *ibid.*, p. 364; P.R.O., Exch., K.R., Mem. Rolls, 'brevia', Mich., 13 Ed. IV, m.4; *C.L.*, doc. no. 12(c).

61. These latter were the terms in which the charge was laid upon him.

ment at the old rate because the profits of the meadow went towards the upkeep of a chantry priest.[62]

In 1474 there was mention of a special receiver, John Beaufitz, appointed to administer the lands formerly held by Alice lady Lovell. He was summoned to the king's Chamber, there to render an account of his office before certain persons assigned to hear him.[63] By this date many crown lands in Nottinghamshire and Derbyshire had been recovered from the duke of Clarence and had been placed under the control of a special receiver whose final account was rendered before a special auditor.[64] From 1477 this receiver was Gervase Clifton who paid over his receipts and accounted for his office at Nottingham castle, before certain persons assigned to hear his account.[65] Edward IV probably kept a regional treasury at Nottingham castle; apart from Clifton's issues, the receiver of Tutbury honour paid in £300 there during 1476;[66] also Richard Welby, receiver of Richmond honour in Lincolnshire, rode from Boston to Nottingham castle with £100 in cash on 26 January 1478 and received an acquittance for it from William Slefeld, the king's esquire.[67]

The greatest single accession of land received by Edward IV in his later years was the very considerable Warwick, Salisbury, and Spencer estates together with many former royal lordships and manors, which passed firmly under his control in the spring of 1478, following the attainder of the duke of Clarence. At first he sent Peter Beaupie, his clerk of the greencloth and formerly in the employment of the earldom of March, to take control of the administration at Warwick.[68] Together with the auditor John Hewyk and others not named, Beaupie had to furnish all relevant accounts for examination by a commission headed by Sir Thomas Vaughan, treasurer of the Chamber and chamberlain to the prince of Wales. The other members were Sir John Say, under-treasurer of England, Sir John Elrington, treasurer of the Household, Sir Robert Wingfield, controller of the Household and Henry Boteler, recorder of Coventry and formerly

62. P.R.O., Exch., Treas. of Receipt, Council and Privy Seal, E.28/91/13 (writ to the auditor).

63. P.R.O., Exch., K.R., Mem. Rolls, 'brevia', Hilary, 14 Ed. IV, m.10; *C.L.*, doc. no. 12(d).

64. *Cal. Pat. Rolls, 1467–1477*, pp. 441, 482.

65. *ibid., 1476–1485*, p. 19.

66. See below, p. 174.

67. P.R.O., Land Revenue, Rentals, etc., L.R., 12/28/988 (account of Richard Welby, receiver, for Mich. 1478–Mich. 1479, audited by John Luthington).

68. P.R.O., Exch. of Receipt, Issue Rolls, E.403/848 (23 October, 18 Ed. IV): Payment to Richard Grenewode (Rougecroix Pursuivant), now of the king's Chamber, sent with letters of privy seal to Peter Beaupie, receiver of lands late of George duke of Clarence, at Warwick, to Nicholas Leventhorpe, receiver-general of the duchy of Lancaster, to Richard Welby, receiver of the honour of Richmond lands in Lincs., and to John Agard receiver of the honour of Tutbury, for certain special causes and matters moving the king and his Council. In commissions to inquire into Clarence's lands (*Cal. Pat. Rolls, 1476–1485*, pp. 109–11, dated 16 March and 20 April 1478), Beaupie acted in eight counties.

employed by the duke of Clarence.[69] They reported to the king and under their guidance the lands were entrusted to a number of receivers, all directly responsible to the king in his Chamber.

Perhaps the most important of such local officers was John Hayes, appointed to administer all lands formerly held by the duke of Clarence in Devon, Cornwall, Somerset, Dorset, Wiltshire, and Hampshire. Although described in his patent of appointment under the great seal merely as receiver, his duties included those of a surveyor, being described as 'riding . . . both to survey and guide the same manors and to levy the lord king's money there and to conduct other business of the lord king there'. He was generally known as 'one of the king's receivers in the West parts of England' and was paid £20 p.a. for his work in collecting money and £24 p.a. for his other duties.[70] John Luthington administered lands formerly held by Clarence in Warwickshire, Worcestershire, Staffordshire, Northamptonshire, and Buckinghamshire. John Harcourt, usher of the Chamber, was in control of other Clarence lands in Gloucestershire, Herefordshire, Worcestershire, Oxfordshire, Warwickshire, Wiltshire, and Berkshire. In addition, there were the following other receivers appointed for Clarence's lands, all of whom seem to have had a special direct responsibility to the king: William Clifford (lordship of Milton and Marden), Richard Welby (Richmond lands in Lincolnshire, where William Huse was appointed to the separate post of surveyor), Thomas Tototh (certain manors in the East Midlands and some lands in Lincolnshire) and John Walsh (receiver and surveyor of the manor and hundred of Barton by Bristol with the great court of the honour of Gloucester there). Various adjustments of areas and some new appointments were made from time to time. By the end of Edward's reign two new receivers, Roger Fitzherbert and Thomas Freebody had been appointed.[71]

These Yorkist receivers were no mere rent-collectors. They were appointed by the king to posts of the highest initiative and trust. Their duties were thus described in a memorandum of 1484: 'to ride, survey, receive and remember on every behalf that might be most for the king's profit and thereof yearly to make report'.[72] Like the special auditors appointed to the king's lands they were required to follow a certain 'circuit' in performance

69. *ibid.*, p. 64 (dated 14 February 1478).

70. P.R.O., Exch., L.T.R., Mem. Rolls, E.358/251, States and Views, Hilary, 18 Ed. IV, m.17.

71. It should be noted that the accounts of the king's receivers drawn up by foreign auditors during the reigns of Edward IV, Richard III, and Henry VII must be sought at the Public Record Office in Ministers' Accounts, Duchy of Lancaster and in Rentals etc., Land Revenue (D.L.29 and L.R.12) as well as in the general series of Ministers' Accounts. Many accounts of the king's lands which had no connection with the duchy are included in the duchy of Lancaster collection. This may have originally been due to the fact that several of the auditors concerned also acted for the duchy.

72. See below, p. 187; *C.L.*, doc. no. 14[32].

of their duties which took them regularly to all the lands under their control. Their yearly reports were presumably made either to the king himself, or to such persons as he assigned to hear them, when they delivered the cash balance of their receipts to him or to his representatives in his Chamber. John Hayes, for example, appeared in the king's Chamber on 31 January 1479, 2 December 1479, 3 December 1480, 22 November 1481, 25 November 1482 and 4 December 1483. Among the items of his account on 2 December 1479 Hayes received acquittance for £472 6s 8d paid into the king's hands. The king received a further cash payment of £100 from him on 12 February 1480 and when he appeared on 3 December 1480 Edward acknowledged the sum of £653 6s 8d as 'paid and delivered unto our own person in our Chamber'. This was in addition to other payments made elsewhere 'by our commandment to him given by our mouth'.[73]

3. ADMINISTRATIVE CHANGES IN THE CENTRAL GOVERNMENT UNDER EDWARD IV

These administrative changes in the organization of the king's lands are indicative of wider changes in the financial machinery of government instituted by Edward IV and his advisers. The English medieval Exchequer in 1461 was divided into two sections, the Lower Exchequer of Receipt, and the Upper Exchequer, Exchequer of Account and Pleas, or Court of the Exchequer. The Exchequer of Receipt was the king's treasury, receiving, storing and issuing his treasure[74] in the form of cash, bullion, jewels, plate, or bearer bonds (tallies and warrants). The Exchequer of Account audited the accounts of the king's officers, taking such action as might be required to ensure that the king received his dues to the full, and supplying such information about the state of his finances as the king might require from time to time.

Under the Yorkist kings two changes were now being made. While the Exchequer of Receipt continued to operate, the king's own coffers in his Chamber became his main treasury involving the transference to it of much more than the issues of crown lands. The Exchequer of Account lost its power to hold full audits for various officers administering the king's land revenues, and retained only the right to receive their audited accounts into custody, to survey them for certain limited purposes, and to preserve

73. Extracts from his accounts as rendered in the king's Chamber are found on the King's Remembrancer's Memoranda Rolls: 'brevia directa baronibus', Hilary, 18 Ed. IV, m.8; Hilary, 19 Ed. IV, m.5, m.9d., m.12d; Hilary, 20 Ed. IV, m.3d, m.4; Mich., 21 Ed. IV, m.17d etc. (writs for his discharge from accounting in full before the Barons of the Exchequer); *C.L.*, doc. no. 12(h).

74. Here also were deposited for safekeeping the most important records of the realm irrespective of their nature, a practice which explains the origin of the miscellaneous collection of documents (at the Public Record Office) now known as Exchequer, Treasury of Receipt.

them for reference. In this sphere the term 'Exchequer of Record' might have been a more fitting description than Exchequer of Account.

From the very beginning of his reign Edward IV began to receive sums of money directly into his Chamber from all manner of sources, without the intervention of any exchequer process. By means of warrants under his signet, his seal of the earldom of March, or by indentures drawn up between the payer and one of the king's officers on his verbal orders, he took money due to him wherever he could obtain it. The Exchequer of Receipt received standing instructions at the beginning of each reign, to provide for the expenses of the various household departments, at the Treasurer's discretion, on a recognized and accepted sale of estimates.[75] These payments of imprests to the different household officers were either sums of cash or assignments. In 1462, as we have seen above, Edward IV gave the additional instruction that all items of his farms and feefarms worth 40s p.a. or more were to go to the Household. But the ability of the Exchequer to supply the king and his trusted officers with prompt payments of ready cash at short notice was limited. The king would not wait for assignments by the system of exchequer tallies, but took his revenues into his own coffers and gave his own receipts. Money from his lands played a big part here. For this purpose efficient local officers able to collect money and carry it about were necessary, while the practice of farming lands from the Exchequer was used less and less, subject as it was to a fossilized system of valuation by extent and to the intervention of preferential grants obtained by petitions on the petitioners' own terms.[76]

For the very years when these new activities, centred on the king's own coffers, became important, there are extensive gaps in the series of records at the Exchequer of Receipt which are almost completely unbroken prior to 1461. The Exchequer of Receipt normally produced two receipt rolls and two issue rolls each year, in triplicate (i.e. for Michaelmas and Easter terms each year, copies for the Treasurer, the king's chamberlain, and the Warwick chamberlain). Yet there are six terms out of a possible fourteen in the first seven years of Edward's reign for which no single copy of a receipt roll survives. There are no surviving issue rolls at all after 1471, except for a single copy in 1479, and they do not reappear until 1567.

The ravages of time could be responsible for these gaps. Alternatively they may be due to developments in late-medieval accounting procedure which have not yet been fully explained by historians. But Dr Anthony Steel

75. e.g. P.R.O., Exch. of Receipt, Warrants for Issues, E.404/72/1, m.7, dated 2 June 1461; *Grants of Edward the Fifth*, ed. J. G. Nichols (Camden Soc., 1854), pp. 68–9, at the beginning of Edward V's reign.

76. The only years between 1461 and 1489 when there were any considerable number of leases of crown lands made at the Exchequer were 1470–1 (during the Readeption of Henry VI), 1485–6 and 1487–9: *Cal. Fine Rolls, 1461–1471*; *ibid., 1471–1485* and *1485–1509, passim.*

has now shown that the importance of the receipt rolls as a guide to the state of the royal finances was undoubtedly declining at this time and this decline appears at least to have been accelerated if not caused by the developments of chamber finance.[77]

Sir James Ramsay long ago calculated from the issue rolls of the Exchequer that Edward IV's Chamber received an annual average of £13,820 from the Exchequer over the first eight years of his reign, reaching £19,600 in one year.[78] It has since been calculated that this figure rose to £21,000 in 1471.[79] Ramsay also noted the disappearance from the enrolled exchequer accounts of 'the large forfeited estates' after the first two or three years, and conjectured that they may yet have continued to contribute to the king's revenues, because he found some of these same estates supplying between £1,100 and £1,400 a year towards the rebuilding of St George's Chapel, Windsor, late in the reign.[80] Dr Anthony Steel found the receipt rolls of the Exchequer for the second half of the reign unable to provide satisfactory information about Edward's benevolences, his French pension and the profits of his trading ventures.[81] Evidence of renewed large-scale financial activity in the royal Chamber after a break which had apparently lasted since the fourteenth century is therefore patchy but real from the beginning of this reign. The most striking absence of all from the receipt rolls of the Exchequer is the yield of the parliamentary lay subsidies granted between 1472 and 1475, equal to four-tenths and fifteenths and apparently making no impact there at all.[82] It is true that the expected yield of this parliamentary generosity, unprecedented since Henry V's French campaigns, was somewhat reduced when Edward IV remitted three-quarters of a tenth and

77. For certain aspects of the operation of the Exchequer in the fifteenth century the reader should consult Dr Anthony Steel's book, *The Receipt of the Exchequer 1377–1485* (C.U.P., 1954), though study of the crown lands under the Yorkist kings suggests some modifications to his conclusions. Information contained in the warrants for issues and the 'brevia directa baronibus' appears to be essential for understanding entries on the receipt rolls of this period. These sources, together with the account rolls of the king's foreign auditors provide evidence of a flourishing system of chamber finance in operation from 1461. Dr Steel does not take such evidence into account in his conclusions. Indeed, one is driven to the conclusion that a fifteenth-century receipt roll had become more of a legal record than a financial document, the main purpose of which was to record the king's obligations to his creditors and theirs to him. In spite of its title, therefore, a receipt roll belonged more to the legal, 'Exchequer of Record' sphere of activities. This perhaps was not new but only becomes clearer in a period like the Yorkist period when government finance was chamber finance and is only recorded on the receipt rolls in this incidental *ex post facto*, legal manner. I am indebted to Dr Gerald Harriss for answering my queries about receipt rolls from his expert knowledge of the period 1435–60. Elucidation of the basic problems presented by the Yorkist rolls must await the publication of his own researches on that earlier period.

78. Ramsay, *Lancaster and York*, ii, 467.

79. Steel, *op. cit.*, p. 326, footnote 1.

80. Ramsay, *Lancaster and York*, ii, 459.

81. *op. cit.*, pp. 311, 354.

82. Steel, *ibid.*, pp. 304–5, 313, 354.

fifteenth on his return to England from his lucrative French venture.[83] Nevertheless, that still leaves close on £100,000 of this direct taxation unaccounted for at the Exchequer.

If we examine specific entries on those receipt rolls which are extant for Edward's reign additional information supplied by the warrants for issues and the 'brevia directa baronibus' makes it quite clear that 'sol' entries (the normal distinguishing mark of a cash payment) did not always now indicate sums of cash paid into the Exchequer of Receipt. For example, an entry of £12,000 cash loan from the mayor, aldermen and citizens of London under the date 22 June 1461 did not signify any payment made by the city at the Exchequer of Receipt at all. The exchequer officials had no knowledge of the transaction until they were ordered by the king's privy seal writ of 24 July 1461 (now among the warrants for issues) to make this entry at the request of the mayor of London. The whole of the money had already been delivered direct from the corporation of London into the king's hands (i.e. to his own coffers) at various dates before 7 April 1461.[84] There are a number of similar examples about the same date.

On each Michaelmas receipt roll up to and including 1470 were entered a series of substantial assignments (enrolled as 'pro' entries, the normal method of distinguishing an assignment from a cash payment) made for the sheriffs on their own issues by authority of privy seal writs. These sums consisted of allowances for amounts which could no longer be levied and for consistent recurrent charges. But for five years from 1471 these sums were entered as 'sol' payments until the traditional method of entry was resumed in 1476. Unless we are to believe that cash receipts from sheriffs suddenly rose by something like 800 per cent during these five years and then suddenly fell again we must conclude that the receipt rolls were not being as carefully kept as formerly because their importance was not what it had been.[85]

83. *ibid.*, p. 307.

84. P.R.O., Exch. of Receipt, Receipt Rolls, E.401/877 (Easter, 1 Ed. IV); Warrants for Issues, E.404/72/1, m.22. The mayor of London was, of course, concerned to make quite sure that the king's liability was recorded. The privy seal writ also ordered an assignment to be made for repayment of the loan, but no reference to such an assignment was entered on the receipt roll, or on the corresponding issue roll (E.403/822).

When considering the interpretation of receipt rolls we must also remember that if K. B. McFarlane's theory of chevisance is correct it is impossible to compile accurate totals of cash receipts at the Exchequer from them even for years before 1461 (see the *Cambs. Hist. Journal*, vol. ix, 'Loans to the Lancastrian Kings'). He has also pointed out (*ibid.*, p. 67) that some of Cardinal Beaufort's cash loans, though entered on the receipt rolls, were not paid into the Exchequer but direct to the king's coffers in France.

85. The change from 'pro' to 'sol' entries can be seen on Receipt Rolls E.401/905, 909, 910, 913, 923, a selection which suggests that it was common to all copies. These rolls should be compared with earlier Michaelmas rolls (e.g. E.401/897, 901, for 1469 and 1470 and E.401/927, 930 for 1476 and 1477). The sums in question are conveniently recorded in MS. Harley 433, fol. 5 as follows: 'The rewards of sheriffs in divers counties: Kent £100, Surrey & Sussex £40, Essex & Herts. £198, Beds & Bucks. £70, Northants. £100, Warws.

There is no evidence that Edward IV wished to abolish the Exchequer of Receipt. No precedent for such action could have been found in any of the earlier periods of English history when government finance had been directed from the Chamber. The Receipt was reduced to the status of a kind of parallel treasury, but one which still received and paid out many of his revenues. However, it appears possible that the Receipt was so starved of money by Edward IV that in later years he had to begin paying sums of cash into it out of his coffers. On 26 August 1478 a total of £7,875 15s 2½d in cash was transported there from his coffers in sixteen convenient sums (the largest being £1,000) by four of his household servants: William Dawbenny, Peter Curtis (keeper of the Wardrobe), John Morton, and Thomas Vaughan (treasurer of the Chamber). Other similar payments followed.[86]

If Edward IV was indeed personally involved through his Chamber in efforts to secure financial economy, solvency and a greater exploitation of that which was his own, then one would expect such efforts to be reflected in the accounts rendered by the treasurer of his Household who was responsible for feeding, clothing and housing the king and his court. He normally received his income as sums of imprest from the Exchequer, in cash or assignments.[87] Under Henry VI small sums were from time to time received by him under the heading 'De Domino Rege' (e.g. in a period of six years 1446–53 a total of £113 6s 8d).[88] They were personal payments from the king for alms, candles etc., on feast days. Under Edward IV the king now became a new substantial source of supply. Sums entered under this heading after 1461 began to rival in importance and even to exceed allocations made from the Exchequer. Sums totalling £1,776 3s 4d were entered under it in the treasurer of the Household's receipts for 1461–2. By 1466–7 these had risen to £9,343 3s 7d. These amounts consisted, in part, of payments from the king's cofferer. Other payments were made by the hand of various yeomen of the Chamber and other household and personal servants of the king like Peter Beaupie, Peter Curteys, Thomas St Leger, Richard Bindewyn, John Parke, John Donne, Thomas Herbert, Richard Jeny etc., who received money from officers of the king's lands and other sources by authority of signet warrants. The king might order a receiver to pay his money over to the Household instead of into his own

& Leics. £160, Notts. & Derbys. £100, Oxon. & Berks. £90, Cambs. & Hunts. £66 13s 4d, Rutland £13 6s 8d, Salop. £100.' These changes from 'pro' to 'sol' entries and back again are not noticed in Dr Steel's book.

86. These payments are noted by Dr Steel (*op. cit.*, p. 310) but he offers no explanation of them: 'There is nothing to show how the money had originally found its way into the royal "coffers" . . .'. The payments are found entered on the receipt roll for Easter, 18 Ed. IV (E.401/931) and on subsequent rolls.

87. See above, p. 169, n. 75.

88. P.R.O., Exch., K.R., Various Accts., E.101/409/20 (controller of Household, 15 November 1446–27, March 1453).

coffers. The clerk entered this money received 'De Domino Rege', not by authority of the Exchequer. Soon the treasurer of the Household was receiving other considerable sums under this chamber authority, such as the issues of the Hanaper and the profits of the Mint.[89] However, just as sums of money were brought to the Chamber by the king's officers and turned over to the treasurer of the Household, so he himself was sometimes required to hand over to the Chamber sums received by him or assignments due to him.[90]

All this was very confusing for the exchequer auditors, who had to audit the accounts of the treasurer of the Household, and it is no surprise to find that in 1474–6 the king had to supply the Exchequer with a declared statement of account for John Elrington, Fogge's successor, under a privy seal writ, as he did for so many other accountants.[91] The Exchequer was holding Elrington to account for sums received by him, which had gone into the king's own coffers or elsewhere at the king's command. The Barons of the Exchequer thus no longer had either the necessary information at their disposal, or the power, to conduct a full audit even of the 'Great Accountants', owing to the financial activities of the king in his Chamber. Their clerks appear to have become uncertain as to the manner of setting up audited accounts,[92] and the matter could only be resolved by the king's Chamber supplying additional information, and by the king ordering verbal declarations to be accepted.

It was in his Chamber that the king made bargains for the sale of forfeitures, wardships, and the keeping of temporalities of bishoprics. Before the letters patent were issued he received payment, cash down, for his own coffers.[93] Here he appointed receivers for his lands by word of mouth and

89. P.R.O., Exch., K.R., Various Accts., E.101/411/11, 13, 14; 412/2 (treasurer of the Household 1461–7). During the same period the treasurer of the Household was also receiving some sums of 'foreign' livelihood by right of special arrangements which concerned neither the Exchequer nor the Chamber: for example, from the committee of household officers which had been set up to administer from Durham the temporalities of the bishopric, the proceeds to go towards household expenses. These were entered in the accounts of the treasurer of the Household as 'Foreign Receipts'. He was also receiving contributions from the duchy of Lancaster, entered under the heading 'Duchy of Lancaster'.

90. For example, P.R.O., Exch., K.R., Mem. Rolls, 'brevia', Easter, 9 Ed. IV, m.4 Easter, 10 Ed. IV, mm.8, 9 (two sums of £799 and £419 7s, the latter from the receiver-general of the duchy of Cornwall); *ibid.*, Mich., 19 Ed. IV, m.6 (an exchequer tally for £1,000); *C.L.*, doc. no. 12(b).

91. P.R.O., Exch., K.R., Mem. Rolls, 'brevia', Mich., 19 Ed. IV, m.6.

92. This seems to have been the case in the treasurer of the Household's accounts for 1473–4. Although divisions 'Exchequer', 'Duchy of Lancaster', 'Of the Lord King', appear, they were scribbled in the margin and were not headings. The receipt side of the account appears to be a chronological record of receipts. Most payments received were noted as by indenture, not tally (E.101/412/3).

93. e.g. sometime before 18 May 1477 Sir John Howard paid £200 into the Chamber for the keeping of the lands late of Walter George. The prior of Chertsey paid 50 marks into the Chamber for the keeping of the temporalities during vacancy. John Sapcote paid

letters missive. They had sometimes held their offices for a year or more prior to the dates of their patents of appointment.[94] He sent orders to the subordinate officers of the royal duchies to dispose of their issues without any reference either to their superior officers in the duchy administration or to the Exchequer. The interest of the Chamber as a central estate office stretched from Cornwall to Yorkshire and knew no barriers. The jealously guarded separateness of the duchy of Lancaster administration is well known. Yet in Edward's reign the receiver of the honour of Tutbury, part of the duchy of Lancaster, was known to deliver his issues into the royal coffers at Nottingham castle by authority of the king's direct command.[95] To cite another example of this outside interference: when the issues of the duchy of Lancaster were not coming in to his satisfaction Edward IV sent a signet letter to the Keeper of the Privy Seal, ordering him to supply the chancellor of the duchy (whom he had commanded to give personal attention to it) with privy seal writs as and when he required them, without any further reference to the king, in order to ensure more speedy and effective collection.[96]

Edward IV was a king with a forceful personality, great energy and thoroughly conversant with his affairs, especially in matters of finance. Nevertheless, a professional officer was required at the centre of his new

£233 6s 8d p.a. into the Chamber for the keeping of lands late of Fulk fitz Warren during minority.

94. John Hayes appointed by word of mouth and letters missive from Mich. 1477, appointed by letters patent under the great seal on 26 January 1479. William Clifford, appointed by word of mouth, had held office for over a year before appointed by patent dated 10 November 1478.

95. P.R.O., Special Collections, Ministers' Accts, S.C.6/1119/19 (Henry Ferrers, king's receiver of Tutbury, 16 Ed. IV). His payment of £372 19s 9d to John Elrington, treasurer of the Household was entered as via the receiver-general of the duchy but another £300 was entered as paid to Gervase Clifton at Nottingham castle by warrant.

96. P.R.O., Privy Seal Office, P.S.O.1/45/2343 (spelling modernized); 'E.R.'

'Edward by the grace of God, king etc. To the Reverend Father in God our right trusty and well-beloved the Bishop of Rochester, Keeper of our Privy Seal, Greeting. For as much as there be many great sums in arrears and unto us due by divers officers and other tenants of our duchy of Lancaster for the nighest recovery and levying of the which we have commanded our trusty and well-beloved councillor Thomas Thwayte, chancellor of our said duchy, to put him in most effectual diligence and devoir and understand that divers and many letters under our said privy seal shall be requisite and necessary to and for the same. We therefore will and charge you that from time to time hereafter ye do make all manner and as many such letters under our said privy seal as our said chancellor shall sue unto you for at any time to thentent aforesaid by warrant hereof signed with our hand and without any other or further suit to be made in that behalf, the premises considered. Given under our signet at our manor of Greenwich the 7th day of July the 18th year of our Reign.

Herbert.'

The vigilance of the Yorkist kings in duchy of Lancaster affairs has recently been described from duchy records: R. Somerville, *op. cit.*, pp. 230–59 *passim*. Sir Robert Somerville, quoting from D.L.5/1, fol. 6, seems to have come upon this same instance of the use of the privy seal but from the internal records of the duchy: *op. cit.*, p. 246.

chamber financial organization. For the first few years of his reign Edward IV seems to have entrusted John Kendal, sometimes called household cofferer and sometimes king's cofferer, with the care of his ready cash. After about 1465, however, he was no longer mentioned in this connection. The officer destined to become the chief instrument of Edward's new financial policy was the treasurer of the Chamber. This title had long been an alternative title for the keeper of the king's jewels. The holder of this office, being so close to the king's person, had on occasion, been a man of considerable standing. For example, under Henry V this office was held by the king's close personal friend Richard Courtenay, bishop of Norwich.[97] However, financial transactions concerning this officer prior to 1461 seem to have been mainly loans periodically raised on the king's jewels. Before 1422 he accounted personally to the king and appears to have received certain allowances under the signet of the Eagle. In 1437 the household chamberlain and a duchy of Lancaster auditor were appointed by patent to audit his accounts. His own appointment was most probably made by word of mouth.[98] In 1465, however, Edward IV appointed his squire of the body Thomas Vaughan to be treasurer of the Chamber during pleasure by letters patent under the great seal, the first time that this procedure was followed.[99] No accounts rendered by Vaughan in this capacity are known to have survived, but he had only to satisfy the king himself and what went into the chamber coffers of medieval English kings was normally their secret. One is reminded of the case of Thomas Hatfield, receiver of Edward III's Chamber, who was instructed by the king in 1344 to burn his accounts.[100]

By contrast the inevitable impact of these changes on the exchequer accounting system did not pass unrecorded. The Exchequer was already familiar with an administrative device, a 'declared account', which had been quite frequently used during the personal rule of Henry VI. From 1444 his advisers seem to have been driven to develop it as an inducement to men to serve as sheriffs, a financial privilege which relieved those sheriffs who were the most vital government supporters in the shires of some of their burdensome and unproductive duties and responsibilities as revenue accountants. This 'declared account' by-passed the 'ancient course of the Exchequer' to give the sheriff immunity against personal expense, inconvenience, and possible financial loss. It gave him exemption in advance from 'all issue trial and averrment' at the Exchequer and from 'answering the summons of the pipe and green wax'. He submitted to no process of charge and discharge under the ancient course of the Exchequer before the Barons. He declared his account on oath, by deputy if he wished, for all

97. See J. H. Wylie, *The Reign of Henry the Fifth*, i, 469; ii, 42–3.
98. *Cal. Pat. Rolls.*, *1436–1441*, p. 91; *ibid.*, *1452–1461*, p. 293.
99. *ibid.*, *1461–1467*, p. 459.
100. Tout, *Administrative History*, iv, 287–8.

that he could levy of his own farm, of the summons of the pipe and green wax. He could not be charged to account for any other items, nor could he be summoned before the Exchequer Court at any subsequent date for any matter arising out of his account. There were only a few instances of sheriffs still obtaining this privilege from Edward IV, indicating that able men were once again more willing to serve without this special financial inducement. But for his receivers, whose loyalties and responsibilities lay with the king in his Chamber, this now became the normal method of freeing them from the time-consuming and financially unproductive annoyance of exchequer intervention in the performance of their duties.[101]

The exchequer accounting system was also affected in another way. Under the terms of the exchequer ordinances of 1323 separate accounting provision had been made for those numerous and important accounts which were not rendered through the sheriff, such as the accounts of the Wardrobe, Gascony, Ireland, Calais, tenths and fifteenths etc., and including 'castles, manors and other lands of the king not let to farm'.[102] During the reign of Edward IV some accounts taken from the king's receivers duly appear on the resulting rolls of 'foreign accounts' (i.e. accounts in this sense 'foreign' to, or outside the main exchequer accounts which were the accounts of the sheriffs enrolled in the annual great roll of the pipe). This was so even in those cases where it is clear from *ad hoc* instructions sent to the Barons that the receivers concerned were only making privileged 'declarations of account' at the Exchequer. In the course of his reign many new lands came into the king's hands, the number of receivers employed grew; yet the number of receivers' accounts appearing on the rolls of 'foreign' accounts does not show any corresponding increase. In fact it decreased, as Sir James Ramsay noticed. The explanation is found in the appointment by letters patent under the great seal of special 'foreign' auditors to draw up the accounts of some of those receivers who were accustomed to receiving their instructions direct from the Chamber by signet warrants and to paying the balance of their receipts, not into the Exchequer of Receipt, but into the king's Chamber. These auditors were 'foreign' in quite a new sense, performing their duties completely outside the jurisdiction of the Barons of the Exchequer. An example of this type of account of the king's receiver John Milewater, drawn up by the auditor John Luthington, has been given above. These 'foreign' auditors appointed by Edward IV were under an obligation to deliver their accounts, after a certain lapse of time, into the custody of the Exchequer, which was still the

101. For further details see my chapter 'The fifteenth-century sheriff and the king's lands' in my Oxford D.Phil thesis 'The Crown Lands and the Parliamentary Acts of Resumption, 1399–1495'. The subject has since been more intensively studied in a wider context by Dr Robin Jeffs in his Oxford D.Phil. thesis 'The Later Medieval Sheriff and the Royal Household'.

102. *The Red Book of the Exchequer* (Rolls Series) ed. H. Hall, iii, 856.

only royal financial court of record, apart from the duchy of Lancaster.[103] This was the practice also recommended under Richard III[104] and ultimately enforced under Henry VII.[105] The Barons of the Exchequer might still need to have the information contained in a receiver's account in order to supply legal exoneration for other lesser accountants such as farmers, bailiffs, tenants, debtors etc. Again, the hearing of accounts for sums of imprest and the checking of payments of salaries, pensions and annuities might require reference to the accounts of one or more of these privileged receivers. But whether the Barons of the Exchequer had before them for purposes of record only the 'declared account' of a receiver, or, ultimately, his full, final account audited elsewhere, they had been deprived of their power and legal duty to subject that receiver himself, his 'foreign' auditor or auditors, or his or their executors, to any account according to the normal processes of the Exchequer Court.[106]

There is thus sufficient evidence to be sure that from the earliest years of his reign Edward IV withheld the accounts of some of his most important receivers from exchequer control, just as he kept the issues of their offices out of the Exchequer of Receipt and free from exchequer assignment. Of course, if exchequer records did reveal the existence of such receivers then they were nevertheless rigorously summoned to account there as the rules of the Exchequer demanded and they required the shield of the king's special protection on all such occasions. But it would be quite wrong to assume that departmental rivalries were consequently generated, or that the venerable Exchequer was fighting for its life. Fifteenth-century English

103. This was stated to be so in the king's order to the Barons of the Exchequer on 26 October 1482 to cease all process against Richard Welby, receiver-general of the Richmond lands in Lincs. for the period during which John Luthington had audited his accounts (P.R.O., Exch., K.R., Mem. Rolls, 'brevia directa baronibus', Mich., 22 Ed. IV., m.6). *C.L.*, doc. no. 12(j).

104. See below, p. 188.

105. See below, p. 207.

106. Typical examples of receivers being given authority to declare their accounts on oath at the Exchequer can be found among the 'brevia' of the K.R., Memoranda Rolls, for Edward IV's reign as follows: Thomas Palmer, Mich., 3 Ed. IV, m.22; William Whelpdale, Hilary, 3 Ed. IV, m.4; John Austin, Easter, 4 Ed. IV, m.1; Richard Spert, Easter, 15 Ed. IV, m.10; Robert Plommer, Trinity, 16 Ed. IV, m.5; John Hayes, Hilary, 18 Ed. IV, m.8.

The following are examples in the 'brevia' of exemptions from the ancient course of the Exchequer given to receivers because they had already rendered account before foreign auditors outside the Exchequer: Richard Croft, Mich., 13 Ed. IV, m.4; Thomas Stiddolf, Mich., 17 Ed. IV, m.1; John Swyft, Mich., 21 Ed. IV, m.1d; Richard Welby, Mich., 22 Ed. IV, m.6.

The following are examples of receivers' accounts (cf. those of John Milewater cited above, p. 164) drawn up by foreign auditors in Edward IV's reign: P.R.O., Duchy of Lancaster, Ministers' Accts, D.L.29/638/10373 (John Harcourt, receiver of former Clarence lands, 19–20 Ed. IV, auditors John Clerk and John Hewyk); P.R.O., Land Revenue, Rentals, etc., L.R.12/28/988 (Richard Welby, receiver of former Clarence lands, 17–18 Ed. IV, auditor John Luthington).

royal servants who participated in the making of policy were not departmentalized. Movements of higher personnel from Household and Chamber to Exchequer or Chancery were common enough. Some of these foreign auditors also appear as exchequer auditors. The writs of exoneration which came from the signet office to the Barons of the Exchequer via the clearing house of the privy seal were quite informative. In many cases they amounted to a brief account taken down in the Chamber by the signet clerks when the receiver concerned appeared there to hand over his receipts and to clear himself. No new court of record had been created. While each receiver was personally protected *ad hoc* from the examination, financial penalties, and constraint which subjection to the ancient course of the Exchequer meant, the Barons still had to be and were provided with sufficient information to enable them to survey the accounts of all other persons involved in the financial transactions of these receivers. Also the Exchequer still had the duty of preserving in legal custody all royal accounts, including those drawn up by 'foreign' auditors outside its control. The only exception to this rule was the duchy of Lancaster which was its own court of record.

It follows nevertheless that the extra-curial activities of these privileged receivers and auditors required some new kind of regular central supervision other than that provided by the attenuated exchequer control to which they were still subjected. Something more was needed to replace the rigours of the ancient course of the Exchequer than a trusted cashier in the king's Chamber ready to lock up their receipts in the king's coffers. The evidence of the existence of central accounting supervision in the king's Chamber under Edward IV is as difficult to come by and to assemble as the evidence of the cash payments he received there. At Easter 1476 Edward IV handed over the custody of the lands late of Alice, lady Lovell, Deyncourt and Gray during the minority of her heir Francis lord Lovell to Gerard Caniziani, towards the payment of a debt of 4,000 marks.[107] An earlier entry on the patent roll shows that these lands were then in the charge of a royal receiver, John Beaufitz, with Thomas Metcalf as auditor.[108] But a privy seal writ to the Barons dated 17 February 1475 further reveals that Edward IV had 'appointed and assigned the said John Beaufitz to account and reckon with us thereof in our Chamber afore certain persons by us thereto assigned' for the hearing of his account, and he was correspondingly released from all exchequer processes, notwithstanding the fact that the Barons were given no details of the lands or their issues, and that it did not appear before them, by matter of record in the Exchequer, that he had accounted in the king's Chamber.[109] In 1478 the receivers and 'foreign' auditors of lands which had belonged to the duke of Clarence were

107. *Cal. Pat. Rolls, 1467–1477*, p. 468.

108. *ibid.*, p. 421.

109. P.R.O., Exch., K.R., Mem. Rolls, 'brevia', Hilary, 14 Ed. IV, m.10; *C.L.*, doc. no. 12(d).

required to submit all their accounts to a committee of five members, headed by Sir Thomas Vaughan, treasurer of the king's Chamber and chamberlain of the prince of Wales, who were called surveyors of the account.[110] The first summary of John Hayes's account for the year ending at Michaelmas 1478 was sent to the Exchequer in the form of a writ of privy seal dated at Westminster on 31 January 1479. This was almost certainly originally written down by a clerk of the signet in the king's Chamber since the privy seal, static in London, normally now merely repeated the date and place of the signet warrant under the authority of its own seal.[111] The Exchequer received its information about Hayes's account for the following twelve months in a writ of privy seal dated at Dorking on 2 December 1479.[112] If the original writ survived it would doubtless also prove to be a signet office writ of the same place and date. The Exchequer similarly received its information about John Luthington's account, covering the two years from Michaelmas 1477 to Michaelmas 1479, in a long writ which was dated at Greenwich on 14 July 1480.[113] The preservation of such statements or 'declarations' of account in exchequer records, originally sent out of the Chamber under the signet, presupposes the existence of supervisors of receivers' accounts in attendance on Edward IV in his Chamber. This would still be so even if, as seem most likely, they were men not yet holding specific appointments as such, but were detailed for this work *ad hoc* from among his councillors in attendance and his household officers.

Contemporaries considered that Edward IV died an extremely wealthy prince,[114] and land revenues undoubtedly played a part in his finances for which there was no precedent since the ill-fated attempts of Edward II and the younger Despenser to create a royal land revenue office in the Chamber. Another new source of revenue was the French pension from 1475. Apart from these two new sources, direct, and especially indirect, taxation continued as the most lucrative source of ready money and as security for cash loans. Except for the years 1472–5 Edward received much less than his predecessor in direct taxation, but his government did not have to bear the crushing burden of a losing French war. The customs revenues were increasing during the second half of his reign. This has been attributed to increased trade, which it is reasonable to link with more settled political

110. *Cal. Pat. Rolls, 1476–1485*, pp. 64, 495.

111. K.R. Mem. Roll, 'brevia', Hilary, 18 Ed. IV, m.8. The original of a special writ of allowance for William Clifford, another of Clarence's receivers which is enrolled among the 'brevia' for Mich. 19 Ed. IV as a privy seal writ dated at Windsor 3 June 19 Ed. IV was actually 'given under our signet' at Windsor 3 June 19 Ed. IV (P.R.O., Privy Seal Office, 1/47/2408).

112. K.R., Mem. Roll, 'brevia', Hilary, 19 Ed. IV, m.5.

113. *ibid.*, 'brevia', Trinity 20 Ed. IV., m.8.

114. *The Usurpation of Richard the Third*, ed. C. A. J. Armstrong (2nd. ed., 1969), p. 70; *Rerum Anglicarum Scriptores*, ed. W. Fulman (Oxford, 1684), i, 559, 564, 567, 575.

conditions,[115] but the Croyland chronicler drew attention to his appointment of special surveyors of the customs throughout the ports, so that administrative reform may well have contributed here also.[116]

The reign does thus stand out for the new economy and striving for efficiency in administration, for the endeavour by the king to 'live of his own'. The economy, which he nevertheless managed to combine with impressive display,[117] was especially noticeable in the royal Household. The management of the crown's landed estate made a material contribution to to the new political and financial stability. In this respect the main interest of Edward's reign lies in piecing together from the records of government those fragments of evidence which, taken over-all, reveal a system of chamber finance in operation from the beginning of his reign. This involved much more than land revenues, but it seems to have originated in the continued payment to his own hands, in his Chamber, of the issues of the efficiently run earldom of March estates. Unlike the jealously guarded separateness and superior efficiency of the Lancastrian inheritance, which had been preserved intact but isolated in the comparable circumstances of 1399, the similar methods of efficient March estate management thus came to permeate the whole central organization of royal finance during the Yorkist period. Heavy series of valuable forfeitures, together with an unusually high number of lucrative custodies during minority, were all, subject to any over-riding political considerations, exploited financially by Edward in his Chamber. Other more lucrative sources of income than land revenues were drawn into the Chamber, but one cannot doubt that Yorkist chamber finance cut its teeth on the problems and opportunities presented by royal estate management and exploitation, while recognizing that the profits of land at his death provided only one of a number of the major sources controlled by it. He had consciously striven to 'live of his own'. Only to those historians who misinterpret this aim as meaning that he should live on the revenues of his landed estate and feudal dues and restrict his expenditure to what their full exploitation could be made to yield does Edward IV's reign in this respect present a picture of failure.

4. RICHARD III AND THE CROWN LANDS

Students of English government during the brief reign of Richard III have a unique advantage which has been little exploited. There survives for the years 1483–5 a docket book of the king's signet office which enables

115. See the tables in Ramsay, *Lancaster and York*, ii, 470–2; and in *Studies in English Trade in the Fifteenth Century*, ed. Eileen Power and M. M. Postan, pp. 2, 401, 406.

116. 'Theoloneorum supervisores exquisititssimos homines, mercatoribus, ut fama tulit, nimis duros, per singulos Regni portus praefecit' (*Rerum Anglicarum Scriptores*, i, 559).

117. Myers, *op. cit.*, pp. 47–8 and sources there given.

government in the king's Chamber to be described from the inside.[118] Parts of it have been in print for a long time, notably those sections dealing with diplomatic correspondence which received very full treatment from James Gairdner,[119] and also those entries which can be identified as belonging to the nominal reign of Edward V, printed by J. G. Nichols as *Grants of King Edward the Fifth*.[120] This latter collection has in fact been given a misleading title, for its contents are really the acts of the Lord Protector. Beginning with an entry made on 5 May 1483 they represent the dispositions, almost entirely appointments to offices, which Richard duke of Gloucester found necessary in order to establish his control over the resources of the Crown and over those of his most powerful opponents. One group of these is very striking indeed, signifying as it does the appointment of Henry Stafford, duke of Buckingham, to replace the prince of Wales's council in what amounted to vice-regal authority in Wales, the Marches of Wales and the West Country.

But grants of land are conspicuous by their absence from this collection, if only because Edward was a minor and the Protector could have no legal power to dispose of royal land at that stage. There were other important regional delegations of authority. While Buckingham was put in to fill the void left by the destruction of the prince of Wales's council at Ludlow, Henry Percy, earl of Northumberland, was strengthened in authority to replace Richard in the North consequent on his own movement down to London. John lord Howard, later to be created duke of Norfolk, and Francis lord Lovell, received key appointments in the Midlands and the South. Nevertheless Richard's advent at the centre of Yorkist authority on the whole entailed few changes of personnel.

Edward IV's treasurer of the Chamber, Sir Thomas Vaughan, had also held the post of chamberlain to the young prince of Wales. He had been prominent among those who administered the prince's lands and was at Ludlow with the prince and his council when the king died. Richard had him beheaded along with Rivers, Grey and Sir Richard Haute, recently appointed the prince's own treasurer, at Pontefract on 25 June 1483.[121] Master Edmund Chadderton, a member of Richard's own council and his household chaplain, became his treasurer of the Chamber and was appointed by patent under the great seal. Unfortunately the printed calendar omits the most interesting details of his appointment. He was in fact ordered to render account only to the king in person as and when required

118. B.M., MS. Harley 433. A selection of documents from this docket book which concern the crown lands is now printed in *C.L.*, pp. 120–39.

119. *Letters etc., Richard III, Henry VII* (Rolls Series), vol. i, Preface, and pp. 1–88 *passim.*

120. Camden Soc., 1854.

121. *Cal. Pat. Rolls, 1467–1477*, pp. 366, 414, 455; J. G. Nichols, *Grants of King Edward the Fifth* (Camden Soc., 1854), pp. xv–xix.

to do so, and to receive his acquittance by the king's sign manual, any statute, act, ordinance or provision to the contrary notwithstanding.[122]

When Richard gained control he and his advisers subjected to careful examination all the arrangements made by his brother for the control and augmentation of his land revenues. Edward IV's treasurer of the Chamber had been too close to his master and to his heir, to survive a revolution but, on the whole, Edward's professional servants accepted Richard as their new master wherever they were given the chance to do so. Perhaps John Hayes wavered. At least he had to confess that the 'great rebel' Thomas marquis of Dorset managed to get from him £39 16s 8d of his issues. But Richard took Hayes into his service on the old terms and wrote off what had passed to Dorset because 'John Hayes hath well and truly endeavoured him in saving the remnant of the said issues and revenues'. He also accepted as true what Hayes told him he had paid out by word of mouth of Edward IV.[123] This treatment may well be contrasted with Henry VII's unwillingness to take any risk when this same important receiver after six years in his service gave him some slight grounds to suspect his loyalty in 1492.[124]

Further appointments of receivers and auditors followed. Richard confiscated the lands held as queen by Elizabeth Wydeville. John Fitzherbert, the king's remembrancer, was appointed as receiver of most of her scattered feefarms and annuities.[125] A number of new receivers were appointed to control groups of manors, some of which had been in her possession, some formerly held by Clarence and some which were later forfeited by the duke of Buckingham. An extensive group of royal lordships in Surrey, Buckinghamshire, Berkshire and Wiltshire were administered from Windsor castle, probably under control of William Harle.[126] Robert Brakenbury, constable of the Tower and formerly treasurer of Richard's household while he was duke of Gloucester, was appointed to administer a group of royal manors in Kent and Essex.[127] King Edward had promised the Gurney lands in Somerset and Dorset to the Herberts in exchange for the lordship of Pembroke and its members, but Richard may either have retained or resumed some or all of them for the time being, placing them under the control of Thomas Sapcote.[128] Richard's treasurer of the Chamber, Edmund Chadderton, later took personal charge of most of Buckingham's forfeited lands as receiver and surveyor[129] (Sir Reginald Bray succeeded him in

122. *Cal. Pat. Rolls, 1476–1485*, p. 449. P.R.O., Chanc., Patent Rolls, C.66/556, m. 3; *C.L.*, doc. no. 13.

123. P.R.O., Exch., K.R., Mem. Rolls, 'brevia directa baronibus', Hilary, 1 Ric. III, mm. 9, 10.

124. See below, p. 201.

125. *Cal. Pat. Rolls, 1476–1485*, p. 451.

126. B.M., MS. Harley 433, fols 217, 290.

127. *Cal. Pat. Rolls, 1476–1485*, p. 385.

128. *ibid.*, p. 364. But see below, p. 304.

129. *ibid.*, p. 453.

this post with the same fee of 100 marks p.a. in December 1485). One receiver of Clarence's lands, John Harcourt, was implicated in Buckingham's rebellion and was replaced by John Cutte.[130] In the North of England a group of manors and lordships were assigned to make payment to John Dawnay, treasurer of the king's household at Sandal, Yorkshire.[131]

New appointments of auditors were made with effect from Michaelmas 1483. William Mistelbroke and John Hewyk were appointed for all the Warwick, Salisbury, and Spencer (i.e. Clarence's) lands. Consequently those receivers of Clarence's lands who had been making declarations of account at the Exchequer under Edward IV now ceased to do so. William Mistelbroke and Richard Lussher were appointed as auditors for the lands of the principality of South Wales, the Pembroke lands, Haverfordwest, the lordship of Abergavenny, the counties of Glamorgan and Morgannok and the lordships of Newport, Hay and Brecknock.[132] John Stanford was appointed auditor for the Mowbray lands, the lands late of Margaret duchess of Somerset and, by a separate charge, to all the king's lands, presumably to cover all the remaining royal manors scattered throughout England for which no other auditor had been appointed.[133] Under Richard, except for one special case, the Exchequer audited no accounts of receivers of royal lands for the two years Michaelmas 1483 to Michaelmas 1485 whatsoever.[134] He appointed sufficient 'foreign' auditors to cover all his lands. A new local council was appointed for the duchy of Cornwall with power to make leases as in Edward IV's reign,[135] but this time the receiver-general of the duchy was instructed to make no appearance before the Barons of the Exchequer at all, and the two duchy auditors were authorized to draw up his final accounts at Lostwithiel.[136]

The '*Grants of Edward the Fifth*' also reveal that Richard had only been in London for a few days when he began to take control of the resources of his opponents and join them to his own. His seizure of the rich Exeter (Holand) inheritance, later confirmed by parliament, which had passed, with accretions, from his deceased sister, the duchess Anne, to her second husband Thomas St Leger, began on 16 May. Piers Courtenay, bishop of Exeter, was ordered to surrender the young 'duchess', their daughter Anne,

130. *ibid.*, p. 505.
131. B.M., MS. Harley 433, fols 269–70; *C.L.*, doc. no. 14[30].
132. *Cal. Pat. Rolls, 1476–1485*, pp. 474–5.
133. *ibid.*, p. 480.
134. P.R.O., Exch., L.T.R., Foreign Accts, E.364/118, 119. The only receiver's account before the Barons for this period was John Fitzherbert's, who was himself the Lord Treasurer's Remembrancer, and was put in charge of ancient exchequer farms and fee-farms confiscated from Queen Elizabeth Wydeville.
135. *Cal. Pat. Rolls, 1477–1485*, p. 461.
136. P.R.O., Exch., K.R., Mem. Roll, 'brevia', Hilary, 1 Ric. III, m. 14d. Order to the Barons to cease troubling John Sapcote Esq., the receiver-general, for any account because he was accounting before Thomas Aleyn and Robert Coorte as instructed to do at his appointment on 18 July 1483; *C.L.*, doc. no. 12(k).

to Buckingham.[137] Edward IV, in return for payment of 5,000 marks, had approved the settlement of these lands, by marriage, on the heir of Thomas Grey, marquis of Dorset, the queen's eldest son.[138] Richard's agents were assuming control of Dorset's own lands from 22 May[139] and of Rivers's lands from 29 May.[140] The Mowbray inheritance which Edward IV had secured for his son Richard was never completely given up by Richard III, even though it had only been acquired by Edward to the heirs male of his body. Buckingham was put in control of the Mowbray lordship of Gower on 26 May.[141]

The royal lands thus continued to be well staffed with receivers, auditors and other officers and the additions of 1483–4 were quickly assimilated. One of the reasons for the later dismal failure of Buckingham's rebellion was most probably the overriding loyalty of such men to whoever held the Crown. They ensured that he was obeyed as the king's representative but not otherwise. In the case of seizures of private lands the normal practice, from the evidence of MS. Harley 433, seems to have been to appoint the existing private officers to the royal service wherever possible *ad interim*, during good behaviour. Richard's signet office docket book contains many instructions to the king's receivers in all parts of the country, irrespective of whether they held office under the Crown, the duchy of Lancaster, or the earldom of March, etc. The steward of the honour of Tutbury, part of the duchy of Lancaster, was sent special instructions under the signet by Richard III how to appoint his subordinates.[142] Under Richard III duchy of Lancaster receivers in the south parts paid their issues direct to the treasurer of the Chamber and the signet office sent out warrants to them direct, ordering them to make payment to the king's creditors. There are numerous entries of receipts given by the treasurer of the Chamber for sums of cash received from various royal receivers. John Kendal, king's secretary, Edmund Chadderton, treasurer of the Chamber, and Thomas Lynom, king's solicitor, were all active taking lands into the king's hands, organizing and administering them.

Among this class of entry (drafts of instructions to issue under the signet) is a signet letter dated at the palace of Westminster on 6 January 1484 to Thomas Freebody 'Receivur of our lands late purchased by the king Edward the iiijth our brother' (the idea that there was a special category of lands purchased by the king was a fiction also maintained by Henry VII). The marginal note is 'Lettres for Recevurs'. It is a second summons to

137. *Grants* etc., p. 11.
138. *Rot. Parl.*, vi, 215–18, the annulment by Richard's parliament is *ibid.*, vi, 242–4.
139. *Grants* etc., pp. 40, 42–3.
140. *ibid.*, pp. 53–4, 57.
141. *ibid.*, p. 49. Edward's acquisition of the Mowbray inheritance through the marriage of the heiress to his son Richard is described in the *Complete Peerage*, ii, 133.
142. B.M., MS. Harley 433, fol. 270; *C.L.*, doc. no. 14[31].

appear before the king 'incontynent upon the sight of thise our lettres by us to you nowe sent all excuses and delayes laid apart'. Freebody, a receiver of lands which had belonged to Clarence, whose patent of appointment is on the patent roll dated 23 January 1482,[143] was commanded: 'be with us in your propre persone in alle goudly hast bryngìng with you alle suche sommes of money as be nowe due unto us by reason of your said office. And also to make your accompte in that behalve before such our Auditours as therunto shalbe assigned. Not failling herof as ye wolle answer unto us at your perille.' There follows a list of nineteen other receivers who were to be sent 'a like lettre'.[144]

The most interesting type of document in this volume are the financial memoranda, some of which no doubt also resulted in instruments sent out under the signet, but which also preserve the results of deliberations by the king and his councillors, or aide-memoires put before them. Thus this volume might well, in part, be described as a council docket book. A good example of this kind of document, the contents of which will be discussed later, is a list of manors, lordships, lands and tenements granted away to various persons, with many annual values and reserved rents stated. This list is undated and in itself gives no clue to its origins.[145] But the reserved rents, new feefarms in effect, had to be notified to the Exchequer, and the writ which accompanied the resulting schedule to the Exchequer on 20 May 1485 reveals how it was prepared. It is worded 'we and oure counsaill be certainly enformed' and 'we by thadvise of oure said counsaill wol and charge you'.[146]

Among such memoranda must be mentioned (1) a list of 'fees and wages granted out of the Crown to divers folk by king Edward IV, whom God pardon', totalled as £9,164 4s 9¾d; (2) a list of fees and wages of officers of the duchy of Lancaster, compiled from the ministers' accounts of 22 Edward IV, and totalled as £1,391 1s 8d; (3) an untotalled list of fees and wages of officers for Salisbury, Warwick and Spencer lands, Devonshire lands, Rivers's lands (including the Isle of Wight), and Wiltshire lands,[147] and (4) a list, with no contemporary heading, but described in a much later hand as 'Officers with their salaries pertaining to the king's houses, lordships and castles'.[148]

There is quite a lot of duplication between the first and the fourth of these lists. The author of the first was concerned to record the names of the recipients of fees and wages and, in general, the office held by each, and he totalled what he had compiled. Entries appear to be recorded by counties

143. *Cal. Pat. Rolls, 1476–1485*, p. 258.
144. B.M., MS. Harley 433, fols 138v.–139; *C.L.*, doc. no. 14[15].
145. *ibid.*, fols 282–9v.
146. P.R.O., Special Collections, Rentals and Surveys, S.C.11/827.
147. B.M., MS. Harley 433, fols 310–16, 317–21, 322.
148. *ibid.*, fols 336–9.

according to the area where payment was received, but the precise source of payment may be omitted. There are certain entries which hardly seem to fit his heading, such as annuity payments to Cecily duchess of York, James earl of Douglas and Lewis de Bruges, earl of Winchester, and a couple of payments for the repair of harbours. On the other hand, if these are taken as legitimate inclusions, one would expect there to be many more of the same kind included. In spite of the total at the end of it, this list, even for England, is territorially incomplete. The fourth list, which consists of titles of offices only and their fees or wages, while not duplicating the offices in the second and third lists (the duchy of Lancaster and the Salisbury, Warwick and Spencer etc., lists) gives complete territorial coverage for England, Wales, Calais, and Ireland. If we combine the information for England and Wales obtainable from all four lists we are still left with certain notable omissions: the offices of the Exchequer, some principal household officers, the sheriffs, and the customers in the ports.

These four lists combined, with duplications eliminated where they have been recognized, suggest that the Yorkist kings had in their gift in England and Wales some 800 offices worth about £13,000 p.a., over and above the omitted categories. Out of these totals some 700 offices, great and small, central and local, had their remuneration secured on crown lands, fee-farms and sheriffs' farms, to a total of about £7,000. The Croyland chronicler attributed the greater political stability of the latter years of Edward IV's reign in part to his effective personal oversight of the distribution of his patronage. The fact that this information should be required by Richard III's advisers is therefore significant evidence of administrative continuity in this respect.

Other important documents of this nature are a list of corrodies and pensions in the king's gift in houses of religion in England and Cornwall[149] (sic); and a certificate of the clear value of the temporalities of the Archbishopric of York for the year ending at Michaelmas 1482.[150] There are also two detailed assignments of £10,574 6s 8d and £1,344, made for a year's maintenance of the king's main Household and for a subsidiary establishment at Sandal, Yorkshire, respectively, and apportioned almost entirely on the revenues from royal lands under the names of the receivers concerned.[151] It is difficult to understand how such statistics could be compiled or such apportionments could be made unless some central record such as a book of summaries of receivers' audited accounts, was maintained in the Chamber.

Two of the numerous documents concerning the royal lands entered among these drafts of signet letters and council memoranda for Richard

149. *ibid.*, fols 335–6.
150. *ibid.*, fols 324–7.
151. *ibid.*, fols 269v.; 290–290v.; *C.L.*, doc. nos. 14[30], 14[33].

III's reign have long been in print: the first, a series of instructions for the better administration of the honour of Tutbury, the second the well known document headed: 'A remembraunce made, aswele for hasty levy of the kynges revenues growing of all his possessions and hereditamentes as for the profitable astate and governaunce of the same possessions.'[152] The latter is a series of observations, jotted down on paper, either as they occurred to a single author, or as points raised in a conciliar committee. It falls naturally into certain sections and may be summarized as follows:

A plea was made for speedy accounting at the Exchequer to facilitate the rapid levying of exchequer revenues which consisted of sheriffs' and escheators' issues, the feefarms of cities and towns, customs and subsidies, the issues of Calais and Guînes, and tenths and fifteenths. No accountant should be allowed more than four months' respite. No officer of the Receipt should hold office in the Court. Exchequer auditors should record all exchequer revenues in a book designed to show the year's income, and its contents should be declared annually before persons assigned by the king. The Treasurer of England should make a yearly declaration of all money received and assigned within his office.

A number of points deal with methods of levying and augmenting the king's land revenues. The system of committing the king's manors at farm to various persons for lump sums ('fermes in certeyn') was not the best. By it the king lost his casual revenues (woodsales and courts), he had no benefit from deductions of farm allowed in anticipation of improvements to be made (because repairs were in fact not carried out), and manors were often set to farm at less than their true value ('within the value'). All the king's lands should have foreign auditors and receivers, charged to 'ride, survey, receive and remember in every behalf that might be most for the king's profit and thereof yearly to make report'. Stewards of the king's lands should be men learned in the law (i.e. professional men), not local lords, knights, or esquires, many of whom might be unlettered and lack the wit and skill to order the king's lands as they should. Also such men extorted fines for their own use, thereby impoverishing the king's tenants and defrauding the king. Wardships in the king's hands during minority, and temporalities of bishoprics, abbeys and priories in the king's hands during vacancy, should be similarly administered and not farmed out.

The remaining points deal with methods of audit. All the king's lands in Wales, the duchies of Cornwall, York and Norfolk, the earldoms of

152. *ibid.*, fols 270–2. Both printed in *Letters etc. Richard III, Henry VII* (Rolls Series), i, 79–85 and the second in *Select Documents of English Constitutional History, 1307–1485*, ed. S. B. Chrimes and A. L. Brown. Both documents are undated. They are entered between documents dated 2 October 1484 and 23 October 1484 respectively; *C.L.*, doc. nos 14[31], 14[32].

Chester, March, Warwick, and Salisbury and all other lands in the king's hands by forfeiture should be audited, not in the Court of the Exchequer, but by carefully selected auditors, assigned for this task only, sufficient in number to audit the king's livelihood between Michaelmas and Candlemas annually. The Exchequer could never have the special on-the-spot knowledge which these examinations of the receivers of the king's lands and their accounts required. Between Candlemas and Palm Sunday each year all auditors, whether of the Exchequer or of foreign livelihood, should make declarations of all the livelihood in their charge, in London, before certain persons assigned to receive them. After this examination they should deliver the accounts in their charge to the Barons of the Exchequer, to be kept in the Exchequer. This delivery to the Exchequer should be made twelve months in arrears so that the most recent accounts were always in the auditors' own hands for reference. This procedure was not to apply to the accounts of the duchy of Lancaster and the lordships of Glamorgan and Abergavenny.[153]

This document undoubtedly represents a survey of the organization of the royal revenues as it existed at the accession of Richard III, with some suggestions for improvements, prepared for the consideration of his Council and based on the experience of twenty years of trial and error under Edward IV.

Contemporary valuations put on them suggest that the main units of estates under Richard's control in 1483 were expected to produce somewhere between £22,000 and £25,000 p.a., and possibly more, over and above recurrent charges, fees and wages. The following, with their approximate valuations, were the principal component parts. The lands of the principality of Wales, Chester and Flint, and the duchy of Cornwall were valued at 10,000 marks a year when set aside for York and his sons in parliament in 1460.[154] To these Edward IV had added the lands of the earldom of Pembroke, though surrendering the Gurney lands in Somerset and Dorset to William Herbert as compensation.[155] Queen Elizabeth had

153. The duchy of Lancaster was its own court of record. The lordships of Glamorgan and Abergavenny were the personal inheritance of Richard III's Queen Anne (died 16 March 1485), through her mother Anne (Beauchamp), dowager countess of Warwick, who in 1474 had been deprived of all her lands 'as if the said countess were now naturally dead' (*Rot. Parl.*, vi, 100). Richard III does not appear to have made any additional provision for his queen and, indeed, Nicholas Spicer, receiver of Abergavenny, was included in the receivers summoned on 6 January 1484.

154. *Rot. Parl.*, v, 380–2.

155. *ibid.*, vi, 202–4. At the end of the fourteenth century the lordship of Pembroke was farmed at 800 marks: *Cal. Pat. Rolls, 1399–1401*, p. 140. Farms collected by receivers of the Gurney manors totalled about £400 a year (e.g. S.C.6/1123/3, Mich., 16–Mich., 17 Ed. IV). Valuations for Welsh lands not subject to English parliamentary taxation or to the English system of justice are even more difficult to ascertain than for English ones. The unsolved, indeed probably insoluble, problems confronting anyone who tries to estimate incomes from land in fifteenth-century England are well brought out by Joel T.

received a jointure reputed to be worth 4,000 marks, though considerably less than earlier fifteenth-century queens. In the year ending at Michaelmas 1467 her receiver-general had handled receipts from land revenues of over £4,500.[156] By the end of Edward's reign she had absorbed most of the income from the south parts of the duchy of Lancaster. Much of the rest of the duchy income would have been absorbed by the provisions of Edward IV's will, but his executors now declined their charge.[157] In 17–18 Edward IV John Luthington had valued the north parts of the duchy at £3,127 7s 7¾d over and above reprises and various other payments, which had included annuities.[158] George duke of Clarence had been guaranteed 'lordships, manors, lands, tenements and other possessions to the yearly value, over all charges, of 5,500 marks, other than fees and wages', together with the reversion of those portions not then free, and valued at a further 1,000 marks.[159] Edward IV had since raised a loan on some of his lands, and had paid some of Clarence's debts with the income from some of the others; he had also allowed the dowager countess of Wiltshire to recover four of the Brian manors which Clarence had held, but, at Richard III's accession, Clarence's lands were still almost completely intact under royal control. As for Richard's own lands, which he already held as duke of Gloucester, it is most improbable that he had been content with anything less than his brother's endowment. Indeed, comparison of their grants on the patent rolls suggests that in the ultimate event he had acquired the larger portion. The lands of York and March were still encumbered with the jointure of Richard's mother, Cecily (5,000 marks less £689 6s 8d borne by the customs) which he confirmed,[160] but the executors of his father's will had already surrendered the lands formerly in their custody,[161] and it does not seem unreasonable to add a further £1,000 for the York and

Rosenthal's study 'The Estates and Finances of Richard, Duke of York (1411–1460)' in University of Nebraska *Studies in Medieval and Renaissance History*, ed. W. M. Bowsky, ii (1965). An admirable picture of Welsh estates where the perquisites of taxation and justice were included is given by T. B. Pugh's *Marcher Lordships of South Wales 1415–1536* (Cardiff, University of Wales History and Law Series no. xx, 1963).

156. *Letters and Papers Illustrative of the Wars of the English in France*, ed. J. Stevenson (Rolls Series, 1864), ii, pt. 2, p. 783; P.R.O., Exch., Treas. of Receipt, Misc. Bks, E.36/207.

157. *Collection of Wills of Kings and Queens of England, etc.*, ed. J. Nichols (Soc. of Antiquaries, 1780), pp. 345–9. The will is printed by S. Bentley in *Excerpta Historica* (London, 1831), pp. 366–79.

158. P.R.O., Duchy of Lancaster, D.L.43/16/1.

159. *Rot. Parl.*, v, 578–9 (1467–8). The household expenses of an ordinary duke in Edward IV's reign were expected to amount to £4,000. Clarence's household expenses in 1468 amounted to £4,505 15s 10¾d (see A. R. Myers, *The Household of Edward IV*, pp. 95 and 238, n. 68). Both Clarence and Gloucester were dependent for their incomes on land revenues, in which I include the valuable exploitation of mineral rights. They did not enjoy grants from the customs revenues, the only other sure source of income for royal dependents.

160. *Cal. Pat. Rolls, 1476–1485*, pp. 441–2, 459.

161. *ibid.*, p. 341.

March lands. The Mowbray inheritance was still under royal control. As always there were valuable lay escheats in hand in 1483. To include only those specifically laid under contribution for household expenses, there were the earldom of Essex (Bourchier) lands (£533 6s 8d) and the Fitzwarren lands (£233 6s 8d).[162]

In the complete absence of central accounts of the kind which only survive from 1503–4 any attempt to give more precise figures would be misleading.[163] Moreover, while not doubting the considerable extent of the royal lands and the essential, central, cameral and conciliar control of them exercised by Richard, it is clear that the ability to expend land revenues locally was always important and, for the moment, especially important to him. The duke of Buckingham had complete discretion to take what he needed locally. In other areas, for example the Isle of Wight, garrison expenses were particularly heavy. This estimate of total value, over and above recurrent charges, fees and wages, must be understood as including such local disbursements.

The additional total of about £7,000 p.a., disbursed in fees and wages from the issues of lands, feefarms and sheriffs' farms, cannot be separated into sinecures and offices requiring actual exercise from the information provided by MS. Harley 433. The inclusion in the list of fees and wages of a few obvious annuities, and the absence of any separate list of annuities charged on royal revenues is puzzling. Richard III certainly granted several large annuities on his land revenues. Thomas Howard, the later victor of Flodden, had £1,000 p.a. to sustain the dignity of earl of Surrey during his father's lifetime, secured on the duchy of Cornwall.[164] William Herbert, earl of Huntingdon, and his wife Katherine, Richard III's illegitimate daughter, had £152 10s 10d from the lands of the principality of Wales until suitable lands should be found for them.[165] Such annuities must therefore be considered as included in the overall total value of between £22,000 and £25,000 for Richard's land revenues, with the addition of some £7,000 p.a. disbursed in fees and wages.

The usurpation had inevitably brought a flood of estates into Richard's

162. Included in the assignment of £10,574 6s 8d for the expenses of the Household from 31 March 1485 (B.M., MS. Harley 433, fols 290–290v.). On the receipt roll for the last year of Richard III appear items of sheriffs' farms, feefarms of towns, payment by bailiffs of liberties, vacant temporalities, wards and marriages, other feudal incidents and farms of royal manors totalling £4,643, but it is doubtful whether any financial calculation should include or exclude these. The receipt rolls by this date seem to be more a legal record of royal obligations to creditors and vice versa than a financial record and, of course, an incomplete record even in this sense (cf. above, p. 170, n. 77; and p. 171, n. 84).

163. My earlier estimates in *E.H.R.* (1956), pp. 19–20, that Richard III enjoyed an income of £25,000 net cash p.a. at the very least from his lands and that they bore charges of something like £10,000 p.a. in annuities and pensions were therefore too high. Further consideration of the MS Harley 433 lists suggests that Yorkist annuities and pensions which were not tied to either local or central offices were rare on crown lands.

164. *Cal. Pat. Rolls, 1476–1485*, p. 479.

165. *ibid.*, p. 538.

hands because he had, in effect, eliminated the whole royal family. His own son did not live long enough to receive any endowment, and his queen appears to have received nothing from him. Her own personal inheritance consisted of the lordships of Glamorgan and Abergavenny, excluded by the author or authors of the 'remembrance for hasty levy of the king's revenues' from the jurisdiction of the chamber auditors, along with the duchy of Lancaster. Their receiver was nevertheless included among those nineteen other receivers summoned to appear there with Thomas Freebody.[166] The availability of something like £22,000 to £25,000 from land revenues, over £11,000 of which could be devoted to the current expenses of the Household, and the rest to Richard's general political objectives, was clearly incompatible with the adequate endowment of a royal family on the traditional scale out of the Crown's landed resources. Such an endowment had been an accepted feature of English government time out of mind, a tradition to which Edward IV had in the main conformed, in spite of the reduced scale of his queen's endowment, and of his experiments in regional government partly financed from their resources.

No fair-minded historian can possibly doubt from the evidence of the sequence of events that the usurpation of Richard III ruined the House of York. Henry of Richmond had been an irrelevance to English politics at the death of Edward IV. Events from June to October 1483 gave him a considerable, if reluctant, following. Speculations about the motives of Richard's many substantial and influential supporters, or of those disillusioned servants of the House of York who raised widespread but easily crushed rebellions throughout the southern counties on 18 October 1483, are largely beyond the scope of this study. On the one side Richard inspired confidence as a ruler; on the other, loyal Yorkists of high principle could not stomach his treatment of the young princes and planned rebellion. They were ultimately driven to invite the intervention of Henry of Richmond; but only when rumours of the murder of the princes became current. This happened at an advanced stage of their preparations.[167] Buckingham clearly inspired no one, not even himself, as an alternative to Richard.

The effects of Buckingham's rebellion upon the royal lands must, however, be considered in some detail. Sir James Ramsay long ago stated that MS. Harley 433 contained a statement of lands given away by Richard to the value of something like £12,000 p.a., without including his grants to the duke of Norfolk, listed there, but not valued.[168] This list has been cited as bearing out Sir Thomas More's contention that 'with large giftes hee get him unsteadfaste frendeshippe' in a state of something akin to panic

166. See above, p. 185, n. 144.

167. This is how I read the account given by the Croyland chronicler, a reasoned, *ex post facto* account by a well-informed, intelligent contemporary (*Rerum Anglicarum Scriptores*, i, 567–8).

168. *Lancaster and York*, ii, 534.

after Buckingham's rebellion.[169] Leaving aside all questions of More's value as a historian, it should be noted that this observation comes in his preliminary character sketch and is not related to any specific events. It is also merely *part* of a sentence, which continues: 'for whiche he was fain to pil and spoyle in other places, and get him stedfast hatred.'[170]

Did Richard pay the price of usurpation by a wholesale dispersal of royal lands? Had Buckingham remained loyal there would probably have been a loss of duchy of Lancaster lands to the value of over £1,000 a year, but, of course, he did not do so.[171] The only effective large-scale alienation prior to the rebellion was a grant of nearly fifty forfeited Oxford (de Vere) and Hungerford manors in Suffolk, Essex, Kent, Cambridge, Cornwall, Wiltshire and Berkshire to John Howard, co-heir to the Mowbray lands, following his creation as duke of Norfolk. Most, if not all of these, had been held by Richard himself as duke of Gloucester. Ramsay was probably correct in assuming that these lands, together with further grants from the newly seized Rivers and Dorset (Grey) lands, confirmed on 28 February 1485,[172] and all included in the MS. Harley 433 list, amounted to £1,000 a year. Against this must be set the fact that from March 1485 Richard could still assign Norfolk (Mowbray) lands to contribute £400 a year to the expenses of the royal Household.[173]

This remarkable MS. Harley list of royal grants, mainly in tail male, bearing annual values of over £12,000 and reserved rents of a little more than £740,[174] can only be adequately discussed after laborious identification in the calendars of chancery rolls, reference to the roll of Richard's parliament, and to the ensuing instructions to the Exchequer which followed its compilation.[175] It proves to represent in fact a ruthless confiscation of the lands of the rebels of October 1483, ninety-five of whom were subsequently attainted in parliament.[176] Their lands were seized and

169. Gairdner, *op. cit.*, p. 159, seems to have been the first to use the quotation from More in this truncated form. It is repeated together with references to Ramsay's list by J. R. Lander in his article 'Attainder and Forfeiture, 1453 to 1509', *The Historical Journal*, iv (1961), 122 and in his book *The Wars of the Roses* (London, 1965), p. 252.

170. For the full original sentence of More see *The Complete Works of Sir Thomas More*, ed. R. S. Sylvester (Yale U.P., New Haven, 1963), ii, p. 8.

171. Dugdale, *Baronage*, i, 168, printed the original letter under the signet and sign manual, dated at Greenwich 13 July I Ric. III, from the Stafford archives, acknowledging Buckingham as the true heir to Henry V's portion of the Bohun inheritance which was to be restored to him in the next parliament as if no act of attainder had been made against Henry VI. Meantime he was to enjoy the profits from Easter 1483. This is also entered in MS. Harley 433, fols 107v.–108v. The list of lands concerned is that of the original division between Anne countess of Stafford and Henry V printed in *Rot. Parl.*, iv, 136 (1421).

172. *Cal. Pat. Rolls, 1476–1485*, p. 359 (25 July 1483); *ibid.*, p. 497 (25 February 1485).

173. B.M., MS. Harley 433, fols 290–290v.

174. *ibid.*, fols 282–289v.

175. P.R.O., Special Collections, Rentals and Surveys, S.C.11/827, correctly described in *Lists and Indexes*, xxv, p. 400, as 'Schedule of rents reserved on grants of forfeited lands'.

176. *Rot. Parl.*, vi, 244–59, 251. This figure does not include the bishops of Ely, Salisbury and Exeter attainted separately, *ibid.*, vi, 250.

redistributed to his loyal supporters on a scale unprecedented in English history since Richard II disinherited his opponents in 1398. Moreover, this confiscation and redistribution proceeded without the normal delaying safeguards of legal inquisition as laid down in several statutes, and parliament subsequently legalized this arbitrary procedure.[177] Inquisitions, the returns of which survive at the Public Record Office, show that by the time these were held the new owners were already in possession, though the jurors declared that they did not know by what authority.[178] The Croyland chronicler, whose accuracy for the events of these years, if not the inferences he drew from them, tends to be borne out by record sources to a remarkable degree, complained bitterly that the people of southern England groaned under a tyranny of northerners imposed by this deliberate 'plantation'.[179] Prominent and less prominent examples of northerners so favoured are easy to identify among the 138 individual grantees in this list.

The list includes much of the Exeter–St Leger inheritance, and of the Rivers and Dorest (Grey) lands. The impact of political events upon family fortunes is well illustrated by the earl of Northumberland's grants included in it, as well as by certain others. Through his mother, Eleanor Poynings, he claimed the extensive Brian and Bures estates in Devon, Dorset, Somerset, Essex, Suffolk and Kent, and the very homelands of the Poynings family in Surrey and Sussex. All these were now summarily granted to him. The young rebel Sir Edward Poynings and his mother received no consideration at all (Sir George Browne the step-father and second husband had also been implicated in the rebellion). Other family claimants to some of these lands, the Butlers and Bourchiers, appear to have fared little better.[180] Francis viscount Lovell put forward a family claim to some of the Exeter lands as an heir of the Holands,[181] and these were included in his grants. There was even one member of the Grey family, Sir Edward, viscount Lisle, uncle of the marquis of Dorset, who was rewarded for his loyalty with a group of his nephew Dorset's manors in Warwickshire and Leicestershire. Richard III thus had an excess of newly forfeited lands of rebel Yorkists, headed by the immense forfeitures of Buckingham, with which to reward his loyal followers. Calculated ruthlessness, not hasty panic, is the explanation of these grants. There had been nothing like these forfeitures in England since the days of Richard II.

Nevertheless, careful study of this remarkable list does reveal more than

177. *ibid.*, vi, 249–50. The relevant statutes governing the taking of inquisitions and the subsequent making of grants were 34 Ed. III, c. 13, 8 Hen. VI, c. 16 and 18 Hen. VI, c. 6.

178. C. 145/330, 'Lands of attainted persons', 2 Ric. III, 22 membranes.

179. *Rerum Anglicarum Scriptores*, i, 570.

180. For the apparent recognition of the Butler and Bourchier claims at this time see J. M. Bean, *The Estates of the Percy Family 1416–1537*, p. 122.

181. *Rot. Parl.*, vi, 254–5.

the devastating thoroughness of his proscription of the rebels, and the consequent exacerbation of a number of private family land feuds. Mention of the Brian lands recalls that Clarence had held these. Acknowledgement of Northumberland's claims therefore diminished the royal estate as it had stood at Richard's accession to power by the amount of their value. Moreover, Richard now took this opportunity to distribute among his most prominent supporters what appear to have been the major part of those earldom of Devon lands formerly also held by Clarence. In disposing of the lands of the Oxford (de Vere) and Devon (Courtenay) lands he was striking at two of the most inveterate supporters of the Lancastrian cause, and giving some of his own most powerful supporters a vested interest in their misfortunes. By relinquishing Brian, de Vere, Courtenay and Hungerford estates to his supporters he may have diminished the crown estates, not by more than £12,000, but by some £2,500 p.a.[182] Against that must be set Mowbray lands, Stafford (Buckingham), Rivers and other forfeited estates which other entries in MS. Harley 433 show he retained in hand, under the control of his receivers and auditors. One conclusion is certain: no later royal act of resumption by his successor, annulling Richard's grants, could appreciably enrich the crown estate. It could only restore the disinherited victims of Richard's ruthless policies and Richmond's own exiled supporters.

182. It would appear that the Courtenay and Brian estates in Clarence's hands were assigned for the expenses of the royal Household by Edward IV in 1482 and may have constituted the whole of the sum of £1,200 p.a. in the list given in *Rot. Parl.*, vi, 198. I do not know the separate value of the Brian lands, but the Courtenay lands in the MS. Harley 433 list (granted to Sir Richard Ratcliffe) were valued at a little under £600 p.a. Allowing the other £600 for the Brian lands and accepting Ramsay's £1,000 for the value of the whole of Norfolk's grant (including the Rivers and Dorset lands), £2,500 seems to be an estimate generous enough to allow for alienations of other individual royal manors which I may have failed to identify in this massive MS. Harley 433 list.

VII
HENRY VII'S LAND REVENUES AND CHAMBER FINANCE*

I. THE COLLAPSE AND RE-ESTABLISHMENT OF THE YORKIST LAND REVENUE ORGANIZATION

Richard III's reign had been an administrative continuation of his brother's reign, indicating that usurpation and political revolution did not necessarily entail disruption of governmental policies or administrative practice. In this respect change depended on the background and character of the new king. As a result of the dissensions within the House of York and the verdict of Bosworth Field, England had now acquired a king whose character made change inevitable. Henry Tudor had grown up in exile; he had no knowledge of English government at all, and no experience gained from having estates of his own. His hunted, foreign up-bringing and the circumstances of his triumph left rooted in his mind a brooding suspicion of impending treachery and an inability to delegate responsibility, which was foreign to the normal run of English kings. His first inclinations were to play safe by relying on the more 'statutory' processes of government. An inevitable suspicion of Yorkist ways and supporters meant at the outset a reliance, wherever possible, on what could also be shown to have been done in the days of Lancastrian rule.

The viability of such a policy and its acceptance by public opinion was, however, very doubtful. Lancastrian days were the bad old days. 'Politique rule and governance' was associated with the House of York. Statements made to the contrary in preambles to Henry's legislation in 1485 were nothing but a polite fiction. Richard III had shocked the public conscience by stooping to infanticide, and his savage proscriptions had driven many able Yorkist servants into the service of Henry Tudor. But execration of his personal acts and their reversal in so far as they affected the lives and property of individuals had perforce to be distinguished from a rejection of the principles of government which he represented.

Greater economy in the royal Household, a greater degree of solvency and a high reputation for the orderly and dignified conduct of their Household had been one of the most acceptable features of Yorkist rule. The House of York had consciously striven to meet the public demand in this respect. But such demands stretched back beyond 1461. Results had

* This chapter is an expanded version of the article which I published in *E.H.R.* (1964), under the same title.

already been achieved with the household appropriations from current revenues, reinforced by the parliamentary acts of resumption, which Lancastrian governments had been prevailed upon to accept from 1450. Thus in 1485 Henry VII at 'the humble supplication made to his Highness by the Commons of this his present Parliament' could sanction a detailed parliamentary appropriation totalling £14,000 p.a. from current revenues for household expenses as a measure with a respectable Lancastrian ancestry. About £9,000 of this sum was charged to land revenues.[1] A further, similar appropriation amounting to £2,105 19s 11d was made for the Wardrobe, of which some £800 was charged on land revenues. This did not quite equal the £11,500 p.a. which MS. Harley 433 reveals Richard III had chosen to devote to the same purpose from his land revenues because Henry VII was pledged to surrender some of Richard's estates. But it did far exceed Edward IV's contribution of £4,500 in 1483. However, with effect from 29 November 1489 £2,700 p.a. of Henry's assignments on his land revenues were withdrawn when he created his infant son prince of Wales and earl of Chester. Substantial further endowment for prince Arthur, mainly from the earldom of March lands, occurred in 1493, followed by the re-establishment of a council in the Marches of Wales and a special act of resumption to declare Arthur's authority over all his lands.[2] The whole household assignment had to be reviewed in 1495 because of complaints from the Commons that it had become ineffective, and only £6,000 p.a. could then be found from land revenues towards the total of £13,059 9s 11d p.a. of a new assignment to replace the 1485 assignment which had broken down.[3]

In accepting these household assignments at all Henry was thus following a tradition which went back to 1450, but the legislation of 1485 has caused confusion in at least one standard modern work on the Tudor period. Professor Mackie maintains in *The Earlier Tudors* that the household appropriations of 1485 were the earliest example of Henry VII's new, exact and successful method of dealing with financial problems by careful estimate and conscious endeavour to live within the estimate.[4] In fact they were identical in conception, form and purpose with the parliamentary legislation of 1450, 1454 and 1455 which had mapped out the lines of subsequent Yorkist policies which had in turn largely rendered such parliamentary assignments unnecessary.

Henry VII's acts of resumption (1485, 1487 and 1495) must also be viewed within the context of the period after 1450, when the collapse of the personal government of Henry VI first forced acceptance of such legislation. Henry's advisers now laid before his first parliament, in its first

1. *Rot. Parl.*, vi, 299–304.
2. *ibid.*, vi, 433, 465–9; *Cal. Pat. Rolls, 1485–1494*, p. 453.
3. *Rot. Parl.*, vi, 497–502. 4. Mackie, *op. cit.*, pp. 63–4.

session, a bill of declaration and resumption with a schedule of protection for Cecily dowager duchesss of York attached to it. This official bill was designed to give Henry possession of the duchies of Lancaster and Cornwall and the earldoms of Richmond and Kendal. A cautious measure, as befitted the situation, it did no more than declare that Henry intended to be accepted as the undoubted heir of his uncle (Henry VI) and of his father (Edmund Tudor, earl of Richmond).[5] The inevitable acts of restitution and attainder followed. The number and importance of restitutions significantly exceeded the number of attainders. Edward IV in 1461 had carried out large-scale forfeitures among the nobility, but the number of his attainders had subsequently followed a downward curve.[6] Richard III had been quite ruthless in the autumn of 1483 and this may have contributed to his downfall. Henry VII, for all his suspicions and uncertainties, was in no position to follow such precedents. His introduction of a bill of attainder containing a modest number of names met with 'considerable censure', or, as one of the members himself put it, 'sore was questioned with'.[7]

The new king had to prove his mettle, but the same desire for co-operation with an effective king, shown by the Yorkist parliaments, was latent in the assembly of 1485. Both Edward IV and Richard III had enjoyed life grants of tunnage and poundage and of the wool subsidies. Henry VII was treated with the same generosity.[8] Moreover, in the second session of his first parliament a petition was presented inviting him 'to seize, have, retain and resume' into his hands all the lands, rents, feefarms annuities etc., which had belonged to Henry VI on 2 October 1455 or at any time since, 'as parcel and in the right and title of the Crown of England and of the duchy of Lancaster, the duchy of Cornwall, the principality of Wales and the earldom of Chester.' The last three (Yorkist) acts of resumption in 1465, 1467 and 1473 appear to have been government measures, presented for the consideration and discussion of parliament on the king's initiative. They symbolized the greater Yorkist concern for the public good expressed in their more frugal distribution and firmer personal control of patronage. But Yorkist precedents could hardly find favour and this so-called 'great resumption' of Henry VII originated in the older Lancastrian form of parliamentary petition. Indeed, the 1485 preamble followed the wording of the 1455 act, even though that act had originally been framed to castigate the Household of Henry VI for its insolvency, dishonourable reputation

5. *Rot. Parl.*, vi, 270–3.

6. See J. R. Lander, 'Attainder and Forfeiture, 1453 to 1509', *The Historical Journal*, iv (1961), 144–5.

7. 'Non transiit tamen sine multa disputatione, seu ut verius dicam, increpatione gestorum', the words of the Croyland chronicler (*Rerum Anglicarum Scriptores*, i, 581); see also the diary of the proceedings as recorded by the burgesses of Colchester (*Red Paper Book of Colchester*, ed. W. Gurney Benham, Colchester 1902), p. 64.

8. Edward IV since 1465, *Rot. Parl.*, v, 508–11: Richard III on accession, *ibid.*, vi, 238–40. Henry VII, *ibid.*, vi, 268–70.

and shameful abuse of the privilege of purveyance. Certain phrases, such as references to the recent disaster to English arms in France had to be discarded. But it had to be a Lancastrian measure and so 'King Henry the Sixth Your Uncle' was glibly substituted for the 1455 reference to the noble Prince Henry V as the example of a ruler who had kept a worshipful and honourable Household, now to be emulated.

Henry's advisers probably had some hand in drafting this new version of an unsuitable Lancastrian act. He was no doubt somewhat mollified to receive a proffer of support for Yorkist policies from the Commons, couched in such diplomatic Lancastrian terms, but the good will did not compensate for the tortuous and ambiguous drafting. All manner of grants made by Richard III were declared to be comprehended within the scope of the proposed resumption although, with the sole exception of grants affecting the earldom of Devon, only grants of offices made by Edward IV and Edward V were specifically mentioned for resumption. All 'resumptions' were to take effect from 22 August 1485, the date of the Bosworth verdict. The petition also invited Henry to resume all his own grants of offices made before 20 January 1486, except for certain principal offices of state which were named. Why this was so must be a matter for some speculation. Was it resentment at the displacement of too many lesser Yorkist servants? Or was it to afford him a welcome opportunity to review his actions in this respect? In any case he accepted the petition as it stood and consequently all recipients of his grants of offices, some of them only a few weeks old, and not yet enrolled, had to sue out clauses of exemption to protect and confirm their appointments.[9]

This was perhaps the most striking result of Henry VII's resumption of 1485. There is no evidence so far as the king's lands were concerned to support the repeated claim of modern historians of the Tudor period that this was a 'great resumption'.[10] Henry Tudor's task was to get himself accepted as the successor of Richard III, who had already held rather more than all the lands to which a king of England could decently lay claim quite firmly in his grasp. This was indeed a 'great' act only in its length (stretching over forty-eight double column, folio pages of the printed *Rotuli Parliamentorum*). This extreme length was due to the 461 clauses of exemption which Henry appended to it, a number far in excess of the total number of exemptions appended to any pre-1485 act of resumption. With the exception of appointments to offices Henry had made few grants himself. The rest of these exemptions were confirmations of the acts of his Yorkist predecessors.

Had the act of resumption, coupled with the attainder of Richard III, given Henry legal possession of the lands of the House of York? It is

9. *ibid.*, vi, 336–84.
10. Dietz, *op. cit.*, p. 21; K. Pickthorn, *op. cit.*, p. 17; Mackie, *op. cit.*, p. 63: 'an enormous act of resumption'.

obvious that he intended to have them, but it appears that the law courts still remained doubtful about his legal title in this respect. Two further legal measures therefore proved necessary as late as 1495, complementary to the legislation of 1485. They were official bills declaring: (1) Henry's undoubted right to all the lands (listed) and the goods which Richard III had held as duke of Gloucester, 'because no office [i.e. inquisition or legal verdict] is yet founden for the King's Highness', and (2) his right to all the lands (listed) which Edward III and Richard II had bestowed upon Edmund Langley, duke of York.[11]

The resumption act of 1487, again based on a Commons' bill, was in quite a different category being designed for specific financial and administrative, not legal, purposes. When Henry met his second parliament (9 November 1487) he was politically more sure of himself. He had defeated Lambert Simnel's army at East Stoke (16 June 1487). It was at this point that the urgent need to deal with problems of finance and to take advantage of the work done by the Yorkist kings and their servants was brought home to him. He may well have seen a memorandum similar to the 'remembrance' of MS. Harley 433 which had been drawn up for Richard III to assist the continuation of the work of his brother's reign. The preamble of this act clearly suggests that the Yorkist administration had been falling apart for lack of royal appreciation and supervision during the previous two-and-a-half years. It states that Henry had been so busy for the defence of the Church of England, his own most royal person and his realm since the beginning of his reign that he and his Council had so far not found time to 'set, make nor ordain receivers, auditors, customers, collectors of customs, subsidies, controllers, searchers, surveyors, alnagers and other officers accountants, such as should be to his most profit and avail, nor providently [to] make leases, grants or other things do for his most profit and approvement of his revenues and commodities, by occasion whereof, his honours, manors, lands, tenements, possessions and inheritaments, be greatly fallen in decay, and further in decay shall daily fall, if remedy in this behalf be not provided....'[12] The act therefore annulled all such grants of offices yet again. In addition all grants of 'lands, tenements and other profits yielding yearly therefor to his Highness any rent' and made for term of life or years by Henry himself, by Edward IV or by Richard III, were resumed. This act of resumption was therefore significantly limited in its scope compared with all the previous acts from 1450 to 1485 because it did not apply to grants in fee or, apparently, to rent-free grants for life or term of years. It was to be effective from Michaelmas 1488 ('Michaelmas next coming').

Record sources confirm that the organization of the Yorkist kings was indeed in fragments. The authority of the Yorkist Chamber had dissolved. Receivers who had managed to secure reappointment were perforce paying

11. *Rot. Parl.*, vi, 459–61.

12. *ibid.*, vi, 403–8.

their issues into the Exchequer of Receipt. Lands which the Yorkist kings had placed under control of receivers were slipping back again into the farming pool.[13] The Barons of the Exchequer, as they were legally bound to do for want of any legislation to relieve them of this duty, or of firm and repeated royal prohibitions, were resuming the powers of audit which had been denied them by Edward IV and Richard III.

On 17 May 1488 a commission was set up with authority under this parliamentary act of resumption either to appoint or confirm receivers and auditors for the king's lands or to let the lands to farm at their discretion. Its members were John lord Dynham, the Treasurer; Robert Lytton, the under-treasurer; William Hody, the Chief Baron; Richard Fox, bishop of Exeter, Keeper of the Privy Seal; Reginald Bray, chancellor of the duchy of Lancaster, formerly receiver-general to Henry VII's mother; and Thomas Savage, clerk.[14] This commission was of course largely dependent on the former servants of the House of York both for advice and to fill the appointments it made or confirmed. Indeed, Sir John Dynham himself had been Richard III's steward and surveyor of the duchy of Cornwall. Other servants of Richard III had secured important posts in the new central government. Avery Cornburgh, experienced in duchy of Cornwall administration and appointed under-treasurer of England by Richard III, had continued in this office, associated with Sir Reginald Bray, until his death in 1487.[15] Sir Richard Croft, Edward IV's receiver-general of the earldom of March and Richard III's treasurer of the Household, continued in office as Henry VII's first treasurer of the Household. John Kendal, Richard's secretary, and Robert Brakenbury, his constable of the Tower, had both been attainted, but their cases were exceptional. Even Master Edmund Chadderton, Richard's treasurer of the Chamber, had survived, though no doubt owing to the protection afforded by his cloth. He was no doubt regarded with the gravest suspicion and given no key post in the new administration, but he was later employed by Henry on several diplomatic missions. Among the receivers of the Yorkist kings who were confirmed in

13. e.g. the following lordships and manors, all in the hands of receivers in 1485, were let out to farm at traditional farms in the first years of Henry VII: Bushey (Herts.), Cold Kennington (Middlx.), Somerton (Lincs.), Milton and Marden (Kent), St Margaret Stratton (Wilts.), Caversham (Oxon.), Cookham and Bray (Berks.). Sir Richard Croft, receiver and surveyor of Woodstock and its members, himself took out a farm of the lands he controlled at £127 16s 6d (the rate of farm operating in the fourteenth and first half of the fifteenth century) plus 3s 6d increment. The bad old farming system was being allowed to come back. Between 1485 and 1489 more leases were made and entered on the fine rolls in the traditional manner than at any time since 1460, except during the 'Readeption' of Henry VI.

14. *Cal. Pat. Rolls, 1485–1494*, p. 230.

15. He may have been responsible for the appointment of a body of six receivers for the royal lands in separate shires or groups of shires to gather issues for Easter Term 1485 on the pattern of the years 1462 and 1471: P.R.O., Special Collections, Ministers' Accts, S.C. 6/3545/88 (Declaration of their Accounts).

office or soon reappointed were John Hayes, John Luthington, John Walsh, Richard Welby, Thomas Lynom, Nicholas Leventhorpe, John Cutte, John Dawnay, and John Agard. Among the Yorkist 'foreign' auditors retained in Tudor service were William Mistelbroke, Richard Sheldon, John Clerk, Robert Coorte, Richard Lussher, Thomas Aleyn, John Luthington, and Richard Greneway. Of newcomers to the administration of the king's lands perhaps the most important were Sir Reginald Bray, who came from the service of the king's mother; Hugh Oldham, later bishop of Exeter; Robert Southwell, and Richard Harper, formerly receiver-general to the duke of Buckingham. Obviously the continuity of personnel was very extensive indeed.[16]

The former servants of Edward IV and Richard III served their new master faithfully and efficiently and were rarely involved in the rebellions against him. But though he gradually came to appreciate the value of the financial policies they represented, the new king seems to have been incapable of taking any risks. The slightest suspicion against a former Yorkist servant disqualified him for future employment. John Hayes, a most efficient receiver, who held the chief office in the Warwick, Spencer and Salisbury lands for almost fifteen years under three kings, was suddenly removed and replaced by Sir Reginald Bray and Hugh Oldham on 20 February 1492. The reason was that he had been approached by an agent of Perkin Warbeck and had handled treasonable correspondence. His personal confession to the king saved his life and even his forfeiture was later rescinded. But his real crime in Henry's eyes seems to have been that he had burnt the correspondence before making his report to the king. Though officially pardoned he was never reappointed to his receiverships.[17]

The disposition of estates under receivers and auditors which emerged from the survey and overhaul carried out by the commission of 1488 was little different, though at first less extensive, than that left by Richard III. Henry had certain weighty obligations to fulfil which somewhat depleted the crown lands. For example, he had felt bound to make some amends to Queen Elizabeth Wydeville whose extensive estates Richard had seized.[18] In 1487 Henry in his turn was also moved to confiscate what he had restored to her, but provision still had to be made for her daughter the new queen, who received crown lands to the value of £3,000 p.a. The king's mother, Margaret countess of Richmond, received a very substantial grant of royal lordships and manors.[19] The king's uncle, Jasper Tudor, was given lands worth £2,000 p.a. Henry had incurred extensive obligations to Sir

16. cf. J. R. Lander's evidence of continuity in the personnel of the Yorkist and Early Tudor Council: 'Council Administration and Councillors, 1461–1485', *B.I.H.R.*, xxxii 1959), 164–5, 178–80.

17. *Cal. Pat. Rolls, 1485–1494*, pp. 21, 45, 46, 368, 377, 429; *Rot. Parl.*, vi, 454–6.

18. *Cal. Pat. Rolls, 1485–1494*, pp. 75–7.

19. *ibid.*, pp. 154–5.

William Stanley. Some restitutions of estates were made. Nevertheless, as regards the remainder, units of management for the king's lands under Henry VII were essentially those evolved by the Yorkist kings.[20]

No discussion of Henry VII's finances can proceed very far without taking into account the extensive and much quoted sets of figures provided by Professor F. C. Dietz for this reign. Dietz began his detailed discussion of Henry VII's land revenues with the statement that whereas the royal income from lands, excluding the farms of the shires and the feefarms of cities, had been £6,471 p.a. during the last year of Edward IV's reign, it rose to £13,633 during the first year of Henry VII.[21] These and other figures have produced a completely misleading picture to which subsequent writers still cling. They were obtained by totalling the receipt rolls which any student of medieval English history knows is a most hazardous process. To mention only one of the more obvious pitfalls, Dietz makes no distinction between cash payments and assignments. All that can safely be said about these figures is that they do seem to suggest a sudden and substantial increase in the ability of the Exchequer to dispose of the revenues of the Crown after the accession of Henry VII which merits investigation. The evidence of the receipt rolls for the last year of Richard III and the first year of Henry VII can perhaps best be stated as follows: excluding sheriffs' farms, feefarms of towns, payments made by bailiffs of liberties and payments for vacant temporalities, but including wardships and marriages, the cash receipts from the king's lands at the Exchequer for Michaelmas Term 1484 and Easter Term 1485 (2 Richard III) were rather less than £700 and assignments made on them a little over £1,800. For Michaelmas Term 1485 and Easter 1486 (1 Henry VII) the comparable exchequer amounts were: cash receipts from land revenues: over £4,700; assignments made on land revenues: over £7,000.[22] The true explanation is now obvious. Those Yorkists receivers of royal lands who survived the revolution, together with a number of new receivers, appointed *ad hoc* in the Exchequer possibly on the under-treasurer's initiative,[23] all began to pay their issues into the Exchequer of Receipt since there was no longer any financial organization in the king's Chamber with authority to accept

20. The organization of the king's lands under receivers and foreign auditors by Edward IV and Richard III is detailed in Appendix 'D'. Under Henry VII they are most conveniently set out in the earliest books of summaries of receivers' accounts, printed for the year 1503–4 in *C.L.*, doc. no. 16.

21. Dietz, *op. cit.*, p. 21, quoting receipt rolls nos 955 and 958. These figures are repeated by Pickthorn, *op. cit.*, p. 17 and Mackie, *op. cit.*, pp. 213–14.

22. P.R.O., Exch. of Receipt, E.401/951, 952, 953, 954, 957, 958. 955 and 956 are incomplete duplicates of 957; 959 is a duplicate of 958. I am assuming for purposes of the calculation that simple 'sol' (non 'mutuum') entries signify cash payments into the Exchequer.

23. John Marlburgh (Herts., Essex, Suff., Norf.), John Alfegh, alias Alseth (Surrey, Sussex, Kent), Thomas Holbache (Cambs., Hunts., Beds., Bucks.), John Dunham (Notts., Derbys.), John Stokker (Middlx.), Richard Welby (Lincs.). See above, p. 200, n. 15.

them. The exchequer officials found that hitherto forbidden sources of assignment were once again open to them. Failure to keep the Yorkist chamber organization intact must have cost Henry VII a great deal of ready cash in 1485. Reverting to the practice of the Lancastrians when English kings did not concern themselves with the management of their estates or with finance in their Chamber, Henry allowed the Exchequer for the moment to regain complete control over the income of the Chamber which appears to have been reduced once more to the position of a minor household department.

However, within a short space of time Henry appears to have been persuaded of the need to make available in the Chamber a substantial sum of ready cash. The habits and achievements of nearly twenty-five years of Yorkist rule could not simply vanish overnight. Three books of Henry's chamber receipts survive, and have been described by Newton[24] and Dietz. These were compiled under the king's eagle eye for his personal perusal and satisfaction. Audited by the king's sign manual, as laid down under Richard III, they were intended for his eyes alone. Nevertheless, his wary chamber treasurers made sure that these books, which constituted their only acquittance, survived the death of their master. They run from 4 July 1487–4 July 1489, from 30 September 1489–1 October 1495 and from 1 October 1502–1 October 1505.[25] The second and third begin with substantial balances in hand. The first shows that Thomas Lovell, as the treasurer of the Chamber, had no balance in hand on 4 July 1487[26] but received £10,491 in the following twelve months. The basis of the account in its earliest stages were payments from commissioners appointed to collect a parliamentary subsidy in the shires. The first two items entered in the surviving chamber accounts as received from the issues of royal lands were on 15 and 18 July 1487: £40 from the receiver of lands late of the earl of Essex and £150 from the receiver-general of the duchy of Lancaster due to the Household in the previous year. The exchequer memoranda rolls of the King's Remembrancer best show how direct payments for the chamber coffers from receivers and farmers of royal lands henceforth increased until ultimately almost the whole of the land revenues were once more going direct to the Chamber.

The rate at which land revenue receipts going to the Chamber (as far as they can be identified as such) increased in relation to the total chamber

24. A. P. Newton, 'The King's Chamber under the Early Tudors', *E.H.R.*, xxxii (1917), 348–72.

25. P.R.O., Exch., K.R., Various Accts, E.101/413/2/1, 2, 3.

26. The absence of any balance in hand on 4 July 1487 does not of course prove that no money had gone to the Chamber at all in the period since Richard III's death. Indeed this book does refer to an earlier account: 'sithen the account ended and determined between our said sovereign lord and the aforesaid Sir Thomas Lovell as appeareth by a book remaining'.

receipts from all sources can be seen from the following figures (given to the nearest £1,000):

	Yearly Average 4 July 1487– 4 July 1489	Yearly Average 1 Oct 1492– 1 Oct 1495	Yearly Average 1 Oct 1502– 1 Oct 1505
Total Receipts	£17,000	£27,000	£105,000
Land Revenues[27]	£3,000	£11,000	£40,000

Henry VII only gradually acquired an appreciation of the nature and purposes of chamber finance and of his need for what the Yorkists had created. Naturally the advantages to be derived from having a private hoard in his Chamber were quickest realized, but an appreciation of all the various methods by which this could be acquired and maintained took much more time.

An examination of the procedure of account after 1485 will probably shed more light on the development of Henry's financial policy than any compilation of figures. The Yorkist practice of holding a cameral and conciliar audit of land revenue which superseded the exchequer audit was unknown to Professor Dietz, who maintained that the repertories to states and views of public accounts and the 'foreign' account rolls in the Public Record Office both show the royal receivers still rendering their accounts at the Exchequer of Account at the beginning of Henry VII's reign in the traditional manner. During the first eight years of Henry's reign, Dietz claimed, these receivers came to the Exchequer in decreasing numbers, and from the eighth year, with a few minor exceptions, they did not come at all.[28] The repertories, the briefest of indexes, are really quite useless for statistical evidence of this kind.[29] Moreover, the entry of an account on the 'foreign' account roll for a certain regnal year does not mean either that the account was rendered for that particular year or that it was heard and determined during that year. The vital information to show when, in what numbers, and for which periods receivers of land revenues did account at the Exchequer during Henry VII's reign is indeed supplied by the 'foreign' account roll, but only with the aid of the auditors' notes written in the left margin at the head of each separate acount. These give the auditors' names and the date of their audit. From this information it is in fact quite clear that during the early years of Henry VII's reign the Exchequer was quietly, persistently and inevitably recovering the audit of accounts which it had so often been prohibited from doing for many years previously.[30] The significance of these auditors' notes was missed by Dietz.

27. For a definition of land revenues see below, p. 219. 28. Dietz, *op. cit.*, pp. 67–9.

29. An entry on a repertory may refer to a full account rendered before the Barons, but equally it may refer to a brief statement on the L.T.R. memoranda roll that the accountant was exonerated from account.

30. E.364/119 *passim* and below, p. 206.

At the same time as receivers of land revenues were being bidden to the Exchequer and were answering the summonses in increasing numbers some of the most prominent and experienced Yorkist 'foreign' auditors, who had grown accustomed to other methods, had secured patents of re-appointment during pleasure or good behaviour.[31] Their influence was bound to be felt. The conflict and confusion which followed shows that Henry took quite a long time finally to make up his mind between the new methods, which were utterly dependent on the king's personal interest and constant management for their survival, and the old, which were hallowed by law and tradition. The practice of freeing individuals from the venerable and relentless exchequer process was not to be lightly undertaken. The advantages of doing so had first to be very clearly demonstrated to him.

For example, during the reign of Edward IV, at least from 1477, a board of auditors had sat in Nottingham castle to determine the accounts of Gervase Clifton, king's receiver in Nottinghamshire and Derbyshire, who was forbidden to render his accounts at the Exchequer. In Michaelmas Term 1486 his successor John Dunham appeared before the Barons of the Exchequer and rendered account for the first time.[32] Richard Croft's accounts for Woodstock and other lands in Oxfordshire had begun to be determined outside the Exchequer in 1472 when the Barons were prohibited from meddling with them. In Hilary Term 1489 Croft, who had prudently obtained a farm of the lands in 1485 in the traditional manner, began to render account at the Exchequer with effect from Michaelmas 1485.[33] The receiver-general of the duchy of Cornwall, Robert Willoughby, whose predecessor had been ordered to make no appearance at the Exchequer by Richard III, secured royal exoneration on 25 May 1487 for failing to account at the Exchequer for the year Michaelmas 1485–Michaelmas 1486.[34] However, in Trinity Term 1489 he was compelled to account before the Barons for the year Michaelmas 1486–Michaelmas 1487.[35] Yet on 28 February 1489 he had already managed to obtain royal protection from exchequer demands for an account covering the year 1487–8.[36] The two most important receivers of lands which had belonged to the duke of Clarence (normally called Warwick, Salisbury and Spencer lands), John

31. E.g. William Mistelbroke to the lordships of Cardiff, Glamorgan, Abergavenny, and Salisbury and Spencer lands in the South-West; Richard Sheldon and John Clerk to Warwick, Salisbury and Spencer lands in the Midlands and South-East; Thomas Aleyn and Robert Coorte to the duchy of Cornwall; John Luthington to the duchy of York, earldom of March and honour and earldom of Richmond. Details are in the *Calendars of Patent Rolls*, and see below, Appendix 'D'.

32. E.364/119, 1 Hen. VII, A.

33. *ibid.*, 3 Hen. VII, D.

34. P.R.O., Exch., K.R., Mem. Rolls, 'brevia directa', Mich., 3 Hen. VII, m.2d. (E.159 264): 'until the time ye shall have from us otherwise commandment'.

35. E.364/119, 3 Hen. VII, H.

36. E.159/265, 'brevia directa', Trinity, 4 Hen. VII, m.10.

Hayes and John Walsh, in spite of their practice under Richard III, both began to render full accounts before the Barons in Hilary Term 1488 with effect from Michaelmas 1485.[37]

According to dates of audit by regnal year, accounts of receivers of land revenues were heard and determined by the Barons of the Exchequer as follows: 1 Henry VII: John Fitzherbert only; 2 Henry VII: John Dunham and John Dawnay;[38] 3 Henry VII: John Hayes, John Walsh (two accounts), Thomas Iden,[39] John Wode and associates;[40] 4 Henry VII: John Hayes (two accounts), John Walsh, John Thomas,[41] Richard Croft,[42] Robert Willoughby. Obviously the Exchequer Court, following a clearly established legal practice, was well on the way to recovering its old accounting supremacy by 1489. Brian Sandeford, for the lordship of Caistor in Lincolnshire, and Richard Cholmeley, as successor to John Dawnay and chamberlain and treasurer of Berwick, began to account for the first time in 5 Henry VII and John Marlburgh[43] and John Peke[44] in 6 Henry VII. But from this date no major new accountants appeared at the Exchequer and some of those accounts already recovered had again ceased to be rendered.

The earliest evidence of a decisive return to Yorkist policy is a long writ to the Exchequer dated at Sheen on 2 March 1493 for Reginald Bray, Hugh Oldham, John Walsh, their heirs and executors, as receivers of the Warwick, Salisbury and Spencer lands, of lands late of William marquis of Berkeley, Lord Morley and Earl Rivers. This reveals that on the advice of his Council Henry VII had instructed them to pay their issues to his own hands and nowhere else and that arrangements had been made for their accounts to be regularly 'over-seen and examined' (i.e. surveyed) by the king and his Council. The writ claimed that the lands concerned 'be not nor have out of time of mind been any parcel of the ancient possessions of our Crown of England but that they be such lands as have now lately come to our hands by way of our purchase and otherwise'.[45] With effect from Michaelmas 1491 the Barons of the Exchequer were straightly charged and

37. E.364/119, 2 Hen. VII, C; 3 Hen. VII, E,F.

38. Receiver-general in Yorkshire, Westmorland, Cumberland and Northumberland. The lands were mainly the patrimony of Richard III as duke of Gloucester. Dawnay had been treasurer of his household at Sandal.

39. Receiver of the manor, lordship and hundred of Milton and Marden, Kent.

40. For lands late of Thomas Pigot.

41. A valet of the king's Chamber, receiver of the castle of Snothill.

42. I include Croft, although he had converted his receivership to a farm on the accession of Henry VII. He had been receiver of these same lands under the Yorkists and exempt from exchequer accounts.

43. Receiver in Herts., Essex, Suff., Norf. of various forfeited lands. See above, p. 202.

44. Receiver of lands late of Henry Neville, lord Latimer, and of Edward lord Roos.

45. It is interesting that Richard III in the signet writ quoted above p. 185, n. 144, refers in like manner to blocks of land which, whatever, their most recent history, did include ancient crown manors.

commanded to cease all process and execution against these three receivers for ever, and charged in future merely to demand regular delivery of their accounts into the Exchequer, from the 'foreign' auditors concerned, only after they had been determined by the king and his Council. Then and only then the Barons were to examine the accounts and preserve them as of record, but were strictly forbidden to make any process whatsoever against Bray, Oldham or Walsh, or against any subordinate accountants charged in the Exchequer who were revealed by perusal of the accounts in question to have accounted with and satisfied the king through these three receivers. The sole remaining duty of the Barons of the Exchequer was to discover whether any subordinate ministers ('bailiffs, farmers, tenants, debtors' etc.) had failed to answer at all for any sums due to the king. In such cases, assisted 'by the allegiance of our said receivers' they were to make due process against the offenders after the course of the Exchequer.[46] On the other hand, since the Barons now had no power to summon the receivers to account, no subordinate minister, bailiff, farmer or tenant could have any action against the receivers in the Exchequer. John Walsh duly made his last appearance at the Exchequer in Hilary Term 1493, accounting up to Michaelmas 1491.[47] Bray and Oldham were the successors to John Hayes and they never actually appeared at the Exchequer, Hayes rendering his final account there (also to Michaelmas 1491) in Trinity Term 1494.[48]

This writ of 1493 exonerating three receivers from exchequer account in certain specified offices for ever meant of course exactly what it said and no more. The heading states that it was for Bray, Oldham, Walsh '*et aliis*', but the others were the heirs and executors of these three men only, not other receivers. The case of each receiver was carefully considered by Henry on the personal reputation and value of the royal servant concerned. For example, Richard Cholmeley, chamberlain and treasurer of Berwick, and receiver of many of the northern lands which Richard III had held as duke of Gloucester, rendered his accounts before the new surveyors of land revenue from Michaelmas 1491 also. But not until 4 March 1496 was he favoured with a general release from exchequer process while he held this office, back-dated to Michaelmas 1491. It appears that in the meantime, between 1491 and 1496, he had been working hard and faithfully establishing his reputation. During this time, on top of his great annual journey from Berwick and his long sojourn before the king's Council (i.e. before the king's surveyors) while his accounts were being determined, he also had to face repeated exchequer summonses and penalties. These could only be staved off by suing out special *ad hoc* royal writs in his defence on each

46. E.159/269 'brevia directa', Trinity, 8 Hen. VII, m.1d; *C.L.*, doc. no. 15.
47. E.364/119, 7 Hen. VII, A.
48. E.364/119, 8 Hen. VII, A.

occasion. Henry VII did not bestow his trust lightly. Chamber servants had to earn it and keep it by constant loyalty and efficiency.[49]

An exoneration from exchequer account was thus always personal to the individual accountant and not to the office. This is further confirmed by what happened when one of these favoured receivers died or was replaced for some reason by another royal servant. On 22 June 1505 Christopher Popham, usher of the king's Chamber, was appointed by patent to succeed Cholmeley in the North. The Barons of the Exchequer duly began all their numerous processses against all concerned with the revenues of these lands, as they were legally bound to do, and as though the new board of surveyors had never existed. Two years later on 4 May 1507 Popham secured his personal, complete and permanent protection against them.[50]

Among all the numerous examples of accountants exonerated from the exchequer process only one instance has been found where the actual members of the board of auditors sitting in the Chamber were named. The accounts of the collectors and receivers of the benevolence granted for the king's journey to France were audited in the Chamber for two years (24 November 1505–23 November 1507) in the kings presence before the king's councillors: Richard, bishop of Winchester; Thomas Lovell, treasurer of the Household; Edmund Dudley; and Henry Wyatt.[51] But this board of auditors do not appear to have been concerned with land revenues. A document dated 20 February 1505 reveals that two other councillors—Roger Leybourn, bishop of Carlisle, and Sir Robert Southwell—were responsible for the surveying of land revenue accounts. This document is an indenture made between them and the Barons of the Exchequer to record an agreement that all manner of exchequer processes pending against various accountants who had appeared before Leybourn and Southwell should be put in suspense in accordance with royal letters missive to the Barons. There follows a list of butlerage and prisage accountants dating from Michaelmas 1500 and of various farmers, bailiffs and receivers of lands who had already answered 'coram consilio Regis'. For what periods and when is mainly not stated in this imperfect document,

49. When Cholmeley received his final exoneration for as long as he held office it was in the same terms as for Bray, Oldham and Walsh. When the year's account finally passed to the Barons of the Exchequer for safe custody, there to remain of record, they could make no process in the Exchequer except 'by the alleging of the said Richard' and any debit balance due from Cholmeley on the account was a matter for the foreign auditors and for those king's councillors appointed to survey his accounts. They entered it at the beginning of Cholmeley's next account. There was no question henceforth of its being put on the next pipe roll of the Exchequer for execution by the sheriff under the traditional summons of the pipe (E.159/274, 'brevia directa', Easter, 13 Hen. VII, m.7). The memoranda rolls of the King's Remembrancer contain other examples of permanent exoneration from exchequer account during tenure of office as well as numerous examples of *ad hoc* exoneration. The phrase used was normally 'has accounted and satisfied us in our Chamber'.

50. E.159/285, 'brevia directa', Easter, 22 Hen. VII, m.5.

51. *ibid.*, 287, 'brevia directa', Mich., 23 Hen. VII, m.7.

but in one case the accounts heard in the king's Council dated from 12 January 1492 and in two others from Michaelmas 1495.[52] It is important to notice that this indenture authorized only the suspension of the accounts. It was a necessary working agreement made between the two bodies of royal servants for their own convenience. They could not pronounce on the king's final pleasure in these matters.[53]

The king and his Council kept their own records of these annual audits in the form of books of summaries or 'declarations' of accounts. They survive, in whole or in part, for the four years 30 September 1502–29 September 1506. According to one of these books of declarations covering the two years ending on 29 September 1503 and 29 September 1504, Roger Leybourn and Robert Southwell were then surveying the accounts of some forty receivers of royal land revenues, some of whom appeared several times for different charges; also of persons owing lump sums (farms, feefarms reserved rents, ulnage or other payments) worth about £2,000 p.a.; and of wards' lands worth about £3,000 p.a. There is a note that certain lands not included were still 'before the king's Council'.[54] A duplicate volume for the year ending 29 September 1504 gives a somewhat fuller list of lands[55] and the volume for the year ending 29 September 1505 is even more extensive. In this volume all wards' lands are charged to William Lichfield as receiver-general, and summaries of accounts of Robert Southwell as chief butler are included for 1502–5. In addition, there is a note that certain accounts not summarized were with Hugh Molyneux, including Calais and Guînes, Berwick, Corbridge, and Shilbottle, and the vacant temporalities of Durham and Chichester.[56]

52. P.R.O., Exch., K.R., Misc. Accts, E.101/517/10. Described at some length by Dietz, *op. cit.*, pp. 69–70, yet he does not reveal that it refers to the accounts of receivers etc., of lands as well as butlerage and prisage.

53. The actual accounting procedure before the conciliar auditors can be partly followed from the original accounts of the receivers concerned. For example, Richard Nanfan appearing before them as receiver-general of the duchy of Cornwall produced fifteen indentures as proof that he had paid £4,284 6s 0½d for the year Michaelmas 1503–Michaelmas 1504 to John Heron for the king's coffers. It took three months for his account to be determined (January, February and March) during which time not only the receiver-general but also the two foreign auditors Robert Coorte and Thomas Hobson had to be available in London to testify, bringing with them all documents subsidiary to the receiver-general's account which they had drawn up. This hearing before the king's councillors was the ultimate, final audit of this account so far as the receiver-general was concerned. In the course of it the work of the foreign auditors was completely re-examined: for example, in Nanfan's account for this year two items of allowance which they had made to him are marked as reduced by command of the bishop of Carlisle and Sir Robert Southwell (P.R.O. Special Collections, Ministers Accts, S.C.6/Hen. VII/1084).

54. P.R.O., Exch. Treas. of Receipt, Misc. Bks, E.36/213.

55. E.36/247.

56. E.36/212. There are two other volumes which properly belong to this series of records: E.36/248 which is a book of declarations of wards' lands for 22 and 23 Hen. VII and Exchequer of Receipt, Misc. Books, E.405/478 (mutilated with only a few pages surviving) being the declarations of the king's lands for 21 Hen. VII (i.e. ending 29 September 1506) including wards' lands and butlerage, followed by summaries of the butlerage accounts for 17, 18, 19, and 20 Hen. VII.

There can be no doubt whatsoever that the work of all these receivers, 'foreign' auditors and conciliar surveyors was under the closest personal supervision of the king. Their appointments, their continuation in office and their accounting methods depended entirely on their giving continued satisfaction to him personally. All the relevant documents reveal the immense personal labour in which the development of his Chamber of Receipt, fed by its own receivers, 'foreign' auditors and conciliar surveyors, relentlessly involved Henry. Professor Dietz noted that he had found no evidence of large sums of money turned over by the treasurer of the Chamber to the king to be stored by him in his private coffers.[57] He did not realize that to search for such sums is futile because the chamber coffers themselves were the king's private coffers. The king himself presided over them and Heron was no more than his cashier. Heron's account book for 1502–5[58] actually opens with four folio sides of memoranda written by the king himself[59] to record financial transactions which he himself had personally handled. These principally concerned his relations with Lewis de la Fava, the Bolognese merchant financier; the receipts of Calais; the French pension and payments of the Spanish and Scottish marriage portions. The king handled crowns of the sun, Flemish pounds, Utrecht guilders, guillelmins, ducats and quite a number of other coins. Some of his conversions to 'good sterling' were made 'after the table of Calais'. Henry paid out as well as received and at the end of his memoranda he estimated the total deposits which resulted from his transactions at £29,000 sterling. Heron then took up the account, recording his receipts 'over and besides all the receipts written by the king's grace in two leaves herebefore in this book by me received'.

Heron closed his account as Henry VII's treasurer of the Chamber on 1 May 1509 with a surplusage of £90 14s 10½d. On 1 July 1509 he paid out a further £9,007 11s 2d for funeral expenses and to meet provisions of the king's will.[60] He also recorded two further payments out on the final page of this issue book totalling £1,333 6s 8d, for Henry VII's executors, to pay the debts of his queen and for the Friars Observant, but he made these latter as Henry VIII's treasurer of the Chamber and they duly appear in the first issue book of the new reign.[61] The final entries for the old reign

57. Dietz, *op. cit.*, p. 87.

58. E.101/413/2(3). These are engrossed accounts, presumably made up from *particule*.

59. Subsequent to forming the opinion that these first four pages in Heron's book are indeed in the king's own hand I discovered that W. B. Sanders, sometime Assistant Keeper of the Records, had reached the same conclusion in *Facsimiles of National Manuscripts*, pt. i (Ordnance Survey Office, 1865). I am most grateful to Mr Neville Williams of the Public Record Office for drawing my attention to this and for finding me an example of Henry VII's handwriting on a Warrant for Issue. I am also indebted to Dr P. D. A. Harvey for finding me another example of Henry VII's handwriting in a Book of Hours.

60. P.R.O., Exch., Treasury of Receipt, Misc. Bks, E.36/214, fol. 167 v. (chamber issue book).

61. B.M., Add. MS. 21481, under dates 29 July 1509 and 4 August 1509 (chamber issue book).

therefore reveal that he had paid out £9,098 6s 0½d in excess of his charge. The explanation seems to lie in the items which Henry VII had himself personally entered in the chamber books and which had resulted in a credit balance 'over and besides' Heron's charge, to use Heron's own words when he referred to them. Some, but by no means all, of Henry VII's personal entries were acquisitions of gold coins made by purchase and therefore Heron had to pay the seller for these. His issue books record his allowance for the purchase money in such cases.[62]

Henry VII's personal entries in the last surviving receipt book up to 1 October 1505 had resulted in total deposits of £29,000 for which Heron had to make payments out for the purchase of gold coins totalling a little under £5,300. We cannot tell from the surviving records of Henry VII's reign to what extent the king himself further augmented the reserves between 1505 and 1509 or to what extent his personal deposits in the coffers had been drawn upon when he died. However, there is a statement made on 23 January 1513, after Henry VIII's advisers had examined Heron's books of the old reign to see whether there was any treasure remaining in his keeping which could be expended on the French expedition. It is clear from this document that a receipt book for the old reign up to at least 30 June 1508 was then extant. The conclusion reached in 1513 was that Heron then still had a little over £10,000 in gold coins, mainly gold current at Calais, but including some English coins, 'particularly entered in your book of receipts by the hands of our most dearest father', and Henry VIII therefore instructed him under his signet and sign manual to deliver it to Sir Gilbert Talbot and Sir Edward Poynings.[63] The first thirteen items specified in this signet letter (numbers of different coins in separate bags) are all items entered by Henry VII in the chamber receipt book ending at 1 October 1505. The remaining items in the signet letter (some £1,400 out of the total of a little over £10,000) were deposits which Henry VII recorded in a later book which is not now extant.

Henry VII's chamber finances, like those of his Yorkist predecessors, were thus his personal hoard, the accumulation and maintenance of which entirely depended on the king's immense application, vigour and constant vigilance. The only auditor for whom the chamber books were intended was the king himself. To this end between October and June 1502 he was still checking and signing Heron's individual receipts and totals to the extent of something like five or six signatures per page. After this date he appears to have been generally content to approve Heron's entries with a

62. This is revealed by entries in the former MS. Phillipps 4104 (chamber issue book), now in the possession of the Robinson Trust, but I only know of these entries from Mr Colvin's transcripts (see below, n. 93).

63. The letter under the signet and sign manual is now bound up as fols 347–348v. of B.M., Add. MS. 21481.

single signature per page.[64] Likewise all the accounts of the receivers of his land revenues, as finally drawn up by those members of his Council appointed to survey them, were regularly checked and signed to his satisfaction. Against all the sums which these surveyors found that Heron had received appears, probably in the king's own hand, 'computatur hoc anno', the entry being usually marked with a large reference mark.[65]

The king's personal authority was constantly brought to bear to extract the last penny from all possible sources of revenue. This can best be illustrated by the considerable numbers of entries in the treasurer of the Chamber's receipts described only as obligations and recognizances. For the year 1504–5 there are over 250 of these, most of them for substantial sums and amounting in all to well over £20,000.[66] Both Professors Dietz and W. C. Richardson have shown that these might and did cover all possible sources of revenue.[67] The essential factor common to them all is that they represent personal arrangements reached with the king himself. In one of the chamber books at the bottom of a page of recognizances Heron actually entered a reminder 'about certain persons which are not yet through with the king's grace. And his said grace hath a bill of their names.'[68]

2. LANCASTRIAN, YORKIST AND EARLY TUDOR LAND REVENUES COMPARED

Having thus considered the nature of chamber finance under Henry VII, its dependence on the methods and personnel of his Yorkist predecessors, the set-back it received in the early years of his reign and the zeal with which Henry subsequently redeveloped it along pre-1485 lines, we can now endeavour to check the impact of all this on the royal finances between 1485 and 1509. Once again the obvious starting point is to review figures supplied by Professor Dietz which have found their way into most text books. He summed up his conclusions thus: 'During the first few years of the reign the total receipts of the Crown from all regularly recurring sources, received at the Exchequer, Berwick and Calais were about £52,000 a year,

64. The sign manual of the early years was an angular signature of many strokes of the pen. The flowing sign manual used for the rest of the reign first appears on fol. 35d. of E.101/413/2(2). On fol. 36 Henry reverted to the old type, but after that the new type continues in unbroken sequence throughout Heron's accounts.

65. See, for example, E.36/212 and E.36/213. Sometimes the entry is 'computatur pro hoc anno' and sometimes just 'computatur'.

66. I make the total for this year about £24,000. Dietz gives £21,565, but he was concerned to classify them under types of revenue and Heron was not. Dietz may have excluded those which he believed he could identify.

67. Dietz, *op. cit.*, ch. iv *passim*; W. C. Richardson, *Tudor Chamber Administration* (Baton Rouge, 1952), pp. 141–58.

68. B.M., Add. MS. 21480, fol. 41.

and the expenditures were so much greater that it was necessary to resort to subsidies and loans. During the last five years of the reign, the receipts averaged £142,000 a year received at the Exchequer, the Treasury of the Chamber, Berwick and Calais, all duplications eliminated.'[69] The sources for the earlier estimate are not given.[70] The figure for the end of the reign is based primarily on a detailed analysis of chamber receipts for a single year, Michaelmas 1504–Michaelmas 1505, classified by Dietz (not Heron) according to sources of revenue,[71] and also on a similar detailed analysis of exchequer receipts and disbursements stated to be for an average year at the end of the reign, Michaelmas 1505–Michaelmas 1506.[72] These exchequer figures are calculated from a Jacobean copy of the earliest known declaration of the under-treasurer which actually runs, not from Michaelmas to Michaelmas but, as stated in its preamble, from Easter 1505 to Easter 1506.

Dietz also claimed that whereas the exchequer revenues increased by 50 per cent during the reign of Henry VII, the 'augmented' revenues increased perhaps ten-fold between 1487 and 1505.[73] To indicate the rate of increase at the Exchequer he gives elsewhere the following figures: cash received during the first year: £1,866 19s 10d, during the eighth year £3,860 17s 3½d, and in the last year £4,717 1s 7d.[74]

Let us begin with the Exchequer, since we have already partly discussed Dietz's misconceptions over the fortunes of the Exchequer during the reign. The sum of cash received at the Exchequer for the last full year of the reign is reliable because it was taken from the cash section of the earliest declaration of the under-treasurer to survive in the original, and represents all cash received at the Exchequer of Receipt, other than the parliamentary subsidy which was now separately handled and reserved for the Chamber. But the two earlier figures were obtained by totalling the pages of a single teller's book. This book may be incomplete. Thomas Stokes who kept it may have kept other books. Certainly he was only one of four tellers at the Receipt of the Exchequer who each received money and kept books. In the early years of Henry VII's reign cash receipts at the Exchequer were in fact higher than they had been for many years owing to the breakdown of chamber activities and they continued to be so for some time. On a single day (18 February 1486) cash entries on the receipt roll far exceeded Dietz's total for the whole year. A summary of the books of the

69. Dietz, *op. cit.*, p. 86. These figures are repeated by Mackie, *op. cit.*, p. 218, though their origin is not given. They are also quoted by Pickthorn, *op. cit.*, p. 19, who was troubled by an inability to reconcile some of Dietz's figures with the rest.

70. The only possible source, in fact, is the receipt rolls, supplemented as regards cash receipts by the incomplete tellers' books and by the chamber accounts from 1487. The difficulties and uncertainties of such calculations are even greater than in an earlier period when the issue rolls at least provided some check on the receipt rolls.

71. Dietz, *op. cit.*, pp. 82–4. 72. *ibid.*, pp. 80–1.

73. *ibid.*, p. 81. 74. *ibid.*, p. 63.

four tellers, Pierson, Stokes, Boteler and Page, for the year Easter 1490–1 March 1491 gives cash receipts at the Exchequer from all sources of over £36,000.[75] The revival and expansion of chamber activities in Henry VII's reign actually entailed a drastic contraction of business at the Exchequer as had previously happened under the Yorkists. Dietz utterly failed to appreciate this. Far from increasing by 50 per cent over the whole reign, cash receipts, and indeed the overall activities at the Exchequer, in fact declined very considerably between 1487 and 1509 as the operations of the Chamber grew.

The task of checking Dietz's other figures bristles with difficulties. In spite of an impression gained from modern writers on Henry VII's reign that great care was taken to ascertain his yearly income and to live within it, none of the surviving documents, even for his later years, can in fact tell us what this yearly income actually was. Indeed, there is no evidence that the first Tudor was at all concerned with such information. Henry VII extracted the most minute reckoning of his charge from his cashier, Heron. but he certainly did not draw up a balance sheet. Even the problem of ascertaining Henry VII's total receipts over several years and averaging them is of much greater complexity than Dietz realized. The only straightforward information comes from Heron's books of chamber receipts. They are indeed a simple chronological record of his cash receipts.[76] In 1503–4 these were less than they had been in the previous year, but they rose spectacularly in 1504–5. Over the three years 1502–5 they averaged £104,863. If the amounts entered as clerical and lay subsidies (direct taxation) are deducted, as they must be if we are to check Dietz's figures for 'regularly recurring sources', this average is reduced to £91,217. On this basis we can attempt to check Dietz's figures of £142,000 for the total annual revenue from all 'regularly recurring sources' at the end of the reign.

The nearest comparable record for the Exchequer would be the tellers'

75. P.R.O., Exch., Treas. of Receipt, Misc. Bks, E.36/124. In contrast to this book the tellers' 'books' (E.405/80) for the last years of Henry VII's reign shows that by then all current receipts from parliamentary subsidies were being entered on a separate roll instead of forming part of the normal receipts as before. They were all paid over to the Chamber. One keeper of this subsidy roll, John Daunce, actually called himself clerk to John Heron, not teller of the Exchequer. Thus by the end of the reign the subsidies had passed out of Exchequer control though the tellers were used to collect and account for them.

76. E.101/413/2/3. This may at first sight be doubted when one reads the numerous entries of obligations, recognizances and some tallies in this book. Nevertheless, careful comparison of these entries with further details of them entered at the back of the corresponding issue book (B.M., Add. MS. 21480) shows conclusively that Heron only included actual cash receipts in the sums initialled by the king and totalled on each page and at various stages of the account. For example, on p. 21 under 23 Nov. 18 Hen. VII appear twenty-two obligations received from John Dawtry amounting to £3,828 19s 8d. This amount is excluded from the receipts entered on this page because these obligations were bonds not cash. In Add. MS. 21480, fol. 150, are further details which distinguish between these payments of Dawtry's in money and obligations.

books, but most exchequer business was still done by assignment, and the tellers were only concerned with cash payments. There are, however, two declarations of the under-treasurer of all cash received and issued and of all assignments made at the Exchequer from Easter 1505 to Easter 1506[77] and from Michaelmas 1507 to Michaelmas 1508.[78] There is a clear contemporary reference to another declaration covering the eighteen months in between,[79] but that declaration itself does not appear to have survived. Each of these declarations is arranged as follows: (1) all cash receipts and issues, except for the parliamentary subsidy; (2) the parliamentary subsidy; (3) assignments by tallies, grouped under the names or offices of the recipients.

It must be stressed that these Declarations of the state of the Treasury are in fact for the major part a record of assignments by tallies, not cash, and were therefore based on the receipt rolls and subsidiary documents just as much as on the tellers' rolls or books. They were produced by the favourite medieval method of 'searching the records': their purpose was to demonstrate how the under-treasurer's office had discharged its liability to the king, and they had no other purpose. These documents are not 'modern' statements of income and expenditure in any sense. Most of the pitfalls lying in the path of researchers who would use medieval receipt rolls in this way apply equally to these declarations.

The most serious criticism of the use made of them from the point of view of Dietz's figures seems to be that, in spite of the impression he gives of being aware of the problem, Dietz in fact failed to appreciate that the major part of all cash receipts and assignments recorded in them were intended for the Chamber, and were included in Heron's receipts as and when they materialized. The declarations themselves reveal this to be so for the following: a substantial sum of miscellaneous cash; the parliamentary subsidy; a batch of assignments to the Chamber for unspecified purposes; assignments to the Chamber for the king's ambassadors, and assignments to the Chamber for the king's works. Furthermore, the chamber books show that Heron was annually bound to advance in working cash to the officers concerned the equivalent of exchequer assignments made for the keeping of the Scottish Marches and the wages of the privy seal office. These exchequer assignments were then paid, not to the warden of the Marches and the Keeper of the Privy Seal, but direct to Heron himself. Again, the arrangement for the king's household expenses were somewhat similar. Heron advanced £12,000 p.a. to the household cofferer, who later repaid this sum in cash to the Chamber in instalments, when he had

77. Known only in the Jacobean transcript (B.M. MS. Lansdowne 156, fols 133–44).
78. P.R.O., Exch. of Receipt, E.405/183.
79. This is shown by payments to a number of clerks for half a year's work searching the records 'pro huiusmodi declaratione facta' covering one and a half years from Easter 21 to Mich. 23 Hen. VII, entered on fol. 48 of E.405/183.

realized his exchequer assignments.[80] Thus the yearly average of Heron's total chamber receipts given above already includes at least £12,000 p.a. of the exchequer assignments for the Household as well as all the other cash and assignments so far listed as far as they were realized.

This tremendous degree of duplication between chamber and exchequer accounts, for which Dietz has made quite inadequate allowance, actually leaves only an average of £12,595 p.a. as cash and assignments (over three-quarters of it being assignments) passing through the Exchequer and not intended for the Chamber.[81] Out of this total the Exchequer provided the fees and wages of its own officers, certain assignments to the Wardrobe, rewards to sheriffs and to customers in the ports, fees and wages to various other persons, assignments for the restitution of desperate tallies and its working balance of cash in hand. The scope of its activities had, in effect, been restricted to the payment of the fees and wages of certain groups of royal officers. Dietz's treatment of Henry VII's finances thus quite conceals the extent to which the augmentation of chamber revenues was made at the expense of the Exchequer.

Apart from the Chamber and the Exchequer there were only two other financial offices receiving and spending money from independent sources at the end of Henry VII's reign.[82] The chamberlain of Berwick expended about £2,000 p.a. on local garrison expenses (derived from land revenues in the North and from the customs of Berwick, Newcastle, and Hull),[83] before turning over his balance to the Chamber. Likewise the treasurer of Calais expended about £7,000 p.a. locally (derived from local revenues and from direct payments by the Society of the Staple on terms agreed in parliament). Any receipts over and above his expenditure had, of course, to be handed over to the Chamber each year.[84] Making allowance for these two minor but independent sources, the total revenues from 'regularly recurring sources' during the last five years of the reign (i.e. excluding the

80. See, for example, the memoranda entered by Heron under 1 Oct. 21 Hen. VII in P.R.O., Exch., Treas. of Receipt, Misc. Bks, E.36/214. These memoranda show clearly the details of the arrangements whereby the Chamber satisfied the immediate cash needs for fees and wages of the Chancery, the king's ambassadors, the warden of the East Marches, the Keeper of the Privy Seal, the cofferer of the Household, the king's works and the household of the prince of Wales.

81. £12,278 in Lansdowne 156, the declaration used by Dietz, and £12,911 in E.405/183.

82. The receipts of the hanaper appear to have gone to the Chamber which paid the chancery officers.

83. Dietz, *op. cit.*, p. 86, quotes this figure, which appears to be reasonable, from the surviving accounts.

84. See *Rot. Parl.*, vi, 523. The total liability of the Staple in return for customs concessions was £10,022 4s 8d p.a. to be paid in fees and wages of the Calais garrison if they amounted to that sum and, if not, the balance to be paid as the king directed, normally to the Chamber. Dietz, *op. cit.*, p. 86, states that the treasurer of Calais' average total receipts were £13,200 and that his expenditure, in 1507, was within his receipts by £6,382. The balance went to the Chamber.

clerical and lay subsidies), probably averaged not more than £113,000. But even in this figure of £113,000 there are still some substantial items which were obviously *ad hoc* payments or arrears, such as marriage money from the king of Spain, and benevolence money. Also some items which cannot be called revenue in any real sense of the word, for example, items of exchequer assignment to sheriffs which investigation shows were allowances for sources of income lost to their offices in some cases as long ago as the fourteenth century.[85]

In attempting to calculate Henry VII's revenues from 'regularly recurring sources' we ought further to note that the records on which these calculations are based show no evidence that their authors were concerned to make such classifications or that they would have meant much to them. The yield of some of the items which made up these sources were very much less predictable than the yield of a parliamentary subsidy and one suspects that contemporaries would have described many such revenues as 'casual' revenues. The really significant points which do emerge from checking Dietz's figures in this way are: (1) the almost total degree of duplication between Exchequer and Chamber; and (2) the revelation that the treasurer of the Chamber financed with a regular supply of cash even those great officers of the king like the treasurer of the Household and the warden of the Scottish Marches, who appeared to be financed by exchequer assignment.

The important, meaningful figure for the years from 1502 to 1505 is the average of £104,863 for the treasurer of the Chamber's total receipts. This constituted, in effect, the complete income of English government. It really had no other financial resources except the sums raised and expended locally at Berwick and Calais, and the allowances made to accountants for fees, wages, annuities, repairs and maintenance.

No strictly comparable figure can be produced for the Yorkist period because we have no accounts of the Yorkist Chamber. For different reasons exact comparison with the Lancastrian period is equally impossible. This can be illustrated by reference back to the financial statements of 1450 and 1433. The amount of cash handled centrally by Henry VI's government (except *ad hoc* from a cash loan, or from any unassigned parliamentary subsidy which happened not to be fully mortgaged before it was due) was very small indeed. In an extreme case, such as the height of the crisis of 1450, it might have available as little as £5,000, with no immediate means of obtaining any more. Cromwell's budget statement of 1433 supplies information for a twelve-month period of: (1) an estimate of gross revenue; (2) what he and his exchequer staff considered from records in the Exchequer to be the amount of income at many local sources which had

85. These are included in the 'absolute figures' of exchequer receipts and issues compiled by Dietz (*op. cit.*, pp. 80–1) from the declarations.

been assigned and paid out or otherwise rendered unavailable there; (3) the amounts still unassigned and, according to his records, still available there; (4) assessments of the unmet current needs of certain vital departments of government; and (5) other outstanding obligations for which no assignment had been made, or for which assignments had been made and had not been honoured. His object in presenting this statement had been to obtain a firm directive of priorities, i.e. how he was to apportion among the current charges and outstanding debts of £225,314 16s 8d the £35,366 2s 0½d which he considered to be still available at dozens of different places throughout the king's dominions. Those departments of government or individuals who were high enough in the priority to get anything at all would then have to arrange to collect it themselves from the source of their assignment, or, in effect, sell their tally at a discount to someone else who was willing to take it over for realization.

The Yorkists and Henry VII, while leaving this sophisticated exchequer system legally in full operation and still partially in operation in fact, created a separate new system of government finance. By the end of Henry VII's reign this new system collected all the king's revenues into the Chamber in cash except for the outposts of Berwick and Calais, the inescapable local costs of administration (fees, wages, and repairs etc.), and what the king chose to give away to individuals in annuities or *ad hoc* payments at local sources. For a complicated system of 'paper' finance, run on the equivalent of bearer bonds, but bearer bonds which had no guarantee of being honoured when presented, there was substituted a simple system in which cash was carried to the centre, stored in the king's coffers and distributed out again under his regular, personal surveyance. When the old system, backed by statute, ordinance and a court of record with its own writs, impeded an officer of the new system, a superior warrant from the king resolved the clash. Alternatively, auditors of the two systems came together to make a working arrangement.

If the Lancastrians had devised and operated such a new system on the basis of the gross revenue totals set out by Cromwell in 1433, its total theoretical potential for England, Wales and Calais would have been a little under £57,000 p.a. less unavoidable deductions for fees, wages, repairs and maintenance etc. This figure is the sum of the various relevant gross amounts in Cromwell's statement, which included no direct taxation. Cromwell wished to present the crisis of priority of assignment confronting him to the Council and to parliament with maximum impact. He therefore arranged his material to this end. However, there are no grounds for supposing that he falsified it, and his figures are probably more reliable than any modern calculations based on the same records but without the expertise of their original compilers. By contrast, for the three years 1502–5 Henry VII was now able to receive into his Chamber an average of something like £90,000 p.a. net cash yield, exclusive of direct taxation granted in parliament. It therefore follows that the revenues of England had been substantially increased in the meantime.

This increase appears to have come from customs revenues and land revenues. In 1433 Cromwell averaged the customs over three years at £30,722 5s 7¾d. Ramsay put them as high as £45,544 for 1477–8.[86] Dietz, basing himself on Georg Schanz's figures, has stated that during the first ten years of Henry VII's reign the customs revenues averaged £32,951 p.a. and during the remainder of the reign they were increased to £40,132 p.a.[87]

It is possible that Henry VII's land revenues may have averaged as much as £42,000[88] in the last five years of the reign. The narrowest possible definition of these land revenues for purposes of compilation and comparison must include the issues of receivers and farmers of estates and property, the sheriffs' issues, feefarms, the issues of bailiffs of liberties, wardships, marriages, vacant temporalities, fines for alienations and other feudal incidents, because the accountants concerned lumped together amounts from all these various sources in such a way that they cannot now be separated. But this definition will also inevitably include items like tallage of Welsh lands, issues of the coinage in the duchy of Cornwall, the ulnage of cloth and, if exchequer accounts are brought into the reckoning at all, items of sheriffs' farms which were partly fictitious. On this definition the amounts identifiable in the chamber accounts alone for the three years 1502–5 average £40,286. The total year's issues net (those marked 'et remanet clare', excluding arrears) in the book of the general surveyors for 1502–3 come to a little under £28,300. For comparison with the other two figures something like £9,250 would have to be added to this one to allow for duchy of Lancaster receipts, according to figures given by the historian of the duchy,[89] making about £38,000. A total of about £40,000 net cash yield p.a. for land revenues, 1502–5, therefore seems reasonable. The gross potential of land revenues contained in Cromwell's statement of 1433 on the same definition amounted to £18,786 13s 1¼d. Reference back to Table 3 on p. 92 above will show that in order to compute the charges (fees, wages, annuities, reparations and necessary expenses, to quote the words of the statement in the case of these items) on this total £1,200 would first have to be added to it for fines imposed in the central law courts, but

86. *Lancaster and York*, ii, 470.

87. Dietz, *op. cit.*, p. 25, based on the table in Schanz's *Englische Handelspolitik gegen Ende des Mittelalters*, ii, 46.

88. This figure is composed of the following averages of land revenue as described on this page: specified in the chamber accounts: £34,644; entered unspecified in chamber accounts but identifiable from the exchequer declarations: £5,642; items in the exchequer declarations in cash and assignments not apparently included in these two sums: £2,313.

89. R. Somerville, *op. cit.*, i, 275.

charged to the sheriffs. Out of the ensuing total of £19,986 13s 1¾d Cromwell considered there was £8,263 0s 10¾d at the government's disposal.

If we added to these 1433 figures the gross and net amounts for the duchy of Lancaster, about which Cromwell had some information, the gross total would be raised to £24,939 6s 5d and the net total to £10,671 9s 5⅛d. But we must remember that Cromwell himself excluded the duchy of Lancaster figures from all his calculations deliberately. The bulk of its estates in 1433 were enfeoffed to perform the terms of Henry V's will and Cromwell's action signifies that the Exchequer had no control over the remainder. This was, of course, the start of the demands that its revenues should be appropriated for the king's household expenses, but for the purpose of our comparison between 1433 and 1502–5 its revenues must be excluded. The figures of the total land revenues of central government in 1433 and 1502–5 are, therefore, something less than £8,263 0s 10¾d compared with about £40,000, provided we remember that the 1433 figure, unlike the figure for 1502–5, did not represent cash received, but amounts considered by the Exchequer to be available for assignment.

It remains to say something about the identity of the lands contributing to this figure of about £40,000 p.a. for 1502–5. Compared with 1433 one can see that the most considerable estates under control of Henry VII's Chamber and not under control of Henry VI's Exchequer in 1433 were: the duchy of Lancaster (for the reasons stated); the earldoms of Richmond and Pembroke (held by Henry VI's uncles); the duchy of York; the earldoms of March and Warwick; the Salisbury and Spencer lands (acquisitions of the Yorkist period); and the forfeitures under the attainders of 1495–1504.

Further analysis shows that one of three most vital factors influencing the high total for these years from 1502 was the utter dearth of members of the royal family able to absorb lands. Paying into the Chamber were the receivers of the principality of Wales, the duchies of Cornwall, Lancaster and York, the earldoms of Chester, March and Pembroke. The death of Prince Arthur (1502) had brought back the revenues of Wales, Chester and Flint, Cornwall and March to the central coffers. Prince Henry had been divested of his title to the lands of York and to the inheritance of his great uncle Bedford (Pembroke etc.) in 1503 on succeeding his brother. The words of the act of divestment that 'by reason [of his brother's death] he hath great and notable possessions'[90] was, however, a fiction as regards their revenues. The issues of Arthur's lands continued to go into the Chamber. The issues of Bedford's lands and of the duchy of York also went into the Chamber. Bedford had died in 1495. So had Cecily dowager duchess of York. Henry's queen died in 1503. This high return of land

90. *Rot. Parl.*, vi, 522–3. His creation as prince of Wales etc., is noticed *ibid.*, vi, 532, as to take place on 23 February 1504.

revenues was largely due, therefore, to the absence, in effect, of any royal family endowments.

The second important reason for this high total of land revenues, and again indicating recent accessions and suggesting possible reasons for impermanence, was the number of estates under chamber control as a result of attainders between 1495 and 1504. Those which merited one or more separate receivers accounting there, and so easily recognizable, were Sir William Stanley's, Lord Fitzwalter's, Edward Ashley's, the Warwick, Salisbury and Spencer lands (though, of course, these had never been surrendered, they were held by reason of the execution and forfeiture of Edward Plantagenet, earl of Warwick, from 1499), the earl of Suffolk's, Lord Audley's, Sir William de la Pole's and Sir James Tyrell's. There may have been others under the control of receivers whom I have not recognized. There were certainly also various annual payments from private persons for forfeited lands let to farm. The preponderance of the entail in fifteenth-century land law and the accepted legal convention that entailed estates should not be for ever lost to the rightful heirs as a result of attainder militated against the permanent retention of lands so held. In addition, the later fifteenth-century trend had been towards the ultimate reversal of attainders, and out of a total of thirty-two subjects above the rank of esquire attainted by Henry VII nineteen had their attainders reversed by him or by Henry VIII.[91]

The third most important factor in this augmentation of land revenues was the personal determination of Henry VII to follow the efforts of his Yorkist predecessors, once he appreciated their significance, in line with the current climate of public opinion, to achieve more effective and economical management of every source of revenue to which he was entitled. As regards land revenues this did not so much mean a drive to increase rents or agricultural yields, as the elimination of accumulated perquisites of officers and farmers, sinecure offices, annuities etc., and the collection of the whole proceeds as cash in the royal coffers. The evidence of his own activities in the records of his chamber treasurers and conciliar surveyors suggests a devotion to drudgery and a refusal to delegate responsibility which, one feels, could not have been matched in inclination by his Yorkist predecessors, and was never palatable to his son. Even when he had the system of chamber finance absorbing and controlling well over four-fifths of the revenues of England, he made no effort to establish the new system by ordinance or statute, and powerful influences in public opinion were already turning against the continuance and development of some of the methods of government involved.

The importance of royal intention and the consequent blessing on administrative change should not be under-estimated. Periods similar to

91. Figures given by J. R. Lander, in the *Historical Journal*, iv (1961), 151.

the years 1502–5 when there had been no substantial endowment of the royal family are hard to find in the whole late middle ages, but in the fifteenth century they were, significantly, 1399–1404, 1447–50, and 1483–5. The first two periods had been crisis periods in the royal finances, with parliamentary criticism concentrated on the disposition of the crown lands. Henry VII followed Richard III in this respect, not his Lancastrian ancestors. As regards the administrative changes the freeing of receivers from any suit in the Exchequer meant that they could not be called to account there by any person (bailiff, farmer, tenants, debtor), who might have claims upon them. Apart from royal petition such persons would now have to resort to the non-revenue courts of law. The Barons of the Exchequer had no claim or power over these receivers. Also subordinate receivers and accountants in Henry VII's reign were bound to render true accounting to the principal receivers by heavy recognizances taken on their appointment to office.[92]

On the other hand the principal receivers, those dealing with Heron, with the conciliar surveyors, and with Henry himself, were themselves subject to long, searching, informed, prompt and regular supervision. Their accounts, first drawn up by the 'foreign' auditors, were scrutinized in the Chamber by men who had full power to allow or disallow items of account, and it seems that the threat of further interminable exchequer suit was deliberately kept hanging over their heads as an additional spur to the production of satisfactory results. Two specific examples of the result of the new policies, now that they had been working for a substantial period can be given. According to Cromwell's exchequer statement of 1433 the gross revenues of the duchy of Cornwall were then £2,788 13s 3¾d. Fees, wages and annuities to various persons, together with reparations and necessary expenses, amounted to £2,637 12s 6½d, leaving for the king's use £151 0s 9¼d. The account of the receiver-general of the duchy, Richard Nanfan, rendered before Henry VII's conciliar auditors for 1503–4, shows that he had delivered to John Heron in cash that year £4,284 6s 0½d. If we examine the current total charge against him for that year (i.e. excluding arrears), we find that this had risen to £4,172 16s 8⅝d, the figure comparable to Cromwell's gross total of £2,788 13s 3¾d. But the total deductions had fallen from £2,637 12s 6½d in 1433 to £601 6s 7½d in 1503–4. The gross revenues of Windsor in 1433 were given as £207 17s 5¼d. They were over-assigned by £72 8s 5¼d. In 1503–4 the current total charge against the receiver there, John Ballson, had risen to £231 10s 10½d, but after the reprises (cost of administration, repairs, wages and annuities) had been met there still remained £55 5s 2¾d unspent. Unfortunately no other comparisons between units of land revenue common to both accounts are possible because all the other lands concerned were in places still subject to

92. e.g. *Cal. Close Rolls, 1500–1509*, pp. 107, 109.

tallages in lieu of parliamentary taxation (North and South Wales, Chester and Flint). Substantial amounts of tallage are specified in all these relevant units for 1503–4, but no breakdown of Cromwell's figures is possible in this respect.

A total of about £40,000 p.a. for what historians have normally considered to be 'ordinary' revenues of the Crown out of a possible total of about £105,000 p.a. for the whole central revenues of England from all sources, and that only in the exceptional circumstances of the last few years of the reign, clearly indicates that even Henry VII did not have the means to 'live of his own', even for a brief period, in the sense in which English historians have generally interpreted that concept.

How solvent was the government of these last few years? A government which could pay its way without running into debt was what contemporaries really meant by the king living of his own. The same minute royal supervision which this concentration of revenues in the Chamber demanded was also exercised in controlling their expenditure.[93] In his later and more affluent years, apart from routine payments, Henry spent most on his soul's welfare and building projects,[94] foreign affairs and the accumulation of treasure. Between 1491 and 1509 he seems to have spent about £200,000 on the purchase of jewels and plate. It is just possible that this figure should be nearer £300,000 because the issue books, like the receipt books, defy accurate classification of entries. John Heron was merely concerned to secure his discharge from the king for the sums he had paid out, and sometimes lumped together in one entry payments of different kinds without specifying in detail how they were made up.[95]

There is no means of knowing how much of this expenditure on jewels and plate was for the normal use and display of monarchy, how much was

93. Dietz's references to the chamber issue books of Henry VII are inaccurate in a number of respects. The surviving ones are P.R.O., Exch., K.R., Various Accts, E.101/414/6, E.101/414/16, E.101/415/3, which cover the whole period from October 1495 to October 1502; B.M., Add. M.S. 21480 which runs from 30 April 1505 to October 1505 and originally covered the whole period from October 1502 to October 1505; and P.R.O., Exch., Treas. of Receipt, Misc. Bks, E.36/214, which runs from October 1505 to the end of the reign. In addition there is B.M. Add. MS. 7099 which contains extracts from chamber issue books between 1491 and 1505 made by Craven Ord who at some time owned Add. MS. 21480. These extracts, where they can be checked, are not always reliable. There is also an original chamber issue book covering the whole period from Michaelmas 1502 to Michaelmas 1505 which appears to duplicate the brief Add. MS. 21480 and is the former MS. Phillipps 4104, described in the Phillipps catalogue as 'Privy Purse expenses of Henry VII from 1503 to 1506'. This is at present in the hands of the Robinson Trust and I only know of its existence through the kindness of Mr Howard Colvin who allowed me to see some transcripts he has been privileged to make from it.

94. His gifts for his new chapel were calculated to produce a regular income of £668 13s 4d, consisting of £437 6s 8d a year from lands and advowsons and £5,150 in cash to buy further specified properties (*Cal. Close Rolls, 1500–1509*, nos. 389–94).

95. Thus on 7 August 1506 Heron entered £88,000 as money sent overseas to buy jewels and plate and for a loan to the king of Castile. On 23 May 1507 he entered £28,000 as money spent on jewels and for a loan to the Archduke.

intended for the king's gifts and how much went towards a royal hoard.[96] After allowing for the payments Heron made in excess of his charge immediately after Henry VII's death, there is record of about £20,000 entered in Heron's books by the king himself and perhaps still in Heron's custody when he began work as Henry VIII's treasurer of the Chamber. It will be recalled that Henry VIII's advisers considered he still had some £10,000 on 23 January 1513. One may reasonably suppose that within these totals was contained the full value of that legendary 'golden fleece' which Henry is reputed to have left to his son. This is a view which does not find favour with most modern historians of the Tudor period. The old view of his tremendous wealth dies hard. The most recent account published states that his financial policy 'produced great, really very great wealth for the Crown'. Although this statement comes in the introduction to a volume of documents executed on the grand scale, no documentary evidence is given to support it.[97] Traditional reports said that he left treasure worth £1,300,000 or even £1,800,000, but then, contemporaries were equally sure that Edward IV left a fortune. Any effective king was reported to have died rich. In a sense we can be surer about Henry V's wealth than Henry VII's because at least it was partially recorded after his death and appears on some twenty-five folio pages of the printed *Rotuli Parliamentorum*. Professor Dietz expresses belief that Henry's accumulated surplus must have been comparable to that credited to him by report because of Henry VIII's lavish expenditure in the first part of his reign, and suggests that a major part of the surplus was in loans, obligations and recognizances. He cites in support of this view at least £260,000 'invested' by Henry in loans to the imperial family.[98] The mere thought of a prudent prince like Henry VII 'investing' such sums in the perennially indigent House of Habsburg, with any expectation of financial return, is ludicrous. The chamber issues do include a total of £226,000 'loaned' to Maximilian, his son Philip and his infant grandson Charles between 1505 and 1509, besides the two large composite entries quoted above, but in only one case (£10,000, 8 January 1509) is mention made of any security (a jewel) being given for repayment.

These 'loans' indicate the cash price which Henry was able and willing to pay in his efforts to make the continent unsafe for pretenders. The establishment of his dynasty among the courts of Europe and his dynastic ambitions there involved him in heavy financial outlay ignored by historians. The only other support quoted by Dietz for his belief in a vast

96. For example, in April 1501 a sum of £14,000 was entered as spent on jewels 'as against the marriage of my lord prince'. In June 1503 £16,000 was spent on jewels, plate and stuffs 'for the queen of Scots and for the king himself'.

97. C. H. Williams, ed., *English Historical Documents, 1485–1558* (London, 1967), p. 18.

98. Dietz, *op. cit.*, pp. 85–7, cf. Mackie, *op. cit.*, p. 218.

accumulated surplus is a total of £87,000 loaned to English and Italian merchants in the last four years of the reign, but we do not know the details of these transactions. For all the years where there is a record of both chamber receipts and issues almost all the receipts were spent. Dietz noted that as late as 1505 the chamber books showed a cash balance in hand of only £22,729,[99] but he did not point out that at the end of the reign Heron's issues exceeded the charge against him and that some of the receipts of the new reign went to meet the obligations of Henry VII's executors.[100]

The 'felicity of full coffers', in Bacon's striking phrase, thus enabled Henry VII in his last years to 'keep state and majesty to the height',[101] as befitted a successful Western European ruler in that 'Age of Princes'. Henry seems to have imported into English kingship a new element of unremitting personal involvement and tireless application to financial matters which earlier monarchs who controlled or attempted to control their finances through their Chamber (Henry II, John, Edward II, Edward III, Richard II, Edward IV, Richard III, to list only uncontroversial instances of chamber finance) would all have considered a debasement of their royal estate. He does not appear to have made any attempt to impart a similar love of cash and accounts to his successor, who reverted to more traditional ways of exercising regal authority. At Michaelmas 1515 it was estimated that the young Henry VIII had already diminished the amount of cash going into his coffers by £24,719 17s 8⅛d p.a. since his father's death as a result of his grants of land, diminished farms, new offices and annuities and the increased expenditure of his Household.[102] By 1509 the landowning and merchant classes were already becoming resentful of the legal and financial implications of Henry VII's 'good governance'. According to Edmund Dudley it was his insatiable appetite for money which lost him the hearts of his subjects.[103] As a symbol of solvent government living economically within his total means from all legal sources, Henry VII, in his last few years, probably represented a near approximation to the ideal of the period 1307 to 1485, that the king should 'live of his own', but this was an ideal which was already turning sour in the very hour of its realization.

99. Dietz, *op. cit.*, p. 87.
100. See above p. 210.
101. *The Moral and Historical Works of Lord Bacon*, ed. Joseph Dewey (London, 1890), pp. 473–4.
102. P.R.O., Special Collections, Rentals and Surveys, S.C.11/837; *C.L.*, doc. no. 22.
103. Edmund Dudley, *The Tree of Commonwealth*, ed. D. M. Brodie (C.U.P., 1948), p. 29.

VIII
CONCLUSION

For several centuries after the Norman Conquest the rulers of England and their advisers devoted constant energy and ingenuity with continuing success to augmenting their financial resources by various kinds of direct and indirect taxation. Whether this was done of necessity or choice may be debatable, but there is no doubt that the role of the royal demesne in English medieval government can only be comprehended in the context of the very long history of superior and more reliable resources from taxation which our medieval English monarchy enjoyed. The idea that 'hereditary' or 'ordinary' revenues derived from royal landed estates had formerly constituted the bedrock of English governmental finance originated in the political and legal theories of the seventeenth century. Enshrined in the law and practice of the constitution by the age of Blackstone, it was taken over by the nineteenth-century pioneers of English medieval studies who, consciously or unconsciously, were concerned to identify in medieval government the infant and adolescent history of their own adult institutions. The late appearance in the medieval period of the plea that English kings should 'live of their own' and not rob their subjects of what was legally theirs, coupled with the fact that this early fourteenth-century plea was a protest against the evils of unlawful 'prises' or purveyance for the royal Household and not against misuse of the king's land revenues, indicated that generally accepted views about the functions of the English royal demesne in medieval English government finance require fundamental revision. Detailed study of the history of the royal demesne to 1509 confirms that certain modern tenets of English constitutional law and history can draw no support from the facts of government finance during the medieval period.

As Sir John Fortescue already realized in the fifteenth century the contrasts between medieval English and French institutions were in some respects more instructive than the similarities. In France the resources of the royal *domaine* provided the financial and other means by which the Capetian kings carried out a piecemeal conquest of their kingdom down the centuries. By contrast, from the Conquest of 1066 the English equivalent of the French *domaine* was the whole kingdom of England, and the English 'royal demesne' subsequently had but a shadowy existence by comparison with the French *domaine*. From the twelfth to the thirteenth century it was a useful concept to describe one aspect of the evolving system of national taxation. On the other hand if it is seen as designating something which had a continuous separate existence and entity from the Conquest to the fifteenth century then it can only be used to describe the constantly fluctuating resources available to the monarchy for the upkeep of the royal family and the dispensation of royal patronage.

From the reign of Henry III, in face of the dissolution of their continental Angevin empire, our Plantagenet kings evinced a growing family interest in the accumulation and disposition of English and Welsh lands which reached its peak in the 'dower' of Queen Isabella, in the substantial and theoretically inalienable fourteenth-century patrimony of the heir to the throne, and in a lavish provision of apanages for younger sons and uncles which assisted the strongest of them to usurp the throne itself in 1399. In addition, as a source of royal patronage, the royal lands, wisely or carelessly used, provided a cement or a solvent of political unity and effective government.

It is possible that the ideal of the king living of his own first became briefly associated with an ideal of an inalienable royal landed patrimony primarily intended for financial purposes due to Edward III's conspicuous, lavish disposal of landed estates when he was endowing his boon companions in the opening stages of his great foreign adventure. There survives one solitary petition from an unofficial source which suggests that this may have been so. That such an association was present in the minds of the parliamentary critics of Henry IV's government cannot be doubted. Viewing the accession of landed wealth which his usurpation brought to the Crown in 1399 they did not doubt that, properly used, the crown lands ought to be able to make a substantial and reliable contribution to the vexatious expenses of an extravagant and unbridled royal Household. But Henry IV was bent on ruling as traditionally as his predecessors and could not accept the limitation of traditional prerogatives which any restriction in his free disposition of his landed resources would represent. The only financial innovations in his reign were further experiments designed to spread the incidence and increase the yield of direct taxation.

Unique abasement of royal authority between 1437 and 1450, culminating in national defeat in war and the collapse of a glorious empire, revived, enhanced, and transformed into practical politics the programme of Henry IV's disgruntled parliamentary knights. If we allow for the many alterations in Sir John Fortescue's *Governance* which were deemed necessary for its ultimate presentation to Edward IV, and for the other passages which no amount of change could render appropriate to that much later and different occasion, then that tract very well expresses the aspirations of government critics in the later 1440s. Elimination of sinecure offices, the removal of unnecessary perquisites attached to those offices which required actual exercise, the annulment of annuities lavishly granted, the reversal of unreasonable alienations of royal lands and rights, and the conciliar supervision of royal grants: all these ideas of Fortescue were embodied in the acts of resumption of 1450–6. By means of detailed parliamentary appropriations these resumed resources were to be devoted to the current expenses of the king's Household. A substantial contribution was confidently expected from the profits of crown lands, but the outcome shows that while the royal family benefited from these resumptions, and government became a little less indigent for a time, there could be no question of achieving by this means a permanent endowment of landed wealth sufficient in itself to enable the king to 'live of his own'. After the most effective of these acts had met the demands of the government's critics in the parliament of 1450–1 the next parliament found it necessary to make one of the most substantial grants of direct and indirect parliamentary taxation ever raised in the later middle ages.

Nevertheless, the Yorkists and Henry VII were pledged to further the policies of economic, solvent government which such acts of resumption represented. At the heart of their efforts to provide more 'politique rule and governance' was the financial exploitation of their crown estate. Conciliar control of grants, always impracticable, became an anachronism under these stronger kings, and parliamentary appropriations for the Household by means of exchequer assignment, whatever their publicity value, ceased to be a vital necessity when a system of chamber finance provided regular cash for household needs. Administrative innovation in English medieval government was never entirely confined to the periods of more active and effective kingship. For example, the graduated income tax of the early years of Henry IV was the direct ancestor of the Yorkist benevolence and the Tudor subsidy. Again, the near chaos of Henry VI's personal rule had produced the declared account which left harassed and reluctant, but vitally important, sheriffs financially free to perform their political and military duties in the shires. But the active concern of strong purposeful monarchs was required to produce financial reorganization on the scale achieved between 1461 and 1509. In this respect, study of the history of the crown lands provides an especially valuable insight into the nature of later fifteenth and early sixteenth-century government.

Two most important aspects of the changes made between 1461 and 1509 were, however, traditional and backward looking. They began with an infusion of ideas from successful large-scale private estate management on the earldom of March lands. The records of Henry VII's receivers under his general surveyors of lands at the end of the period were thus couched in the normal, long-established form of the charge and discharge account as used in the central office of any late-medieval complex of private estates. This was, of course, identical with the methods of the duchy of Lancaster which had not been allowed to make any impact on the 'ancient course of the Exchequer' or the 'summons of the pipe' under the Lancastrians.

Secondly, the normal direct process of cash payment of issues into the lord's coffers was also in line with traditions of English governmental finance which were older and, in certain ways, superior in authority, simplicity and effective technique to exchequer methods, belonging to periods when the royal Chamber had normally been the 'centre and controlling organ of the financial system'.[1] Throughout the whole of the period 1461 to 1509, the development of an administrative technique and organization unknown to the central government of England under the Lancastrian kings can most readily be traced in operation by following the role played by the crown lands in government.

The full central accounts of chamber receipts and issues, and the parallel receivers' accounts as surveyed by the king's general surveyors, enable the composition and amount of the revenues of England to be indicated for the last years of Henry VII's reign with a reasonable degree of conviction unattainable for any earlier years. It has generally been supposed that the reign of Henry VII was a time, if never before, when an English king 'lived of his own'. As the culminating achievement of very important changes in governmental aims and practices evident from 1461 land revenues were indeed made to provide a substantial portion of his total income. But even Henry VII's 'own' in his final days of comparative affluence consisted of very much more than the profits of his landed estate. It was not that a venerable medieval ideal proved impossible of fulfilment even in the person of the most capable of English royal financiers. When Henry VII died the demand that the king should 'live of his own' had indeed been raised in the estates of the realm many times over the preceding two centuries and the first Tudor had at last come very close to meeting it. But the doctrines of seventeenth and eighteenth-century statutes and law books, especially as adopted by the founder of English medieval historical studies, have both concealed the true origins of that plea of the later middle ages that the king should 'live of his own' and obscured its true meaning and significance during its first two centuries of existence.

1. H. G. Richardson and G. O. Sayles, *The Governance of Mediaeval England from the Conquest to Magna Carta*, p. 239.

APPENDIX 'A'

LANDS OF THE ROYAL FAMILY 1327–77

1. QUEEN ISABELLA (died 1358). GRANTS IN ENGLAND AND WALES

25 July 1317 (*Cal. Pat. Rolls, 1317–1321*, pp. 8–9)

	During pleasure, all the king's castles, towns, manors, lands and tenements in the county of Cornwall with the shrievalty [valued as the equivalent of £1,094 1s 4d in 1318]

5 March 1318 (*Cal. Pat. Rolls, 1317–1321*, pp. 115–16)

	Assignment as dower to the value of £4,500 p.a.:
Lincs.	manor of Long Bennington, value £160
Northants.	manor of Kingsthorpe, value £60
	manor of Easton, value £40
	hundred of Fawsley, value £12
	manors of Torpel and Upton, value £100
	£25 of farm of manor of Gretton rendered to the Exchequer by Laurence de Preston
Kent	manor of Ospringe, value £60
	manor of Milton with hundreds etc., value £240
	manor of West Cliffe, value £40
Oxon.	mills of Oxford with the Kingsmeadow, value £52
	manor of Bloxham, value £35
	castle of Wallingford and honours of Wallingford and St Valery with members in Oxfordshire and other counties, value £300
	manor of Watlington, value £60
	manor of Woodstock, value £100
Sussex	honour of the Eagle with members, value £230, excepting Pevensey castle and the manor of Laughton held for life by John Duvedale of Edward I
Surrey	manor of Banstead, value £30
Essex	manor of Havering with part and forest, value £140
	manor of Nayland, value £100
Herts.	castle, town and honour of Berkhamsted, value £72 15s 8d
Notts. & Derbys.	* castle and honour of High Peak with its chace, value £291 13s 4d
Wilts.	castle and town of Marlborough with the barton and hundred of Selkley, value £20
	castle and town of Devizes with the parks and forests of Melksham, Chippenham and Pewsham with the purprestures and the manor of Rowde, value £80
	manor of Woodrow, value £14 10s
	manor of Sevenhampton with the boroughs of Cricklade and Highworth and the manor of Stratton, value £200
	castle and manor of Mere with park, value £78
Leics.	manors of Bowden and Market Harborough, value £42 13s 4d
Hants.	town of Southampton with petty rents in the county, value £201 3s 2d
	manor and town of Alton with hundred of Alton and petty rents in the town, value £88 15s 6d

farm of the town of Andover with the increment and the hundred, value £104 12d

manor and town of Basingstoke with hundred and a rent out of a tenement late of Walter Merton in the town, value £80 15s

castle of Southampton, manor of Lyndhurst with park and the New Forest, bailiwicks and hundred of Redbridge and 40s of rent for a forest tenement due of the abbot and convent of Reading, value £150

castle of Christchurch of Twinham with borough and manor of Westover and hundred of Christchurch, value £120

manor of Ringwood, value £80

Worcs. — farm of the town of Droitwich, value £89 5s

Dorset — manor of Gillingham with the barton, the forest, and 74s of rent out of the purpresture, value £80

Gloucs. — * £100 of the farm of the manor of Lechlade of the abbot and convent of Hailes

* £200 of the issues of the castle, town and barton of Bristol

Cambs. — * £31 of the farm of the manor of Chesterton of the prior and convent of Barnwell

Chester — * manor of Macclesfield, value £175 8s

* manor of Overton, value £126

Wales — £20 of the farm of the manor of Ellesmere by the hand of John de Knokyn, life tenant of Edward II

* manors of Rhosfeir, Dolpenmayn, Pennehan and the commote of Menai, value £170

25 April 1318 (*ibid.*)

Wilts. — forest of Savernake as part of the grant of the castle and town of Marlborough

30 October 1318 (*Cal. Pat. Rolls, 1317–1321*, pp. 222–3)

the county of Cornwall as above but in dower, in recompense for the above items [*] now granted for the maintenance of the king's children John and Eleanor.

6 November 1319 (*Cal. Pat. Rolls, 1317–1321*, pp. 400–1)

surrender to the king of the manor of Long Bennington, Lincs., the farm of the town of Droitwich, Worcs., the manors of Torpel and Upton and the manor of Easton, Northants., the manor, town and hundred of Basingstoke, manor, town and hundred of Andover, manor, town and hundred of Alton, Hants., and the manor of Bloxham, co. Oxon., all as above, receiving in exchange as dower the following:

Suffolk — the manor of Haughley

castle and manor of Eye with hamlets of Dallinghoo, Alderton and Thorndon

Norfolk — £20 rent of the manor of Bacton from the prior and convent of Bromholm

Lincs. — castleward and free court of the honour of Eye, extent £11, with a yearly rent pertaining to the honour in Essex., Lincs., Norf. and Suff.

manor of Kirton with members

Oxon. — manor of Handborough

1 May 1320 (*Cal. Pat. Rolls, 1317–1321*, p. 453)

restoration to Isabella during pleasure of all those items [*] above surrendered in October 1318, since she has the burden of the upkeep of the king's son John and his daughter Eleanor.

10 January 1327 (*Cal. Pat. Rolls, 1324–1327*, p. 346)

	at Kenilworth Queen Isabella restored to herself the county of Cornwall with castles, fortresses, towns, manors, lands, farms and divers places lately granted to her by the king for life in dower, but afterwards resumed by him for certain causes. Mandates issued to keepers of lands etc., in 15 other counties.

16 August 1327 (*Cal. Pat. Rolls, 1327–1330*, p. 177)

Northants.	for life, manor of Brigstock, value 49 marks

1 February 1327 (*Cal. Pat. Rolls, 1327–1330*, pp. 66–9)

	for life, to the yearly value of £8,722 4s 4d to augment her dower to 20,000 marks p.a.:
Norfolk & Suffolk	£125 18s 4d of the farm of Norwich, £60 0s 1d of the farm of Ipswich, £55 of the farm of Yarmouth
Suffolk	Lands and tenements in Clopton formerly of Margaret late countess of Cornwall, value 20 marks
Norfolk	manor of Burgh with the park, value £30; manor of Causton, value £60; manor of Aylsham, value £83; manor of Fakenhamdam, value £80
Hunts.	manors of Glatton and Holme, value £100
Cambs.	£10 of yearly farm paid by the heirs of Nicholas de Kyriel for manor of Hinton
	£68 4s 10d of the farm of Cambridge
	manor of Soham, value £100
	£31 of yearly farm paid by canons of Barnwell for manor of Chesterton
London	£50 of the farm of Queenhithe, city of London
Middlx.	manor of Isleworth with park, value £128
Essex	£35 0s 2d of the farm of Colchester
	£10 of yearly farm paid by prior of Christ Church Canterbury for part of manor of Borley
	manors of Eastwood and Rayleigh with park and hundred of Rochford [value £100 in 1330 as granted to Queen Philippa]
	castle and town of Hadleigh with park, value £16 10s
Herts.	castle, town and honour of Hertford, value £100
	manor of King's Langley with park, value £38
Essex	manor of Thundersley, value £17 5s
Kent	£33 7s 4d of the yearly farm of Canterbury
	£50 of yearly farm paid by Henry de Cobham for castle and city of Rochester
	castle and town of Sandwich, value £70
	castle and manor of Leeds, value £21 6s 8d
	manor of Chetham, value £38
	manor of Bockenfield with park, value £25
	manor of Gravesend, value £20
	manor of Eltham with park, value £40
Leics.	hundred of Gartree, value £16
Warws.	£12 of yearly farm paid by heirs of Nicholas de Segrave for manor of Kington
Leics.	£12 18s 5½d of yearly farm paid by heirs of Roger Beler for hundred of Framland
Wilts.	**[1] manor of Berwick (St James), value £25

1. These Lacy manors etc. (**) were either ultimately reunited with the Lancaster estates by grant of Edward III to Henry of Grosmont first duke of Lancaster, or were recovered by John of Gaunt and his wife Blanche or passed to the heirs of William Montague earl of Salisbury, by virtue of a reversionary grant to him and his heirs male of

manor of Chelworth, value £22
manor of Tockenham, value £20
manor of Brodeton, value £10
manor of Seend with park, value £50
** manor of Winterbourne (Earls), value £30
manor of Compton, value £40
manor of Wootton, value £54
manor of Vasterne with parks, value £50
** manor of Aldbourn with chace, value £26
** manor of Upavon and Netheravon, value £100
manor of Marden, value £34
£31 10s of yearly farm paid by the heirs of the earl of Gloucester for the manors of Westcomb and Bedwin
£20 of yearly farm paid by abbot and convent of Malmesbury for town of Malmesbury

Oxon. manor of Whitchurch, value £28
£81 of yearly farm paid by Richard Damory and his heirs for manor of Headington and hundred without the North Gate of Oxford

Berks. manor of Bray, value £84
manor of Cookham value £95
manor of Crookham with park of Fremantle, value £30

Beds. £30 of the farm of Bedford (except £10 assigned to the Lady Lestraunge)

Bucks. manor of Wycombe, value £58
£18 8s 8d of yearly farm of town of Wycombe
manor of Risborough with park, value £84
manor of Cippenham, value £64
manors of Langley Marish and Wyrardisbury with the park, value £110

Northants. castle of Rockingham with forest and stewardship of forest between bridges of Oxford and Stamford,[2] value £80
£118 0s 5d of farm of Northampton
£100 of yearly farm paid by Simon de Daventre and his heirs for the manor of Fawsley
£20 of yearly farm paid by Eustace de Burneby and his heirs for a tenement in Watford
manor of King's Cliffe, value £62
town of Rockingham, late of the earl of Cornwall, value £7
manor of Geddington value £52

Worcs. £30 6s 3d of yearly farm of Worcester
towns of Norton and Bromsgrove (except £100 which Matilda de Mortuo Mari used to receive of it), value £10
town of Feckenham with forest, value £46

Dors. £12 of the farm of the town court of Shaftesbury
£16 of the farm of town of Bridport
town of Dorchester, value £20
town of Lyme, value £35 10s

Som. borough of Ilchester late of earl of Cornwall, value £21

Salop £10 of yearly farm paid by burgesses of Bridgnorth for the mill of Pendlestan
£12 of yearly farm paid by Nicholas Daudele for the manor of Ford

18 March 1337. For details see Somerville, *op. cit.*, p. 35–6. Queen Philippa had meantime held Pontefract from 1330–48 (see below).

2. Included the forests of Barnwood (Gloucs.), Whittlewood (Northants.), Whauberge, Clive (Salop.) and Salcey.

County		Item
		hundred of Bradford, value 24 marks
		castle of Montgomery, value 85 marks
		manor of Claverley, value £17 2s
		castle and manor of Ellesmere with park (except £20 already paid to Isabella as dower), value £60
N. Wales		manors of Rhosfeir, Dolpenmayn, Pennehan and commote of Menai, value £170
Chester		manor of Macclesfield with park and forest, value £174 8s
Flint		manor of Overton, value £126
Pembs.		borough of Haverford, value £128 10s 10d
Brecon		castle and cantred of Builth, value £113 6s 8d
Staffs.		£10 of yearly farm of manor of Rowley
		hundred of Tatemundeslowe, value 23 marks
Heref.		£43 6s 1d of yearly farm of city of Hereford
Yorks.		£27 0s 1d of yearly farm paid by the heirs of Peter de Brus for the wapentake of Langbarugh
		castle and honour of Knaresborough with forest, value £533 6s 8d
		manor of Burstwick with parks, value £800
	**[3]	manor of Whitgift, value £80
	**	manor of Cowick with town of Snaith, value £50
		castle and town of Tickhill with members, Wheatley and Gringley, value £333 15s 9d
	**	castle and borough of Pontefract with members and parks, value 1,000 marks
Lancs.	**	castle of Clitheroe and manors of Penwortham, Tottington and Rochdale with hamlets and free chaces and the
Yorks.	**	manor of Slaidburn with hamlets and free chace of Bowland, value £400
Surrey		£54 16s 6d of yearly farm of town of Kingston
		bailiwick of Southwark, value £11
		castle and town of Guildford with park, value 30 marks
		manor of Byfleet, value £40
		manor of Sheen, value £30
Sussex		town of Winchelsea, value £46
		manor of Laughton, value £80
Gloucs.		castle of St Briavel's with forest of Dean, value £160
		£16 16s 10½d paid by abbot and convent of Hailes for the farm of Pinnockshire
		castle, town and barton of Bristol, value £210
		castle, barton and *tyna* [prise of ale] of Gloucester, value £110
Derbys.		£46 10s of farm of town of Derby
Notts.		£10 of yearly farm paid by abbot of Welbeck for the mill of Radford
		£15 of yearly farm of towns of Darlton and Ragnall
		£10 of yearly farm of town of Retford
		£10 of yearly farm paid by Hugh de Nevill for the town of Arnold
Derbys.		castle of Horston, value £20
		castle, town and honour of High Peak with forest, value £291 13s 4d
Notts.		manor of Mansfield with soke and farm of Linby and mill of Carburton, value £54 15s 8d
Southants.		£18 4s 8d of yearly farm of town of Portsmouth
		city of Winchester, value 100 marks
		castle and town of Porchester, value 25 marks
		castle and manor of Odiham with park, value £60

3. Lacy manors, see above, p. 232.

manor of Polhampton with pasture called Kyngeslese, value £12 18s 4d

May 1327 (*Cat. of Anc. Deeds*, A. 10947, 8; *Cal. Close Rolls, 1327–1330*, p. 267; *Cal. Pat. Rolls, 1334–1338*, pp. 129–30, 551)

By purchase with 10,000 marks from a parliamentary grant of a twentieth and a tenth: the lands of Robert de Montalt, with remainder to John of Eltham and his heirs, and the king and his heirs, with later compensation to the widow agreed at £400 p.a. for life:

N. Wales	manors of Mold and Hawarden
Chester	manors of Lea, Bosley and Neston
Staffs.	manor of Walton-on-Trent
Warws.	manor of Cheylesmore
Norfolk	manors of Castle Rising, Snettisham and Kenninghall
Suffolk	manors of Kessingland and Framsden
	[Framsden later surrendered to a collateral heir. Snettisham alienated in fee simple to her yeoman Walter de Chesthunt, in reversion after her death, with the king's approval (*Cal. Pat. Rolls, 1334–1338*, p. 519, 1 September 1337)]

1 December 1330 (*Cal. Pat. Rolls, 1327–1330*, p. 48)

Surrender of lands assigned to her in dower, and grant of £3,000 p.a. at the Exchequer.

THE REDISTRIBUTION

15 November 1331 (*Cal. Pat. Rolls, 1330–1334*, p. 195) in lieu of part of the exchequer grant to the yearly value of £2,000, for life from Michaelmas last:

Lancs.	castle of Clitheroe, manors of Penwortham, Tottington, Rochdale
Yorks.	manor of Slaidburn, free chace of Bowland, park of Ightenhill
Norfolk	manor of Aylsham
Hunts.	manors of Glatton and Holme
Herts.	castle, town and honour of Hertford
	manor of King's Langley
Kent	castle, manor and park of Leeds
Wilts.	manors of Woodrow, Chelworth, Tockenham, Winterbourne, Compton, Marden
Berks.	manor of Bustlesham [a Despenser forfeiture later granted for life to Alice, widow of Ebulo L'Estrange, *ibid.*, p. 74]
Northants.	manor and park of Kings Cliffe, manor of Geddington
	manor and park of Brigstock, manor of Kingsthorpe
	£20 of Eustace de Burneby for the town of Watford
	£25 of Laurence de Preston for the town of Gretton
Chester	manor, park, and forest of Macclesfield
Surrey	manor of Sheen, £54 8s 10d of the town of Kingston and 3 other small farms there
Notts.	manor of Mansfield with soke and farm of Linby, Carberton mills, £10 of farm of Radford mill of the abbot of Welbeck, £14 of the towns of Darlton and Ragnall, £10 of the town of Retford
Oxon.	manor of Whitchurch
Heref.	£43 6s 1d of the farm of the city of Hereford and two other small farms there
Derbys.	£46 10s of the farm of the town of Derby with the increment
Hants.	£18 4s 8d of the farm of Portsmouth
	£66 13s 4d of the farm of the city of Winchester

	£201 3s 2d of the farm of the town of Southampton with small rents and appurtenances
Cambs.	£31 yearly farm of manor of Chesterton of the prior of Barnwell

20 November 1331 (*Cal. Pat. Rolls, 1330–1334*, pp. 225–6) in lieu of the rest of the exchequer grant to the value of £1,000:

N. Wales	manors of Rhosfeir, Dolpenmayn and Pennehan, commote of Menai
S. Wales	castle and borough of Haverford with islands, mills, rents of St Ismael and Penrhos and appurtenances [acquired, together with the honour of Hertford by exchange from Mary, widow of Aymer de Valence, earl of Pembroke]
Worcs.	£30 6s 3d of the farm of Worcester and two small farms there
Wilts.	£20 of farm of town of Malmesbury with its three hundreds of the abbot and convent there
Leics.	the hundred of Gartree and £12 18s 5½d of the yearly farm of the hundred of Framland of the heirs of Roger Beler
Cambs.	£67 9s 10d of yearly farm of Cambridge with increment and small farms
Essex	£35 of farm of Colchester
Kent	£100 of yearly farm of Rochester castle and city paid by Henry de Cobham
Northumb.	£100 of farm of Newcastle-on-Tyne
Beds.	£32 of farm of borough of Bedford beyond £10 assigned to Lady Lestraunge
Cumb.	£200 paid by Ralph de Nevill for manors of Penrith and Sowerby p.a. for 10 years, with full possession when that term is expired, as of value £200
	£80 of farm of Carlisle and of mills and fishery in river Eden
Suffolk	£60 of farm of Ipswich and a rent there

11 May 1332 (*Cal. Pat. Rolls, 1330–1334*, p. 280)

Norfolk	Because £40 of farm of Derby not available due to a previous life grant which the king wishes to stand, grant of the hundreds of North and South Erpingham as of value £40

4 November 1332 (*Cal. Pat. Rolls, 1330–1334*, p. 367)

Norfolk	manor of Fakenhamdam, as of value £80
Surrey	manor of Eltham and appurtenances to stay in at pleasure

13 December 1334 (*Cal. Pat. Rolls, 1334–1338*, p. 60)

Wilts.	manors of Vasterne and Wootton for surrender of £100 of Newcastle-on-Tyne and 45s 10d of Ipswich

26 May 1344 (*Cal. Pat. Rolls, 1343–1345*, p. 263)

Norfolk	£100 of farm of Norwich for surrender of manors of King's Langley and Eltham

23 November 1348 (*Cal. Pat. Rolls, 1348–1350*, p. 217) at request of the king, greatly in his debt for services to the Crown: surrender of Blackburnshire and Bowland to Henry earl of Lancaster for £600 p.a. compensation at the hanaper

26 August 1358 (*Cal. Fine Rolls*, vii, *1356–1368*, p. 85)
Order to escheators for taking her lands into the king's hands in the counties of Lincs., Norf., Suff., Essex, Derbys., Leics., Warwks., Som., Dors., Wilts., Hunts.

2. QUEEN PHILIPPA (died 1369). GRANTS IN ENGLAND

12 April 1330 (*Cal. Pat. Rolls, 1327–1330*, p. 508)

Leics.	manor of Loughborough [Despenser forfeiture]

1 January 1331 (*Cal. Pat. Rolls, 1330–1334*, pp. 55–6) towards a dower of £4,000 p.a.:

Essex	manors of Eastwood and Rayleigh with hundred of Rochford, value £100
	manor of Nayland, value £100
Middlx.	manor of Isleworth, value £128
Bucks.	manors of Langley Marish and Wyrardisbury, value £110
Berks.	manor of Bray, value £84, of Cookham, with purprestures, value £95
	manor of Stratfield Mortimer, value £52 [Mortimer forfeiture]
Sussex	honour of the Eagle in divers counties except Pevensey castle and manor of Laughton, value £230
Cambs.	manor of Soham, value £100
Gloucs.	castle, town and barton of Bristol, value £210
Northants.	castle of Rockingham and stewardship of the forest between Oxford and Stamford bridges, value £80
Derbys.	castle, town and honour of High Peak, value £291 13s 4d
Yorks.	castle, town and honour of Knaresborough with forest and members, value £533 6s 8d
	manor of Cowick with town of Snaith, value £50
	castle, borough and honour of Pontefract in divers counties, value 1,000 marks [already held since 12 February 1330, *ibid.*, p. 501]
	castle and town of Tickhill with its members of Gringley and Wheatley in Yorks. and Notts., value £333 16s 5d
Wilts.	castle and town of Devizes with park and forest of Melksham, Chippenham and Pewsham and the manor of Rowde, value £80
	castle and town of Marlborough with barton and hundred of Selkley, value £120
	manor of Sevenhampton with the boroughs and hundreds of Cricklade and Highworth and the manor of Stratton, value £200
Worcs.	town of Feckenham with forest and woods, value £46
Dors.	manor of Gillingham with barton, 74s rent of purprestures and forests, value £80
Surrey	manor of Banstead with park, value £30
Hants.	castle of Southampton, manor of Lyndhurst with park, the forest, bailiwick and hundred of Redbridge with a rent for a forest tenement, value £150

25 February 1331 (*Cal. Pat. Rolls, 1330–1334*, p. 78)

Chester	the issues of the county of Chester for the Chester support of the king's son Edward and his sister Eleanor from the time of Roger Mortimer's arrest. Farmed to Oliver de Ingham, justice of Chester, for 1,000 marks p.a. (*ibid.*, p. 2)

20 July 1331 (*Cal. Pat. Rolls, 1330–1334*, p. 161)

in recompense for certain portions of the honour of Knaresborough (value £44 5s 10d) and of the honour of Pontefract (value £50) surrendered to the king for the support of his stud:

Hants.	castle and manor of Odiham, value £60
Northants.	hundred of Fawsley, value £12
Suffolk	hundreds of Bosmere and Claydon, value £20
	45s 10d of the farm of Ipswich

24 May 1333 (*Cal. Pat. Rolls, 1330–1334*, p. 439)

Kent — manor of Milton with hundred and appurtenances from death of John of Florence who had held it since Queen Isabella surrendered it, value £240

20 November 1342 (*Cal. Pat. Rolls, 1340–1343*, p. 569)

Yorks. etc. — custody of the lands etc., of the earldom of Richmond for the upkeep of the king's son John, earl of Richmond, granted to him in tail by charter. Manor of Danby Wiske added on 20 May 1343, previously held by Geoffrey le Scrope, deceased, by life grant of John of Brittany (*ibid.*, p. 42)

8 August 1347 (*Cal. Pat. Rolls, 1345–1348*, p. 371)

Yorks. — custody of all the lands of John de Warenne, late earl of Surrey, beyond Trent which reverted to the king at his death, for the upkeep of the king's son Edmund de Langley to whom they have been granted in tail male.

18 November 1348 (*Cal. Pat. Rolls, 1348–1350*, p. 217) at request of the king, greatly in his debt for services to the Crown, surrender of the honour of Pontefract to Henry earl of Lancaster for £1,000 p.a. out of the customs of London or failing them Kingston-upon-Hull and Boston.

26 June 1359 (*Cal. Pat. Rolls, 1358–1361*, pp. 237–9) for life to supplement her dower which is insufficient for her household, chamber and other expenses, to the value of £2,000 p.a. including an annuity of £60 at the Exchequer:

Yorks.	hundred of Staincliffe as of value £18 13s 4d
Norfolk	£100 of the farm of Norwich
	manor of Aylsham as of value £84
	manor of Fakenhamdam as of value £79
	hundreds of North and South Erpingham as of value £48
Hunts.	manors of Glatton and Holme as of value £80
Wilts.	manor of Woodrow as of value £13 6s 8d
	manors of Vasterne, Wootton, Chelworth, Tockenham, Winterbourne, Compton and Marden as of value £266 13s 4d
	£20 of the farm of the town of Malmesbury with its three hundreds, of the abbot and convent there
Northants.	manor and park of Kings Cliffe as of value £64
	manor of Geddington as of value £52
	manor of Kingsthorpe as of value £60
	manor and park of Brigstock as of value £46
	£20 of Eustace de Burneby for the town of Watford
	£25 of Laurence de Preston for the town of Gretton
Surrey	£54 8s 10d of the town of Kingston and 3 other small farms there
Notts.	£10 of the farm of Radford mill of the abbot of Welbeck
	£14 of the towns of Darlton and Ragnall
Heref.	£43 6s 1d of the farm of the city of Hereford and two other small farms there
Derbys.	£6 10s of the farm of the town of Derby with the increment
Leics.	£12 18s 5½d of the yearly farm of the hundred of Framland of the heirs of Roger Beler
Hants.	£18 4s 8d of the farm of Portsmouth
	£66 13s 4d of the farm of the city of Winchester
	£201 3s 2d of the farm of the towns of Southampton with small rents and appurtenances
Worcs.	£30 6s 3d of the farm of Worcester and two small farms there

Cambs. £67 9s 10d of the yearly farm of Cambridge with increment and small farms

£31 paid by the prior of Barnwell for the manor of Chesterton

Beds. £32 of the farm of the borough of Bedford beyond £10 assigned to Lady Lestrange

Cumb. manors of Penrith and Sowerby as of value £200

£80 of the farm of Carlisle and of mills and a fishery in the river Eden

Suffolk £57 14s 2d of the farm of Ipswich and a rent there.

Grant to her further because she has surrendered at the king's request the castle of Southampton, the New Forest and the manor of Lyndhurst to the value of £160:

Norfolk manor of Snettisham as of value £66 13s 4d

hundred of Smithden as of value £14

the king's part of the tolbooth of Lynn.

Grant also that in recompense of £66 of the yearly value of the said castle, forest and manor, and of 42s 7d of the said £2,000 yearly still deficient, she shall have for life the honours, manors, hundred, cities, towns, lands, farms, rents and other places aforesaid with all knights' fees, advowsons, wards, marriages and escheats, chaces, parks, woods, warrens, fairs, markets, waters, ways, fisheries, commons and assarts, wastes and purprestures and the arrenting thereof, with fines for entry into them, courts, views of frank pledge, hundreds, wapentakes, wreck and waif, royal liberties, free customs and other appurtenances. Grant to her also of all fines, ransoms and amercements, of men and tenants of the premises and in the honours etc. and in all cities, towns, hundreds and other places whence the farms and rents now granted arise, issues forfeit, year, day and waste, forfeitures and murders.

Also held by Queen Philippa at her death in 1369:

Essex manor of Havering-atte-Bower and members [value £116 in 1370]

Hants. manors of Tytherley and Lockerley [value £45 in 1372]

3. JOHN OF ELTHAM, THE KING'S BROTHER, EARL OF CORNWALL (died 1336) GRANTS IN ENGLAND

4 December 1330 (*Cal. Charter Rolls*, iv, *1327–1341*, p. 198)

to support the dignity to himself and the heirs of his body with remainder to the king and his heirs, all surrendered by Queen Isabella:

Cornwall £20 of the issues of the county

Suffolk manor of Haughley

castle and manor of Eye with hamlets of Dallinghoo, Alderton and Thorndon and yearly rent of the honour of Eye in Norf., Suff., Lincs. and Essex with castle guard and free court in Lincs.

Norfolk £20 of manor of Bacton of prior of Bromholm

lands and tenements in Clopton

Herts. castle, town and honour of Berkhamsted

Bucks. manor of Risborough

manor of Cippenham

Oxon. castle and town of Wallingford with members and honours of Wallingford and St Valery

mills of Oxford and the Kingsmeadow there

Lincs. manor of Kirton

Leics. manors of Bowden Magna and Market Harborough

Surrey	manor of Byfleet
Northants.	town of Rockingham
	(value £20 of the county and 2,000 marks so far)
Suffolk	hundreds of Hartismere and Stow
London	a yearly farm from Queenhithe
	(these to value of 100 marks of land in exchange for the manor of Mileham, Norf., surrendered to the king)

4. EDWARD PRINCE OF WALES, DUKE OF CORNWALL AND EARL OF CHESTER (died 1376). GRANTS IN ENGLAND AND WALES

18 March 1333	(*Cal. Charter Rolls*, iv, 300) earldom of Chester to Edward the
Chester	king's eldest son and his heirs, kings of England, with the castles
and	of Chester, Rhuddlan and Flint and all the king's lands there, the
Flint	castle of Beeston and the cantred and land of Englefield (co. Flint) with the remainder of castle, manor and lands of Hope in
Salop	Wales which John de Crombewell held for life of Edward I's grant

17 March 1337 (*Reports from the Lords' Committee touching the Dignity of a Peer of the Realm*, v, *Appendix*, 35–8, London 1829)

	duchy of Cornwall to him and his heirs, eldest sons of the kings of England: the sheriffdom of Cornwall,
Cornwall and Devon	castle, borough, manor and honour of Launceston with park and appurtenances
	castle and manor of Trematon with the town of Saltash and park and appurtenances
	castle, borough and manor of Tintagel
	castle and manor of Restormel with park and appurtenances
	manor of Climsland with park of Carybullock and appurtenances
	Tybesta with bailiwick of Powder and appurtenances
	Tewington with appurtenances
	Helston in Kerrier with appurtenances
	Moresk with appurtenances
	Tywarnhaile with appurtenances
	Penkneth with appurtenances
	Pelynt with park and appurtenances
	Rillaton with beadelry of East Hundred and appurtenances
	Helston in Trigg with the park of Helsbury and appurtenances
	Liskeard with park and appurtenances
	Calstock with a fishery there and appurtenances
	town of Lostwithiel
	the stannaries with the coinage of the stannaries[4]
	the water of Dartmouth
	£20 annual farm of the citizens of Exeter
	prises and customs of wine in the water of Sutton
Oxon.	castle of Wallingford with the honours of Wallingford and St Valery with appurtenances in Oxfordshire and elsewhere
Herts, Bucks., Northants.	castle, manor and town of Berkhamsted with park and honour, with appurtenances
Surrey	manor of Byfleet with park and appurtananances

4. The grant of the stannaries and coinage of the stannaries in Cornwall was subject to a reservation of 1,000 marks p.a. granted by the king to William Montague, earl of Salisbury, and the heirs male of his body until he received in reversion certain lands held for life by John de Warenne, earl of Surrey, and his wife Joan, valued at 800 marks p.a., plus 200 marks of land. The Warenne lands were finally secured by Montague's son in 1361 on the death of Joan.

Wilts. £80 rent of castle and manor of Mere of John de Mere, life grantee of the king

And in reversion on the death of Queen Philippa:
Yorks. castle, manor and honour of Knaresborough with members in Yorks. and elsewhere
Middlx. manor of Isleworth

And in reversion on the death of Margaret, wife of Hugh Audley, earl of Gloucester:
Devon castle and manor of Lydford with appurtenances and chace of Dartmoor
manor of Bradninch

And in reversion on the death of John de Mere:
Wilts. castle and manor of Mere

4 September 1337 (*Cal. Charter Rolls*, iv, *1327–1341*, 428) for the increase of the duchy of Cornwall:
Surrey manors of Kennington and Vauxhall with a meadow in Lambeth and Newington, inalienable as above

1 October 1337 (*ibid.*, p. 432) for the increase of the duchy of Cornwall in reversion:
Norfolk castle and manor of Rising with a 4th part of the Tolbooth of Lynn
Warws. manor of Cheylesmore with £98 6s 8d rent in Coventry, to be annexed inalienably to the duchy of Cornwall on the death of Queen Isabella

12 May 1343 (*Reports . . . Dignity of a Peer, etc.*, v, *Appendix*, 43–4)
Wales to himself and his heirs, kings of England, all the king's lordships and lands in North Wales, West Wales and South Wales with the lordship, castle, town and county of Caernarvon, the lordship, castle and town of Conway, the lordship, castle and town of Criccieth, the lordship, castle and town of Beaumaris, the lordship, castle and town of Harlech, the lordships and counties of Anglesea and Merioneth, the lordship, castle, town and county of Carmarthen, the lordship, castle and town of Llanbadarnfawr (co. Cardigan), the lordship and seneschalry of Cantref Mawr (co. Carmarthen), the lordship, castle, town and county of Cardigan, the lordship, castle and town of Newcastle in Emlyn (co. Carmarthen), the lordship, castle and town of Builth, the lordship, castle and town of Haverford, the lordship, castle and town of Montgomery and all lands, etc., which were of Rees ap Meredith and came to the hands of Edward I.

5. JOHN OF GAUNT (1340–99), EARL OF RICHMOND AND DUKE OF LANCASTER. GRANTS IN ENGLAND

6 March 1351 (*Reports . . . Dignity of a Peer etc.*, v, *Appendix*, 478)
Yorks. etc. confirmation of the earldom of Richmond and its possessions:
the county, honour, castle, manors, lands, tenements etc., of the earldom to him and the heirs of his body with remainder to the king and his heirs, as formerly held by John duke of Brittany.

20 May 1360 (*Cal. Pat. Rolls*, *1358–1361*, p. 428)
Herts. castle, town and honour of Hertford with Bayford, Essendon and Hertingfordbury (cf. *ibid.*, *1374–1377*, p. 359, grant converted to tail male)

25 June 1372 (*Cal. Pat. Rolls, 1370–1374*, p. 183)

Derbys. castle, manor, honour and free chace of High Peak

Yorks. castles, manors and honours of Tickhill and Knaresborough with the wapentake of Staincliff, and the manors of Gringley and Wheatley, Notts.

200 marks farm of the abbot and convent of St Mary, York, for the manor of Whitgift

Suffolk manor of Wighton

Norfolk manors of Aylsham, Fakenham, Snettisham, the hundreds of North Greenhoe, North and South Erpingham and Smithdon

Hunts. manors of Glatton and Holme

Sussex castle and lowey of Pevensey

manors of Willingdon and Maresfield

bailiwick of Endlewick

free chace of Ashdown

Cambs. manor of Soham

Also included in the grant were the advowsons of Staindrop and Brancepeth churches, of the free chapels of Tickhill and High Peak, of the church and free chapel of Maresfield, of the free chapel within Pevensey castle, of the priory of Wilmington (cell of St Mary de Greston, Normandy), of the priory of Withyham (cell of the abbey of St Martin de Meremest in Touraine) and of the house of St Robert of Knaresborough.

The whole grant was made in return for the surrender of the possessions of the earldom of Richmond which Edward III now required to give to John de Montfort, duke of Brittany to bind him in alliance.

In 1377 John of Gaunt petitioned for and received a supplementary charter naming the towns of Grinstead (previously considered to be part of the manor of Maresfield), Seaford (previously considered to be part of the castle and lowey of Pevensey) and Laughton-in-le-Morthen (previously considered to be part of the honour of Tickhill) as included in the original grant, with the liberties and privileges which Queen Philippa, the former life tenant enjoyed in them (*ibid., 1337–1381*, pp. 24, 69–70; and *ibid., 1396–1399*, p. 76, an exemplification).

6. EDMUND OF LANGLEY (born 1341) EARL OF CAMBRIDGE AND DUKE OF YORK. GRANTS IN ENGLAND

6 August 1347 (*Cal. Charter Rolls*, v, *1341–1417*, p. 63) to himself and the heirs male of his body with reversion to the king's other sons John and Lionel and the heirs male of their bodies and to the king and his heirs, all the lands of John de Warenne, late earl of Surrey, beyond Trent, subject to a dower of £200 p.a. for the countess of Warenne, and the custody granted to Queen Philippa during pleasure

These were (*Cal. Inq.*, ix, no. 54 by writs of 2 July 1347):

Yorks. the castle and manor of Sandal and the town of Wakefield with members (Alverthorpe, Stanley, Thornes, Ossett, Hipperholme, Sowerby with Sowerbyshire and the park of Erringden, Harbury, Rastrick, Holmfirth, Warley and Scammoden), together with the castle and manor of Conisborough and the manor and town of Doncaster

Also the manors of Hatfield and Thorne, Fishlake and Stainforth with Braithwaite, and Donsthorpe, Newenge, Muscroft, Ashfields park and fisheries of Went and Bramwith

8 May 1363 (*ibid.*, p. 178) to support the dignity of earl of Cambridge:

Lincs. the castle, manor and town of Stamford and the manor, soke and town of Grantham, also previously held by John de Warenne for life

25 May 1377 (*Cal. Pat. Rolls, 1374–1377*, pp. 474–5) to him and Isabel his wife in tail male, following on the death of Mary de Sancto Paulo, countess of Pembroke who had a life interest:

Northants. castle and manor of Fotheringhay with members (Nassington and Yarwell)

Herts. castle and manor of Anstey with members

Wilts. manor of Vasterne with the manors of Wootton Bassett, Winterbourne Bassett, Tockenham and Chelworth, value 500 marks, with the reversion of the manor of Compton Bassett, value 50 marks, on the demise of Bernard Brocas, knight (the manors of Westmill, Little Hormead and Meesden (Herts.) to revert to the abbot and monks of St Mary Graces by the Tower of London following the death of the said countess as a condition of this grant).

[N.B. Edmund Langley, duke of York, received to himself and his heirs Wendover, Bucks., Compton Bassett, Wilts., and the reversion of the honour, town, fair and market of Rayleigh, Essex, the manors of Thundersley, Eastwood and Newport, Essex, Sevenhampton and the hundreds of Highworth and Cricklade, Wilts., in reversion after John of Brittany and his heirs, who held them so long as the king held Brest. John of Brittany died without heirs in 1399. These lands were thus lost to the Crown until the Yorkist accession (*Cal. Pat. Rolls, 1385–1389*, pp. 530, 636; *ibid., 1388–1392*, p. 377)].

7. ISABELLA, THE KING'S DAUGHTER (1332–(?)79), COUNTESS OF BEDFORD. GRANTS IN ENGLAND

23 October 1353 (*Cal. Pat. Rolls, 1350–1354*, p. 504) for life

Northants. manor of Weedon Lois

Wilts. manor of Corsham

Berks. manor of Swalclyve [? Swallowfield]

7 March 1355 (*ibid., 1354–1355*, p. 185) for life

Yorks. all the king's manors and hamlets of Burstwick, Bondburstwick, Skeckling, Little Humber, Keyingham, Cleton, Skipsea, Owthorne, Withernsea, Lelley-Dyke, Elsternwick, Burton Pidsea, Preston, Sproatley, Hedon, Paull, Skefling, Kilnsea, Easington and Ravenser

Lincs. lordship and town of Barrow

Wilts. manor of Corsham (second grant)

Northants. manor of Wedon Lois (second grant)

Berks. manor of Swallowfield (? second grant)

(all as fully as any king of England or count of Albemarle held them)

10 March 1355 (*ibid.*, p. 190) appointed for her dwelling place

Wilts. manor of Ludgershall (granted for life *ibid.*, p. 405, 4 June 1356)

29 November 1355 (*ibid.*, p. 317) for life

Hants. the castle, lordship and honour of Carisbrooke and the manors and towns of Bowcombe, Wroxall, Newtown, Pan, Newport, and Yarmouth, Isle of Wight

And the reversions of the manor of Whitfield with the liberty of the town of Brading and the manor and liberty of Thorneye, both held for life by William de Dale

20 March 1356 (*ibid.*, p. 361) for life
Wilts. manor of Marston Maisey held for life by John Darcy the son, deceased

before 30 August 1357 (*ibid.*, p. 636)
Berks. manor of Carswell [in Bray]

17 April 1361 (*ibid.*, *1361–1364*, pp. 5–6) for life
Berks. two thirds of the manor of Hampstead Marshall, late of William Danvers deceased, plus the third part on the death of Mary dowager countess of Norfolk
manor of Speen which William de Hadham held for life

1 October 1367 (*ibid.*, *1367–1370*, p. 16) jointly with her husband Ingram de Coucy, earl of Bedford, to them and the heirs male of their bodies
Kent manors of Tremworth and Vanne
Wilts. manors of Haselbury Plucknett and Somerford Keynes (the whole grant as of the value of 300 marks p.a.)

3 October 1375 (*ibid.*, *1374–1377*, p. 180)
Bucks. shown as holding the manor of Salden for the life of Isabella (cf. *ibid.*, p. 462, dated 13 May 1377)

They were survived by their daughter and heir Philippa duchess of Ireland.

APPENDIX 'B'

THE PROPOSED CONFISCATION OF TEMPORALITIES OF THE CHURCH IN 1404

THE ST ALBANS CHRONICLER AND THE COVENTRY PARLIAMENT

Since the most important of contemporary chroniclers, Thomas Walsingham, gives an account of the Coventry Parliament of 1404 which differs in essentials from events as stated on the roll of the parliament, some examination of the chronicler's story must be attempted. He was the author of three accounts of these years found in the *Annales Henrici IV*, the *Historia Anglicana* and *Ypodigma Neustriae*.[1]

One firm fact about the Coventry Parliament was that the king had varied the usual form of the writ of summons ordering elections in the shires; he ordered the sheriffs to prevent the election of lawyers or men learned in the law.[2] On the strength of this interference Walsingham described the parliament as one lacking in learning, composed of men no wiser than rustics or heathen, stupid men, secular in their beliefs and loyalties, who could think of no better proposal than to plunder the established ecclesiastical order of the endowments it had received from generations of worthy and pious men. The assembly thus became the 'Unlearned Parliament'. The king's intervention had almost certainly been made, not without precedent, to exclude lawyers who took up the time of parliament by using their membership to present hosts of petitions for clients. The presentation of private petitions during parliamentary sesssions had become a most important method of obtaining legal redress. Hence the especially favourable position of lawyer members in their profession. This assembly was summoned to Coventry to help the king out of an urgent and critical financial situation. There was to be no time for the other normal parliamentary activities.[3] Of course the king may have had other motives in attempting to exclude lawyers (there is no evidence that he succeeded). They were presumably great talkers and procrastinators and perhaps trouble makers, but it is going too far to say that this change in the form of the writ of summons produced a stupid assembly.

Walsingham's story is that the knights of parliament not only worked for a general resumption of all crown lands, but also pressed the king to confiscate the temporal possessions of the church. The church was fortunate in her champion, Archbishop Arundel, who led the prelates in opposition to the act of resumption, won the gratitude of the temporal lords for this, and thereby secured their support in resisting the attack on church lands. He was aided by the eloquent bishop of

1. Professor V. H. Galbraith in his introduction to *The St Albans Chronicle 1406–22*, pp. xii, lx, proves conclusively that he was the author of all three accounts.

2. *Reports . . . touching the Dignity of a Peer*, iii, 372.

3. There was a precedent for this in 1372: *Rot. Parl.*, ii, 310; *Statutes of the Realm*, i, 394. The king had recently been compelled to declare a financial moratorium by an order in Council dated at Lichfield 28 August 1404: *Cal. Close Rolls, 1402–1405*, p. 382. J. H. Wylie, *History of England under Henry the Fourth*, noticed that this was first enrolled under the date 5 July at Pontefract but crossed through. It appears that Henry had already cancelled his unwelcome decision once. The parliament met in the middle of this acute financial crisis.

Rochester, Arundel's 'Mercury', who made a rousing speech which quite discomfited the knights. The latter's most weighty point was that the knights were rendering themselves liable to excommunication under the provisions of Magna Carta. They ended by begging Arundel's pardon[4] and the chronicler rounded off his story of this triumph with a suitable epigram from Martial.[5]

The roll of the parliament has no mention of an attack on the temporalities of the church and supplies a different account of the outcome of the secular act of resumption. Some of the facts of Walsingham's account will not bear close examination. He made Sir John Cheyne, the alleged renegade deacon and despoiler of alien priories, Speaker of the Commons in this parliament and leader of their attack. He put into his mouth a fine anticlerical speech. Cheyne was certainly not Speaker of the Coventry Parliament,[6] and he was probably not even elected to it.[7] Also Walsingham kept John Bottlesham, bishop of Rochester, alive until 1405,[8] whereas he died on 17 April 1404,[9] some time before the parliament met. There was no bishop of Rochester at all during the Coventry Parliament.[10]

Of all the political events of the times an attack on church endowments tainted with lollardy and made in parliament was most likely to rouse the ire of the chronicler of the wealthy abbey of St Albans. He wrote his chronicle primarily for the glory of God and this struck at the basis of the faith. It looks as though he combined the incidents of two parliaments (1399 and 1404) to make a better story, or else, writing his account a few years later, and with the dreadful climax of the heretical lollard petition of the 'milites pocius Pilati quam Parliamenti' of 1410 fresh in his mind, he inadvertently mixed the chronology of the earlier years.

There are grounds for placing the attack on the temporalities of the church in Henry's first parliament of 1399 rather than at Coventry in 1404. Cheyne was then elected Speaker and an earlier Bottlesham, William, a prelate especially renowned for his eloquence,[11] was then bishop of Rochester. While the roll of that parliament, like the roll of the 1404 parliament, has no mention of an attack on ecclesiastical temporalities the next parliament which met on the Octave of Hilary 1401 was given

4. 'Annales Ricardi et Henrici IV,' ed. H. T. Riley, in *Johannis de Trokelowe et Henrici de Blaneforde Chronica et Annales* (Rolls Series), pp. 392–4. *Historia Anglicana* (R.S.), ed. H. T. Riley, ii, pp. 266–7. *Ypodigma Neustriae* (R.S.), ed. H. T. Riley, pp. 410–11.

5. *Martial*, xii, 6, addressed to Helvidius Priscus who had been exiled under Domitian and returned under Nerva, so that it would have been more appropriate to the circumstances of 1399 when Arundel returned from exile, than to five years later.

6. William Sturmy was Speaker: *Rot. Parl.*, iii, 546.

7. *Returns of Names of Members of Parliament*, i, 265–6.

8. *Ann. Hen.*, p. 397.

9. *Handbook of British Chronology*, p. 165; Dugdale, *Monasticon* (new ed. 1817–30), i, 156.

10. Richard Yonge, bishop of Bangor, was nominated to succeed John Bottlesham on 28 July 1404 but did not accept. Writing to the king from Calais on 7 April 1405 he spoke of himself as Richard, bishop of Bangor: *Proc. and Ord.*, i, 257. The see of Rochester was still vacant on 22 December 1406: *Rot. Parl.*, iii, 582–3. Even as bishop of Bangor he was unlikely to have been present at the Coventry Parliament. He was in Scotland on 24 September 1404: J. H. Wylie *op. cit.*, p. 140, quoting duchy of Lancaster records. On 12 November 1404 the king appointed him to treat with the ambassadors of the duchess of Burgundy and the business of a truce kept him abroad until May 1405: *Proc. and Ord.*, i, 238–40; *Foedera*, viii, 375. He was not a close associate of Arundel, who seized his temporalities and would not give them up until application had been made to Rome: Dugdale, *loc. cit.*

11. Dugdale described him as: 'Much esteemed for his learning, but more for his eloquence in the pulpit, which procured him the favour of Richard II. . . .' There can be little doubt that he was Arundel's 'Mercury'. Walsingham was confused about the two Bottleshams, for he made them both Johns in announcing the death of the first and the appointment of the second: *Ann Hen.*, p. 337.

an extra strong and unusual warning by command of the king that the position of Holy Church would be maintained.[12] This warning may well have been occasioned by the activities of the previous assembly.

12. The additional warning is at *Rot. Parl.*, iii, 454. For the traditional assurance see *ibid.*, pp. 166 (1384), 257 (1389), 277 (1390), 347 (1398).

APPENDIX 'C'

THE CROWN LANDS AS AFFECTED BY THE ACTS OF RESUMPTION, 1450–61

Notes

In this appendix, a grantee is described as sheriff, escheator, M.P., or officer of the duchy of Lancaster if he held the position at any time during the reign of Henry VI, since the object is to give a general picture of status and interests.

Alienations are marked with an asterisk.

Regrants to the original grantee with a dagger.

Resumed lands granted to members of the royal family with a plus sign above the line.

The extents quoted are those made by the sheriffs and escheators under the acts.

Sources

Exch., K.R., Various Accts, E.101/330 (a collection of the 'particule compoti' of sheriffs and escheators under the acts of 28 and 29 Hen. VI).

Exch., K.R., Escheators' Accts, E.136/238/3 (the 'particule compoti' of the escheator of Essex and Herts. under the act of 29 Hen. VI).

Exch., K.R., Sheriffs' Accts, E.199, *passim* (a number of 'particule compoti' for all three acts).

Exch., L.T.R., Sheriffs' Seizures, E.379/175 (the enrolled accounts for the act of 28 Hen. VI).

Exch., L.T.R., Escheators' Accts., E. 357/41 (the enrolled accounts for the act of 29 Hen VI.)

Exch., L.T.R., Sheriffs' Seizures, E.379/174 (the enrolled accounts for the act of 33 Hen. VI).

The details of regrants are mainly from the Fine Rolls.

BEDFORDSHIRE AND BUCKINGHAMSHIRE

	Terms until 1450 (rent paid etc.)	Later terms etc.
Lands and tenements in Chalfont.	7s 2d as long as in king's hands. Nicholas Willoughby rec. gen. & attorney gen. to Hen. VI's duchy feoffees. Wm. Michell, king's clerk.	2 Dec. 1451 at 12s as long etc. Richard Dynton, John Ford and Thos. Clerk.
2 parts of manor of Saldin with lands and rents in Weston Turville, Hoggeston, Beauchampton, Horwood Magna, Horwood Parva, Kimble, Wendover, Ewell, Luton and Fennelsgrove.	*1d sold to Cardinal Beaufort who had resold to Sir Robt. Whitingham, treasurer of Calais, M.P. (son M.P., in Household).	†2 June 1450 at £12 13s 4d for 7 years but cancelled 11 August 1450 and sales upheld.

	Terms until 1450 (rent paid etc.)	Later terms etc.
Manor of Wyrardisbury.		15 Mar. 1456. At rate of extent from Mich. 1455 for 10 years. David & John Brecknock.
200 acres in Cranfield, Shutlington, Barton in the Clay, Flatwick, Cravenhurst and Sutton.	7s 6d for 20 years. John Browne, under clerk of king's kitchen. Bartholomew Willesden, of the Exchequer.	Extent (with 7 acres called Beancroft at Harrow, Middx.). £2 13s 4d Grant confirmed in 1457.
A messauge and virgate of land in Padbury.	Nil. Joint lives. Ric. Dalby, M.P., yeoman porter, king's servant. Ric. Waynfleet, porter of Berkhamsted, keeper of Hinckley park.	Extent £1
The King's park of Princes Risborough.	Nil. Life. John Brecknock of Horsenden, J.P., sheriff, M.P., rec. gen., duchy of Cornwall, feodary Richmond honour in Lincs. and Notts., clerk of Household.	Extent £1.
CAMBRIDGESHIRE AND HUNTINGDONSHIRE		
Castle & honour of Huntingdon and honour of Peverel, Boulogne and Hagenet in Bucks., Northants. and Leics.	£3 6s 8d. Life. Roger Hunt, M.P., king's attorney in Exchequer, deputy steward, duchy of Lancaster, South Parts.	27 April 1451 at £5 from 6 Nov. 1449 for 24 years. John Burcestre, Roger Thorpe, Thos. Crosse.
		7 Feb. 1456 at £5 3s 4d from Mich. 1455 for 20 years. Thos. Thorpe.
		26 Aug. 1460 at £5 6s 8d from Mich. 1460 for 24 years. Wm. Neville, lord Fauconberg.
2 parts of manors of Bassingbourn and Babraham.	*Nil. Alienated to Edmund Beaufort, duke of Somerset, fee tail male (*Rot. Parl.*, V, 446–7).	7 June 1450 at rate of extent from Easter 1450 for 20 years. Thos. Cotton.

	Terms until 1450 (rent paid etc.)	Later terms etc.
		20 Sept. 1450 at £66 13s 4d with lands in Dorset and Somerset from Easter 1450 for 10 years. Henry duke of Exeter, Thos. Mannyn, John Chancy and Thos. Hugan.
		+ Edmund Tudor, probably tail male. ? date. Seized of, at death.
		15 April 1457 for life to his widow, Margaret Beaufort, to a certain value.
Assarts, wastes and purprestures between bridges of Oxford and Stamford.	Nil. Probably in hands of the Roos family cf. Northants.	10 Feb. 1453 at £60 from Mich. 1449 for 10 years Henry Skenard. & Wm. Bertram.
		10 Feb. 1453 Ric. Wydeville & Jacquette joint lives to value of £60.
Park of Fleming Mede in Burwell	7s for 12 years Robt. Carlyle, J.P., M.P.	
A messuage and 5 acres in Offord Darcy.	2s 6d for 15 years. John Randes.	
4 acres 3 roods meadow at Godmanchester.	13s 4d as long as in king's hands. John Frere, Reginald Quenyve.	

CUMBERLAND AND WESTMORLAND

	Terms until 1450 (rent paid etc.)	Later terms etc.
Fisheries in Eden called Armathwaite, Ternwathlane and le Glashouse.	John Skelton, sheriff, M.P., king's sergeant.	
10 acres of pasture in Inglewood Forest.	Richard Trott.	Waste and no value.
A fishery in Eden called Kingsgarth.	Mayor and bailiffs of Carlisle.	

	Terms until 1450 (rent paid etc.)	Later terms etc.
Plumpton lawn.	*Alienated in fee. Nil. Richard earl of Salisbury.	Extent £22. This grant confirmed 1452.
Lands in Inglewood Forest. Armathwaite, Thowthwaite, Morton Hasket, Wollaikes, Nonclos and Blabirthwaite.	Joint lives £17 19s od John Skelton, snr. and jnr.	Extent £17 19s od.
Clothihowe.	£1 13s 4d. Sir Hen. Fenwick, J.P., sheriff.	Extent £1 13s 4d. 22 Mar. 1452 to these added various subsidies due to king in Carlisle excluding hides and woolfells, from Mich. at £31 10s od for 20 years. Richard earl of Salisbury.
A fishery called the Frithnet or Sheriff's net in river Eden.	£1 18s 4d for 60 years. Sir Thos. Curwen, esch., J.P., sheriff, M.P.	6 August. 1454 further added feefarm of Carlisle and city mill £80 for 20 years. Richard earl of Salisbury. Amount remitted to him as fee for office of warden of king's forests beyond Trent.
A fishery by Eden bridge with meadow land at Carlisle and Bridgend.	£15 os 10d for 20 years. Richard Neville, earl of Salisbury.	By Act of 33 Hen. VI he lost this £80, and office of warden and justice of king's forest beyond Trent changed from entail to joint lives of himself and his son Richard earl of Warwick.
Land in Inglewood Forest: closes of Itonfield, Barrockfield and Brumgill and some demesne lands of Carlisle.	£8 6s 8d, joint lives. Roger Beetham and wife. br. of Sir Edward Beetham of B., J.P., M.P., who was allied to Nevilles by marriage.	†2 April 1451 £8 6s 8d from Easter 1451 for 12 years. 23 July 1451 agreement with others to pay more for lease of 24 years. Henry Percy, lord Poynings.

	Terms until 1450 (rent paid etc.)	Later terms etc.
		†19 Feb. 1456 £8 13s 4d from Mich. 1454 for 20 years.
60 acres in Castle Field, Carlisle.	£3. William Buk.	Extent £3.
100 acres in Armathwaitebank in Inglewood Forest.	80 years at 8s 4d. John Skelton.	Extent 8s 4d.
Lands at Weryholme by Carlisle.	£1. Sir Thos. Parre, esch., undersheriff, J.P., M.P.	Weryholme and market etc. at Kendal. 26 June 1451 £4 from 25 Mar. 1451 for 20 years. Robt. Danby and Thos. Colt.
2 parts of toll of fair and market at Kendal (lordship of Kendal).	£3. Sir Thos. Parre.	†7 July 1451 £4 3s 4d from Easter 1451 for 12 years.
1 part of 2 parts of lordship or manors of Grasmere, Loughrigg, Langdale, Casterton and Ambleside and herbage of the Dalehead above Troutbeck Park (lordship of Kendal).	The portion of the lordship of Kendal held by the widow of John Beaufort, late earl of Kendal.	Exempt from Act of 28 Hen. VI. 1 June 1451 £13 1s 0d for 24 years. Thomas Harrington.
2 parts of manors of Applethwaite, Lower Mill beck and Dalehead, a cornmill, a fishery in Windermere and a place called Calgarth (lordship of Kendal)	£22 9s 6d term of years. Sir Thomas Harrington, J.P., M.P., steward of Amounderness, duchy of Lancaster.	
2 parts of manor of Troutbeck, meadows, mills, pastures and parks and Windermere Holme (lordship of Kendal).	Nil. Probably life. Thomas Danyell Esq., sheriff, J.P., bailiff W. Derby, duchy of Lancaster, chamberlain of Chester, king's remembrancer, member of king's Household, m. sister of duke of Norfolk.	Applethwaite etc., and Troutbeck etc. 5 July 1451 £41 14s 11d from Easter 1451 for 24 years. Thomas Harrington.
Mill of Upperby and 3 waste places.	15 years at 7s 8d. James Kelom, Chancery, gent.	

	Terms until 1450 (rent paid etc.)	Later terms etc.
Andrew Harclay's lands.		10s from Mich. 1454 for 10 years. Thos. de la More.
Land at Cheton.	£5. Joint lives.	Extent £5.
Land at Braithwaite and Midelstogh.	£5 6s 8d. Joint lives. Roger Beetham and wife.	Extent £5 6s 8d.
2 parts of manor of Strickland–Kettle, Crossthwaite, Hutton, Helsington and a fishery in waters of Kent and a place called Forstwaite (lordship of Kendal).	Life. £25 12s 10d. Sir Richard Tunstall, M.P., king's carver, later rec. of Lancs. and Ches., baron of exchequer at Lancaster, duchy of Lancaster.	Extent £25 12s 10d.
2 parts of manors of Grasmere, Loughrigg, Ambleside, Casterton, Kirkby in Kendal and a farm called le Burgh and Lithouse (lordship of Kendal, the inheritance of Margaret, da. and heir of John Beaufort).	20 years at £33 2s 6d. John Tunstall, M.P. (uncle of Sir Richard), Thos. Colte, M.P., member of York's council, chamberlain of Exchequer 1454–9 (Richard earl of Salisbury surrendered grant that they might have this. He had a 50 mark annuity on it).	Extent £39 9s 8d. + 24 Mar. 1453 to Edmund and Jasper Tudor, the keeping during minority of heir.
2 parts of herbage and pannage of Troutbeck park (lordship of Kendal).	£2. Henry Warenne, gent., yeoman of Chamber, keeper of Kingston Lacy manor (Dors.), duchy of Lancaster.	Extent £2.

Note + On 6 March 1453 all the lordship of Kendal lands were granted to Edmund earl of Richmond, and came under control of his officers (Ministers Accts., D.L. 29/644/10444). His receiver was Robert Duket.

Windermere Island (lordship of Kendal).	Life. Nil. Wm. Thornburgh, J.P., king's esquire.	

DEVON AND CORNWALL

Manors of Trematon, Calstock and burgh of Saltash.	£80 apparently reserved rent. Fee tail male to John Holand, duke of Exeter.	Apparently allowed to stand at first on plea of earlier grant of 25 June 16 Ric. II.

	Terms until 1450 (rent paid etc.)	Later terms etc.
		†9 July 1456 at rate of extent which Exchequer said should be £133 14s od from Easter 1456 for 10 years. Henry duke of Exeter and others.
Forest of Dartmoor and castle, town and manor of Lydford and manor of South Teign.	£66 13s 4d joint lives. Sir Philip Courtenay, M.P., summoned to Council. Sir Edmund Hungerford, sheriff, J.P., king's carver, M.P., sergeant-at-law, chamberlain of duchy of Lancaster, steward of South Parts, duchy of Lancaster.	12 Oct. 1451 Sir Philip Courtenay and Sir Edmund Hungerford forcibly expelled by Robert Burton, sheriff of Devon. 1451–2 charged to sheriff in Foreign Accounts. 3 Feb. 1453 restored by order of the king (Patent Roll). £66 13s 4d from Mich. 1452 for life. Sir Wm. Bonville of Chewton. Not enrolled (Resumption Accts., 33 Hen. VI).
Fishery in the Exe.	*Nil. Alienated to Thos. Courtenay, earl of Devon.	Still in hand in 1456 (Resumption Accts., 33 Hen. VI).
Manor of Helston in Kerrier. Burgh of Helston.	Nil. Joint lives. John Arundel Esq., of Lankerre, J.P., John Trevelyan Esq., esch., steward of duchy of Cornwall, M.P., member of king's Household.	24 May 1451 at £50 for 7 years. John Nanfan.
Herbage and pannage of Liskeret park.	Thos. Bodulgate.	Extent £1 16s 8d.
4 messuages in Grampound Tregoys, Chypys and Penryn.	Nil. As long as in king's hands. John Trevelyan Esq.	†25 Oct. 1451 at £1 for 7 years.

	Terms until 1450 (rent paid etc.)	Later terms etc.
Manors of Restormel, Pelynt, Penkneth, Tintagel, Moresk and Tewington. Burghs of Lostwithiel and Camelford.	£80 for 7 years. Thos. Bodulgate Esq., J.P., M.P., king's squire, lawyer. John Trevelyan Esq.,	15 July 1451 at £90 for 10 years. Thos. Appleton. †14 Nov. 1451 at £91 from Easter 1451 for 10 years. Trevelyan and duke of Exeter. 3 Mar. 1455 at £93 10s 0d from Christmas 1454 for 10 years. Sir Wm. Bonville and Appleton. †24 Sept. 1456 at £94 10s 0d from Mich. 1455 for 10 years. Trevelyan and Exeter.
Waters of Fowey.	Extent 10s. John Trevelyan Esq.	

Note: +All these lands in Devon and Cornwall together with all other duchy of Cornwall lands passed under the control of the ministers of Edward prince of Wales, from Mich. 1456.

ESSEX AND HERTFORDSHIRE

Manor of Hunsdon.	*Freehold. Richard duke of York.	
Tenement in Gosfield Mochemes and pts in Gosfield, Bocking and Finchingfield.	1s. Life. Richard Somer of Hertford, yeoman purveyor of Household.	£2 13s 4d extent, but regranted at 1s in Sept. 1451.
A messuage and 3 acres of arable called Clemens Doddes and rents at Reynham.	6d for 80 years. Thos. Scargill, M.P., usher of Chamber, troner and peser in Ipswich, rider in Waltham Forest, keeper of Havering.	17s extent. †15 June 1453 at 6d from 6 Nov. 1449 for 20 years.
A messuage in town of Offley.	4d. Life. Wm. Hawes of King's Walden.	5s extent.

	Terms until 1450 (rent paid etc.)	Later terms etc.
Lordship of manor of Havering atte Bower.	Life. £36 13s 4d. Thos. Brown, king's squire, J.P., sheriff, M.P., under treasurer of Exchequer, steward of Middleton and Marden (terms £86 13s 4d with £50 p.a. remitted).	9 Nov. 1451 at £100 from 25 Mar. 1451 for 10 years. Robert Browne. + 1 Mar. 1453 livery to Queen Margaret for life value £92 (Close Roll).
Herbage and pannage at Havering.	Nil. Life. Thos. Scargill Esq., M.P., member of Household.	†15 Feb. 1452 at £4 for 10 years.
Manor of Hadleigh.	*Richard duke of York had reversionary grant in fee tail male, after death of Humphrey duke of Gloucester.	18 May 1450 rate of extent from Mich. 1449 for 7 years. John Everdon. 7 Sept. 1450 surrendered. 20 Nov. 1450 at £14 from Easter 1450 for 20 years. Henry Holand, duke of Exeter. + 1 Mar. 1453 livery to Queen Margaret for life, value £14 (Close Roll).
2 parts of manor of Bradwell.	£7. 10 years. John Poutrell, gent., customer in port of London, farmer of ulnage Bristol.	†10 Aug. 1651 at £67 for 40 years. + 1 Mar. 1453 livery to Queen Margaret for life, value £72 (Close Roll).
A messuage called le Hyde, 100 acres arable, 2 acres pasture, 20 acres wood at Abbots Langley.	£3 2s 6d. Life. Bartholomew Halley, M.P., king's servant.	†12 July 1451 at £3 6s 8d for 12 years.
A fishery and ford near Colchester.	*Alienated to John earl of Oxford.	1457 Town of Colchester established their right to it in Exchequer Court (L.T.R. Mem. Roll).
7 acres of arable in town of Panfield.	4s 4d. John Othoo of Panfield.	19 April 1459 at 4s 8d for 50 years. John Levechilde.

	Terms until 1450 (rent paid etc.)	Later terms etc.
A salt pond called 'le Rye at Wose' in parishes of Leigh and Hadleigh.	Nil. Life. Thos. Barton, M.P., yeoman of the Chamber.	
A tenement called Chamberlains, in Ashingdon.	Nil. Life. Philip Wentworth, J.P., M.P., sheriff, squire of the body, constable of Clitheroe castle, duchy of Lancaster.	
Manor called Chamberlains in hundred of Rochford.	Nil. Life. Henry Everingham, esch., M.P., squire of the Household.	
Manor of Lawford.	*Nil. Alienated to John Say, esch., J.P., M.P., chancellor duchy of Lancaster, squire of the body, and heirs.	
A kidell called the Horned Weir.	Nil. Life. John Byrkyn, valet of king's larder.	Reversion to Eton.
Some 4 acres in Waltham Forest called Peryhull or Mount John.	Nil. Life. Wm. Stafford, chaplain (according to Resumption Accts.).	*Recte*. Richard de la Felde, king's sergeant who had life grant in 1447 (Pat. Roll).
	GLOUCESTERSHIRE	
2 parts of Forest of Dean.	Nil. Joint lives. £40 rent charge but remitted as separate life grant. John lord Beauchamp, Ralph lord Sudeley.	†28 Oct. 1451 at £40 for joint lives and order to sheriff not to molest occupants, one of whom was the Treasurer himself (Patent Roll).
Manor of Stantway in Rodley in Westbury parish.	Nil. Joint lives. Richard Boulton, J.P., M.P., gent., of Lincoln and London. Morgan Meredith Esq., of Carmarthen and Kent, M.P., keeper of the armouries in Wales 'notwithstanding that there are no armouries'.	
	HAMPSHIRE	
Herbage and pannage of pigs in forest of Woolmer and Alice Holt.	10s for 12 years. John Berewe Esq.	Extent 10s.

	Terms until 1450 (rent paid etc.)	Later terms etc.
Lands in East Worldham, Nutley and Benesworth with 33 acres of Woolmer forest imparked in E. Worldham park.	*Rose at midsummer. Fee simple. Wm. de la Pole, marquis of Suffolk and wife. Formerly Thos. Chaucer Esq.	Extent £5 11s 7d.
Manors of Combe and Monxton.	Nil. Life. John de Rinell, clerk, king's secretary.	Supposed value at time of grant £31 13s 4d but Exchequer valued it at £44 from the reversion roll.
Manor of Odiham.	£36. Life. John Basket Esq., J.P., sheriff, M.P., king's servant, bailiff, attorney.	£12 May 1451 at £50 from Mich. 1449 for 12 years. John Basket and Humphrey Stafford. 1 July 1453 at £51 from Midsummer 1453 for 20 years. Richard Merston and John Grenefield. 10 Oct. 1453 at £51 for 20 years. Richard Merston.
Castle and manor of Porchester with forest and warren.	Life, apparently nil. Robert Fiennes Esq., nephew of Say and Sele, J.P., M.P., sheriff, Household.	17 Feb. 1452 appropriated for keeping of the seas.
Manor of Bowcombe, I.O.W.		5 April 1451 at £66 13s 4d for 12 years. John Baker Esq., to be paid to receiver or farmer of I.O.W.
Isle and lordship of Wight with castle and lordship of Carisbrooke, king's manors of Whitefield, Brading, Wroxall, Niton, Bowcombe, Freshwater, Thorley, burghs of Newport and Yarmouth, forest of Bordwood, chace of Parkhurst, liberties of Eastmede and Westmede and all alien priory lands in the island.	According to the Resumption Accounts: alienated to Edm. Beaufort, earl of Somerset, after death of Humphrey duke of Gloucs. According to the Enrolled Foreign Accounts: granted for life to Richard duke of York from whom it was resumed. York had the issues until 24 June	Resumed under Act of 28 Hen. VI. and on 7 June 1450. John lord Beauchamp appointed lieutenant and steward for life. 6 Nov. 1449–25 June 1452 at £139 16s 11½d p.a. charged to Thos. Chamberlain, valet of Chamber, receiver of king's lordships within the island (E.163/8/6). He was appointed by

	Terms until 1450 (rent paid etc.)	Later terms etc.
	1450, through his servants there. This latter is correct (see *Rot. Parl.*, v, 204–5).	patent dated 27 June 1450. 6 Sept. 1452 alienated in fee tail male to Edmund duke of Somerset. Resumed under Act of 33 Hen. VI. 18 Mar. 1456 at £139 16s 11½d from Mich. 1455 for 7 years. Eleanor duchess of Somerset. 5 Nov. 1457 at £139 16s 11½d from Mich. 1457 for 12 years. Henry duke of Somerset.
The Channel Islands.	*Rose at midsummer. Entailed on Henry Beauchamp, duke of Warwick (died 1446) in reversion after the death of Humphrey duke of Gloucester (died 1447) in exchange for gift to the king of the reversion of the manor of Leighton Buzzard (Beds.). Guardianship of heir given to Suffolk who appointed Wm. Bertram as keeper with power to collect rents.	From 2 March 1450 Richard earl of Warwick in possession and still in possession 12 July 1451. John Nanfan, king's esquire took up post as warden and governor there with his company 22 July 1452. Appointed in Close Rolls 24 Sept. 1452 for 5 years. Mustered 130 archers on 9 Aug. 1452 (Issue Rolls).
HEREFORD AND MARCHES OF WALES ADJACENT		
Castle and lordship of Pembroke with castles and lordships of Cilgerran, Emlyn-Is-Cych and Dyffryn Breuan.	*Wm. de la Pole, marquis of Suffolk alienated in fee tail.	Resumed under act of 28 Hen. VI (Close Roll). 28 May 1450 Philip Wentworth appointed receiver of lordship of Cilgerran. Castle and lordship of Pembroke only: 31 May 1450 at extent from Mich. 1449 for 12 years. John lord Beauchamp.

	Terms until 1450 (rent paid etc.)	Later terms etc.
		Cilgerran etc. 16 Dec. 1450 at extent from Mich. 1450 for 12 years. Henry Griffin ap David ap Thomas and William Johns Esq.
		Cilgerran etc. 18 April 1451 at £53 6s 8d from Mich. 1450 for 12 years to same.
		+ The whole: 23 July 1451 livery to Queen Margaret at an extent of £400 2s 8d taken 26 May 1451 (Close Roll).
		+ The whole: 6 March 1453 to Jasper Tudor in fee tail male.

Note: A special commission to discover the true yearly value of the lordship of Pembroke and all these lands had been appointed on 17 April 1451 (Pat. Roll).

A garden at Hereford Castle and the King's Orchard there. 100 acres arable, 12 acres meadow at Makeley. 60 acres arable, 6 acres meadow and messuage at Stretton.	Nil. Joint lives. Henry Lockard, of king's cellar, and wife.	†22 June 1451 at £3 6s 8d from Mich. 1450 for 10 years.
Land in King's Capel, Baysham, Brockhampton and How Caple.	Fee simple. Henry Oldcastle Esq., M.P. (son of Sir John).	Alleged to be his father's forfeited lands but his possession upheld in Exchequer Court in 1456 by agreement of king's proctor (L.T.R. Mem. Roll).

SALOP AND MARCHES OF WALES ADJACENT

Chirk and Chirklands.	*Nil. Fee simple. Sale to Cardinal Beaufort. Held by his heir Edmund Beaufort.	Sale upheld by the acts as a genuine one.

	Terms until 1450 (rent paid etc.)	Later terms etc.
Forest of Morfe and hays of Bentley and Shirley (Cannock).	*Nil. Entail to John Hampton, squire of the body etc.	Value nil beyond reprises, by extent.

OTHER LANDS IN MARCHES OF WALES

(no resumption accounts found for N. Wales or Chester)

Castle and manors of Mold and Hawarden in Marches of Wales.	*Nil. Alienated in fee tail male. Sir Thomas Stanley, controller of Household etc. 15 Oct. 1443 (Pat. Roll).	Resumed by act of 29 Hen. VI (Evidence of entry on Pat. Roll, 16 March 1452). †Regranted as before. Sometime before 12 March 1451 (K.R. Mem. Roll). Not exempted from the resumption of 33 Hen. VI.

SOUTH WALES

An agistment in the forest of Glyncothy and 2 water mills there.	Nil. Life. David Lloyd, M.P., king's squire, Queen Margaret's master cook.	Extent £6 13s 4d.
2 water mills at Cardigan called Abertive and in the new town of Carmarthen called Cokmill.	Nil. Life. Geoffrey Williams, page of queen's kitchen, bedel of divers commotes, king's carpenter in S. Wales.	12 April 1452 at £8 from Easter 1452 for 10 years. Edmund Wigmore Esq. To be paid at Carmarthen exchequer.
Demesne lands of Gerardston or Treferedd in Tremain co. Cardigan.	Nil. Life. William Johns, king's servant.	25 Oct. 1451 at £4 15s 0d from Mich. 1452 for 20 years. Thos. Cokes. To be paid at Carmarthen exchequer.

Note: Special auditor of all accounts of chamberlains, receivers and other ministers of king's lands etc. in Cardigan and Carmarthen, Walter Gorfen, appointed 21 June 1451 during pleasure. William Welwik and Thomas Snelle appointed on same terms 11 May 1452, but with no control over the accounts of the chamberlain of South Wales.

KENT

A moiety of Hawodestenement at Canterbury.	As long as in king's hands at 1s. Wm. Billington of Canterbury	28 Feb. 1455 at 1s 1d from Mich. 1454 for 7 years. Thos. Mareschall and Roger Ridley.

	Terms until 1450 (rent paid etc.)	Later terms etc.
		26 Nov. 1455 at 1s 8d from Mich. 1455 for 7 years. Mareschall and Ridley.
		9 May 1456 at 1s 4d from Midsummer 1455 as long as in the king's hands. Thos. Deynold.
Manor, lordship and park of Leeds.	£24 for 20 years. Prior and convent of Leeds.	†17 Nov. 1451 at £24 from 6 Nov. 1449 for 10 years.
		†1 June 1459 at £24 1s 0d from 6 Nov. 1459 for 20 years.
Messuage and holding of *c.* 46 acres at Preston, Ash, Staple and Wingham, 2 messuages and gardens at Ickham and Littlebourne.	£1 6s 8d. Warden and canons of Wingham.	11 Dec. 1451 at £1 13s 4d from Mich. 1451 for 20 years. John Holme.
		17 May 1453 at £2 from May 1453 for 20 years. Wm. Stede.
		6 June 1453 at £2 from Easter 1453 for 20 years. John Holme.
		†10 June 1453 Letters patent to canons of Wingham restoring it to them.
		20 Feb. 1459 at £2 1s 0d from Mich. 1458 for 7 years. George Brown.
Manor of Keston.	£4 13s 4d for 7 years. Thos. Lebysham, clerk.	6 Dec. 1451 at £5 from Mich. 1451 for 10 years. Robt. Chamberlain and Philip Reynold.
		12 Nov. 1458 at £5 0s 8d from Mich. 1458 for 7 years. Nicholas Lathell and John Wybarn.
Manor of Eltham and members.	10 years at £40 which was nearly absorbed by fees and wages. Robt. Dawson, yeoman of the	†10 July 1451 at £40 from Mich. 1450 for 12 years. (Haydock).

	Terms until 1450 (rent paid etc.)	Later terms etc.
	Crown. Wm. Haydock, customer.	†29 June 1452 at £44 1s 0d from Easter 1452 for 12 years. (Haydock). 17 July 1452 at £44 from Easter 1452 for 10 years. Wm. Wetenale and Thos. Goly.
		18 July 1452 to same for same period at £46 1s 0d.
		†7 June 1453 at £46 2s 0d from Easter 1453 for 7 years.
		13 May 1457 at £46 5s 4d from Easter 1457 for 12 years. Thos. Stratton.
		26 Nov. 1460 at £46 6s 8d from Mich. 1460 for 10 years. Thos. Neville, kt.
A house called Corbyhall at Eltham with 42 acres arable.	Life. Nil. Philip Reynold, clerk of household chapel, king's servant.	19 May 1457 at £1 0s 6d from Easter 1457 for 7 years. Thos. Bulkley.
Rents of free tenants at Rochester.	Life. Nil. Sir John Steward, knight of the body, keeper of Eleanor duchess of Gloucester.	Resumed. Value £36. Granted to Alexander Iden as a reward for capture of the rebel Cade. To spend £16 p.a. of it in repairing the castle of Rochester committed to him.
Manor of Huntingfield and messuage in Chelsfield.	*Nil. Fee simple. James Fiennes, lord Say and Sele, chamberlain of Household.	28 June 1451 at £10 from 25 Mar. 1451 for 10 years. Thos. Broune Esq.
		23 Mar. 1452 rent free to value of £12 for life. John Hithe or Hayde.
		7 May 1456 extent from Mich. 1455 for 10 years. James Hithe (now kt.).

	Terms until 1450 (rent paid etc.)	Later terms etc.
		28 Feb. 1458 at £10 from Mich. 1457 for 16 years. Hithe.
5 acres of pasture in Mersham parish.	John Chichele, late seneschal to archbishop of Canterbury.	Extent 5s.
Hospital of White Ditch at Rochester and a house built upon its foundations.	Arnold Knight, falconer.	Extent 1s.
Manors of Penshurst, Bayhall, Ensfield, Haysden and Stepham.	*Nil. Freehold exchange. Humphrey duke of Buckingham. Late Gloucester's lands.	Extent £18. Exempt from Act of 33 Hen. VI, because it was an exchange made with the king for the church of Fordingbridge.
2 messuages and lands in Frindsbury.	3s 4d for 30 years. Andrew Kebyll, M.P., controller of the pipe of the Exchequer, and Henry Belle, jointly.	Extent 3s 4d.
	LINCOLNSHIRE	
2 parts of manor of Ludford (Richmond land).		+ 1 Feb. 1453 from Mich. 1452 to Edmund and Jasper Tudor and heirs for ever.
Manor of Bonby.	Life. Nil. Thos. Cumberworth, J.P., esch.	11 April 1451 £10 for 20 years. John Holme. 10 July 1451 at £10 1s 0d for 30 years. John Holme and son John. + 1 May 1453 to Edmund and Jasper Tudor and heirs for ever.
2 parts of manor of Burwell. Reversion of 3rd part (Richmond land).	*Freehold. Nil. Alienation to Ralph lord Cromwell, chamberlain of Household.	8 Nov. 1456 at £41 13s 4d from Mich. 1456 for 10 years. Richard Welles, kt. 20 Jan. 1458 increased to 12 years.

	Terms until 1450 (rent paid etc.)	Later terms etc.
		23 Nov. 1459 increased to 30 years for good service.
		23 Oct. 1460 at £42 from Mich. 1460 for 12 years. Thos. Neville, kt.
2 parts of manor of Leadenham, with reversion of 3rd part (Richmond land).	*Freehold. Nil. Alienation to Ralph lord Cromwell, chamberlain of Household.	
2 parts of manor of Washingborough with advowson of Fulbeck church. Reversion of 3rd part (Richmond land).	*Freehold. Nil. Alienation to Ralph lord Cromwell, chamberlain of Household.	Leadenham and Washingborough etc. 26 Sept. 1458 at £20 from Mich. 1457 for 16 years. John viscount Beaumont.
2 parts of manors of Frampton and Wykes and soke of Skirbeck and reversion of 3rd part (Richmond land).	*Nil. Alienated to John viscount Beaumont entail. Great Chamberlain and Constable of England.	1 July 1451, 15 Dec. 1451 and 25 May 1452 at £122 from Easter 1450 for $11\frac{1}{2}$ years. Gervase Clifton Esq. John Scott Esq.
		+ 23 Nov. 1453 to Edmund Tudor and heirs male.
2 parts of manor of Boston and sokes of Kirton, Gayton and Mumby and reversion of 3rd part (Richmond land).	*Nil. Alienated to John viscount Beaumont entail.	7 June 1451 Beaumont confirmed as steward for life with fees and wages.
Manor of Holywell in Castle Bytham with manor of Stretton, Rutland.	Life. Nil. Thos. Pulford Esq., sergeant-at-arms in Ireland, yeoman of the Crown.	†25 Mar. 1451 at £10 granted to Mich. 1451 and on 22 July 1451 for 1 year more.
		†20 Oct. 1453 at £10 from Mich. 1452 for 2 years.
		3 July 1454 at £10 3s 4d from Mich. 1454 for 7 years. Hen. Forster and Robert Lawrence.

	Terms until 1450 (rent paid etc.)	Later terms etc.
		23 Nov. 1455 at £11 3s 4d from Mich. 1455 for 7 years. Wm. Zouche and Hen. Chaterton.
		18 Feb. 1456 at £13 6s 8d from Mich. 1454 for 10 years. Edmund s. and h. of Thomas Roos and Hen. Forster.
		8 Nov. 1456 at extent from Mich. 1456 for 10 years. Richard Welles.
		27 Mar. 1460 at £13 10s od from Mich. 1459 for 7 years. Peter Idle, Philip Nele and Everard Digby.
		28 Mar. 1460 at £13 11s od from Mich. 1459 for 10 years. Wm. Boteler.
2 parts castle and lordship of Somerton.	£15 6s 8d for 12 years. John Tailboys sen., esch., sheriff, M.P., and John Tamworth, esch., feodary of Richmond, rec. of duchy of Lancaster in Lincs.	†24 Feb. 1451 at £15 6s 8d from Easter 1451 for 12 years. 22 Jan. 1456 at £16 6s 8d from Christmas 1455 for 12 years. John Beek, kt.
Lordship of Magore in marches of Wales, and Gloucs., a dovecote, 6½ acres arable, 6 pasture, a court, 66s 8d rent (Sometime Montalt land always accounted under Lincs.).	£6 15s od for 24 years. John viscount Beaumont.	†26 Mar. 1451 at £6 15s 4d from Mich. 1450 for 20 years. 6 May 1452 put in charge of a receiver, Thos. Morgan during pleasure. 24 July 1453 to Edmund and Jasper Tudor and heirs.
2 parts of manor of Colby called Northall.	£3 term of years. John Tamworth, Wm. Stanlowe, M.P., king's sergeant, Robt. Bailflete.	†12 Nov. 1452 at £3 for 8 years if so long in king's hands from 25 March 1451. Thos.

	Terms until 1450 (rent paid etc.)	Later terms etc.
		Rothwell Esq., and Wm. Stanlowe.
4 bovates of arable, 3½ of pasture and 2 cottages at Corringham.	10s for 40 years. Richard Waterton Esq., lord of Corringham, sheriff, M.P., several times feoffee for Cromwell.	Extent beyond 10s not known.
A bovate of land at Somerby, 5 acres at Bassingthorpe, 20 acres at Witham.	6s 8d for 7 years. Robert Clerk of Eston.	Extent beyond 6s 8d not known.

Note: 5 August 1451 a special auditor, Thomas Pygge, appointed during pleasure to audit all the accounts of all officers of resumed lands of the lordship and honour of Richmond in Lincs., Norf., Suff., and Cambs., with special mention of Ludford, Lincs. (Pat. Roll).

LONDON

Shelleys Tenement in parish of St. Mary Staining.	*Nil. John Doreward Esq., J.P. To alienate in mortmain.	†3 July 1451 at £1 6s 8d from 6 Nov. 1450 for 2 years.
		8 Nov. 1452 at £1 7s 2d from Mich. 1452 for 40 years. Thos. Vaughan.
		†14 Dec. 1452 at £2 13s 4d from 6 Nov. 1451 for 12 years.
Messuages and lands on Tower Wharf.	3s 4d for 90 years. Stephen Cote, valet of Chamber.	†30 June 1452 at 10s from 6 Nov. 1449 for 45 years.
Tenements in Colemanstreet, pa. of St Stephen and in Old Jewry pa. of St Lawrence.	Wm. Apuldrefeld, of London, gent., Cromwell's deputy at Exchequer.	†10 July 1451 at £7 6s 8d from Easter 1451 for 16 years.
A hall and chambers 2 shops and 3 stables in Pentecost Lane, pa. of St Nicholas.	Nil. John Hampton, J.P., M.P., sheriff, squire of the body. John Aleyn, king's servant. Thos. Mayn, M.P., Hampton's esquire, king's sergeant, beheaded by Cade.	24 Jan. 1455 at £5 from Mich. 1453 for 20 years. Richard Whele.

	Terms until 1450 (rent paid etc.)	Later terms etc.
A tenement in Grubstreet, pa. of St Giles without Cripplegate.	8s 8d. Andrew White, butcher.	†15 Nov. 1451 at 10s from Mich. 1451 for 20 years.
A messuage in Watling Street, pa. of All Saints.	1d. John Penycock, J.P., esch., sheriff, M.P., squire of the body.	18 May 1452 at £2 from 25 March 1451 for 20 years. Ralph Holand.
A garden, a dovecote, 3 cottages and gardens in Houndsditch without Aldgate.	John Barowe, groom of the Chamber.	†24 Nov. 1451 at £1 6s 8d from 25 March 1451 for 20 years.
5 messuages in Old Jewry, pa. of St Lawrence.	Prayers for king and queen. St Olave's Church.	2 July 1451 at £6 13s 4d from 25 Mar. 1451 for 6 years. John Gournay and John Berew.
		†9 July 1456 committed to churchwardens of St Olave's from Mich. 1455 at rate of extent.
Queen Joan's Wardrobe, consisting of 12 tenements, 1 messuage, 1 stable at Aldersgate, pa. of St Anne.	Nil. Life. Thos. Aldenham, of Middx., gent., groom of the Chamber, feodary duchy of Lancaster in home counties.	23 July 1451 at £4 plus increment for 24 years. Henry Percy, lord Poynings.
A wharf and crane in Vintry ward and 2 parts of all property there late of duke of Bedford.	Nil. Life. Derek Pile.	15 Mar. 1456 at £6 13s 4d from Mich. 1455 for 10 years. Nicholas Sharp.
		26 Oct. 1458 cancelled by privy seal writ and given to Eton College.
The Coldharbour, pa. of All Saints Dowgate.	Nil. Henry duke of Exeter.	†Leased to Exeter at rate of extent plus increment.
7 tenements and 4 gardens in Coleman street, pa. of St Stephen.	In free alms. Church of St Stephen.	10 July 1452 at £7 11s 8d from Easter 1452 for 20 years. John Rokle and Thos. Chamber.
2 tenements in St Benet Shorebury. 2 tenements in St Martin's Lane.	Life. 8d. John Ripon, king's yeoman harbinger.	†10 August. 1451 at 10s from 25 Mar. 1451 for life. Proved £100 spent on them and

	Terms until 1450 (rent paid etc.)	Later terms etc.
		reward for 29 years service to king.
The Lamb, a brewhouse in the venel called Distaflane.	John Blakeney, esch., M.P., clerk of signet, usher of Chamber. John Barowe.	†26 May 1450 at £5 4s od from Mich. 1449 for 10 years. Discovered to be in ruins.
		26 Nov. 1451 at £1 3s 4d from Easter 1451 for 24 years. Richard Cokkes.
The Welshman and 2 shops in Fleet Street without Ludgate, pa. of St Martin.	Henry Langton, M.P., yeoman of Household, marshal of Marshalsea. John Croke, of London, gent., customer, attorney in duchy exch., clerk of Exch., king's servant.	†15 Nov. 1451 at £4 19s 8d from Mich. 1449 for 12 years.
A tenement in Smithfield.	Master John Somerset, ? bastard of Somerset, J.P., M.P., keeper of mint, chancellor of Exch., physician to the king.	10 Mar. 1454 at 3s 8d from 25 Mar. 1455 for 80 years. Robert Wilkinson.
The Leaden Porch, a tenement in St Martin's in Orgarlane and Crookedlane.	6d. 40 years, John Merston, treasurer of the Chamber and wife.	8 Nov. 1451 at £2 from 25 Mar. 1451 for 20 years. Clause of exemption for both their lives. Act of 33 Hen. VI. Ruinous and wasted. Proved they had spent 200 marks on it.
A tenement in pa. of St Botolph without Aldersgate.	Nil. Joint lives. Gilbert Parr, squire of the body and wife.	5 June 1451 for lives of Parr and wife to Eton College paying nothing.
A forge and chamber at Baynards Castle, pa. of St Andrew's.	4d. Richard Whityngdon, king's yeoman farrier.	Value not known.
Lands late of Agnes late wife of Wm. atte Mille, jeweller in pa. of St Michael at Corne.	Nil. Joint lives. John Weston, king's servant. Peter Preston, king's servant.	Extent £6 13s 4d.

	Terms until 1450 (rent paid etc.)	Later terms etc.
A certain place in the Tower for keeping the king's lions and leopards.	Nil. Joint lives. Robert Manfield, sheriff, M.P., squire of the body, and Richard Manfield.	For the discharge of his office as keeper.
A piece of Tower wharf.	Nil. Life. John Pury, J.P., M.P., king's avenor.	For the discharge of his office, for handling grain.
	MIDDLESEX	
Manor of Sutton by Chiswick.	*A rose at midsummer. Fee simple. Ralph lord Cromwell.	Resumed by 1456. Farm assigned to Household in 1456.
Manor of Ruislip.	Life. Nil. Master John Somerset.	Extent £140. Given to Eton who already had the reversion.
A place in Westminster palace.	Nil. Joint lives. Thos. Stok, yeoman, of Westminster, bailiff of Savoy manor, duchy of Lancaster, rec. of Queen Margaret, and Robert Stok.	Extent £1 6s 8d.
A message in Holborn.	Up to 24s rent free. Life. John Clayton, page of king's buttery.	Extent £2.
A message rented to John Arderne, Baron of Exch. in Westminster palace.	Nil. Life. Wm. Cleve, clerk of king's works.	Extent £2.
A cottage in the palace of Westminster.	Nil. Life. John Gurnay, yeoman of the kitchen.	Extent £1 6s 8d.
A house at Westminster by the Clock House.	Nil. Life. Wm. Dawtre, Household.	Extent £2 13s 4d.
A message called Garlike in Brookstreet Stepney.	6d for 80 years, Oliver Chorley, of Stepney.	12 Feb. 1452 at 3s 6d from Mich. 1449 for 30 years. Thos. Franceys and wife. 30 Mar. 1453 to Thos. Vaughan in fee tail. 15 Nov. 1456 to Jasper Tudor and Thos. Vaughan in fee tail.

	Terms until 1450 (rent paid etc.)	Later terms etc.
		+ 12 Feb. 1460 Jasper Tudor in tail male.
Manor of Kempton (Cold Kennington).	£18 2s 1d. Joint lives of which £18 0s 5d wages and 20d to Exchequer. John Hampton, John Somerton Esq., customer.	†16 April 1450 at £18 13s 4d from Easter 1450 for 25 years.
A vacant house beneath the king's Treasury with a 'pitcher house' (Palace of Westminster).	John Randolph Esq., Exchequer, keeper of council chamber.	†23 Nov. 1451 at 13s 4d from 25 Mar. 1451 for 20 years.
2 vacant pieces of land at West Smithfield.	1s 8d John Norman, groom of the robes.	3 Nov. 1451 at £4 from Mich. 1451 for 20 20 years. John Hewit Esq.
	NEWCASTLE-ON-TYNE	
Prize of fish brought to port.	John Felton	†29 Jan. 1452 at £1 from Christmas 1451 for 21 years. 17 Oct. 1454 at £1 0s 8d from Mich. 1454 for 21 years. John Broune. 4 Dec. 1458 at £1 6s 8d from Mich. 1458 for 7 years. Robert Botiller. 16 Feb. 1459 at £1 12s 8d from Mich. 1458 for 20 years. John Broune.
	NORFOLK AND SUFFOLK	
Manor of Great Wratting and townships of Wratting, Harewell, Great Thurlow and Withersfield and advowson of Great Wratting.	*Alienated to Richard duke of York and heirs, after death of Humphrey duke of Gloucester (had been Mortimer land).	He probably lost it by the resumption acts for in 1455 the Commons petitioned that it should be used to pay Humphrey's debts. He may have lost it in 1450 or in 1453.

	Terms until 1450 (rent paid etc.)	Later terms etc.
2 parts of manor of Swaffham.	Nil. In lieu of 50 marks wages, for attendance at Council. Wm. de la Pole, marquis of Suffolk.	Easter term 1450 at £32 5s od from 6 Nov. 1449. Hugh Brice of Bishop's Lynn. £45 6s 8d from Easter 1450 for 12 years. Sir Thos. Stanley and Hugh Fenne. £40 from Easter 1451 for 12 years. Hugh Fenne and Thos. Boteright, clerk.
Lands and rents in town of Great Wratting.	Richard duke of York.	25 May 1450 at £4 from 6 Nov. 1449 for 24 years. Hugh Fenne. 2 May 1453 at £5 from Easter 1453. Wm. Lawshull, king's servant, for good service. Grant disallowed and resumed by 33 Hen. VI act. Assigned for payment of duke Humphrey's debts. *Rot. Parl.*, v, 339 (1455). cf. Polstead Hall manor Norfolk, Duke Humphrey's wardrobe at Baynard's Castle.
Manor of Stanhoe.	Lawrence Danyell, gent. (father of Thomas, squire of the body, according to Parkin's *Norfolk*, x, 382–3).	26 June 1453 at £6 14s 4d from Mich. 1453 for 10 years. Wm. White and Thos. Ailward. 16 May 1454 at £6 17s 4d from Easter 1454 for 10 years. John Twyer and Wm. Bosom.
Manor of Westley.	Life. 13s 4d. Stephen Cote.	3 June 1450 at £5 from Mich. 1449 for 7 years. John Blakeney Esq., and Wm. Fastolf.

	Terms until 1450 (rent paid etc.)	Later terms etc.
		†29 Oct. 1451 at £5 from Mich. 1451 for 10 years.
		†20 Feb. 1451 at £5 13s 4d from 25 March 1450 for 12 years.
Lordship of Castle Rising (duchy of Cornwall land).	£20 for 10 years. Ralph lord Cromwell.	4 Mar. 1456 at £20 1s 8d from death of Cromwell for 20 years. Henry Bourchier and Thos. Sharne-bourne.
Manor of Polstead Hall in Burnham.		30 July 1451 at £16 Easter 1451 for 10 years. Robt. Foulman Esq.
		27 Oct. 1453 at £16 6s 8d from Mich. last for 20 years. Edmund Blake Esq.
		18 Dec. 1453 at £16 6s 8d from Mich. 1453 for 20 years. Rob. Foulman. Agreed to pay higher rate being the prior farmer.
		+
		19 Oct. 1454 extent plus increment from Mich. 1454 for 5 years. Jasper Tudor, earl of Pembroke.
		1455 Parl. petition that it be used to pay Duke Humphrey's debts.
		3 Nov. 1460 at £16 8s 4d from Mich. 1460 for 20 years. Wm. Calthorpe Esq.
		8 Dec. 1460 at £16 10s od from Mich. 1460 for 10 years. Robert Foulman.

NORTHAMPTONSHIRE AND RUTLAND

	Terms until 1450 (rent paid etc.)	Later terms etc.
A tenement in Great Houghton.	Nil. Life. John Parke of Great Houghton, gent., clerk of king's counting house, king's sergeant.	Extent £1 4s od.
Hundred of Fawsley.	Term of years. £10. Thos. Bradley Esq., John Greene, yeoman.	21 Feb. 1455 at £10 1s od from Mich. 1454. Thos. Willoughby. 8 May 1456 at £10 1s 8d from Mich. 1456 for 10 years. Thos. Rothwell and John Aleyn.
Manor of Geddington.	Nil. Life. Thomas Danyell, squire of the body.	2 June 1450 at £28 from Mich. 1449 for 10 years. Richard Wydeville, lord Rivers. 12 Nov. 1454 at £29 from Mich. 1454 for 20 years. Philip Nell and Thos. Mulso Esq.
Castle and lordship of Moor End.	*Nil. Alienated in fee tail male, to Sir Robt. Roos, king's carver, M.P. (Henry, his son and heir aged 15 in 1450).	†25 Oct. 1451 at £29 6s 8d from 25 Mar. 1451 for 20 years. To his son and Nicholas Husee. + 1 March 1453 livery to queen for life valued at £30 (Close Roll). 24 July 1453 a grant to Edmund and Jasper Tudor and heirs cancelled.
Castle of Rockingham and seneschalry of forest.	*Nil. Alienated in fee tail male to Sir Robt. Roos.	†8 Feb. 1453 at £33 13s 4d for 20 years. John Roos and John Merbury. Exemption for life, act of 33 Hen. VI for Henry Roos, son and

	Terms until 1450 (rent paid etc.)	Later terms etc.
		heir of Robert, but on all offices etc. held profits not to exceed £10 p.a.
Manor of Little Weldon.	Either: life at 3s 4d to Isabel late wife of John Cheyne (Pat. Roll). Or: Thos. Osbarne, Sergeant-at-arms. Terms unknown (esch. resumption returns).	9 July 1451 at £9 2 6d from 25 Mar. 1451 for 20 years. Thos. Osbarne.
		10 Nov. 1454 at £9 3s 0d from Mich. 1454–Mich. 1455. Rich. Streech.
		12 Nov. 1455 at £9 3s 0d from Mich. 1455 for 30 years. Robert Catesby.
	NORTHUMBERLAND	
Castle and lordship of Bamburgh.	£72 9s 3½d for 20 years. Sir John Heron, esch., Sheriff, M.P., and John Fynkell.	23 July 1451 at £72 9s 3½d from Easter 1449 for 20 years. John Trayn and Robt. Sumpton.
		16 March 1458 at £88 15s 11½d from Easter 1458 for 20 years. Ralph Percy, kt.
		17 Aug. 1459 at £88 from Easter 1459 for 20 years. Wm. Heron and John Heron.
		28 May 1460 at £89 15s 11½d from Easter 1460 for 20 years. W. & J. Heron.
A desolated township Newtown or Wernmouth pa. of Bamburgh.	Life. Wm. Greydon.	† ? at £2 10s 0d from Mich. 1449 for 14 years.
		12 Nov. 1460 at £2 11s 0d from Mich. 1460 for 12 years. Rowland Horsele.
King's Meadows by the Tyne.	Life. Nil. John Felton, sergeant of king's chamber.	†29 Jan. 1452 at £2 from Christmas 1451 for 21 years.

	Terms until 1450 (rent paid etc.)	Later terms etc.
		20 Oct. 1458 at £2 0s 8d from 1 Nov. 1458 for 21 years. Alan Brydde.
		20 Feb. 1459 at £2 1s from Mich. 1458 for 20 years. John Penreth
Fisheries in the Tweed called Hoxstell, Cedman and Stert.	Life. Nil. Thos. Browne, J.P., M.P. Sheriff, under treasurer of Exch., king's esquire, etc.	24 Mar. 1451 at £12 from Mich. 1450 for 10 years. John Ogle and Robert Werk.
		20 Nov. 1451 at £12 from 25 Mar. 1451 for 12 years. Ogle and Werk.
		17 Mar. 1457 at £12 1s 0d from 1 April 1457 for 12 years. Wm. Heron and Robert Crawcestre.
Other fisheries there called Crabwater, Lawe, Aldstell, Abstell, Calet, Tudyngford, Edermouth, Newewater, Northyarawe and Hendewater	Nil. In surveyorship. Sir Robert Roos and Henry, his son.	23 July 1451 at £40 from 25 Mar. 1451 to Henry Percy, lord Poynings.
		Recovered by Henry Roos as result of writ sued out 12 Oct. 1451 (Pleas in Chancery).
		Resumed by Act of Resumption 33 Hen. VI.
Foucherhouses in lordship of Wickham and Gillettes lands in Bishopton and Barmston (Northumberland forfeitures under Hen. IV).	Joint lives. Nil. Roger Thornton, J.P., sheriff. On numerous local commissions. And son Roger.	Charged to sheriff in Foreign Accounts, 1451–2.
		20 Feb. 1455 at £6 10s 6d from Mich. 1454 for 6 years. John Thirkild and Richard Myles.
NOTTINGHAMSHIRE AND DERBYSHIRE		
Bailiffry of Morleston and Litchurch.	Life. £17 2s 0d. Walter Blount Esq., J.P., M.P.	Resumed under Act of 29 Hen. VI. Not farmed out.

	Terms until 1450 (rent paid etc.)	Later terms etc.
		+
		24 July 1453 to Edmund and Jasper Tudor and heirs.
30 acres of arable called Pylefield at west end of Clipstone Park.	4s for 28 years. William Folyambe, feodary of duchy of Lancaster in Lincs.	†17 July 1451 at 14s from 25 March 1451 for 30 years.
		1 Sept. 1453 at 17s 4d for 30 years. Ralph Waldiswyke Esq.
		†5 Jan. 1458 at 17s 4d from Mich. 1457 for 30 years.
200 acres in Sherwood forest called Hardwyk Closes for enclosing and holding in severalty.	*1d. Alienated freehold to Richard Illingworth, J.P., M.P., of Lincoln's Inn, deputy chief steward N. Parts duchy of Lancaster, Chief Baron of Exchequer.	†20 July 1451 at 3s 8d from Mich. 1449 for 40 years. Ralph Illingworth *et al.*
		†10 Oct. 1452 at 3s 8d from Mich. 1449. Illingworth, the Dean of Lincoln and Nicholas Stathum.
		†From Mich. 1445 at 4s for 20 years. Illingworth, with Sir John Fortescue, John Leyntun, Wm. Broune (Ric. Illingworth, gent., the main-pernour).
Manor or lordship of Bolsover.		Resumed under Act of 29 Hen. VI.
		+
		24 July 1453 to Edmund and Jasper Tudor and heirs.
30 acres arable in fields of Norwell. 2 messuages and *c.*200 acres at Bathley and 60 at N. Carlton.	1s as long as in king's hands. John Tysyng, of Cathorp.	28 Oct. 1451 at 13s 8d from Mich. 1451 for 10 years. John Skelton.
		10 May 1456 extent from Easter 1456 for 10 years. George Strangeways.

	Terms until 1450 (rent paid etc.)	Later terms etc.
Castle and lordship of Horston in Horsley.	£12 term of years. John Stathum Esq., of Morley, Derbys., esch., sheriff.	†4 Nov. 1451 at £12 from Mich. 1451 for 20 years.
		+ 4 July 1453 to Edmund and Jasper Tudor and heirs for ever.
Manors of Mansfield, Linby and Clipstone.	£40 12s 0d for 12 years. John Cokfield, esch., sheriff. Wm. Heton Esq., J.P., esch., sheriff (associate of Lord Roos and of Tailboys). Robert Cowsell, clerk, and Wm. Stanlowe, M.P., king's sergeant, etc. (associate of Cromwell who gave them the lease. He had assignment for his wages as member of Council on it.)	+ 24 July 1453 to Edmund and Jasper Tudor and heirs.
OXFORDSHIRE AND BERKSHIRE		
7 Hundreds of Cookham and Bray.	£8. Richard Philip and John Martin now dead.	†20 Nov. 1455 at £8 1s 0d from Mich. 1454 for 21 years. Thos. Combes and Richard Philip.
Manors, lordships of Cookham and Bray, Binfield and Sunninghill.	£101 for 20 years. John Noreys, squire of the body etc., his son Wm. and 2 other Noreys.	†21 July 1451 at £105 from Easter 1448 for 20 years.
		†3 March 1457 at £116 13s 4d from Mich. 1455 for 20 years.
Manor of Benham Lovell.	*Nil. Alienated fee tail. John Noreys.	†30 June 1453 at £11 11s 0d from Mich. 1452 for 20 years. 8s for Hurst and Ashridge.
200 acres of wood at Hurst, and hundred of Ashridge.	6s 8d. Life. John Noreys.	3 Mar. 1457 at £11 13s 0d from Mich. 1455 for 20 years.

	Terms until 1450 (rent paid etc.)	Later terms etc.
2 parts of Manor of Swallowfield with reversion of 3rd.	*Pair of gilt spurs. Alienated fee tail. John Penycock, squire of the body etc.	†22 May 1452 tail male at £13 6s 8d and after reversion at £20.
		†15 Mar. 1456 extent from Mich. 1455 for 10 years.
		†2 Mar. 1457 at £13 6s 8d from Mich. 1456 for 40 years.
Manor of Hampstead Marshall.	*£13 6s 8d. Alienated to Sir Edmund Hungerford in fee tail male, king's carver etc.	†13 July 1451 at £20 from 25 March 1451 for 4 years.
		1 Feb. 1457 at £18 from 25 Mar. 1456 for 20 years. John Hubard.
		12 Mar. 1457 at £21 from Easter 1457 for 40 years. Henry Spencer, yeoman of Crown.
Manor of Woodstock, Hanborough, Wootton and Stonesfield and Wootton Hundred.	Wm. de la Pole, marquis of Suffolk. Life. Nil.	24 May 1453 at £127 16s 6d (Pat. Roll), Ralph lord Sudeley from Mich. 1450.
		1 Mar. 1457 at £127 16s 6d Ralph lord Sudeley from Mich. 1455 (Pat. Roll).
		30 Oct. 1457 at £127 16s 6d from Mich. 1455. John, earl of Shrewsbury and Sudeley in survivorship.
Shillingford ferry.	Wm. Annesley, purveyor for the Household.	
The lodge, herbage and pannage etc. of Beckley Park.	Nil. Life. Sir Edmund Hampden, J.P., M.P., squire of the body, queen's carver, chamberlain to prince of Wales 1456.	Extent £5. Exempted by act of 28 Hen. VI to value of 50s only. From 28 Hen. VI onwards accounted for as part of

	Terms until 1450 (rent paid etc.)	Later terms etc.
		honours of Wallingford and St. Valery, part of the duchy of Cornwall.
The manor of Watlington consisting of site of manor house, 24 acres of meadow, a wood and the king's park.	Nil. Life. Richard Lyllyng, king's sergeant.	Extent £3 5s 4d. From 28 Hen. VI also as part of duchy of Cornwall.
Manor of Nettlebed.	Life to value of 60s. John Wattes, valet of Household, keeper of Eleanor duchess of Gloucester.	Extent £3. From 28 Hen. VI also as part of duchy of Cornwall.
Sandford ferry.	Robert Hyd.	Extent £2.
Forest of Wychwood.	Nil. Life. Ralph Butler, lord Sudeley, steward of Household.	Appointed master and surveyor in lieu of. 11 December 1451.
Manor of Folly John.	Nil. Life. John lord Beauchamp, chamberlain of Household etc.	
Herbage and pannage of Windsor forest.	Nil. Life. Nicholas Walton, king's sergeant, keeper of Windsor Forest, gent.	
Issues of forestry of Batell Bayly in Windsor Forest and of pannage and keeping of Cranborne.	Nil. Life. Thomas Warde, M.P., yeoman of the ewery.	
	SOMERSET AND DORSET	
The King's wood called Brewcombe with lands and pastures there, in forest of Selwood.	*3s reserved rent. Entail on John lord Stourton, treasurer of Household, etc.	No extent possible.
Forest of Filwood. Forest and park of Gillingham with courts of wood court and swainmote, rents called wood-silver, a court called woodshire held at Knolle and a fishery called Stapleton Water.	*Nil. By fealty only. Entail on John St Loo (d. 1448), sheriff, M.P., squire of the body, constable of Bristol.	

	Terms until 1450 (rent paid etc.)	Later terms etc.
Manor of Henstridge and Charlton Camville.	*Nil. Freehold. Sale to Cardinal Beaufort.	
Manor of Canford with Poole.	*Nil. Freehold. Sale to Cardinal Beaufort. Held by Edm. Beaufort, his heir.	Exempted as a genuine sale from the acts.
Manors of West Harptree, Norton, Withycombe, Farrington Gurney, Welton, English Combe, Stratton on the Fosse, Stoke under Hampden, Curry Mallet, Milton Falconbridge and moiety of Shepton Mallet, Somerton (Soms.) and Ryme (Dors.).	*Nil' Alienated to Edmund Beaufort in fee tail male (*Rot. Parl.*, v, 446–7).	16 Dec. 1450 at £246 13s 4d from Easter 1450 for 10 years. Henry duke of Exeter, Sir John Holand, John Chancy, jnr., Thos. Manning, clerk, Peter Powle. First made 20 June 1450. Rate of extent.
		20 Sept. 1451 at £246 13s 4d from 25 Mar. 1451 for 10 years at same to same.
		6 Sept. 1452 to Edmund Beaufort, duke of Somerset, entail.
		Resumed under act of 33 Hen. VI. On 14 Mar. 1456 Wm. Browning took Curry Mallet at £14 14s 10d for 7 years from Mich. 1455. Rate of extent.
		17 Mar. 1456. Sir John Fortescue took Farrington Gurney at extent. £13 6s 8d from Mich. 1455.
		†18 Mar. 1456 Eleanor duchess of Somerset took rest at rate of extent £123 13s 10d from Mich. 1455 for 7 years.
		†8 Nov. 1456 Henry duke of Somerset at extent or as much as

	Terms until 1450 (rent paid etc.)	Later terms etc.
		may be agreed with Treasurer from Mich. 1456 for 10 years. Curry Mallet only. + From Mich. 1456 the whole was granted by the king to Edward prince of Wales and passed under control of his ministers.
A message and 20 acres in Oakford.	£1. 20 years. John Batescombe, of Dorset, gent.	8 July 1451 at £1 1s 0d from Mich. 1450 for 10 years. Wm. Lovell and Wm. Geer.
Manor of Fordington.	Life. Nil. Wm. Stafford Esq., J.P., M.P., sheriff. Slain by Cade while reconnoitring for the king's forces.	21 Nov. 1450 from death of Wm. Stafford at £70 for 5 years to 7 farmers. John Parker the younger and others.
		8 June 1451 at £70 from death of Stafford for 6 years. John Parker the younger and others.
		24 May 1452 at £73 6s 8d from Easter 1452 for 20 years. James earl of Wiltshire.
Manor of Seavington.	Joint lives. £4. Thos. Mayn and wife. M.P., king's servant. Beheaded by Cade. Reversion in tail to Sir John Stourton, treasurer of Household etc.	17 April 1451 at £9 6s 8d from Mich. 1450 for 12 years. Wm. Bulman.
	STAFFORDSHIRE	
The hundred of Seisdon under which name were included the farms of the manors of Clent and Mere, Swinford, Wolverhampton, and Rowley Regis, of land	*Nil. Alienated to John lord Dudley, prominent member of Household in 1450 etc.	Extent £54 4s 1d. Exempted from Act of Resumption of 28 Hen. VI to value of £50. Resumed by Act of 29 Hen. VI. Resumption confirmed by Act of 33 Hen. VI.

	Terms until 1450 (rent paid etc.)	Later terms etc.
in Kinver forest, of a mill and various rents including one in Stafford, besides sheriff's aid, view, etc.		
Hays of Teddesley, Canelegh, Allerwas, Chiselyn, Hopewas and Bentley, i.e. forest of Cannock.	*£1 3s 7d for 20 years. Humphrey Whitegreve, M.P., steward of Newcastle-under-Lyme, duchy of Lancaster. Reversion in fee to Thos. Swinnerton, king's squire, whose family had seneschalry of Cannock in fee.	22 July 1451 at £2 from Mar. 1451 as for 12 years. Rice Griffith and Ralph Wolsey. 27 Feb. 1456 at £2 1s 0d from Christmas 1456 for 12 years. Richard Lockwood Esq.
	SURREY AND SUSSEX	
Manor of Claygate and Henley on the Heath.	Nil. In survivorship. Richard Ludlow, J.P., sergeant of the cellar and his son Richard.	Extent £6 13s 4d
Manor of Worplesdon.	1d. Joint lives. Thos. Montgomery, king's squire (elder brother John, M.P., king's sergeant), nephew of Sudeley and his father.	†12 Sept. 1451 at £18 from 25 Mar. 1451 for 10 years. + 1 June 1453 to Jasper Tudor in tail male.
Manor of Witley.	*Alienated in fee simple. Nil. Wm. lord Say—to his father Lord Say, chamberlain of Household, Treasurer, etc., now dead.	†20 July 1451 at £33 from 25 Mar. 1451 for 10 years. 20 Feb. 1453 at £33 0s 10d from Mich. 1452 for 7 years. John Merston, esq. and wife. + 1 June 1453 to Jasper Tudor in tail male.
Manor of Old Shoreham.	Life. £10. Wm. Dawtre, esch., member of Household.	Still holding date of 33 Act. + 19 Oct. 1454 at extent from Mich. 1454 for 7 years. Edmund earl of Richmond.

	Terms until 1450 (rent paid etc.)	Later terms etc.
Manor of Walton on the Hill, Banstead and lands in Charlwood.	Nil. 3 lives and then frankalmoign. Sir Ralph Rockford, John Merston, keeper of king's jewels etc. and wife, then to Eton College.	†26 Mar. 1456 at extent extent from Mich. 1455 for 7 years. John Merston. †12 Mar. 1457 at £40 (Pat. Roll). John Merston and wife survivorship.
Manors of Sheen, Petersham, Ham and island of Crowet.	Life. £16 14s 7d John Somerset, king's physician etc.	19 Nov. 1451 at £23 4s 4d from Mich. 1451 for 20 years. Wm. Hulyn and Thos. Barton. 12 April 1456 at £23 4s 4d from Mich. 1456 for 20 years to same.
Manor of Kennington.	30 years. £13 6s 8d. Ralph Legh Esq., member of Household.	24 Oct. 1451 at £14 from Mich. 1451 for 10 years. Ralph Harris. 10 May 1452 Legh got confirmation of wages as keeper. †20 May 1452 Legh secured revocation of Harris's grant in Chancery as a result of a writ sued out on 17 Nov. 1451 (Pleas in Chancery). †20 Mar. 1455 at extent from Mich. 1454 for 20 years. Ralph Legh.
Manor of Higham by Winchelsea.	£1 1s 8d. Life. Wm. Dawtre.	Still held date of 33 Act. 10 March 1457 at £1 3s 0d from Mich. 1456 for 7 years. John Haysand Esq. †5 Dec. 1458 at £1 3s 4d from Mich. 1458 for 10 years.

	Terms until 1450 (rent paid etc.)	Later terms etc.
Manor and park of Byfleet and pts in Weybridge, Bisley and Effingham.	£10. Life. John Penycock.	†17 Aug. 1451 at extent from 25 Mar. 1451 for 40 years.
		†5 July 1452 at £15 from Easter 1452 for 20 years.
		†15 Mar. 1456 at extent. From Mich. 1455 for 10 years.
WARWICKSHIRE AND LEICESTERSHIRE		
Manors of Solihull and Sheldon.	£33 6s 8d. Life. Edmund Mountford Esq., sheriff, M.P., king's carver.	†3 July 1452 at £33 6s 8d for 10 years.
		+
		1 July 1453 to Edmund and Jasper Tudor and heirs for ever.
Manor of Atherstone.	Life. Nil. Humphrey Stafford, duke of Buckingham.	6 July 1451 at £33 6s 8d from 25 Mar. 1451 for 10 years. John Heston and Clement Draper.
		6 Sept. 1451 at £33 6s 8d from 25 Mar. 1451 for 10 years. Same and John abbot of Merevale.
		+
		4 April 1453 to Edmund Tudor in fee tail.
		24 July 1453 cancelled.
Manor or pasture of Whatborough.	John lord Dudley.	Extent £6 13s 4d. Lost by Acts of Resumption of 29 and 33 Hen. VI.
Prior's Wood in Leicester Chace.	10d. Wm. Babthorpe (brother of Ralph of Household), esch., lawyer, steward of Leicester honour, duchy of Lancaster, Baron of the Exchequer.	

WILTSHIRE

	Terms until 1450 (rent paid etc.)	Later terms etc.
Manor of Marston Maisey.	Life. £12. John Norreys Esq., sheriff, M.P., J.P., feodary of Leicester honour, duchy of Lancaster, member of Household.	12 July 1451 at £12 for 20 years. Sir Edmund Hungerford and George Houton. 9 Nov. 1456 at £20 1s 8d from Mich. 1456 for 20 years. Hungerford and Houton.
Castle and lordship of Mere.	Life. Nil. Sir Edmund Hungerford.	†12 July 1451 at £100 for 10 years. †8 Nov. 1456 at £100 for 2 years.
Manor of Corsham.	Life. Nil. Sir Edmund Hungerford.	†12 July 1451 at £66 13s 4d for 10 years. †8 Nov. 1456 at £73 6s 8d from Mich. 1456 for 7 years.
Castle of Old Sarum.	*Alienated in fee tail male to Sir John Stourton.	
Castle, manor, park and town of Ludgershall.	*Alienated in fee tail male to Wm. Ludlow, sheriff, M.P., steward of Monmouth, duchy of Lancaster, yeoman of king's cellar.	+ 1456 to Edmund Tudor in tail male.
Herbage of King's Hay of Hippenscombe in Tidcombe, forest of Chute.	50 years at 13s 4d. Sir John Lysle, J.P., M.P., sheriff.	†21 Nov. 1457 at 13s 8d for 40 years, from Mich. 1455.
Manors of Amesbury, Winterbourne Earls and Wilton.	*Nil. Freehold sale to Cardinal Beaufort.	
Manors of Bedwyn and Wexcombe (probably only a feefarm rent).	Nil. Life. Humphrey Stafford, duke of Buckingham.	†12 June 1451 confirmed in possession of £31 10s 0d from it for 14 years as part of fee as constable of Dover.

WORCESTERSHIRE

	Terms until 1450 (rent paid etc.)	Later terms etc.
20 acres arable, 2 acres wood, 1 acre meadow, pa. of Redmarley D'Abitot.	*Rose at midsummer. Alienated to Wm. Gloucester.	1 Dec. 1451 at 18s from Mich. 1451 for 3 years. Sir Hugh Mortimer.

YORKSHIRE

2 parts of manor of Thornton in Lonsdale (Lancs.) (lordship of Kendal).		1 June 1451 at £8 12s 0½d from Easter 1450 for 24 years. Sir Thos. Harrington.
2 parts of manors or lordships of Kneeton and Middleton (lordship of Kendal).	12 years. £4 8s 10d. Christopher Boynton, bailiff, honour of Richmond in Yorks.	23 July 1451 extent and increment from Easter 1451 for 24 years. Henry Percy, lord Poynings.
		†19 Oct. 1451 at £4 8s 10d from Easter 1451 for 20 years.

Note: +6 March 1453 Thornton, Kneeton and Middleton granted to Edmund earl of Richmond with the other lordship of Kendal lands and came under the control of his officers.

2 parts of manor and lordship of Forcett.	40 years. £2. Brian Roucliffe, J.P., Baron of Exchequer.	†24 July 1451 at £2 6s 8d from Mich. 1449 for 40 years.
2 messuages in Kirby Sigston. 8 messuages in Northallerton.	*Alienated to Master John Somerset. 1d 'for defence of the realm'.	23 Oct. 1453 at £1 8s 4d from Mich. 1453 for 20 years. Thos. Crosse and George Scalby.
Manor of Laverton.	Nil. 7 years. Heirs of Ric. Florneys.	27 Jan. 1451 at £3 6s 8d from 6 Nov. 1449 for 10 years. Sir James Strangeways and Robt. Kelsey.
2 parts of castle, manor and lordship of Wressell.	Nil. Life. Ralph lord Cromwell.	12 Mar. 1456 at £5 6s 8d from Easter 1456 for 10 years. Sir Jas. Pickering.
		12 Dec. 1456 at £6 from Mich. 1456 as long as in king's hands. Jas Talbot Esq., John Joskyn Esq., Robert Croppell.

	Terms until 1450 (rent paid etc.)	Later terms etc.
2 parts honour and lordship of Richmond in Yorkshire. Reversion of 3rd part.	*Alienated in fee tail to Ric. earl of Salisbury. £2 7s 11¾d reserved rent and after reversion £21 10s 7¾d.	†14 Feb. 1452 previous grant confirmed to Ric. earl of Salisbury at £9 1s 6¼d. + 1454–5 granted to Edmund Tudor and heirs male of his body with reversion of 3rd part. Mich. 1456–Mich. 1457 charged to sheriff of Yorks. Resumed by Richard Hanford, esch. and Thos. Harrington, sheriff on 24 Sept. 1456. Accounted for at £43 1s 3¾d plus £10 0s 8d for Richmond fees from that date. Given back to Salisbury minus castle and fee farm of town by clause of exemption 33 Hen. VI act.
	YORK CITY	
4 small tenements in Mekillith in suburbs.	Nil. Joint lives. Nic. and Thos. Sharpe. Nic: feodary in Wilts., attorney gen., duchy of Lancaster, auditor for Eton and king's judge. Thos: yeoman of Crown.	11 May 1452 at 4s from Mich. 1451 for 20 years. Brian Roucliff.
Castle Mills.	Nil. Life. John Langton Esq., king's sergeant, foreign apposer (his son Henry, M.P., and yeoman of Household).	†22 Nov. 1451 at extent from 25 Mar. 1451 for 10 years. †14 Feb. 1452 at £9 from 25 Mar. 1451 for 10 years. 30 June 1452 in frankalmoign. Hospital of St Leonard's York, exchange for rights in forest of Galtres which

	Terms until 1450 (rent paid etc.)	Later terms etc.
		if recovered to revert to them as before.
		30 Jan. 1457 at £9 6s 8d from Mich. 1455 for 4 years. Robert Drax.
		†6 Feb. 1459 at £9 10s od from Mich. 1458 for 4 years.
		26 Feb. 1460 at £9 13s 4d from Mich. 1459 for 8 years. Thos. Eldyrton.
DUCHY OF LANCASTER LANDS (NO RESUMPTION ACCOUNTS FOUND)		
Manor of Kilbourne (Yorks.).	*Alienated to Byland Abbey 1446.	Exempted in act of 1451.
Thorley manor (Lincs.).	*Alienated in fee to Ralph lord Cromwell 1443 (R. Somerville, *Duchy of Lancaster*).	Presumably covered by his exemption in acts of 28 and 29 Hen. VI and resumed by act of 33 Hen. VI.
Caldicot and Newton manors (Mon.).	*Alienated in fee tail to John lord Beauchamp (Somerville, *D. of L.*).	+ Both resumed. 30 Mar. 1453 Caldicot granted in fee tail to Jasper Tudor.
Manor of Withyham or Monkcourt (Sussex).	*Alienated to James lord Say.	Extent £20. Resumed. He had granted a reversion to the king's college of Eton in exchange for a gift of the manor of Witley from the king. Eton now received Withyham.
Manor of Southam (Gloucs.).	Life grant rent free to John lord Beauchamp	In hand by 1458 at latest.
Manor of Walton on Thames (Surrey).	Life grant to John Penycock at £15 p.a. but allowed £15 p.a. remittance, therefore rent free in effect.	Still holding it at date of 33 Hen. VI act (Resumption Returns). Extent £23.

APPENDIX 'D'

THE MANAGEMENT OF THE CROWN LANDS 1461–85

LISTS OF OFFICERS

A. RECEIVERS

Appointments of receivers alias surveyors, supervisors or approvers, to administer the king's lands and to augment and collect his land revenues, 1461–85 (excluding appointments under duchy of Lancaster seal).

References are given only where additional information has been obtained from sources other than the *Calendars of Patent Rolls*.

	Date and terms of appointment, if known	Area of control
*Thomas Mauncell[1]	13 Mar. 1461, for life.	Devizes, Marlborough, Corsham (Wilts.), Gillingham (Dors.), Odiham (Hants.).
Geoffrey Kidwelly	8 May 1461, during good behaviour.	The honour of Wallingford, the manor of Berkhamsted, the king's woods of Nettlebed, the warren and park of Watlington, accounting to duchy of Cornwall auditors.
John Lylbourne	28 May 1461 to collect all arrears up to March 1461.	Devizes, Marlborough, Corsham (Wilts.), Gillingham (Dors.), Odiham (Hants.).
Otwell Worsley	24 June 1461 for life.	Chirk and Chirklands and offices of steward and constable.
John Smyth	8 July 1461 for life.	The lordship of Clare and Rayleigh and other possessions of the duchy of York and earldom of March, in Norf., Suff., Essex, Kent, Surrey, Sussex, Cambs., Hunts., Herts.
Vincent Pitelsden	15 July 1461 so long as they remain in the king's hands.	All lands etc., late of James earl of Wiltshire, in Wilts., Dors., Soms., Devon.
Henry Thwaites	3 Aug. 1461, during pleasure. Fees and expenses for rec. and 1 auditor £40 p.a.	All lands within the realm, late of Henry Percy, earl of of Northumberland.

1. Note: * throughout indicates that there are biographies of these men in *History of Parliament 1439–1509, Biographies.*

	Date and terms of appointment, if known	Area of control
*Thomas Blount	3 Aug. 1461 during pleasure. 8 Aug. 1461, during good behaviour.	All lands etc. late of Edmund earl of Richmond within the realm, of Thomas Roos of Hamelake and Richard Tunstall, in Lincs., and city of Lincoln.
*Richard Fowler	9 Sept. 1461, during pleasure (30 Jan. 1462, replaced by John Milewater).	Lands etc., late of John earl of Shrewsbury during the minority of his heir, in Derbys., Salop, Staffs., Chester, Gloucs., Bucks., Wilts., and elsewhere in England.
John Milewater (S.C.6/1305/15)	From Mich. 1461. Fee £60 p.a., incl. expenses.	Various castles, lordships, manors and lands of King Edward IV as of the earldom of March, as of the duchy of Lancaster, as of the Crown, and other lands late of Humphrey duke of Buckingham, in king's hands during the minority of his heir. In Denbigh, Montgomery, Radnor, Heref., Brecon, Mon., Carmarthen, Glam., Pembroke, Salop.
John Milewater	30 Jan. 1462, during pleasure. Fee £10 p.a., incl. expenses.	King's lands in Forest of Dean, Gloucs., Haverfordwest, South Wales. All lands etc., in Gloucs., Heref., Worcs., Salop, Wales and Marches of Wales, late of John duke of Norfolk during minority, Humphrey duke of Buckingham during minority, John earl of Shrewsbury during minority, Henry duke of Somerset by forfeiture, James earl of Wiltshire by forfeiture.
*John Birde (alias Bridde) (Fine Roll)	24 Feb. 1462, during pleasure (enrolment), during good behaviour (Treasurer's Bill).	All the king's lands etc., in Notts., Derbys., Staffs., Yorks., York, Hull, Nottingham.
John Austin	26 Feb. 1462, during pleasure.	All the king's castles, lordships, manors, tenements, feefarms, and mills, in Wilts., Oxon., Berks., Gloucs., Bristol, Worcs., Salop, Heref.

	Date and terms of appointment, if known	Area of control
*John Sturgeon	25 Feb. 1462, during pleasure.	All the king's lands etc., in Beds., Bucks., Herts., Cambs., Hunts.
William Whepdale	26 Feb. 1462, during pleasure. Fee 3s *per diem* incl. expenses.	All the king's lands etc., in Norf., Suff., city of Norwich, Essex.
*Thomas Palmer	26 Feb. 1462, during pleasure. Fees and expenses £26 13s 4d p.a.	All the king's lands etc., in Warws., Leics., Northants., Rutland.
*Thomas Mauncell	26 Feb. 1462, during pleasure.	All the king's lands etc., in Soms., Dors., Devon, Cornwall.
*Thomas Blount	26 Feb. 1462, during pleasure.	All the king's lands etc., in Lincs., and the city of Lincoln.
*Richard Waller	26 Feb. 1462, during pleasure.	All the king's lands etc., in Kent, Surrey, Sussex, Hants., Southampton.
*Thomas Mauncell	10 March 1462, during pleasure.	All lands etc., in the king's hands in Soms. and Dors. by reason of the act of resumption in the last parliament at Westminster.
*Robert Plomer	26 Mar. 1472, during pleasure.	All the king's lands etc., including the farm of the ulnage of cloth, in Cambs., Hunts., Herts., Essex, Suff., Norf.
William Brent	26 Mar. 1472, during pleasure.	All the king's lands etc., in Kent, Surrey, Sussex, Hants.
*Richard Spert	26 Mar. 1472, during pleasure.	All the king's lands etc., in Lincs., Rutland, Northants., Leics., Warws., Bucks., Beds.
Thomas Hunte	26 Mar. 1472, during pleasure.	All the king's lands etc., in Notts., Derbys., Salop, Staffs.
Maurice Kidwelly	26 Mar. 1472, during pleasure.	All the king's lands etc., in Heref., Gloucs., Worcs., Wilts., Berks., Oxon.
Geoffrey Kidwelly	26 Mar. 1472, during pleasure.	All the king's lands etc., in Soms., Dors., Devon, Cornwall.

	Date and terms of appointment, if known	Area of control
Nicholas Leventhorpe	26 Mar. 1472, during pleasure.	All the king's lands etc., in Yorks., Westmorland, Cumb., Northumberland (York and Carlisle added 8 April, and Hull and Newcastle on 15 April).
*Robert Plomer	4 Aug. 1472, during pleasure.	As above, with Beds., Bucks., city of Norwich added. His manors etc. now stated to be specified in a special roll and no sum below 40s p.a. to be collected by him.
William Brent	4 Aug. 1472, during pleasure.	As above, with Southampton town and Canterbury city added, and further details set out as for Robert Plomer.
*Richard Spert	4 Aug. 1472, during pleasure.	As above, less Leics., Warws., Beds., Bucks. City of Lincoln added, and further details set out as for Robert Plomer.
Thomas Hunt and John York	4 Aug. 1472, during pleasure.	As above for Thomas Hunt, with Warws., Leics., city of Coventry, city of Nottingham added, and further details set out as for Robert Plomer.
Maurice Kidwelly	4 Aug. 1472, during pleasure.	As above, plus town of Bristol, with further details as for Robert Plomer.
Geoffrey Kidwelly	4 Aug. 1472, during pleasure.	As above, with further details as for Robert Plomer.
Nicholas Leventhorpe	4 Aug. 1472, during pleasure.	As above, with further details as for Robert Plomer.
*Richard Croft	4 Dec. 1472, during pleasure.	Lordships of Woodstock, Handborough, Wootton and Stonesfield, with hundred of Wootton (George Neville's lands).
*Thomas Stidolff	19 Oct. 1473, as long as in the king's hands.	Lands in Berks., Wilts., Gloucs., of George earl of Shrewsbury, during his minority.
*Richard Croft	19 Oct. 1473, as long as in the king's hands.	Lands in Heref., Salop, of George earl of Shrewsbury, during his minority.

	Date and terms of appointment, if known	Area of control
John Beaufitz 'brevia', Hilary, 14 Ed. IV m.10[2]	10 Feb. to Easter 1474.	Lands late of Alice lady Lovell.
Thomas Bingham	22 April 1474, during pleasure. Fee 10 marks p.a.	Horston in Horsley, Bolsover, Chesterfield, Mansfield, Linby, Edwinstowe, Clipstone, Bulwell, Darlton, Ragnall, Arnold, Retford, Basford, Nottingham, and all the king's other lands in Notts., and Derbys (Clarence lands).
John Swift	2 June 1474.	Lordship of Hallam and Worksop with appts., in Yorks., and Notts., during minority of George earl of Shrewsbury.
Gervais Clifton	28 Feb. 1477, during pleasure. Fee £10 p.a.	As for Thomas Bingham, but further specified, the bailiwick of the honour of Peverel, manors of Whatton, Aslockton, Gedling, Shelford, and Stoke Bardolph.
John Hayes 'brevia', Hilary, 19 Ed. IV, m.5	From Mich. 1477, appointed by word of mouth, and letters missive. By patent, 26 Jan. 1479, as long as in the king's hands. Confirmed Feb. 30 (sic) 1484.	All lands late of George duke of Clarence, in Devon, Cornwall, Soms., Dors., Wilts., Hants.
William Clifford 'brevia' Mich., 19 Ed. IV, m.14d. MS. Harley 433	From Mich. 1477, appointed by word of mouth. By patent, 10 Nov. 1478, for life. Fee 20 Marks p.a. (replaced by Robert Brakenbury 25 Jan. 1484).	Lordship of Milton and Marden, Kent, late of duke of Clarence.
John Luthington 'brevia', Trinity, 20 Ed. IV, m.8. MS. Harley 433	From Mich. 1477. Fee £4 p.a. From Mich. 1478 (replaced by Roger Fitzherbert on 22 Dec. 1481, excl. Bucks.; replaced by John Agard sometime before 22 June 1484). Fee £6 13s 4d p.a.	Cheshunt, Flamstead, Clavering, Northwell. All lands late of duke of Clarence in Warws., Worcs., Staffs., Northants., Bucks.

2. All 'brevia' references are to the King's Remembrancer's Memoranda Rolls.

	Date and terms of appointment, if known	Area of control
*Richard Welby	2 Mar. 1478 for life. Fee £13 16s 8d p.a.	All lands of the lordship of Richmond in Lincs., with the lordship of Somerton (Clarence lands).
*William Huse	3 Mar. 1478 for life (as surveyor only).	All lands late of duke of Clarence in Lincs.
John Walsh	17 June 1478.	Manor and hundred of Barton by Bristol with office of feodary of great court of honour of Gloucester (Clarence lands), during minority.
*Peter Beaupie E.403/848	Before 23 Oct. 1478.	Lands late of duke of Clarence with headquarters at Warwick.
Thomas Tototh	12 Nov. 1478, as long as in the king's hands. For life. Fee 5 marks p.a.	All lands late of duke of Clarence in Rutland, Colly Weston, Easton, Freiston and Boston on the west side of the water, Lincs.
*Robert Wingfield	25 Dec. 1478 for life. Fee 10 marks p.a.	Richmond lands in Norfolk and Suffolk and office of steward.
John Harcourt D.L. 29/638/10373	By Mich. 1479. On 11 Jan. 1485 and with effect from Mich. 1484 replaced by John Cutte (Harcourt was implicated in Buckingham's rebellion).	Tewkesbury and other lands in Gloucs., Heref., Worcs., Oxon., Warws., Wilts., Berks. Spencer and Salisbury (Clarence lands).
*John Sapcote	7 Nov. 1480.	Lands late of Fulk Bourchier in Salop and Staffs., during minority.
John Thomas	25 Jan. 1481 during minority.	Lordship of Gower and members S. Wales.
Thomas Freebody	23 Jan. 1482, for life. Fee 100s p.a.	Hanley, Beaudesert, Solihull, Fulbrook, Sudeley, Moor End, Colly Weston, Newport Pagnell, a third part of Bassingbourn, part of the possessions of Richmond honour in Cambs., viz. in hundred of 'Armyngford' and 'Stowe', 'Papworth', 'Northstowe' and Chesterton, 'Wecherley' and 'Thyplowe' (late Clarence lands).

	Date and terms of appointment, if known	Area of control
*Thomas Sapcote	20 July 1483, during pleasure.	Lands late of Matthew Gurney in Dors., Soms., Wilts., and elsewhere (taken from Clarence by Resumption of 12 Ed. IV, and given to prince of Wales. Exchanged with W. Herbert for Pembroke, 1482).
Richard Huddleston	20 July 1483, during pleasure. Annuity 20 marks out of the issues.	All lands in Cumb., and Lancs., late of Thomas marquis of Dorset.
Henry Argentine MS. Harley 433	1483. Fee £10 p.a.	Rivers lands in Norf., Herts., Northants.
John Penler	Before Jan. 1484.	Lands late of Queen Elizabeth.
William Harle	Before Jan. 1484.	Lands late of Queen Elizabeth.
Thomas Holbech	Before Jan. 1484.	Lands late of Queen Elizabeth
Richard Grenway	Before Jan. 1484.	Not specified.
Thomas Fowler	Before Jan. 1484.	Manor of Bushey.
John Bardfeld	Before Jan. 1484.	Lands late of Queen Elizabeth.
John Issham	Before Jan. 1484.	Lands late of Queen Elizabeth.
Robert Court	Before Jan. 1484.	Lands late of Queen Elizabeth.
John Woderowe	Before Jan. 1484.	Wakefield.
Oliver Sutton	Before Jan. 1484.	Wiltshire lands.
Nicholas Spicer	Before Jan. 1484.	Abergavenny and elsewhere.
Martyn Hawte	Before Jan. 1484.	Lands late of Queen Elizabeth.
David Midilton	Before Jan. 1484.	Denbigh.
Thomas Totothe	Before Jan. 1484.	Honour of Richmond.
Richard Croft	Before Jan. 1484.	Earldom of March.
(all the above 15 receivers, among others already listed were summoned to account in the Chamber on this date: MS. Harley 433, fols 138 v.–139).		
John Cutte MS. Harley 433	24 Feb. 1484.	All lands in the king's hands by forfeiture in Soms., Dors.
Robert Brakenbury	8 Mar. 1484, for life.	Writtle, Havering, Boyton, Hadleigh, Rayleigh, Rochford (Essex), Tonbridge, Hadlow, Penshurst, Milton and Marden

	Date and terms of appointment, if known	Area of control
		(Kent), (some late Clarence, some late Queen Elizabeth).
John Fitzherbert	24 Mar. 1484, during pleasure. Fee £20 p.a.	Various crown farms and feefarms, mostly taken from Queen Elizabeth. Value *c.* £1,000 p.a.
Probably William Harle (mentioned in instrument under the signet as receiver of various crown manors 'in circuitu Johannis Stanford' about 31 Mar. 1485). MS. Harley 433	Before 15 May 1485 (date of Commission under signet to mayors, bailiffs, and other local officers of the lands concerned).	New Windsor, Guildford, Kingston-on-Thames, Amersham, Chesham, Langley Marish, Wyrardisbury, Wendover, Datchet, Swallowfield, Cookham, Bray, Bagshot, Worplesdon, Claygate, Pirbright, Kempton, St Margaret Stratton. Crown lands and feefarms to be administered from Windsor castle (late Clarence, Queen Elizabeth, and others).
Edmund Chadderton (treasurer and receiver of the Chamber)	22 May 1484, during pleasure. Fee 100 marks p.a.	Desning, Shardlowes in Cavenham, 'Cresseneres', 'Talmages', and 'Passelowes', Suffolk; Fobbing, 'Haydon' (?Horndon), Essex; Tysoe, 'Estall', 'Westall', and Sheldon, Warws.; Little Brickhill and Bourton, Bucks., with tenements in Thames Street, London (late of Henry duke of Buckingham).
William Colwyck MS. Harley 433	?1484.	Lands late of the duke of Buckingham in Staffs.
Thomas Overton MS. Harley 433	By 31 Mar. 1485.	Lands of duchy of Norfolk.
Ralph Willoughby	12 May 1485 for life. Fee 10 marks p.a.	Lands of honour of lordship of Richmond in Norf. & Suff., and office of steward.
John Plomer MS. Harley 433	By 24 May 1485.	Lands late of the earl of Essex.
'Irping' MS. Harley 433	By 24 May 1485.	Latimer lands 'in the south parts'.
John Marlburgh S.C.6/3545/88	Receiving issues from Easter 1485.	King's lands in Herts., Essex, Suff., Norf.
John Alfegh alias Alseth S.C.6/3545/88	Receiving issues from Easter 1485.	King's lands in Surrey, Sussex, Kent.

	Date and terms of appointment, if known	Area of control
Thomas Holbache S.C.6/3545/88	Receiving issues from Easter 1485.	King's lands in Cambs., Hunts., Beds., Bucks.
John Dunham S.C.6/3545/88	Receiving issues from Easter 1485.	King's lands in Notts., Derbys.
John Stokker S.C.6/3545/88	Receiving issues from Easter 1485.	King's lands in Middlx.
Richard Welby S.C.6/3545/88	Receiving issues from Easter 1485.	King's lands in Lincs.

B. 'FOREIGN' AUDITORS

Appointments of auditors for the king's lands, 1461–85 (excluding appointments under duchy of Lancaster seal).

References are given only where additional information has been obtained from sources other than the *Calendars of Patent Rolls.*

1. Those for whom no evidence has been found that they audited any accounts other than those of subordinate officers on the lands concerned.

	Date of appointment etc.	Evidence of exchequer control or otherwise.
John Broke, and Thomas Aleyn	9 Sept. and 23 July 1461. Joint auditors of ministers of the duchy of Cornwall, including foreign manors and of the rec. gen. of Wallingford honour, who was subordinate to the rec. gen. of the whole duchy.	William, lord Hastings as rec. gen. accounted at Exchequer until 10 Ed. IV when duchy given to prince of Wales.
William Stork of Selby Yorks. S.C.6/1121/11	From 1461 appointed by exchequer writ, auditor of lands late of earl of Northumberland.	Rec. gen. declared his account at the Exchequer: E.159/240, 'brevia' Mich. 3 Ed. IV m.3d.
Richard Byndewyn	16 Sept. 1462 for life. Various manors in Wilts., Hants., Dors. (Devizes, Marlborough, Corsham, Gillingham, Odiham).	Receiver's accounts at Exchequer, 1–4 Ed. IV on foreign acct. roll E.364, 4 Ed. IV, D.
Robert Hanbury (late auditor to earl of Wilts.)	1 July 1461, appointed by Treasurer's bill, during good behaviour, for all lands in England, late of earl of Wilts., as he had been during the lifetime of the earl.	
Henry Harper (late auditor to	23 April 1478, during pleasure, from Mich. 1477, of lands late	Rec. gen. declared his account at the

	Date of appointment etc.	Evidence of exchequer control or otherwise.
Clarence), Ralph Aylesbury (assoc. with him from 14 Jan. 1481 when Leics. & Soms. omitted & Salop, Bucks & Rutland added)	of duke of Clarence during minority of the heir (Warwick and Spencer lands) in Warws., Staffs., Leics., Northants., Oxon., Wilts., Berks., Soms., Gloucs., Worcs., Heref.	Exchequer: E.159/257, 'brevia' Trinity, 20 Ed. IV m.8. which also shows Harper holding audits at Warwick with fee of 100s p.a.
Robert Coorte (cf. below)	27 April 1478 for life. All lands etc. late of earldom of Devon, earldom of Richmond, late of Sir Guy de Bryan (all late Clarence lands) assigned for expenses of the Household.	
*John Tonke, Tooke or Toke (late auditor to Clarence; also to Margaret lady Hungerford and Botreaux). S.C.6/1119/15	By Mich. 1478 lands late of Clarence in Cornwall, Devon, Soms., Wilts., Hants. (S.C.6/1118/1 acct. of rec. gen. John Hayes) MS. Harley 433 shows Tonke receiving £6 13s 4d p.a. for Salisbury lands & £5 p.a. for Warwick lands.	Rec. gen. declared this account at the Exchequer, e.g. E.159/255 'brevia' Hilary 18 Ed. IV m.8. E.159/256 'brevia' Hilary 19 Ed. IV m.5. E.159/257 'brevia' Hilary 20 Ed. IV m.3d etc.
John Hewyk	11 Oct. 1478 during pleasure. All lands etc., of the honour of Richmond and all lands late of duke of Clarence in Yorks., Lincs., Norf., Suff., Cambs., Hunts., Herts., Essex, Middlesex, London, Kent, Surrey.	
Robert Coorte	24 Nov. 1478 during minority of lands late of Clarence in Devon, Soms., Dors., Hants., Wilts. MS. Harley 433 shows Coorte received £4 p.a. for Spencer lands, £6 13s 4d p.a. for Devonshire lands, 66s 8d p.a. for Wiltshire lands.	Rec. gen. John Hayes declared his account at the Exchequer (refs. as for Tonke).
Robert Coorte	18 Feb. 1480 ministers' accounts on lordship of Cranbourne for life.	
John Clerk	7 Aug. 1480 for life. Lordships of Hanley, Beaudesert, Solihull, Fulbrook, Sudeley, Moor End, Newport Pagnell, Caversham, Cookham.	Recs. gen. (e.g. Thomas Tototh, Thomas Freebody, Roger Fitzherbert) appear to have

	Date of appointment etc.	Evidence of exchequer control or otherwise.
	Fee 100s p.a. 16 Dec. 1481 for life, Ditton and Datchet, Bushey, Moor Park, Hunsdon, Clavering, East & West Worldham, Colly Weston, Rock and Sneed, Wotton under Edge and one third of Bassingbourn with the honour of Richmond in Cambs.	accounted at Exchequer for most of these: foreign acct. roll E. 364, 21 and 22 Ed. IV.

2. Those who may also have audited accounts of receivers general outside the Exchequer.

Henry Elham *Hugh Hulse	27 Nov. 1461, during good behaviour. Chester and Flint in North Wales.	No exchequer accts.
John Harper	1 Jan. 1462, during good behaviour. Buckingham, Norfolk and Shrewsbury lands in Wales, Heref., Salop, Gloucs. King's lands in North and South Wales, Chester, Flint and St Briavels and Forest of Dean, Gloucs.	No exchequer accts. for these lands (except Forest of Dean) during the Yorkist period.
John Harper William Weldon	4 July 1462, during pleasure, and several times renewed by 1465. North and South Wales, Chester and Flint (cf. below Mistelbroke and Lussher entry)	No exchequer accts. during the Yorkist period.
William Weldon Peter Bowman	11 April 1461, during pleasure. South Wales.	No exchequer accts. during the Yorkist period.
Henry Harper *William Clerk	20 Feb. 1467, during pleasure. South Wales.	No exchequer accts. during the Yorkist period.
John Josselyn MS. Harley 433 fol. 14 (v.)	After 4 April 1483. Lands late of Henry Bourchier, earl of Essex in king's hands by reason of minority of the heir.	
William Mistelbroke MS. Harley 433 fol. 322	1483. Rivers lands in Herts., Northants., Norf. Fee £6 13s 4d p.a.	
John Touke *ibid.*	1483 Salisbury, Warwick and Spencer lands.	
Robert Coorte	1483. Spencer lands.	

	Date of appointment etc.	Evidence of exchequer control or otherwise.
ibid.	Devonshire lands. Wiltshire lands.	
Robert Browne MS. Harley 433 fol. 126	After Jan. 1484. Auditor of lands late of marquis of Dorset, who was retained as king's auditor there (formerly auditor there) to hear and finally determine the accts as auditor for this time only at Mich. last past.	
William Croke MS. Harley 433 fol. 126	After Jan. 1484. Auditor of lands late of Marquis of Dorset, and of Thomas Saintleger in Yorks., Cumb., Chester, Derbys., Rutland, Essex, Sussex, Wilts., Warws., Northants., Leics., and Wales. Retained as king's auditor there. Similar authority for Mich. last past.	

3. Those who certainly held a final audit for the accounts of receivers general at various places outside the Exchequer.

John Luthington	4 Dec. 1461. Life. Auditor of honour and earldom of Richmond lands. Held a final audit at Boston. E.159/259, 'brevia', Mich. 22 Ed. IV m.6. L.R.12/28/988 D.L.29/639/10379 (Richard Welby's rec. gen's acct. audited by him for 17–18 Ed. IV).	Prohibition by the king, dated 26 Oct. 1482, against exchequer demand for account from rec. gen. for 1478–8 referring to 1461 appointment.
John Luthington	Appointed by letters of privy seal, auditor of North Wales and Chester at 5s *per diem* as John Browne had. S.C.6/1217/4, 5, 7 S.C.6/1236/9, 11 S.C.6/1305/15, 23	Luthington audited an account of chamberlain of N. Wales, 1464–5. Paid £10. There was no audit at the Exchequer for N. Wales or Chester during the Yorkist period. Audited the accounts of John Milewater, king's rec. gen. in Wales and the Marches, from 1461 onwards, at Hereford.
*John Eltonhead (sometime auditor of Lincoln's Inn	1. 24 July 1461, during pleasure. Auditor of all lands late of the earl	No rec. gen. accounted at Exchequer. For most of period, but

	Date of appointment etc.	Evidence of exchequer control or otherwise.
accounts, of duchy of Cornwall 1454, and of various magnates throughout England)	of Richmond. 2. 14 Feb. 1467. All lands late of William lord Zouch and Seymour during minority. Fee £10 p.a. and 5s *per diem*.	not all, these lands in hands of Edward IV's brothers.
The king's auditors (not named)	28 Dec. 1462. The lands of bishopric of Durham put in hands of treasurer of Household, controller of Household, and Thomas Colt. Money paid to treasurer of Household.	Ordered to render account before the king's auditors in the exchequer of the bishopric of Durham.
John Hewyk	30 Sept. 1471. For life. All lands, formerly of Richard duke of York, in Yorks., Essex, Dors.	No record of any duchy of York lands being accounted for at the Exchequer.
Thomas Aleyn	4 Dec. 1472. By terms of appointment during pleasure to audit the accounts of Richard Croft, rec. gen. of Woodstock, Handborough, Stonesfield, Wootton and members. Held at Woodstock. Fees 100s and 33s 4d.	Prohibition against demand for account at Exchequer dated 14 Nov. 1472. Foreign accounts for these lands first appear at the Exchequer after this date in 6 Hen. VII, for years 4–7 Hen. VII.
Richard Grenewey	14 Sept. 1473, during good behaviour. Held at Sheffield. All lands etc., late of John earl of Shrewsbury during minority.	Prohibition against demand for account at Exchequer dated 2 Feb. 1482. Held final audit at Sheffield.
Richard Grenewey	14 Sept. 1473, during good behaviour. To audit the accounts of Thomas Stiddolf, rec. gen. of Shrewsbury lands in Berks., Wilts., Gloucs. Also of Richard Croft, rec. gen. of Shrewsbury lands in Heref., Salop.	Prohibition against demand for account at Exchequer dated 18 Feb. 1477. Prohibition against demand for account at Exchequer dated 21 Feb. 1477.
Certain persons in the king's Chamber (not named), 'brevia', Mich. 13 Ed. IV m.4	To audit the accounts of John Beaufitz, rec. gen. of lands late of Alice lady Lovell, 10 Feb.–Easter 1474.	To be audited in the king's Chamber before certain persons assigned. Prohibition against demand for account at Exchequer dated 17 Feb. 1475.

	Date of appointment etc.	Evidence of exchequer control or otherwise.
John Durant	13 Jan. 1475. Auditor of the king's lands in Notts. and Derbys. Fee £3 6s 8d.	No record of exchequer accounts of these lands. (listed in *Cal. Pat. Rolls 1467–1477*, p. 482).
Certain persons appointed (not named)	28 Feb. 1477. To audit the accounts of the king's rec. gen. in Notts., and Derbys.	To be audited at Nottingham castle before certain persons appointed. These lands appear in foreign accounts at Exchequer for 1 Hen. VII, but not before (listed in *Cal. Pat. Rolls, 1476–1485*, p. 19).
*Sir Thomas Vaughan, treasurer of king's Chamber. *Sir John Say, under-treasurer of England. *Sir Robert Wingfield, controller of Household. *Henry Boteler, Recorder of Coventry.	14 Feb. 1478 (*ad hoc* appointment). To examine the accounts of lands late of duke of Clarence, which would be produced by John Hewyk and others, and by *Peter Beaupie, clerk of the Greencloth of the Household, and to certify thereon to the king.	
John Clerk John Hewyk	27 Oct. 1480 during minority. All lands etc., late of Clarence in Warws., Worcs., Staffs., Salop, Heref., Oxon., Berks., Wilts., Northants., Gloucs., Rutland.	By authority of privy seal writ dated 2 Nov. 1480 held final audit of rec. gen. John Harcourt outside Exchequer: D.L.29/638/10373, acct. of Harcourt 19–20 Ed. IV.
*Richard Sheldon and John Clerk	7 July 1482 for life. Lands of the duchy of York and earldom of March. Fee 20 marks p.a. In king's hands by demise of Richard duke of York's feoffees.	No record of exchequer acct.
Thomas Aleyn and Robert Coorte 'brevia' Hilary 1 Rich. III	Auditors of the duchy of Cornwall, on the appointment of John Sapcote as rec. gen. of the duchy (21 May 1483,	No foreign account of rec. gen. of duchy of Cornwall exists at the Exchequer between 10

	Date of appointment etc.	Evidence of exchequer control or otherwise.
m.14d	confirmed 18 July 1483), authorized to audit the account of the rec. gen. as well as of subordinate officers, at Lostwithiel (They had probably begun to do this as auditors of the prince of Wales and duke of Cornwall, now become king).	Ed. IV and 4 Hen. VII, when the Barons again secured the right to hear the accounts, and audited the account for 2–3 Hen. VII. Richard III had prohibited their attempt on 25 Feb. 1484.
'Such auditors as shall be assigned'	6 Jan. 1484, to audit the accounts of 20 named receivers in the king's Chamber. MS. Harley 433, fols 138(v.)–139.	
William Mistelbroke and John Hewyk	25 Sept. 1484, during pleasure, to audit accounts of all ministers and officers of Warwick, Spencer and Salisbury lands from Mich. 1483 in Staffs., Derbys., Warws., Salop, Gloucs., Heref., Worcs., Northants., Rutland, Oxon., Berks., Herts., Essex, Middx., London, Kent, Hants., Wilts., Soms., Dors., Devon, Cornwall and Isle of Wight.	There are no accounts for these lands on the enrolled foreign account rolls after 22 Edward IV until 3 Henry VII. An entry in MS. Harley 433 confirms that receivers general accounted before local auditors.
William Mistelbroke and Richard Lussher	25 Sept. 1484, during pleasure, to audit accounts of all ministers and officers of principality of S. Wales in the counties of Carmarthen and Cardigan and castle of Pembroke, lordship of Haverfordwest, of Langharne (co. Carmarthen) and Walwyn's Castle (co Pembroke) in S. Wales, lordship of Abergavenny and counties of Glamorgan and Morgannok, pertaining to the king by right of his consort Queen Anne, lordships of Newport, Hay and Brecknock late of the rebel Henry duke of Buckingham. All with effect from Mich. 1483.	Formerly auditors under authority of prince of Wales's appointments for lands in S. Wales, auditing the chamberlain of S. Wales's accounts as well as other ministers': Mistelbroke since 6 March 17 Ed. IV, Lussher since 5 March 12 Ed. IV (e.g. S.C.6/1225/8, Mich. 20–Mich. 21 Ed. IV) Fees £10 p.a. each. No enrolled Foreign Accts.
John Stanford	8 Aug. 1484 for life, to audit accounts of all ministers and officers of lands late of John	

	Date of appointment etc.	Evidence of exchequer control or otherwise.
	duke of Norfolk and Margaret duchess of Somerset including lordships of Bromfield and Yale. From Mich. 1483. Fee 20 marks p.a. of manors of Wing (Bucks.) and Sileby (Leics.).	
John Stanford	8 Aug. 1484 for life, to audit accounts of all ministers and officers of all lands pertaining to the Crown throughout England [not provided with other auditors]. From Mich. 1483. Fee £10 p.a. of manors of Bradwell (Essex) and Corsham and Rowde (Wilts.). 3s 4d *per diem* expenses.	

INDEX

Abergavenny, 183, 188, 191, 205, 296, 304
Abbots Langley, 256
Agard, John, 166, 201, 294
Ailward, Thomas, 272
Aldbourn, 233
Alderton, 231, 239
Aldenham, Thomas, 268
Aleyn, Thomas, 160, 165, 183, 201, 205, 267–8, 274, 298, 302, 303
Alfegh (Alseth), John, 202, 297
Alien priories, 61, 92, 95, 106, 125, 127, 132, 242, 246, 258; *and see* Exchequer
All Soul's College, Oxford, 106, 126
Alton, 230, 231
Alverthorpe, 242
Ambleside, 252, 253
Amersham, 297
Amesbury, 286
Amounderness, 252
Ancient demesne, 17, 21, 22, 23, 24–6, 28, 29; *and see* Exchequer
Andover, 231
Anglesey, 76, 241
Anne, queen of England, 30
Anne, queen of Richard II, 56, 58, 60, 64, 65, 66, 98
Anne (Neville), queen of Richard III, 188, 191, 304
Annesley, William, 279
Anonimalle Chronicle, 49
Anstey, 243
Apanages, 52–8, 227, 239–40, 241–3
Applethwaite, 252
Appleton, Thomas, 255
Appletrefeld (Apuldrefeld), William, 110, 267
Aquinas, St Thomas, 40
Arderne, John, 270
Ardeyn, Sir Thomas, 64
Argentine, Henry, 296
Arnold, 234, 294
Arnold, Richard, 113, 124
Arundel, earls of, *see* FitzAlan
Arundel, John, 254
Arundel, Thomas, archbishop of Canterbury, Chancellor of England, 80, 245–7
Ash, 262
Ashford, 62
Ashingdon, 257
Ashley, Edward, 221
Ashridge, 278
Aslockton, 294
Atherstone, 102, 285
Audley, Hugh, earl of Gloucester, 59
Audley, James, 57, 58
Audley, lord, *see* Tuchet
Auncell, Sir John, 64
Austin, John, 177, 291
Aylesbury, Ralph, 299
Aylsham, 232, 235, 238, 242

Babraham, 102–3, 129, 135, 249
Babthorpe, Ralph, 285
Babthorpe, William, 285
Bacton, 231, 239
Bagshot, 297
Bailflete, Robert, 266
Baker, John, 258
Bale, Robert, 116
Balliol College, Oxford, 165
Ballson, John, 222
Bamburgh, 275
Bangor, bishop of, *see* Yonge
Banstead, 37, 230, 231, 285
Barmston, 276
Barnstaple, 19, 20, 57
Barnwell, prior and convent of, 231, 232, 236, 239
Barowe, John, 268, 269
Barrow, 243
Barton Buckwell, 62
Barton-in-the-Clay, 249
Barton, Thomas, 112, 257, 284
Basford, 294
Basket, John, 258
Basingstoke, 231
Bassingbourn, 102–3, 129, 135, 240, 295, 300
Batescombe, John, 282
Bath, 19
Bayford, 241
Bayhall, 264
Baysham, 260
Beauchamp, Henry, earl and duke of Warwick, 127, 259
  Anne, sister and heir of, 154, 188
Beauchamp, John, lord, 109, 110, 125, 128, 129, 130, 257, 258, 259, 280, 289
Beauchamp, Thomas, earl of Warwick, 80
Beauchamp, William, lord St Amand, 128
Beauchampton, 248
Beaudesert, 295, 299
Beaufitz, John, 166, 178, 294, 302
Beaufort, Edmund, marquis of Dorset, duke of Somerset, 102, 103, 121, 123, 129, 130, 131, 134, 135, 152, 249, 258, 259, 260, 281
  Eleanor, wife of, 103–4, 259, 281
Beaufort, Henry, duke of Somerset, 103–4, 108, 153, 164, 165, 259, 281, 291
Beaufort, Henry, cardinal, 88, 106, 120–1, 125, 129, 152, 171, 248, 260, 281, 286

Beaufort, John, earl of Kendal, duke of Somerset, 121
Margaret (Beauchamp), wife of, 183, 252, 305
Margaret, countess of Richmond, daughter of, 200, 201, 250, 253
Beaumaris, 241
Beaumont, John, viscount, 108, 110, 127, 128, 265, 266
Beaupie, Peter, 147, 166, 172, 295, 303
Beckley, 279
Bedford, 233, 236, 239
earl and duke of, *see* Lancaster; Tudor
Bedfordshire, 171, 202, 233, 236, 239, 248–9, 292, 293, 298
Bedwyn, 233, 286
Beek, Sir John, 266
Beeston, 76, 240
Beetham, Roger, 251, 253
Beetham, Sir Edward, 251
Beler, Roger, 232, 236, 238
Belle, Henry, 264
Benham Lovell, 278
Berd, Robert, 108
Berew, John, 268
Berewe, John, 257
Berkeley, William, marquis, earl of Nottingham, 206
Berkhamsted, 104–5, 107, 230, 239, 240, 290
Berkshire, 106, 110, 135, 167, 172, 182, 192, 200, 233, 235, 237, 243, 244, 278–80, 291, 292, 293, 295, 299, 302, 303, 304
Bertram, William, 250, 259
Berwick, 206, 207, 209, 212, 213, 216, 217, 218
Berwick (Wilts.), 232
Bewper, 62
Billington, William, 261
Bindewyn (Byndewyn), Richard, 172, 298
Binfield, 278
Bingham, Thomas, 294
Birde (Bridde), John, 291
Bishopton, 276
Bisley, 285
Blackburnshire, 236
Blackstone, Sir William, 40–1, 226
Blacman, John, *Henry the Sixth*, 119–20, 121–2
Blagdon, 57
Blake, Edmund, 273
Blakeney, John, 269, 272–3
Blount, Thomas, 291, 292
Blount, Walter, 276
Blount, Walter, lord Mountjoy, 164
Bloxham, 230, 231
Bocking, 255
Bocking, John, 139
Bockenfield, 232
Bodulgate, Thomas, 254, 255
Bohun, Humphrey, earl of Essex, Hereford and Northampton, 76
Mary, daughter and coheiress of, 53, 75, 76
Bohun, William de, earl of Northampton, 59, 60
Bolsover, 277, 294
Bonby, 264
Bondburstwick, 243
Bonville, Sir William, 254, 255
Borley, 232
Bosley, 235
Bosmere, 237
Bosom, William, 272
Bossiney, 57
Boston, 166, 238, 268, 294, 301
Bosworth, battle of, 195, 198
Boteler, Henry, 166–7, 303
Boteler, William, 266
Boteright, Thomas, 272
Botiller, Robert, 271
Bottlesham, John, bishop of Rochester, 246
Bottlesham, William, bishop of Rochester, 246
Boulton, Richard, 257
Bourchier, Fulk, lord Fitzwarren, 174, 190
Bourchier, Henry, 273
Bourchier, Henry, earl of Essex, 190, 297, 300
Bourchier, Thomas, archbishop of Canterbury, 147
Bourton, 297
Bovey Tracey, 57
Bowden, 230, 239
Bowland, 234, 235, 236
Bowman, Peter, 300
Boynton, Christopher, 287
Boyton, 296
Bracton, Henry de, 26
Bradford, 234
Bradley, Thomas, 274
Bradninch, 63, 241
Bradwell, 135, 256, 305
Braithwaite, 243, 253
Brakenbury, Robert, 182, 200, 294, 296
Bramwith, 242
Brancepeth, 242
Bray, 135, 200, 233, 237, 244, 278, 297
Bray, Sir Reginald, 128, 200, 201, 206, 207, 208
Brecknock, 183, 234, 291, 305
Brecknock, David, 249
Brecknock, John, 249
Brent, William, 160, 292, 293
Brian estates, 189, 193, 194, 299
Brice, Hugh, 272
Brickhill, Little, 297
Brictric, lands of, 19–20
Bridgend, 251
Bridgnorth, 233
Bridport, 233
Brigstock, 63, 64, 68, 135, 232, 235, 238
Bristol, 63, 64, 93, 256, 280, 291, 293
Bristol Barton, 167, 231, 234, 237, 295
Brittany, dukes of, as earls of Richmond, 64, 77, 238, 241, 242, 243
Broad Clyst, 57
Brocas, Sir Bernard, 243

Brockhampton, 260
Brodeton, 233
Broke, John, 160, 298
Bromfield, 58, 305
Bromholm, prior and convent of, 231, 239
Bromsgrove, 233
Broune, John, 271
Broune, Thomas, 263
Broune, William, 277
Browe, Sir Hugh, 80
Brown, George, 262
Brown (Browne), Thomas, 110, 114, 256, 276
Browne, John, 249, 301
Browne, Robert, 256, 301
Browne, Sir George, 193
Browne, Sir Thomas, 158
Browning, William, 103, 281
Bruges, Lewis de, earl of Winchester, 186
Brus, Peter de, 234
Bryan, Sir Guy, 299
Brydde, Alan, 276
Buckingham, dukes of, *see* Stafford
Buckingham's rebellion, 191–4, 295
Buckinghamshire, 167, 171, 182, 202, 233, 237, 239, 240, 243, 244, 248–9, 291, 292, 293, 294, 298, 299, 305
Builth, 76, 234, 241
Buk, William, 252
Bulkley, Thomas, 263
Bulman, William, 282
Bulwell, 294
Burcestre, John, 249
Bures estates, 193
Burgh, 232
Burgh, Hubert de, 45
Burgh, Walter de, 66
Burley, John de, 64
Burley, Sir Simon, 60, 80
Burneby, Eustace de, 233, 235, 238
Burnham, 273
Burstwick-in-Holderness, 58, 71, 234, 243
Burton Pidsea, 243
Burton, Robert, 254
Burwell, 101, 250, 264
Bushey, 200, 296, 300
Bustlesham, 235
Butler, James, earl of Wiltshire, 164, 185, 282, 290, 291, 296, 298, 299, 300–1
  Eleanor (Beaufort), wife of, 189
Butler, Ralph, lord Sudeley, 99, 109, 110, 111, 125, 128, 129, 154, 257, 279, 280, 283
Buxhall, Sir Alan de, 63
Byfleet, 234, 240, 285
Byland, abbey, 289
Byrkyn, John, 257

Cade's rebellion, 118, 123, 124, 130, 141, 263, 267, 282
Caernarvon, 76, 241
Caistor, 206
Calais, 85, 90, 115, 126, 133, 136, 147, 176, 186, 187, 209, 211, 212, 213, 216, 217, 218
Caldicot, 289
Calstock, 57, 106, 204, 253
Calthorpe, William, 273
Cambridge, 232, 236, 239
Cambridgeshire, 76, 102, 103, 134, 135, 164, 172, 192, 202, 231, 232, 236, 237, 239, 242, 249–50, 290, 292, 293, 295, 298, 299
Camelford, 57, 255
Canford, 281
Caniziani, Gerard, 178
Canterbury, 232, 261, 293
  archbishop of, *see* Arundel; Bourchier; Chichele
  prior of Christchurch, 124, 232
Cantref, 76, 241
Carburton, 234, 235
Cardiff, 205
Cardigan, 76, 134, 135, 241, 261, 304
Carisbrooke, honour, 243
Carlisle, 236, 239, 250, 251, 252, 293
  bishop of, *see* Layburne; Lumley
Carlton, 277
Carlton le Moorland, 64
Carlyle, Robert, 250
Carmarthen, 76, 134, 135, 241, 266, 291, 304
Carnwell, 244
Carybullock, 240
Casterton, 252, 253
Castle Bytham, 265–6
Castle Rising, 63, 64, 100, 101, 235, 241, 273
Catesby, Robert, 275
Catesby, William, 161
Catherine of Valois, queen of Henry V, 87, 95, 108, 111
Causton, 232
Cavenham, 297
Caversham, 200, 299
Chadderton, Edmund, 181, 182, 184, 200, 297
Chalfont, 248
Chamber, the king's, 65, 69, 70, 81, 85, 87, 90, 106, 115, 120, 147, 175, 180–1
  receipt and issue books of, 203–4, 210–12, 214–17, 223–5
  land revenues in, 71–2, 148, 166–80, 182–5, 188–91, 202–25, 228–9, 296, 302, 304
Chamber, Thomas, 268
Chamberlain, Robert, 262
Chamberlain, Thomas, 130, 258
Chancy, John, 250, 281
Channel Islands, 71, 77, 259
Charlton Camville, 281
Charlwood, 284
Chaterton, Henry, 266
Chaucer, Thomas, 258
Chelsfield, 263
Chelworth, 233, 235, 238, 243
Chertsey, prior of, 173

Chesham, 297
Cheshunt, 294
Chester, 76, 240
earldom and palatine county, 53, 76, 107, 108, 161, 162, 163, 223, 231, 234, 235, 237, 240, 300–1
Chesterfield, 294
Chesterton, 231, 232, 236, 239, 295
Chesthunt, Walter de, 235
Chetham, 232
Cheton, 235
Cheylesmore, 235, 241
Cheyne, John, 275
Cheyne, Sir John, Speaker of the Commons, 246
Chichele, Henry, archbishop of Canterbury, 106
Chichele, John, 264
Chichester, 209
Chirk and Chirklands, 58, 87, 106, 120, 121, 152, 154, 260, 290
Cholmeley, Richard, 206, 207, 208
Chorley, 100
Chorley, Oliver, 270
Christchurch, 231
Cilgerran, 76, 100, 129, 135, 259–60
Cinque Ports, 129, 133
Cippenham, 233, 239
Clare, 290
Clarence, duke of, *see* Lancaster; Lionel; Plantagenet
Clavering, 294, 300
Claverley, 234
Claydon, 237
Claygate, 283, 297
Clayton, John, 270
Clemens, Thomas, 160
Clent, 282
Clerk, John, 177, 201, 299, 303
Clerk, Robert, 267
Clerk, Thomas, 248
Clerk, William, 300
Cleton, 243
Cleve, William, 270
Cliffe, William, 135
Clifford, William, 167, 174, 179, 294
Clifton, Gervase, 166, 174, 205, 265, 294
Climsland, 240
Clinton, William, earl of Huntingdon, 59
Clipstone, 108, 277, 278, 294
Clitheroe, 234, 235, 257
Clopton, 232, 239
Clun, 58
Cobham, Eleanor, duchess of Gloucester, 98–9, 263, 280
Cobham, Henry de, 232, 236
Cockfield (Cokfield), John, 108, 278
Cokes, Thomas, 261
Cokkes, Richard, 269
Colby, 266
Colchester, 232, 236, 256
Coldbridge, 62
Colly Weston, 295, 300
Colt, Thomas, 108, 147, 163, 164, 302
Colwyck, William, 297
Combe, 258
Combe Martin, 58
Combes, Thomas, 278
Compton, 233, 235, 238, 243
Connisborough, 242
Conway, 76, 241
Coorte (Court), Robert, 183, 201, 205, 209, 296, 299, 303
Cookham, 135, 200, 233, 237, 278, 297, 299
Corbridge, 209
Corby, William de, 63
Corfe, 153
Cornburgh, Avery, 147, 200
Cornwall, 155, 167, 174, 186, 192, 230, 231, 232, 239, 240, 292, 293, 294, 299
earldom and duchy, 53, 54, 55, 56, 57, 58, 63, 64, 66, 67, 76, 92, 94, 95, 96, 100, 102, 104, 116, 134, 140, 149, 152, 160, 162, 173, 183, 187, 188, 190, 197, 200, 205, 219, 240, 253–5, 280, 298, 303–4
earl and duke of, *see* Edmund; Edward; Edward V; Gaveston; Henry V; John; Lancaster
Corringham, 267
Corrodies, the king's, list of, 186
Corsham, 243, 286, 298, 305
Cote, Stephen, 129, 127, 272–3
Cotton, Sir Robert, 97, 99, 104, 144
Cotton, Thomas, 129, 249
Cotton, William, 135
Coucy, Ingram de, earl of Bedford, 65, 244
Council, the king's, 61, 65, 73, 74, 81, 82, 83, 84–5, 86–7, 88, 90, 103, 104, 106, 108, 111, 114, 116, 118–23, 131, 132, 144, 145, 149, 185, 187–8, 199, 201, 206–7, 209, 212, 218, 228, 245, 271, 272
Council in the North, 148
Council in Wales and the West, 148, 181, 196
Courte, Sir Francis de, 80
Courtenay, Piers, bishop of Exeter, 183, 192
Courtenay, Richard, bishop of Norwich, keeper of the king's jewels, 175
Courtenay, Sir Philip, 254
Courtenay, Thomas, earl of Devon, 108, 254
Coventry, 77, 83, 155, 163, 166, 241, 293
Cowick, 234, 237
Cowick Ordinances, 37
Cowsell, Robert, 108, 278
Cranbourne, 280, 299
Crane, John, 125
Cranfield, 249
Cravenhurst, 249
Crawcestre, Robert, 276
Crepping, Robert de, 67
Criccieth, 76, 241
Cricklade, 230, 237, 243
Croft, Sir Richard, 147, 164, 165, 177, 200, 205, 206, 293, 296, 302
Croke, John, 269
Croke, William, 301

Crombewell, John de, 240
Cromwell, Ralph, lord, 43, 89, 90, 91, 93, 94, 99, 100, 101, 106, 108, 109, 110, 114, 115, 121, 125, 128, 136, 149, 217, 218, 219, 220, 222, 223, 264, 265, 267, 270, 273, 278, 287, 289
Crookham, 233
Croppell, Robert, 287
Crosse, Thomas, 249, 289
Crossthwaite, 253
Crowet Island, 284
Crowmer, William, 118
Cumberland, 20, 80, 129, 206, 236, 239, 250–3, 293, 296, 301
Cumberworth, Thomas, 264
Curry Mallet, 102, 103, 104, 281–2
Curtis (Curteys), Peter, 172
Curwen, Sir Thomas, 251
Cutte, John, 183, 201, 295, 296

Dalby, Richard, 108, 249
Dale, William de, 244
Dalehead, 252
Dallinghoo, 231, 239
Damory, Richard, 233
Danby Wiske, 238
Daniel (Danyell), Thomas, 129, 252, 272, 274
Danos, Mundina, king's nurse, 65
Danvers, William, 244
Danyell, Lawrence, 272
Darcy, John, 244
Darlton, 234, 235, 238, 294
Dartford, 136
Dartmoor, 241, 254
Dartmouth, 240
Datchet, 297, 300
Daudele, Nicholas, 233
Daunce, John, 214
Daventre, Simon de, 233
Dawbenny, William, 172
Dawley, 58
Dawnay, John, 183, 201, 206
Dawson, Robert, 108, 262
Dawtre, William, 270, 283, 284
Dawtry, John, 214
Dean Court in Thanet, 62
Denbigh, 291, 296
Denys, Thomas, 129
Derby, 234, 235, 236, 238
  earl of, *see* Henry IV
Derbyshire, 155, 165, 166, 172, 202, 205, 230, 234, 235, 236, 237, 238, 242, 276–8, 291, 292, 293, 294, 298, 301, 304
Desning, 297
De Speculo Regis, 48
Despenser, Hugh, 71, 179
Devizes, 107, 230, 237, 290, 298
Devon, 19, 20, 55, 56, 57, 58, 76, 129, 155, 176, 193, 240, 241, 253–5, 290, 292, 293, 294, 299, 304
Devon, earl of, *see* Courtenay
Devon, earldom of, 185, 194, 198, 299, 301
Deynold, Thomas, 262
Dialogus de Scaccario, 18, 20, 21, 31, 33
Digby, Everard, 266
Ditton, 300
Dolpenmayn, 231, 234, 235
Domaine (Capetian and Valois), 26, 34, 38–40, 226
Domesday Book, 17–20, 26, 30–1, 32, 33–4, 35
Doncaster, 242
Donne, John, 172
Donsthorpe, 242
Dorchester, 233
Doreward, John, 267
Dorking, 179
Dorset, 102, 106, 110, 129, 135, 140, 153, 154, 155, 160, 167, 182, 188, 193, 231, 233, 236, 237, 280–2, 290, 292, 293, 294, 296, 298, 299, 302, 304
  marquis of, *see* Grey
Douglas, James, earl of, 186
Dover, 118, 129, 133, 286
Dower of queens of England, 54–6, 60, 61–2, 81, 87, 95, 108, 136, 137, 139, 227
Draper, Clement, 102, 285
Drax, Robert, 289
Drayton, William de, 65
Droitwich, 231
Dunbar, George, earl of March of Scotland, 80
Dudley, John, lord, 109, 110, 282, 285
Dudley, Edmund, 208, 225
Duket, Robert, 253
Dunham, 80
Dunham, John, 202, 205, 206, 298
Durant, John, 303
Durham, 67, 164, 173, 209, 302
Duvedale, John, 230
Dyffryn Breuan, 259–60
Dynham, John, lord, 200
Dynton, Richard, 248

Eagle (Pevensey), honour, 230, 237
  signet of, 175
Easington, 243
Eastling, 62
Easton, 230, 231, 295
Eastwood, 63, 232, 237, 243
East Worldham, 258, 300
Eden, river, 236, 239, 250, 251
Edith, queen, 19, 20
Edmund of Almaine, earl of Cornwall, 56
Edmund of Langley, earl of Cambridge, duke of York, 58, 60, 80, 137, 199, 238, 242–3
  Isabel, wife of, 243
Edward the Confessor, 19, 26, 34
Edward I, 28, 29, 43, 45, 48, 53, 54, 56, 70, 74, 144, 230, 240, 241
Edward II, 29, 43, 44, 48, 54, 55, 56, 57, 59, 71, 72, 75, 86, 93, 179, 225, 231
Edward III, 43, 48, 49, 52, 53, 54, 55, 56, 57, 58, 59, 60, 61, 62, 64, 65, 70, 71,

72, 73, 74, 75, 79, 80, 84, 86, 87, 93, 95, 111, 175, 199, 225, 227, 235, 242
Edward of Woodstock, the Black Prince, 54, 66, 75, 111, 237, 240–1
Edward of York, duke of York, 80
Edward IV, 117, 119, 120, 143–205 *passim*, 224, 225, 227
Edward V, 169, 181, 191, 198
  as prince of Wales, 148, 154, 166, 179, 181, 296, 298, 304
Edwinstowe, 296
Effingham, 285
Eldyrton, Thomas, 289
Eleanor, daughter of Edward II, 231, 237
Elizabeth, queen of Henry VII, 201, 210, 220
Elizabeth (Wydeville), queen of Edward IV, 153, 155, 164, 182, 183, 188, 191, 201, 296, 297
Elham, 62
Elham, Henry, 300
Ellesmere, 231, 236
Elmrugge, Roger, 68
Elmstone, 62
Elrington, Sir John, 147, 166, 173, 174
Elsternwick, 243
Eltham, 108, 121, 232, 236, 262, 263
Eltonhead, John, 162, 301
Ely, bishop of, *see* Morton; Nigel
Emlyn-Is-Cych, 259–60
Endlewick, 242
Engayne, Walter, 66
Engelfield, 240
English Combe, 102, 281–2
Ensfield, 264
Erpingham, 236, 238, 242
Erringden, 242
Essendon, 241
Essex, 33, 63, 110, 135, 154, 171, 182, 192, 193, 202, 206, 230, 231, 232, 236, 237, 239, 243, 255–7, 290, 292, 293, 297, 299, 301, 302, 304, 305
  earl of, *see* Bohun; Bourchier
Estate management, private, 161–2, 228–9
  of Yorkist kings, 158–61, 162–8, 180–94, 290–305
  of Henry VII, 195–225 *passim*
Eston, 267
Eton College, 125, 131, 132, 257, 268, 269, 270, 284, 289
Everdon, John, 129, 256
Everingham, Henry, 257
Ewell, 248
Exchequer, 24, 31, 32, 35, 37, 46, 57, 59, 60, 77, 81, 92, 96, 106, 109, 128, 130, 131, 138, 141, 148, 149, 157, 162, 164, 165, 169–80, 183, 185, 186, 192, 200, 204–9, 228, 230, 235, 238
  Declarations of the State of the Treasury in, 213–17
  keepers of ancient demesne in, 66
  land leases in, 60–5, 67–9, 97–104, 108, 133–5, 159–60, 169, 187–8, 200, 202–3, 248–89 *passim*
  Ordinances of 1323, 176
  stewards of the demesne in, 66–7
  stop of annuities in, 80, 81, 245
  surveyors of alien priories in, 68
  tellers of, 213–15
Exe, river, 254
Exeter, 19, 240
  bishop of, *see* Courtenay; Fox; Oldham
  dukes of, *see* Holand
Extenta maneria, statute of, 67
Eye, honour, 231, 239

Fakenham, 242
Fakenhamdam, 236, 238
Farrington Gurney, 102, 103, 281–2
Fastolf, Sir John, 139
Fastolf, William, 272–3
Fauconberg, lord, *see* Neville
Fava, Lewis de la, 210
Fawsley, 135, 230, 233, 237, 274
Feckenham, 107, 233, 237
Felde, Richard de la, 257
Felton, John, 271, 275
Fenne, Hugh, 114, 129, 272
Fennelsgrove, 248
Fenwick, Sir Henry, 251
Ferrers, Henry, 164, 174
Fiennes, James, lord Say and Sele, 99, 106, 109, 110, 118, 125, 128, 130, 258, 263, 283, 289
Fiennes, Robert, 258
Fiennes, William, lord Say and Sele, 283
Fillongley, Richard, 68
Financial surveys, 43, 89–96, 99, 113–15, 149, 217–18
Finchingfield, 255
Fishlake, 242
FitzAlan, Richard, earl of Arundel (d. 1376), 87
  Joan, daughter and heiress of, 87
FitzAlan, Richard, earl of Arundel (d. 1397), 58, 80
FitzAlan, William, earl of Arundel, 80, 127
Fitzherbert, John, 182, 183, 206, 297
Fitzherbert, Roger, 167, 294, 295, 299
Fitzwalter, lord, *see* Radcliffe
Fitzwarren, lord, *see* Bourchier
Flamstead, 294
Flatwick, 249
Flint, 76, 240
  palatine county of, 53, 76, 107, 188, 223, 234, 240, 300
Flint, Richard, 103–4
Florence, John of, 238
Florneys, Richard, 287
Fobbing, 297
Fogge, Sir John, 147, 173
Folly, John, 280
Folyambe, William, 277
Forcett, 287
Ford, 233
Ford, John, 248
Fordingbridge, 106, 264
Fordington, 282

Forests, 19, 20, 151
Alice Holt, 257; Ashdown, 242; Barnwood, 233; Cannock, 261, 283; Chute, 286; Clive, 233; Dean, 153, 234, 257, 291, 300; Feckenham, 233, 237; Filwood, 280; Galtres, 288–9; Gillingham, 231, 237, 280; Glyncothy, 261; Havering, 230; High Peak, 234; Inglewood, 250, 251, 252; Kinver, 283; Knaresborough, 234, 237; Macclesfield, 234, 235; Melksham, Chippenham and Pewsham, 107, 230, 237; Morfe, 261; New, 231, 237, 239; Porchester, 258; Rockingham, 135, 233, 235, 274; Salcey, 233; Selwood, 280; Sherwood, 68–9, 277; Waltham, 255, 257; Whauberge, 233; Whittlewood, 233; Windsor, 280; Woolmer, 257, 258; Wychwood, 280
Form of Proceeding on the Judicial Visitation, 21
Forster, Henry, 266
Fortescue, Sir John, 9, 36, 41, 42–3, 103–4 113, 115, 119, 120, 121, 131, 136, 137, 226, 227–8, 277, 281
Foster, John, 153
Fotheringhay, 163, 243
Foucherhouses, 276
Foulman, Robert, 273
Fowey, river, 57, 255
Fowler, Sir Richard, 147, 291, 296
Fox, Richard, bishop of Exeter, Keeper of the Privy Seal, 200; bishop of Winchester, 208
Framland, 232, 236, 238
Frampton, 265
Framsden, 235
Franceys, Thomas, 270
Frank, John, 106
Freebody, Thomas, 167, 184, 185, 191
Freiston, 295
Fremington, 58
Frere, John, 250
Friars Observant, 210
Frodsham, 76
Fulbeck, 101, 265
Fulbrook, 295, 299
Fynkell, John, 275

Gartree, 232, 236
Gate, Geoffrey, 154
Gaveston, Peter, earl of Cornwall, 56, 72, 233
Gayton, 265
Geddington, 129, 135, 233, 235, 238, 274
Gedling, 294
Geer, William, 282
George, Walter, 173
Gerald of Wales, 22
Gillingham, 231, 237, 290, 298
Glamorgan, 183, 188, 191, 205, 291, 304
Glanvill, 17, 21, 26
Glatton, 232, 235, 238, 242
Glendower, Owen, 80
Gloucester, 153, 234
dukes of, *see* Thomas; Lancaster; Plantagenet
Gloucester, William, 287
Gloucestershire, 107, 110, 153, 167, 231, 233, 234, 237, 266, 291, 292, 293, 295, 299, 300, 302, 303, 304
Godmanchester, 250
Goly, Thomas, 263
Gore in Upchurch, 62
Gorfen, Walter, 261
Gosfield, 255
Gower, 184, 295
Grampound, 254
Grantham, 243
Grasmere, 252, 253
Gravesend, 232
Great Houghton, 274
Great Thurlow, 271
Great Wratting, 129, 271, 272
Greene, John, 274
Greenhoe, 242
Green Wax, fines of, 92, 94, 175, 219–20
Greenwich, 179, 192
Grenefield, John, 258
Greneway (Grenway), Richard, 164, 201, 296, 302
Grenewood, Richard, 166
Gretton, 230, 235, 238
Grey, Elizabeth, wife of Sir John, *see* Elizabeth, queen of Edward IV
Grey, Edward, viscount Lisle, 193
Grey, Richard, lord, 181
Grey, Thomas, marquis of Dorset, 182, 184, 192, 193, 296, 301
Greydon, William, 275
Griffith, Harry, 161
Griffith, Rice, 283
Gringley, 234, 237, 242
Grinstead, 242
Guildford, 234, 297
Guînes, 187, 209
Gurnay (Gournay), John, 268, 270
Gurney, Matthew, lands of, 102–4, 107, 129, 134, 135, 140, 154, 155, 160, 182, 188, 296

Habsburgs, loans to, 223, 224
Hadham, William de, 244
Hadleigh, 129, 135, 232, 256, 257, 296
Hadlow, 296
Hailes, abbot and convent of, 231, 234
Hallam, 294
Halley (Hawley), Bartholomew, 126, 256
Ham, 62, 284
Hampden, Sir Edmund, 279
Hampshire, 167, 230, 231, 234, 235, 237, 238, 239, 243, 290, 292, 293, 294, 298, 299, 304
Hampstead Marshall, 244, 279
Hampton, John, 110, 129, 261, 267–8, 271
Hampton, Richard de, 64
Hanbury, Robert, 298

Handborough, 129, 165, 231, 279, 293, 302
Hanford, Richard, 288
Hanley, 295, 299
Harbury, 242
Harclay, Andrew, 253
Harcourt, John, 161, 177, 183, 295, 303
Harle, William, 182, 296, 297
Harlech, 75, 241
Harold, earl, 19, 20, 34
Harper, Henry, 298, 299, 300
Harper, John, 300
Harper, Richard, 201
Harrietsham, 62
Harrington, Sir Thomas, 252, 287
Harrington, Thomas, 288
Harris, Ralph, 284
Harrow, 249
Hartington, Adam, 68
Hartismere, 240
Haselbury Plucknett, 63, 65, 244
Hastings, William, lord, 160, 298
Hatfield, 242
Hatfield, Thomas, 175
Haughley, 231, 239
Haukeston, John, 108
Haute, Sir Richard, 181
Haverfordwest, 76, 100, 107, 183, 234, 236, 241, 291, 304
Havering, 63, 110, 135, 230, 239, 255, 256, 296
Hawarden, 110, 235, 261
Hawte, Martyn, 296
Hay, 183
Haydock, William, 108, 262–3
Haydon, 297
Hayes, John, 167, 168, 174, 177, 179, 182, 201, 206, 207, 294, 299
Haysand, John, 284
Haysden, 264
Headington, 80, 233
Hedon, 243
Helsbury, 57, 240
Helsington, 253
Helston in Kerrier, 57, 240, 254
Helston in Trigg, 57, 240
Henley-on-the-Heath, 283
Henry I, 23, 25, 33, 43
Henry II, 20, 21, 22, 25, 30, 31, 33, 35, 36, 43, 44, 45, 50, 70, 225
Henry III, 43, 45, 47, 52, 53, 54, 70, 227
Henry IV, 52, 56, 57, 58, 73, 75, 77, 81–7, 95, 98, 115, 119, 137, 145, 227, 228
  as duke of Lancaster and Hereford, earl of Derby, Leicester, Lincoln and Northampton, 51, 76, 162
Henry V, 76, 79, 87, 88, 93, 95, 102, 106, 107, 116, 118, 120, 122, 126, 136, 139, 140, 145, 146, 170, 175, 192, 198, 220, 224
  as prince of Wales, etc., 52, 58, 77, 87, 94, 95
Henry VI, 58, 88, 89, 93–126 *passim*, 131–160 *passim*, 169, 172, 192, 196, 197, 198, 200, 217, 220, 228
Henry VII, 68, 75, 119, 127, 142, 148, 149, 150, 156, 167, 177, 182, 184, 191, 195–225, 228, 229
Henry VIII, 210, 211, 221, 224, 225
  as prince of Wales, etc., 220
Henry Griffin ap David ap Thomas, 260
Henstridge, 281
Herbert, Thomas, 172
Herbert, William, earl of Pembroke, later Huntingdon, 154, 188, 190, 296
  Katherine, wife of, 190
Herbert, William, lord, 153
Hereford, 19, 163, 164, 234, 235, 238, 260, 301
  earl and duke of, *see* Bohun; Henry
Herefordshire, 19, 33, 167, 234, 235, 238, 259–60, 291, 292, 293, 295, 299, 300
Hermesthorp, John de, 64
Heron, Sir John, 209–16, 222, 223, 224, 225, 275
Heron, William, 275, 276
Hertford, 255
  honour, 232, 235, 236, 241
Hertfordshire, 33, 107, 135, 171, 200, 202, 206, 230, 232, 234, 235, 239, 240, 241, 243, 255–7, 290, 292, 293, 296–7, 299, 300, 304
Hertingfordbury, 241
Heston, John, 285
Heton, John, 102
Heton, William, 108, 278
Hewik (Hewyk), John, 164, 166, 177, 183, 299, 302, 303, 304
Hewit, John, 271
Higham by Winchelsea, 284
High Peak, honour, 230, 234, 237, 242
Highworth, 230, 237, 243
Hinton, 232
Hipperholme, 242
Hithe, Sir James, 263, 264
Hobson, Thomas, 209
Hody, William, 200
Hoggeston, 248
Holand, Henry, earl of Huntingdon, duke of Exeter, 103, 108, 129, 250, 254, 255, 256, 268, 281
  Anne (Plantagenet), wife of, 183
Holand, John, earl of Huntingdon, duke of Exeter (d. 1400), 57–8
  Elizabeth, wife of, 57–8
Holand, John, earl of Huntingdon, duke of Exeter (d. 1447), 104–5, 106, 253
Holand, Ralph, 268
Holand, Sir John, 281
Holand, Thomas, earl of Kent, duke of Surrey, 57
Holbache (Holbech), Thomas, 202, 296, 298
Holborn, 270
Holdsworthy, 57
Holme, 232, 235, 238, 242
Holme, John, 262, 264
Holmfirth, 242
Holt, 58, 154

Holt, John, 127
Hope, 58, 76, 240
Hopedale, 58
Hormead, 243
Horsele, Rowland, 275
Horsenden, 249
Horsley, 278, 294
Horston, 234
Horwood, 248
Household, the king's, 48, 64, 65, 81, 85, 87, 90, 92, 106, 108, 109, 110, 111, 112, 115–17, 120, 124, 126, 127–8, 129, 134, 135, 137, 138, 140, 141, 145, 147, 148–9, 159, 160, 164, 166, 172–3, 178, 180, 186, 190, 191, 192, 194, 195–6, 197–8, 203, 215–16, 217, 225, 226, 227, 228, 299
Houton, George, 286
Howard, John, duke of Norfolk, 181, 191, 192
Howard, Sir John, 175
Howard, Thomas, earl of Surrey, 190
How Caple, 260
Hubard, John, 279
Huddleston, Richard, 296
Hugan, Thomas, 250
Hull, 216, 238, 291, 293
Hulse, Hugh, 300
Hulyn, William, 284
Humphrey, duke of Gloucester, *see* Lancaster
Hundred Rolls, 35
Hungerford, Margaret, Lady Hungerford and Botreaux, 161, 162, 299
Hungerford, Robert, lord, lands of, 192, 194
Hungerford, Sir Edmund, 105, 110, 128, 254, 279, 286
Hunsdon, 255, 300
Hunt, Roger, 249
Hunt (Hunte), Thomas, 160, 292, 293
Huntingdon, 249
  earl of, *see* Clinton; Herbert; Holand
  honour, 249
Huntingdonshire, 164, 172, 202, 232, 235, 236, 242, 249–50, 290, 292, 293, 298, 299
Huntingfield, 263
Hurst, 278
Huse, William, 167, 295
Husee, Nicholas, 274
Hutton, 253
Hyd, Robert, 280

Ickham, 262
Iden, Alexander, 263
Iden, Thomas, 206
Idle, Peter, 266
Ightenhill, 235
Ilchester, 233
Illingworth, Richard, 277
Ingham, Oliver de, 235
Ipre, Sir John de, 64
Ipswich, 139, 232, 236, 237, 239, 255
Isabella, countess of Bedford, daughter of Edward III, 58, 65, 72, 243–4
Isabella, queen of Edward II, 54, 55, 56, 57, 59, 60, 61, 62, 71, 77, 227, 230–6, 238, 239, 241
Isleworth, 63, 64, 102, 132, 137, 241
Issham, John, 296

Jacquette of Luxemburg, wife of John, duke of Bedford, 99, 101, 127; wife of Richard Wydeville, earl Rivers, 154, 250
James I, 29, 97, 104, 144
Jeny, Richard, 172
Joan of Navarre, queen of Henry IV, 52, 56, 68, 77, 80, 87, 94, 106, 111, 137
John, duke of Bedford, *see* Lancaster
John, king of England, 32, 43, 44, 70, 225
John of Eltham, son of Edward II, earl of Cornwall, 54, 57, 59, 77, 231, 235, 239–40
John of Gaunt, duke of Lancaster, *see* Lancaster
John le Scot, earl of Chester, 53
Johns, William, 260, 261
Joskyn, John, 287
Josselyn, John, 300

Kebyll, Andrew, 264
Kelom, James, 252
Kelsey, Robert, 287
Kemp, John, archbishop of York, 106
Kempton (Cold Kennington), 129, 200, 271, 297
Kendal, 252
  earl of, *see* Beaufort
  lordship, 108, 137, 252, 253, 287
Kendal, John, 175, 184, 200
Kenilworth, 232
Kenninghall, 235
Kennington, 241, 284
Kent, 64, 80, 106, 107, 108, 110, 118, 129, 153, 171, 182, 192, 193, 200, 202, 206, 230, 232, 235, 236, 238, 244, 261–4, 290, 292, 293, 294, 297, 299, 304
Kent, river, 253
Kessingland, 235
Keston, 262
Keyingham, 243
Kidwelly, Geoffrey, 147, 155, 160, 290, 292, 293
Kidwelly, Maurice, 147, 160, 292, 293
Kilbourne, 289
Kilnsea, 243
Kimble, 248
King's Capel, 260
King's Cliffe, 233, 235, 238
King's College, Cambridge, 125, 131, 132
King's Langley, 232, 235, 236
Kingsthorpe, 135, 230, 235, 238
Kingston, 234, 235, 238, 297
Kingston Lacy, 253
Kington, 232
Kirby Sigston,

Kirkby, 253
Kirton, 231, 239, 265
Knaresborough, 234, 237, 241, 242
 honour, 56, 234, 237, 241, 242
Kneeton, 287
Kneton, Geoffrey, 68
Knight, Arnold, 264
Knokyn, John de, 231
Knole, 118
Kyriel, Nicholas de, 232

Lacy, Henry, earl of Lincoln, 55
 Alice, daughter of, 55
 lands of, 55, 232, 233, 234
Lambeth, 241
Lampeter, 76
Lancaster, royal county and honour, 53, 67
 duchy and palatine county, 75, 76, 95, 96, 107, 109, 110, 111, 117, 133, 139, 151, 152, 161, 162, 163, 167, 173, 174, 177, 178, 180, 184, 185, 186, 188, 189, 191, 192, 197, 220, 228, 232, 234, 235, 248–89 *passim* (offices in), 296
Lancaster, Edmund Crouchback, earl of, 53
Lancaster, Edward of, prince of Wales, duke of Cornwall, 103–4, 120, 140, 255, 282
Lancaster, Henry of Grosmont, earl and duke of, 55, 232, 236, 238
 Blanche, daughter and coheiress of, 75, 76, 232
 Maud, daughter and coheiress of, 76
Lancaster, Humphrey of, duke of Gloucester, earl of Pembroke, 77, 80, 88, 95, 98, 101, 111, 112, 121, 122, 256, 258, 259, 264, 271, 272, 273
 Eleanor, wife of, *see* Cobham
Lancaster, John of, duke of Bedford, earl of Richmond and Kendal, 77, 80, 88, 95, 98, 102, 111
 wife of, *see* Jacquette
Lancaster, John of Gaunt, duke of, 49, 53, 58, 75, 76, 130, 232, 238, 241–2
Lancaster, Thomas of, duke of Clarence, 77, 80, 111
 Margaret (Holand), wife of, 95
Lancaster, Thomas of, earl of, 55
Langbarugh, 234
Langdale, 252
Langharne, 304
Langley Marish, 233, 237, 297
Langton, Henry, 269, 288
Langton, John, 288
Langton, Walter, Treasurer of England, 71
Lanteglos, 57
Lathell, Nicholas, 262
Latimer lands, 297
Laughton (Sussex), 230, 234, 237
Laughton (Yorks.), 242
Launceston, honour, 240
Laverton (Som.), 102
Laverton (Yorks.), 287
Lawford, 257
Lawrence, Robert, 265
Lawshull, William, 272
Layburne (Leyburn), Roger, bishop of Carlisle, general surveyor, 208, 209
Lea, 235
Leadenham, 101, 265
Lebysham, Thomas, 262
Lechlade, 231
Leeds (Kent), 63, 64, 232, 235, 262
Leges Edwardi Confessoris, 44
Leges Henrici Primi, 20
Legh, Ralph, 284
Leicester, 114, 124, 125, 126, 129, 131, 132
 earl of, *see* Henry IV
Leicestershire, 33, 161, 165, 172, 193, 228, 229, 230, 232, 236, 237, 238, 239, 285, 292, 293, 294, 299, 301, 305
Leigh, 257
Leighton Buzzard, 259
Lelley-Dyke, 243
L'Estrange, Ebulo, 235
L'Estrange (Lestraunge), lady, 233, 236, 239
Levechilde, John, 256
Leventhorpe, Nicholas, 147, 166, 201, 293
Leybourne, 62
Leybourne, Juliana de, countess of Huntingdon, 60, 62
 lands of, 62, 63, 80
Leyntun, John, 277
Lichfield, William, 209
Linby, 64, 68, 69, 108, 234, 235, 278, 294
Lincoln, 291, 292, 293
 dean of, 277
 earl of, *see* Henry IV; Lacy
Lincolnshire, 59, 64, 76, 101, 110, 162, 166, 167, 200, 202, 206, 230, 231, 236, 237, 243, 264–7, 291, 292, 293, 295, 298
Lionel of Antwerp, duke of Clarence, 242
Liskeard, 240
Liskeret, 254
Litchurch, 276
Littlebourne, 262
Little Humber, 243
Little Weldon, 275
Littleworth, 106
Llanbadarnfawr, 241
Lloyd, David, 261
Lockard, Henry, 260
Lockerley, 239
Lockwood, Richard 283
Lollardy, 246
London, 101, 106, 118, 132, 136, 163, 171, 181, 183, 188, 232, 238, 301, 304
 parishes, churches, places and properties in, 58, 92, 124, 131, 134, 147, 162, 232, 240, 243, 256, 267–70, 297, 299, 301
Long Bennington, 230, 231
Lostwithiel, 57, 76, 183, 240, 255, 304
Loughborough, 237
Loughrigg, 252, 253
Lovell, Daincourt and Gray, Alice, lady, 166, 178, 294, 302

Lovell, Francis, lord, 178, 181, 193
Lovell, Henry, lord Morley, lands of, 206
Lovell, Sir Thomas, 203, 208
Lovell, William, 282
Ludford, 264, 267
Ludgershall, 110, 243, 286
Ludlow, 163
Ludlow, Richard, 283
Ludlow, William, 110, 286
Lumley, Marmaduke, bishop of Carlisle, Treasurer of England, 109
Lussher, Richard, 183, 201, 300, 304
Luthington, John, 162, 163, 166, 167, 176, 177, 189, 201, 205, 294, 301
Luton, 248
Lydford, 19, 20, 57, 241, 254
Lylbourne, John, 290
Lyllyng, Richard, 280
Lyme, 233
Lyndhurst, 231, 237, 239
Lynn, 239, 241, 272
Lynom, Thomas, 184, 201
Lysle, Sir John, 286
Lytton, Robert, 200

Macclesfield, 231, 234, 235
Magore, 266
Magna Carta, 48, 246
Malmesbury, 233, 236, 238
  abbot and convent of, 233
Malore, Sir Angetill, 64
Manfield, Richard, 270
Manfield, Robert, 270
Manning (Mannyn), Thomas, 250, 281
Mansfield, 63, 64, 68, 69, 108, 234, 235, 278, 294
March, earldom of, 75, 152, 161, 162, 163, 164, 166, 169, 180, 184, 188, 189–90, 196, 200, 205, 220, 228, 290, 291, 296, 303
Marden, 107, 110, 167, 200, 206, 233, 235, 238, 256, 294, 296
Maresfield, 242
Mareschall, Thomas, 261–2
Margaret, countess of Kent (widow of Edmund of Woodstock), 77
Margaret (de Clare), wife of Peter Gaveston, 56, 232; wife of Hugh Audley, 59, 241
Margaret of Anjou, queen of Henry VI, 56, 99, 100, 107, 108, 111, 117, 118, 122, 125, 136, 137, 138, 139, 152, 256, 260, 270
Margaret, queen of Edward I, 56, 68
Market Harborough, 230, 239
Marlborough, 107, 230, 231, 237, 290, 298
Marlburgh, John 202, 206, 297
Marsh, Richard, 45
Marston Maisey, 135, 244, 286
Matilda, queen of William I, 19, 20
Martin, John, 278
Martin, Master Richard, auditor, 164
Mauncell, Thomas, 290, 292
Mayn, Thomas, 267–8, 282
Meesden, 243
Menai, commote of, 231, 234, 235
Menwennek, William, 160
Merbury, John, 274
Mere (Staffs.), 282
Mere (Wilts.), 230, 241, 286
Mere, John de, 241
Meredith, Morgan, 257
Meres Court in Rainham, 62
Merevale, abbot of, 285
Merioneth, 76, 241
Mersham, 264
Merston, John, 135, 269, 283, 284
Merston, Richard, 258
Merton, Walter, 231
Metcalf, Thomas, 178
Middleton, *see* Milton
Middlesex, 64, 106, 129, 200, 202, 232, 237, 241, 268, 298, 299, 304
Midilton, David, 296
Mileham, 240
Milewater, John, 163, 164, 176, 177, 291, 301
Mille, William atte, 269, 270–1
Milton, 107, 110, 167, 200, 206, 231, 238, 256, 287, 294, 296
Milton Falconbridge, 102, 281–2
Mistelbrook, William, 183, 201, 205, 300, 304
Mold, 110, 235, 261
Molyneux, Hugh, 209
Monkecourt, 106
Montague, William, earl of Salisbury, 55, 59, 232, 240
Montalt inheritance, 55, 59, 64, 235, 266
de Montfort lands, 53
Montgomery, 76, 234, 241, 291
Montgomery, John, 283
Montgomery, Thomas, 283
Monxton, 258
Moor End, 63, 65, 274, 295, 299
Moor Park, 300
More, Sir Thomas, 191–2
Moresk, 57, 240, 255
Morgan, Thomas, 266
Morgannok, 183, 304
Morley, 278
Morley, lord, *see* Lovell
Morleston, 276
Mortimer, Sir Hugh, 287
Mortimer, Roger, 237
Morton, John, 172
Morton, John, bishop of Ely, 192
Mountford, Edmund, 285
Mowbray, John, duke of Norfolk (d. 1432), 92
Mowbray, John, duke of Norfolk (d. 1461), 130, 291
Mowbray, John, duke of Norfolk (d. 1476), 305
Mowbray, Thomas, duke of Norfolk, 80
Mowbray lands, 183, 184, 190, 192, 194
Mulso, Thomas, 274
Mum and the Sothsegger, 78–9
Mumby, 265

Muscroft, 262
Myles, Richard, 276

Nanfan, John, 254, 259
Nanfan, Richard, 209, 222
Nassington, 243
Nayland, 230, 237
Nele, Philip, 265
Nell, Philip, 274
Neston, 235
Netheravon, 233
Nettlebed, 280, 290
Nevill, Hugh de, 234
Nevill, Ralph de, 236
Neville, George, archbishop of York, Chancellor of England, 147, 155, 165, 293
Neville, Henry, lord Latimer, 206
Neville, John, 154
Neville, Ralph, earl of Westmorland, 77, 80
Neville, Richard, earl of Salisbury, 108, 251, 253, 288
Neville, Richard, earl of Warwick, 108, 120, 130, 147, 155, 251, 259
Neville, Sir Thomas, 263, 265
Neville, William, lord Fauconberg, 249
Nevin, 76
Newcastle in Emlyn, 76, 241
Newcastle on Tyne, 216, 236, 293
Newenge, 242
Newington, 106, 241
Newport (Mon.), 183, 304
Newport (Essex), 243
Newport Pagnell, 295, 299
Newton, 289
Newtown, 243
Nigel, bishop of Ely, 44
Nomina Villarum, 35
Norfolk, 59, 64, 76, 100, 129, 135, 139, 202, 206, 231, 232, 235, 236, 238, 239, 240, 241, 242, 271–3, 290, 292, 293, 295, 296, 297, 299, 300
  duchy of, 187, 192, 194, 297, 300
  duke of, *see* Howard; Mowbray
  Mary, dowager countess of, 244
Norman, John, 271
Norreys (Noreys), John, 110, 112, 278, 286
  William, son of, 278
Northallerton, 287
Northampton, 163, 233
  earl of, *see* Bohun; Henry IV
Northamptonshire, 33, 64, 65, 106, 110, 129, 135, 161, 167, 171, 230, 231, 232, 233, 235, 237, 238, 240, 243, 292, 293, 296, 299, 300, 301, 303, 304
Northlew, 57
Northumberland, 165, 206, 236, 275–6, 293
  earls of, *see* Percy
Northwell, 294
Northwich, 58
Norton (Midsomer Norton), 102, 281–2
Norton (Worcs.), 233
Norwich, 129, 139, 232, 236, 238, 292, 293
  bishop of, *see* Courtenay
Nottingham, 155, 166, 174, 205, 291, 293, 294, 303
Nottinghamshire, 64, 68, 80, 108, 110, 155, 166, 172, 202, 205, 230, 234, 235, 237, 238, 242, 276–8, 291, 292, 293, 294, 298, 299, 300, 301, 302, 303
Norwell, 277
Nutley, 258

Oakford, 282
Odiham, 234, 237, 258, 290, 298
Offices, the king's, lists of, 185–6
Officers, the king's, 248–289 *passim* (1422–1461); 158–194 *passim*, 290–305 (1461–1485); 195–212 *passim* (1485–1509)
Offley, 255
Offord Darcy, 250
Ogle, John, 276
Oklee, Thomas, 63
Oldcastle, Henry, 260
Oldcastle, Sir John, 260
Oldhall, Sir William, Speaker of the Commons, 130
Oldham, Hugh, bishop of Exeter, 201, 206, 207, 208
Old Sarum, 286
Ordinances of 1311, 48, 73
Oriel College, Oxford, 106, 124
Osbarne, Thomas, 275
Ospringe, 230
Ossett, 242
Oswestry, 58
Othoo, John, 256
Overland, 62
Overmarsh, 58
Overton, 231, 234
Overton, Thomas, 297
Owthorne, 243
Oxford, 230, 233, 239, 250
  earls of, *see* de Vere
Oxfordshire, 19, 33, 65, 80, 110, 135, 165, 167, 172, 200, 205, 230, 231, 233, 235, 239, 240, 278–80, 291, 292, 293, 295, 299, 303, 304

Packmanstone, 62
Padbury, 249
Palmer, Thomas, 177, 292
Panfield, 256
Parke, John, 172, 274
Parker, John, 282
Parker, Thomas, 126
Parliament, 43, 55, 60, 69, 74, 77, 78, 84–6, 87, 114, 115–17, 122, 123, 143–4, 146, 147, 183, 184, 192, 193
  clerk of, 157
  composition of, 112 (1439–1459), 136 (1450–1453), 245 (1404)
  resumption of lands, etc., in, 79–84, 245–7 (1399–1404); 113 (1451); 114 (1450); 116 (1449); 124–42, 227–8 (1450–1456); 150–8 (1461–1473); 196–200 (1485–1495)

Speakers of the Commons in, 150, 156, *and see* Cheyne; Oldhall; Say; Sturmy
Parr, Gilbert, 105, 269
Parre, Sir Thomas, 252
Paston, John, 129
Paston, Sir John, 155
Paull, 243
Peke, John, 206
Pelynt, 57, 240, 255
Pembridge, Sir Richard de, 62
Pembroke, 76, 80, 259–60, 304
county and lordship, 76, 80, 95, 99, 107, 129, 134, 135, 137, 153, 154, 182, 183, 188, 220, 259–60, 291, 296, 304
earl of, *see* Herbert; Lancaster; Tudor
Pembroke Hall, Cambridge, 132
Pendlestan, 233
Penkneth, 57, 240, 255
Penler, John, 296
Pennehan, 231, 234, 235
Penreth, John, 276
Penrhos, 236
Penrith, 236, 239
Penryn, 254
Penshurst, 106, 264, 296
Pensions, the king's, list of, 186
Penwortham, 234, 235
Percy, Henry, earl of Northumberland (d. 1408), 76
Percy, Henry, earl of Northumberland (d. 1461), 135, 164, 290, 298
Eleanor, wife of, *see* Poynings
Percy, Henry, earl of Northumberland (d. 1489), 181, 193, 194
Percy, Henry, lord Poynings, 251, 268, 276, 287
Percy, Sir Ralph, 275
Percy, Thomas, earl of Worcester, 76
Perrers, Alice, 65, 80
Petersham, 284
Pevensey, 230, 237, 242
Peverel, honour, 249, 294
Philip, Richard, 278
Philippa, duchess of Ireland, 244
Philippa, queen of Edward III, 56, 60, 62, 63, 77, 233, 237–9, 241, 242
Pickering, Sir James, 287
Pigot, Thomas, 206
Pile, Derek, 268
Pinnockshire, 234
Pipe Rolls, 20, 21, 27, 31, 32, 33, 35, 36, 37, 176, 208
Pirbright, 297
Pitelsden, Vincent, 290
Plantagenet, Anne, countess of Stafford, 76, 192
Plantagenet, Cecily, duchess of York, 162, 186, 189, 197, 220
Plantagenet, Edward, earl of Warwick, 221, 299
Plantagenet, Edward, son of Richard III, 191
Plantagenet, George, duke of Clarence, 147, 153–4, 155–6, 158, 160, 162, 164–5, 166, 167, 177, 178, 179, 182, 183, 185, 189, 193, 205, 294, 295, 296, 297, 299, 302, 303
Plantagenet, Richard, duke of Gloucester (Richard III), 148, 153–4, 155–6, 162, 189, 192, 302
Plantagenet, Richard, duke of York, 99, 103, 108, 111, 122, 129, 130, 131, 134, 135, 136, 138, 139, 145, 147, 152, 157, 188, 255, 256, 258, 271, 272, 302, 303
Plantagenet, Richard, duke of York (son of Edward IV), 184, 191
Plomer, John, 297
Plomer (Plommer), Robert, 160, 177, 292, 293
Plumpton, 251
Pole, Edmund de la, earl of Suffolk, 221
Pole, Michael de la, earl of Suffolk, 60, 65, 69, 80, 105
Pole, Sir William de la, 221
Pole, William de la, duke of Suffolk, 99, 100, 104, 108, 110, 114, 118, 119, 122, 123, 124, 125, 129, 130, 258, 259, 272, 279
Polhampton, 235
Pontefract, 163, 181, 234
honour, 233, 237, 238
Poole, 281
Pope, Thomas, 126
Popham, Christopher, 208
Porchester, 234, 258
Portsmouth, 234, 235, 238
Poutrell, John, 256
Powder, 240
Powle, Peter, 281
Poynings, Eleanor, countess of Northumberland, 193
Poynings, Sir Edward, 193, 211
Poynings, lord, *see* Percy
Preston (Kent), 62, 262
Preston (Yorks.), 243
Preston, Laurence de, 230, 235, 238
Preston, Peter, 269
Princes Risborough, 249
Provisors, statute of, 139
Pulford, Thomas, 265
Purprestures, 21, 230, 231, 237, 239
Purveyance, 48–9, 116, 117, 124, 126, 140, 144, 147, 148, 149, 198, 226
Pury, John, 270
Pwllheli, 76
Pygge, Thomas, 267

Quartayse, John, 64
Queenborough, 63
Quenyve, Reginald, 250

Radcliffe, John, lord Fitzwalter, 221
Radclyff, Sir John, 94
Radford, 234, 235, 238
Radnor, 291
Ragnall, 234, 235, 238, 294
Ramesey, Adam de, 64

Randes, John, 250
Randolph, John, 271
Rastrick, 242
Ratcliffe, Sir Richard, 194
Ravenser, 243
Rauf, Walter, 65
Rayleigh, 232, 237, 243, 290, 296
Reading, abbot and convent of, 231
Redbridge, 231, 237
Redmarley D'Abitot, 287
Rees ap Meredith, 241
Reigate, 58
Restormel, 57, 240, 255
Retford, 234, 235, 294
Reynham, 255
Reynold, Philip, 262, 263
Rhosfeir, 231, 234, 236
Rhyddlan, 76, 240
Richard I, 32, 43
Richard II, 43, 47, 49, 50, 53, 54, 55, 56, 57, 58, 60, 63, 64, 66, 70, 72, 73, 75, 77, 80, 82, 83, 84, 86, 105, 136, 150, 192, 193, 199, 225, 246
Richard III, 148, 149, 153, 160, 162, 167, 177, 180–207 *passim*, 222, 225
Richard, duke of York, *see* Plantagenet
Richmond, 76
  earldom and honour, 76, 77, 95, 100, 102, 107, 109, 134, 137, 153, 155, 162, 164, 165, 166, 167, 177, 197, 205, 220, 238, 241, 242, 264, 265, 266, 267, 287, 288, 295, 296, 297, 299, 300, 301–2
Richmond, countess of, *see* Beaufort
Ridley, Roger, 261–2
Rillaton, 240
Rinell, John de, 258
Ringwood, 231
Ripon, John, 268
Risborough, 233, 239
Rivers, lord, *see* Wydeville
Rochdale, 234, 235
Roche, Sir John, 64
Roches, Peter des, 45
Rochester, 232, 236, 257, 263, 264
  bishop of, *see* Bottlesham, John and William; Russell
Rochford, 63, 232, 237, 257, 296
Rock, 300
Rockford, Sir Ralph, 284
Rockingham, 233, 237, 240, 274
Rokle, John, 268
Roos, Edmund, 266
Roos, Edward, lord, 206
Roos, Henry, 274–5, 276
Roos, John, 274
Roos, Sir Robert, 110, 274–5, 276
Roos, Thomas, 266
Roos, Thomas, lord, 164, 291
Rothwell, Thomas, 266–7, 274
Roucliffe, Brian, 287, 288
Rowde, 230, 237, 304
Rowley, 234
Rowley Regis, 282
Ruislip, 270
Russell, John, bishop of Rochester, Keeper of the Privy Seal, 174
Rutland, 172, 292, 293, 299, 301, 303, 304
Ryme, 281

St Albans, battle of, 103, 138
St Amand, lord, *see* Beauchamp
St Briavels, 135, 234, 300
St Ismael, 236
St Leger, Thomas, 172, 183, 301
  Anne, daughter of, 183
St Loo, John, 110, 280
St Margaret Stratton, 200, 297
Salden, 244, 248
Salisbury, 299
  bishop of, *see* Wydeville
  earl of, *see* Neville; Montague
  earldom of, 188
Saltash, 57, 106, 240, 253
Sandal, 183, 186, 242
Sandeford, Brian, 206
Sandford, 280
Sandwich, 232
Sapcote, John, 173, 182, 183, 295, 296, 303
Savage, Thomas, 200
Say, John, 110, 257
Say, Sir John, Speaker of the Commons, 146, 147, 166, 303
Say and Sele, lord, *see* Fiennes
Scalby, George, 287
Scales, lord, *see* Wydeville
Scammoden, 242
Scargill, Thomas, 255
Scotland, marches of, 90, 115, 126, 215, 217
Scott, John, 265
Scott, Sir John, 147
Scrope, Geoffrey le, 238
Seaford, 242
Seavington, 282
Seend, 233
Segrave, Nicholas de, 232
Seisdon, 282
Selby, 298
Selkley, 230, 237
Sevenhampton, 230, 237, 243
Shaftesbury, 233
Sharnebourne, Thomas, 273
Sharp, Nicholas, 268
Sharpe, Nicholas, 147, 288
Sharpe, Thomas, 288
Shaw, Edmund, 163
Sheen, 206, 234, 235, 284
Sheffield, 164, 302
Sheldon, 285, 297
Sheldon, Richard, 201, 303
Shelford, 294
Shepton Mallet, 102, 281–2
Sheriffs, declared accounts of, 175–6, 2–8
  farms of, 31–2, 33, 35, 92, 94, 171–2, 175–6, 186, 187, 190, 202, 219
  rewards to, 171–2, 216, 217
Shilbottle, 209
Shillingford, 279
Shoreham, 283

Shotwick, 76
Shrawadine, 58
Shrewsbury, 136
  earls of, *see* Talbot
Shropshire, 110, 161, 172, 233, 240, 260–1, 291, 292, 293, 295, 299, 300, 302, 303, 304
Shutlington, 249
Sileby, 305
Simnel, Lambert, 199
Skeckling, 243
Skefling, 243
Skelton, John, 250, 251, 252, 277
Skenard, Henry, 250
Skirbeck, 265
Skipsea, 243
Skipton in Craven, 154
Slaidburn, 234, 235
Slefeld, William, 166
Smithden (Smithdon), 239, 242
Smithfield, 271
Smyth, John, 290
Snaith, 234, 237
Sneed, 300
Snelle, Thomas, 261
Snettisham, 235, 239, 242
Snothill, 206
Soham, 232, 237, 242
Solihull, 285, 295, 299
Somer, John, 114
Somer, Richard, 255
Somerford Keynes, 244
Somerby, 267
Somerset, 19, 20, 57, 102, 107, 110, 129, 135, 140, 153, 154, 155, 160, 167, 182, 188, 193, 233, 236, 280–2, 290, 292, 293, 294, 296, 299, 304
  dukes of, *see* Beaufort
Somerset, John, 269, 270, 284, 287
Somerton in Boothby, 63, 64
Somerton (Lincs.), 100, 101, 200, 266, 295
Somerton (Som.), 281–2
Somerton, John, 271
Southam, 289
Southampton, 136, 230, 231, 236, 237, 238, 239, 292, 293
South Molton, 58
South Teign, 254
Southwark, 37, 234
Southwell, Sir Robert, general surveyor, 201, 208, 209
Sowerby, 236, 239, 242
Speen, 244
Spencer, Henry, 279
Spert, Richard, 160, 177, 292, 293
Spicer, Nicholas, 188, 296
Sproatley, 243
Stafford, countess of, *see* Plantagenet
Stafford, Henry, duke of Buckingham, 163, 181, 182, 183, 184, 190, 201, 297, 300, 304
  Humphrey, brother of, 163
Stafford, Humphrey, 258
Stafford, Humphrey, duke of Buckingham, 99, 102, 106, 108, 111, 127, 132, 264, 285, 286, 291, 300
  Anne (Neville), wife of, 161
Stafford, Humphrey (of Southwick), lord, 160
Stafford, William, 257, 282
Staffordshire, 110, 161, 165, 167, 234, 235, 282–3, 291, 292, 293, 294, 295, 297, 299, 303, 304
Staincliffe, 238, 242
Staindrop, 242
Stainforth, 242
Stamford, 163, 243, 250
Stanford, John, 183, 297, 304, 305
Stanhoe, 272
Stanley, 242
Stanley, John, 126
Stanley, Sir Thomas, 110, 112, 128, 129, 261, 272
Stanley, Sir William, 154, 202, 221
Stanloe, William, 108, 267, 278
Staple, 262
Staple, merchants of the, 136
Stathum, John, 278
Stathum, Nicholas, 277
Staunton, 57
Stede, William, 262
Steeple Aston, 165
Stepham, 264
Stephen, king of England, 33, 43, 71
Stepney, 270
Steward, Sir John, 263
Stidolff, Thomas, 164, 177, 293, 302
Stok, John, 270
Stok, Robert, 270
Stoke Bardolph, 294
Stoke sub Hamdon, 102, 281–2
Stokker, John, 202, 298
Stonesfield, 129, 165, 279, 293, 302
Stork, William, 298
Stourton, John, lord, 109, 110, 128, 138, 280, 282, 286
Stow, 240
Strangeways, George, 277
Strangeways, Sir James, 287
Stratfield Mortimer, 237
Stratton, Thomas, 263
Stratton-on-the-Fosse, 102, 281–2
Stratton (Wilts.), 230, 237
Streech, Richard, 275
Stretton (Heref.), 260
Stretton (Rutland), 265–6
Strickland-Kettle, 253
Sturgeon, John, 292
Sturmy, William, Speaker of the Commons, 246
Sudeley, 154, 295, 299
Sudeley, Ralph, lord, *see* Butler
Suffolk, 59, 76, 129, 139, 192, 193, 202, 206, 231, 232, 235, 236, 237, 239, 240, 242, 271–3, 290, 292, 293, 295, 297, 299
  earl or duke of, *see* de la Pole; Ufford
Sumpton, Robert, 275

Sunninghill, 278
Surrey, 65, 110, 171, 182, 193, 202, 230, 234, 235, 236, 237, 238, 240, 241, 283–5, 290, 292, 293, 297, 299
  earl of, *see* Howard; Warenne
Surveyors, board of, for land revenues, 206–9, 219, 229
Sussex, 110, 171, 193, 202, 230, 234, 237, 242, 283–5, 290, 292, 293, 297, 301
Sutton, 249
Sutton by Chiswick, 106, 270
Sutton Courtenay, 19
Sutton, Oliver, 296
Sutton, water of, 240
Swaffham, 129, 135, 272
Swalclyve, 243
Swallowfield, 243, 279, 297
Swift, John, 164, 177, 294
Swinford, 282
Swinnerton, Thomas, 283
Syon, nuns of, 102

Tackbeare, 58
Tailboys, John, 266
Talbot, George, earl of Shrewsbury, 294
Talbot, James, 287
Talbot, John, earl of Shrewsbury (d. 1453), 127
Talbot, John, earl of Shrewsbury (d. 1460), 279, 291, 300
Talbot, John, earl of Shrewsbury (d. 1473), 291, 302
Talbot, Sir Gilbert, 211
Talman, John, 64
Tamworth, John, 266
Tatemundeslowe, 234
Taxation, benevolences, 70, 217, 228
  customs and subsidies on wool, etc., 30, 60, 61, 70, 83, 91, 92, 93, 116, 117, 134, 136, 146, 149, 187, 216, 228, 251
  danegeld, 23
  incomes from land, etc., 81, 83, 117, 146, 228
  sales, 113, 136
  scutage, 23, 24, 28
  tallage, 21, 22–4, 25, 27, 28, 29, 30, 36, 219, 223
  tenths and fifteenths, etc., on movables, 27–8, 29, 30, 47, 48, 61, 70, 83, 90, 117, 136, 146, 154, 170–1, 176, 187, 203, 214, 215, 217, 228, 235
  tunnage and poundage, 91, 136
Templars, lands of, 71
Temporalities, ecclesiastical, 61, 94, 116, 164, 173, 186, 187, 190, 202, 209, 219, 245–7
Tenby, 76
Terrae datae, 30–2, 35, 46
Tewington, 57, 240, 255
Tewkesbury, 295
Thirkild, John, 276
Thomas, duke of Clarence, *see* Lancaster
Thomas, John, 206, 295
Thomas of Woodstock, duke of Gloucester, 58, 80
Thorley, 289
Thornburgh, William, 253
Thorndon, 231, 239
Thorne, 242
Thornes, 242
Thornton in Lonsdale, 287
Thornton, Roger, 276
Thorp, Thomas, 104
Thorpe, Roger, 249
Thorpe, Thomas, 249
Thundersley, 232, 243
Thwaites, Henry, 290
Thwayte, Thomas, 174
Tickhill, 234, 237, 242
Tintagel, 57, 240, 255
Tiptoft, John, lord, 102, 103
Tockenham, 233, 235, 238, 243
Tonbridge, 296
Tonke (Toke, Tooke, Touke), John, 162, 299, 300
Torpel, 230, 231
Tototh (Totothe), Thomas, 167, 295, 296, 299
Tottington, 234, 235
Tours, truce of, 122
Trayn, John, 275
Treasurers of War, 49, 81
Tremain, 261
Trematon, 57, 106, 240, 253
Tremworth, 244
Trevailly, 57
Trevelyan, John, 108, 254, 255
Trott, Richard, 250
Troutbeck, 252, 253
Tuchet, John, lord Audley, 221
Tudenham, Sir Thomas, 129
Tudor, Arthur, prince of Wales, 196, 220, 224
Tudor, Edmund, earl of Richmond, 58, 111, 113, 137, 139, 152, 153, 197, 250, 253, 264, 265, 266, 274, 277, 278, 283, 285, 286, 287, 288, 291
Tudor, Jasper, earl of Pembroke, duke of Bedford, 58, 111, 113, 137, 139, 152, 201, 220, 235, 260, 264, 266, 270, 271, 273, 274, 277, 278, 283, 285, 289
Tunstall, John, 108, 253
Tunstall, Sir Richard, 253, 291
Tutbury, honour, 155, 184, 187
Tweed, river, 276
Twyer, John, 272
Tybesta, 240
Tyle, Ralph, 63
Tyne, river, 275
Tyrell, Sir James, 221
Tysoe, 297
Tysyng, John, 277
Tytherley, 239
Tywarnhaile, 240

Ufford, Robert, earl of Suffolk, 59, 60
Upavon, 233

Upperby, 252
Upton, 230, 231

Vacche, Sir Philip de la, 68
Valence, Mary, widow of Aymer de, earl of Pembroke, 236
Vanne, 244
Vasterne, 233, 236, 238
Vaughan, Sir Thomas, 147, 148, 157, 166, 172, 175, 178, 181, 267, 270, 303
Vauxhall, 241
Veer, Aubrey de, 63
Vere, John de, earl of Oxford (d. 1462), 108, 256
Vere, John de, earl of Oxford (d. 1513), 192, 194

Wadley, 106
Wadling, 62
Wakefield, 242, 296
Waldgrave, Sir Richard, 65
Waldiswyke, Ralph, 277
Wales, marches of, 100, 110, 163, 181, 186, 187, 259–61, 266, 291, 301
principality of, 53, 54, 58, 76, 92, 94, 95, 107, 135, 140, 152, 162, 163, 181, 183, 186, 187, 188, 190, 197, 220, 223, 231, 234, 235, 236, 241, 261, 291, 295, 300, 301, 304
statute of, 53
Waller, Richard, 294
Wallingford, 230, 239, 240
honour, 230, 239, 240, 280, 290, 298
Walsh, John, 167, 201, 206, 207, 208, 295
Walton Ordinances, 89
Walton, Nicholas, 280
Walton-on-the-Hill, 284
Walton on Thames, 108, 289
Walton on Trent, 63, 64, 235
Walwyn's Castle, 304
Warbeck, Perkin, 201
Warde, Thomas, 280
Wardrobe, the king's, 65, 69, 70, 81, 85, 87, 90, 115, 137, 138, 172, 176, 216
Wards' lands, 49, 61, 92, 94, 116, 173, 187, 190, 202, 209, 219
Warenne estates, 59, 60
Warenne, Henry, 253
Warenne, John de, earl of Surrey, 59, 238, 240, 242, 243
Warley, 242
Warwick, 166, 299
earls and duke of, *see* Beauchamp; Neville
Warwick, Salisbury and Spencer lands, 154, 155–6, 166, 183, 185, 186, 188, 201, 203, 206, 220, 221, 299, 300, 304; *and see* Plantagenet, George
Warwickshire, 102, 161, 167, 171, 193, 232, 235, 236, 241, 285, 292, 293, 294, 295, 299, 301, 303, 304
Washingborough, 101, 265
Wateringbury, 62
Watford, 233, 235, 238
Waterton, Richard, 267
Watlington, 230, 280, 290
Wattes, John, 280
Waynfleet, Richard, 249
Weedon Lois, 106, 243
Welbeck, abbot of, 234, 235, 238
Welby, Richard, 166, 167, 177, 201, 202, 295, 298, 301
Weldon, William, 300
Welles, Leonard, lord, 127
Welles, Sir Richard, 264, 266
Welton, 102, 281–2
Welwik, William, 261
Wendover, 243, 248, 297
Went, river, 242
Wentworth, Philip, 129, 257, 259
Werk, Robert, 276
Westbury, 257
Westby, Gregory, 161
West Cliffe, 230
West Harptree, 102, 281–2
Westley, 129, 272
Westmill, 243
Westminster, 63, 104, 114, 121, 130, 157, 160, 163, 179, 184, 270, 271
Westmorland, 80, 108, 129, 206, 250–3, 293
earl of, *see* Neville
Weston Turville, 248
Weston, John, 269
Weston, William de, 65
Westover, 231
Westwood, Roger, 98
West Worldham, 300
Wetenale, William, 263
Wexcome (Westcomb), 233, 286
Weybridge, 285
Whatborough, 285
Whatton, 294
Wheathampsted, John, abbot of St Albans, 157
Wheatley, 234, 237, 242
Whele, Richard, 267
Whelpdale (Whepdale), William, 177, 292
Whitchurch, 63, 65, 233, 235
White, Andrew, 268
White, William, 272
Whitegreve, Humphrey, 283
Whitgift, 234, 242
Whitingham, Sir Robert, 248
Whittingham, Robert, 98
Whityngdon, Richard, 269
Wickham, 276
Wight, Isle of, 124, 129, 190
lordships and manors in, 71, 77, 135, 154, 185, 243–4, 258–9, 304
Wighton, 262
Wigmore, Edmund, 261
Wilkinson, Robert, 269
Willesden, Bartholomew, 249
William I, 18, 19, 26, 33, 34, 43, 44, 73, 76
William II, 43
William of Hatfield, second son of Edward III, 54
Williams, Geoffrey, 261

Willingdon, 242
Willoughby, Nicholas, 248
Willoughby, Robert, 205, 206, 297
Willoughby, Thomas, 274
Wilmington, priory of, 242
Wilton, 286
Wiltshire, 33, 64, 107, 110, 135, 153, 160, 167, 182, 192, 200, 231, 232, 235, 236, 237, 238, 241, 243, 244, 286, 290, 291, 292, 293, 294, 295, 296, 298–9, 300–5 *passim*
  earl of, *see* Butler
Winchelsea, 234, 284
Winchester, 114, 116, 125, 234, 235, 238
  bishop of, *see* Fox
  cathedral, cartulary of, 74
Windermere, 252, 253
Windsor, 92, 121, 170, 179, 182, 222, 297
Wing, 305
Wingfield, Sir Robert, 166, 295, 303
Wingham, 262
Winterbourne Bassett, 243
Winterbourne Earls, 233, 235, 238, 286
Witham, 267
Withernsea, 243
Withersfield, 271
Withycombe, 102, 281–2
Withyham, 242, 289
Witley, 63, 65, 106, 283
Wode, John, 206
Woderowe, John, 296
Wolsey, Ralph, 283
Wolverhampton, 282
Wooderowe, John, 64
Woodrow, 63, 64, 230, 235, 238
Woodstock, 68, 129, 135, 165, 200, 205, 230, 293, 302
Wootton, 129, 165, 233, 236, 238, 293, 302
Wootton Bassett, 243
Worcester, 233, 236, 238
  earl of, *see* Percy
Worcestershire, 129, 167, 231, 233, 236 237, 238, 287, 291, 292, 293, 294, 295, 299, 303, 304
Worksop, 294
Worplesdon, 283, 297
Worsley, Otwell, 290
Wotton under Edge, 300
Wressell, 287
Writtle, 296
Wyatt, Henry, 208
Wybarn, John, 262
Wycombe, 233
Wydeville, Anthony, lord Scales, earl Rivers, 154, 184, 185, 192, 193, 194, 296, 300
Wydeville, Elizabeth, queen of Edward IV, *see* Elizabeth
Wydeville, Lionel, bishop of Salisbury, 192
Wydeville, Richard, earl Rivers, 127, 129, 154, 181, 206, 250, 274
  wife of, *see* Jacquette
Wye, college of St Gregory and St Martin at, 106
Wykeham, William, Chancellor of England, 63
Wyrardisbury, 233, 237, 249, 297

Yale, 58, 305
Yarmouth, 232
Yarwell, 243
Yonge, Richard, bishop of Bangor, 246
York, 242, 288–9, 291, 293
  archbishop of, *see* Kemp; Neville
  duchy of, 164, 187, 189, 205, 220, 290, 302, 303
  duke of, *see* Plantagenet
York, John, 160, 293
Yorkshire, 76, 154, 174, 183, 186, 234, 235, 237, 238, 241, 242, 243, 287–8, 291, 293, 294, 298, 299, 301, 302
Ystlwyf, 76

Zouch, William, lord Zouch and Seymour, 266, 302